The Richards
BIBLE STORY BOOK

The Richards

BIBLE
STORY BOOK

by Jean Hosking Richards

Illustrations by Dorothy Teichman

ZONDERVAN PUBLISHING HOUSE
GRAND RAPIDS MICHIGAN

1st Printing, October, 1968

THE RICHARDS BIBLE STORY BOOK

Library of Congress Catalog Card Number 68-27465

Printed in the United States of America

And thou shalt teach them diligently unto thy children, and shalt talk of them when thou sittest in thine house, and when thou walkest by the way, and when thou liest down, and when thou risest up.

Deuteronomy 6:7

PREFACE

The Bible is a book of many stories, and yet it tells one story—God's dealing with man; at first through a family, then through a nation, and finally through the new family of God, the Church. No Bible storybook aims to be a substitute for the Bible but is more of an introduction to it.

The Bible abounds in drama, and children of all ages have a keen appreciation for drama; but the Bible is an adult book and in order for children to find enjoyment and meaning for themselves its stories need to be adapted.

Adapting Bible stories for children means more than simplifying the vocabulary. It also involves selection of stories and details, emphasis within the story, and its implied interpretation.

No attempt has been made to "draw a lesson" from each story; but by presenting these stories dramatically as the Bible gives them, we hope to have laid a foundation for a mature Christian faith in the boys and girls who will hear or read them.

The Bible is not one, but a collection of books, including different types and forms of literature, ranging from routine historical records to poetry. Throughout this literature we find one central unfolding story of God's redemptive work. In the Zondervan Bible Storybook we have brought out this overall story, as well as given the individual stories that make up the history of God's people, from Genesis to Revelation.

The characters the children read about in the Bible were not perfect; nor are they always good examples to follow. God is the hero of the Bible. Many of these men and women did have a strong conviction that the sovereign God was working in the events around them. Because of this faith they were used by God in His plan to bring men back to Himself.

In each story we have brought out the background facts about the world in which these people lived in order to make the story more meaningful to the boys and girls of today.

The Bible contains some exciting stories, but to provide exciting reading was not God's purpose in giving us the Bible. In the

Bible we have a record of God's revelation to man; although we must keep in mind the fact that God's greatest revelation is to be found in the person of Jesus Christ.

Accordingly, our purpose in presenting this book is that it help children to respond in love and trust to God and to joyfully accept Jesus Christ as Savior and Lord.

TABLE OF CONTENTS
Old Testament

PART ONE: FIRST STORIES

PART TWO: THE PEOPLE OF GOD

PART THREE: THREE RULERS

PART FOUR: KINGS AND PROPHETS

PART FIVE: A NEW CHANCE FOR GOD'S PEOPLE

New Testament

PART ONE: THE MESSIAH COMES

PART TWO: "GOD WAS WITH HIM"

PART THREE: "HE GAVE HIMSELF"

PART FOUR: GOD'S PEOPLE, THE CHURCH

THE OLD TESTAMENT

PART ONE

FIRST STORIES

We live in a world that is very old. Our planet Earth is a small one. Around us are billions of stars and other planets. Men have always wondered, "How did all this happen? When did it begin? Who made this universe? Who made me?"

In the beginning of the Bible we find the truth that God made all things. The whole universe and whatever it holds is God's creation. Nothing was made without Him.

We are important to God, not because we are strong or clever, not because we are always good, but because we are made by God, and God loves us.

The first stories in the Bible tell us how once man walked close to God but then disobeyed Him. The world became so full of wrongdoing that God's judgment had to come. But with the judgment came a new beginning, and a new chance for people to walk with God.

1. A World That Was Very Good

The universe is so vast that no man can even imagine how large it is. God is over all the universe. He is its Creator. God created the heavens and the earth. It is all a result of His plan, and a part of His great purpose; and we are a part of that plan and purpose.

At first our world, or planet, was overshadowed with darkness. It was lifeless, barren and covered with water; but God was at work.

God spoke: "Let there be light." And there was light.

God continued His work, and our world began to look like the world we know. There was daytime and nighttime. There was the bright blue sky overhead and fresh breezes. The waters were gathered together into seas, and the dry land appeared.

Now our world was ready for something very special to happen. Life began. Green appeared on the earth. Plants and trees started to grow. Fragrant blossoms for the first time filled the air with sweetness. The trees bore fruit in their branches, many different kinds of trees and fruit.

These flowers and fruits contained seeds from which new plants and trees could grow. This was God's way for each kind of life to continue, year after year.

God looked at all this green, growing life which He had brought to pass and said, "It is good."

In the sky the sun shone brightly during the day. At night there were the stars and our own silver moon.

Looking up from our planet we can mark the paths the different stars travel about the sky. The moon seems to change shape, because we do not always see all of it. By studying these movements we can count time—days, months, and years. This was part of God's purpose in giving us the sun, moon, and stars.

God looked at these heavenly lights and said, "It is good."

In the waters a new kind of life appeared. Fish and others creatures of the deep filled the seas. Overhead, birds flew across the sky. The birds made melody as they called to one another. There were many kinds and varieties, and all had the wonderful ability to reproduce creatures like themselves.

God was very pleased with this part of His work. He said, "Be fruitful and multiply and fill the waters in the seas, and let birds multiply on the earth."

God had further plans for our world, all to be brought about by His power and wisdom.

The animals of the land came and made their homes in the dense forests and open plains. Some were very large —larger than any animals we know today. Others would look more familiar to us. Swarms of tiny insects made clouds in the sky, and many small creatures crept along the ground.

As all these living creatures gave birth, they spread over the earth, making it a busy, humming world. God looked at all this work of His and saw that it was all good.

But God had not finished. There was something important to come.

God wanted someone to take care of this world of beauty and wonder. He would have to be a wise creature. He would need to know and love God so that he could work with God.

Therefore God decided to make man, and to make him in the image of God. This meant that man was like God in some ways. Man could think and remember and plan. He knew that he was a person. He had the ability to know and love God. He could choose between right and wrong.

God made a man and a woman. He said, "Let them rule over all the earth, the fish of the sea, the birds of the air, and every living thing."

God planned that these two would have a family. In this way mankind would grow and spread over the world.

God paused in His work. He looked at these special creatures whom He had made to know and love Him. He looked over the world He had given to them. God saw everything that He had made. It was very good.

Genesis 1; 2:1-4

2. Trouble in the Garden

The name of the first man whom God made was Adam. Adam lived in a beautiful place. God's creatures were all around him. The flowers were bright and made the air sweet. There were plants and fruit trees which gave him food to eat. But until God made Eve, a woman to help him, Adam was lonesome. Having someone like himself with whom he could talk and work made everything perfect.

Adam and Eve had many happy days in the garden. They had been told to take care of the plants and trees and to gather the food they needed. Everything around them belonged to them. There was only one thing that they must not do.

Adam told Eve about this special commandment of God. He said, "God told me, 'You can eat of every tree of the garden except the tree of the knowledge of good and evil. If you eat of the tree of the knowledge of good and evil you will die.' "

"I'll remember," Eve promised.

Adam and Eve were made in the image of God. This meant that they could know God. Every evening when the heat of the day was gone, Adam and Eve walked and talked with God.

Adam and Eve also had the ability to choose for themselves. They could obey God or disobey God.

God wanted man to love Him enough to obey Him, so He gave man a test. Would they leave the tree of the knowledge of good and evil alone?

Up to this time Adam and Eve had not done anything wrong. They did not know what evil was like. Nor had they ever felt pain or grief.

But one day Eve was alone, standing near the forbidden tree. A serpent came up and talked to her. He brought temptation to Eve.

This serpent did not look like those we know. He stood erect and he could talk.

He had a question: "Did God tell you not to eat the fruit from these trees?"

"We can eat any fruit," said Eve, "except the fruit of this tree, the tree of the knowledge of good and evil. We can't even touch this tree. If we do, we will die."

Then the serpent began to speak against God. He told Eve that God was not being fair with them. He hinted that God was keeping something good from them.

"You won't die," he said. "God knows that if you eat this fruit you will become wise. You will know good and evil. You will have more power. You will be more like God."

Eve should have run away. Instead she looked at the tree more closely. It was a beautiful tree. The fruit looked good to eat. Then she began to doubt what God had said.

"If this fruit will make me wiser, why shouldn't I have it?" she asked herself.

Eve reached up and took a piece of the fruit. It looked good. She ate some of it. Then she ran to Adam.

"Look, I have some of the forbidden fruit," she cried.

Instead of remembering God's command and refusing it, Adam took and ate the fruit.

At first nothing happened. Then they felt guilty and afraid. They were ashamed. Now they knew what it was to do wrong, but it had not made them happier.

As the sun set and the cool evening breezes swept through the trees, God came for the evening walk.

Adam and Eve hid behind the bushes and trees. They did not want to see God. For the very first time they were afraid of Him.

"Adam, where are you?" they heard God call.

Finally they came out and faced God. Adam said, "I heard your voice, and I was afraid."

God knew what Adam and Eve had done. "Have you eaten the fruit which I told you not to eat?" He asked.

They confessed that they had disobeyed. But then they refused to take the blame. They started to blame each other.

"Eve, the woman you made for me, gave me the fruit," said Adam. He was hinting that God was partly responsible.

But Eve didn't want to be blamed either. "The serpent tricked me into eating the fruit," she said.

The serpent was nearby. As a punishment God changed the shape of the serpent so that it crawled on the ground.

There had always been friendly feelings between men and animals, but now God said to the serpent, "You and man will be enemies; but man will overcome."

The serpent had brought temptation. Now he stood for all that was evil; but God promised that one day Someone would come who would overcome evil.

God turned to the woman. "From now on you will have much sorrow and pain," He said.

God said, "You will now very hard. It will be more get food from the land be- eds. You, too, will know what ke."

There was another special tree in the garden, called the tree of life. Now that man was a sinner, a creature who did wrong, it would no longer be a blessing to live forever. God did not want Adam and Eve to eat of this tree.

"You must leave this garden," God told them. "Outside it will be harder to get the things you need, but this is your punishment for disobeying."

Yet God still cared for them. He brought them clothes of animal skins to wear. He loved them and watched over them as they made a life for themselves outside.

But Adam and Eve no longer felt close to God. This was part of what God meant by saying they would die. They would continue to do wrong, and more and more evil would come to the world. Years later they would die. Sorrow and grief and death had become a part of life.

Genesis 2, 3

3. A Man Who Killed His Brother

Childen were born to Adam and Eve. They grew up and had families of their own. In time the families grew so large they became tribes. Men learned many things about finding food, building shelters, living together. They learned how to plant seeds and care for them so that they would have a good harvest. They learned how to care for flocks of animals so that they could use their wool, skins, and milk.

Among Adam and Eve's children were Cain and Abel. Cain was one of the farmers. Abel was a shepherd. Each thought their work was most important. Sometimes the shepherds and farmers quarreled over the use of the land.

Although men were not close to God as Adam and Eve had been in the garden, they knew something about God. Sometimes they prayed to God and brought offerings to Him.

One day both Cain and Abel brought an offering to God. Cain brought an offering from the harvest of his fields. But something was wrong. Cain realized that God had not accepted his offering. He became very angry.

"I brought the best I had," he grumbled. "What does God want?"

God knew Cain's heart. Cain did not love God nor did he want to live God's way. He was not grateful for the good harvest God had given him.

Abel brought one of his lambs as an offering. God knew that Abel loved Him and that his offering was an expression of thanksgiving from a humble heart. He accepted Abel's offering.

Abel was thankful and happy. He felt the joy of God's presence.

When Cain realized that Abel was accepted by God and he was not, he grew very angry at his brother. He was jealous.

God spoke to Cain. "Why are you so angry? If you do well you will be accepted by Me. Temptation is very near you, Cain; you must overcome it."

But Cain did not want to overcome temptation. He hated his brother and wanted to get rid of him. He proved that his heart was not right before God by what he did.

Cain pretended to be friendly with Abel. "Let us go out to the countryside," he suggested.

Abel agreed and they went out to the open plains. When they came to a lonely spot, Cain jumped on Abel and killed him.

As he started home, Cain thought he had been successful in getting rid of his brother. Who would know that he had done it?

Then God spoke to Cain again. "Where is Abel your brother?"

Cain was angry that God should question him. "I do not know," he lied. "Am I my brother's keeper?"

God knew what Cain had done. The blood of Abel was even now running into the ground beside his slain body.

God told Cain what his punishment would be. "You will be a fugitive and a wanderer from now on," He said. "The ground will no longer grow food for you."

Cain was afraid. All of Abel's relatives would want to kill him. If he had to go away, he couldn't count on the protection of his own family.

"My punishment is too great," he complained. "I will be driven away from all the people I know and from your face."

Cain did not realize that God was everywhere. He thought if he left home, God would no longer be able to help him. "And everybody I meet will want to kill me," he added.

Now Cain realized the seriousness of his crime. He realized that others might want to do to him what he had done to Abel.

But God showed mercy on Cain. He promised that no one would kill him.

Cain went away from his home and started a new family and tribe and built a new village. His children, like himself, were known for their cruel ways. Wrongdoing had come into the world and was getting worse.

Adam and Eve grieved over the murder of their son, Abel. Then Seth, another son, was born to them. This son, like Abel, loved God and Seth's children learned to love God. Men began to call on God and ask for His help.

Genesis 4

4. Another Chance for Men

The first tribes of men lived in a green, fertile land between the Tigris and Euphrates Rivers. This land of Mesopotamia extended down to the Persian Gulf. On the other side of the Tigris River were high, rugged mountains of what was later known as Persia. On the other side of the Euphrates River was what today we call the Arabian desert. This is where we believe men first lived.

Many generations had passed since the first family. Men did not care about God. More and more evil was done. Violence and wickedness were everywhere. No one was safe. From early childhood people were taught to do wrong. There were few good examples to follow.

But there was one family who did love God and tried to do what was right. This was Noah and his family. One day God spoke to Noah about the way the world had grown wicked.

"I will destroy man," God said. "There is nothing but violence in the earth, and it is man's fault. But you have found favor in My sight, Noah, because you have tried to obey Me."

This was terrible news. Yet Noah had to agree that the world needed judgment. Men couldn't continue in such wickedness.

God told Noah His plan. "I want you to make a ship, Noah. It is for you and your family. A great flood will come upon the earth and destroy mankind, but you and your family will be saved."

Noah set to work on the ship. His wife and his three sons, Shem, Ham and Japheth and their families helped him. There were three decks on the ship and one window that continued around all sides. The ship was of wood and made waterproof with pitch or tar.

"A great flood of waters will come," God warned him. "All men and animals outside the ship will perish. I want you to collect different animals so that you have a male and female of each. These should come into the ship, along with your sons and their families. Be sure to take food for yourselves and the animals."

So the family worked to get ready. They were sure God meant what He said. Others wondered what Noah was doing.

When the people heard about a coming judgment they laughed. They did not believe it. They did not repent of their wrongdoing and ask for forgiveness. They kept doing wrong right up to the time the rain began.

Noah had done as God asked. His family and the animals were safe in the ship. A heavy rain began to fall. Suddenly there was water overflowing everywhere. An earthquake shook the ground, and the sea and rivers overflowed the wide, level plain. The ship was carried away in the swift waters, but those inside were safe.

The rain continued for forty days. The high hills were covered. Then not even the mountains could be seen above the rushing waters. Still the sky overhead was dark with storm clouds. Noah and his family were frightened, but they trusted that God would save them.

At last the rain stopped. The sky cleared, and the ship sailed peacefully. Gradually the waters began to go down. After many days, Noah and his family looked out and found that their ship had settled on the top of Mt. Ararat.

Day by day they watched as the waters decreased. Now they could see the tops of other mountains and hills around them.

Noah and his family were happy to be safe. Still they wondered how they were going to be able to come down from these mountains and build new homes. Everything would need to start over. Perhaps they could go back to the place where they used to live.

"We must find out if the waters still cover the plains," Noah said. He sent out a raven, but the bird did not come back. After a few days he had found some place to stay.

Then Noah sent out a dove, but after a short time the dove came back. Doves are fussier about where they live. Noah knew it was not yet time to try to leave the ship.

A week later Noah again sent out the dove. All the family were waiting when it returned, an olive leaf in its mouth.

"The waters must be low now," said Noah. "The olive is a low growing tree, and now we know its leaves are above water."

Still they waited another week to send out the dove again. This time the dove found a place for itself and did not return.

"Now it is safe to leave," God told Noah.

They opened the doors, and the animals scampered away, glad for their freedom. Noah, his wife, and his sons and their families stepped out on the ground.

God had judged the human race, but He had saved it too. Now with Noah's children and grandchildren it could begin again. Perhaps this time it would become more what God wanted it to be.

"Have children and spread out on the earth," God commanded.

God wanted the land to be again filled with animals and people.

Noah and the rest of his family looked around them. Everything was fresh and green. It felt good to be alive. They were glad and thankful, but they were sober too. Now they realized that God was righteous. He would not just overlook wickedness. God had brought judgment on the world.

Perhaps, the sons thought, *we will also displease God, and He will destroy us, too. Who knows but what another flood will come.*

But Noah built an altar. "We must thank God," he said. "We have been delivered."

Noah brought an offering to God and prayed to Him, thanking Him for this chance to begin again.

God knew Noah's family were afraid of what might be in the future. He made a promise that the ways of nature could be counted upon.

God said, "While the earth remains, seedtime and harvest, cold and heat, summer and winter, day and night shall not cease."

Then God blessed Noah and his family. He looked down with love on them. He was glad that there had been this one family with whom He could work in making a new world.

"Have children and refill the earth," He said.

Then God had a special message for Noah as head of the family. It was a promise to man.

"This promise is for you and your children and their children," said God. "There will never again be such a flood to destroy all human life. In the sky is a sign that I promise this."

Noah and his sons and their wives and children looked up and there was a rainbow shining. An arc of color stretched across the sky where the sunshine met some lingering rain.

"This is the sign," God said. "I promise you and every living creature throughout all generations that the waters will never again become a flood to destroy all life."

Noah and his family looked up at the rainbow. It made them feel safe. It made them realize that though God was strict, He was just. If they walked in His ways they would find blessing and happiness.

Genesis 4-9

5. God Chooses a Man

Noah's family grew larger. His children and grandchildren had families. The families became tribes, and gradually they moved apart. Some went north, some south, some to the east. The Hebrew people counted Shem as their ancestor. Some of Shem's people went to live in Mesopotamia where Noah had lived.

But men did not love God as they should. They forgot how He had delivered their ancestor Noah. They began to do much that was wrong.

One group of people, in the broad plains of what would become Babylonia, decided to build a great city and a tower. In disobedience to God's command, they decided to stay in one place.

"We will not scatter over the earth," they said. "We will stay here and become powerful."

They made bricks from clay and started to build. Higher and higher they went. The building probably looked like the ziggurats which were often built later. "Our tower will reach into the heavens," they boasted.

But God judged their pride and rebellion by confusing their speech. When they had trouble understanding each other, they stopped their project, and went elsewhere to live. The building became known as the Tower of Babel.

As families and tribes migrated, they crossed rivers and mountains. They forgot the friends they left behind. They made customs of their own. As they met different conditions, they developed different ways to live. Sometimes tribes fought each other for possession of the best land.

With all of this, they forgot about the One God. They forgot the true story of how God had created them and the world they lived in. They created explanations of their own that told of many gods who quarreled with one another.

They believed these many gods had charge of specific activities such as harvest, war or hunting. They imagined harmful spirits were everywhere and tried to make friends with the spirits by giving them gifts.

They were afraid of the world around them, because they had forgotten the God they could trust.

As centuries passed, men built large cities. They wrote on tablets of stone. They made beautiful pottery.

People found it was a good idea to build their cities near water. Two great centers of civilization were near water. One was in Mesopotamia. The other was in Egypt, along the Nile River.

The people learned how to build canals so that the rivers did not com-

pletely overflow the land in springtime with the rains. They used the canals to travel by boat. They traded with one another and with people further away who could also travel by boat.

Sometimes the different people lived in peace, but often there were wars. Sometimes tribes from the desert would come to the cities and conquer them.

The people of Babylonia, in the southern part of Mesopotamia, built wonderful temples called Ziggurats. Each story on the building was higher but smaller than the last. But they did not worship God in the temple room at the very top.

Marduk was their chief god, but the Babylonians worshiped a great many gods. Some of their gods represented the moon and the stars. Many families had their own personal god, and in their homes the idol would have a place of honor.

The knowledge of God who had created the world, judged the world, and saved Noah was almost lost. But God had a plan to keep the truth about Himself alive.

God found a man whom He could use to start His plan. It would take centuries, but this plan would bring men back to Himself, and help them to be at last what God wanted them to be.

The name of the man God chose was Abram.

Genesis 10, 11

6. Abram Leaves All for God

Abram lived in Babylonia as his family had for generations. He and his brothers grew up in the busy, thriving city of Ur of the Chaldeans on the bank of the Euphrates River.

Abram had been given a good education. His father was a merchant and they lived in a fine home. In time the brothers married. Abram's wife was called Sarai.

As Abram looked around at the wonders of the created world, he could not believe the religion of many gods which he had been taught. He could not love or serve these gods who quarreled and did wrong, just like men.

After one of his brothers died, Abram moved north with his father Terah, and Lot, his brother's son. They settled in the smaller city of Haran some six hundred miles away. It was a city where important caravan trails met. Here as in Ur the temple to the moon-god was in the center of the city.

Abram was rich. He owned many herds and flocks. He and his wife, Sarai, had many servants. But Abram was not happy in spite of his comforts and success.

One day God Himself spoke to Abram, "Leave this country and your relatives. Come to a land which I will show you. I will make your descendants a great nation. I will bless you, and because of you all the families of the earth will be blessed."

This was Abram's chance to learn about and follow the One true God.

But the price was high. He must leave all his relatives and friends. He must leave his comfortable city home and become a nomad.

Life in the wilderness was hard. Here

and there were patches of grass and water, but the nomad shepherds had to travel a long way from one good spot to another. They had no place to really call their home. They lived in tents made from black goathair.

But out in the open spaces, as chieftain over his tribe, he would come to know God. Because Abram was sure of this, he made plans to leave.

Getting ready was a lot of work. Abram was glad he had many servants to help. Out in the desert the servants would be shepherds of the flocks and herds. There would be much for everyone to do.

Abram took along his nephew Lot. Terah, Abram's father, had died. Lot also had a wife, servants, and flocks and herds. The families of the servants were also included. They were slaves and had no choice but to go.

Finally the caravan of several hundred persons, as well as flocks and herds, made its way out of the city.

Friends who saw them leave wondered. "Abram is foolish to leave our fine city for the wilderness," they said. "What does he expect to find out there?"

But Abram knew what he was doing. He was going to find out the truth about God.

Slowly the large caravan entered the desert. They made their way through Syria into Canaan, some three hundred miles away from their starting place in Haran.

Canaan was a small, narrow land on the Mediterranean Sea. It lay between Mesopotamia and Egypt.

In Canaan Abram built an altar to God. He led the tribe in worshiping God. As he worshiped, God spoke to him.

"I will give this land to your children," God said.

Canaan was the land God had promised to show Abram. It was the land that would figure as most important in God's plan to bring men back to Himself.

Abram and Lot went from place to place in search of pasture. Water was even harder to find. As they moved from campsite to campsite they had to remember where certain wells and springs were located. Then they would return to these places.

Here and there were walled cities. Although all of this land was under Egyptian rule, the cities had their own kings.

The nomads were permitted to roam the hills and plains with their flocks. Some nomads made raids on the cities or stole the harvest from the fields outside a city wall. But neither Abram or Lot's people did this. They were peaceful people.

When a famine came to the land, it grew even harder to find the pasture they needed. Abram and Lot decided to spend some time in Egypt. Often the nomads did this, because Egypt was a fertile land. But it was not their home, and they were not permitted to stay once the famine was over.

Genesis 12

7. Lot Takes the Best

When the famine was over, Abram and Lot went back to Canaan; but their group was too large. Often Lot's servants and Abram's servants quarreled over where their flocks should graze or who should have first chance at the precious water.

One day Abram called Lot apart.

"Lot," he said, "I don't want your herdsmen and my herdsmen to quarrel. I do not want strife to be between you and me. Let us remember that we are of one family. There is much land around us. We had better separate."

Abram led his nephew up a hill to where they could see all the surrounding countryside. As the uncle, he had every right to tell Lot what to do. Instead he generously said, "You choose, Lot. If you take the left hand, then I will go to the right; or if you go to the right, then I will go to the left."

"All right, Uncle," Lot agreed.

Then Lot looked around. Here was his chance to make sure his family found a good place to stay. He did not like wandering around in the hills where it was hard to find water and grass.

Lot saw the plains which were watered by the Jordan River. They would have no long search to find water and grass here. Of course, it would leave little in the way of good land for Abram. As far as Lot could see in the other directions, there were only bare, limestone hills. Here pasture lands would be far apart. Still, his uncle had told him to choose.

"We will go to the Jordan Valley," he told Abram. "We will pitch our tents among the cities of the plain."

So Lot made his way to the best land. Abram was not angry at Lot for being selfish. He still loved the younger man. They made friendly farewells.

Lot pitched his black goathair tents near the city of Sodom, a city which was known for its wicked, violent ways.

Abram's herdsmen wondered why their chief had been so generous in letting Lot take the best. But Abram was sure God had some great plan for him. He wanted to go where God led.

After Lot left and as Abram looked around the countryside trying to decide in what direction to go, God said, "Look around you, Abram. Look to the north and the south and the east and the west. I will give your descendants all this land. You will have many descendants, Abram. They will be like the dust of the earth—everywhere. As you wander through all this land, remember that I will give it all to you."

So Abram called the caravan to march. They made camp as soon as they found good pasture. The first thing Abram did was to build an altar to God to thank Him for his continuing guidance.

Some time later as Abram wandered through the hills of Canaan a messenger came to him. He was an escaped prisoner and he brought Abram news that Lot and all Lot's family had been taken as prisoners.

An army from Mesopotamia had raided the Jordan Valley. Even though the kings, including the king of Sodom, had fought hard, these raiders had overcome them. The soldiers had taken much treasure from the cities of the plain and many prisoners.

In those days, every tribal chieftain

had to have men trained in war to defend his possessions and his rights to pasture. When Abram heard that Lot was captured he gathered his trained men together to fight. They pursued the enemy and overcame them, freeing all the prisoners and bringing back the treasure.

Abram brought Lot and his family back to Sodom. The king of Sodom was so grateful to Abram for fighting his enemies, he wanted to give him some of the treasure, but Abram did not want any reward.

Lot and his family again settled in the valley near Sodom; but this city grew more wicked than ever. Lot tried to keep his family living in good ways, but it was hard.

Meanwhile Abram went from place to place throughout the hill country of southern Canaan. God blessed him and increased his wealth. Abram was confident that God's promise would come true. And yet sometimes he wondered. For, you see, Abram had no son.

Genesis 13, 14

8. A Son Is Promised

Life as a nomad was hard. Abram realized now more than ever that there was danger all around. He had been involved in one war. Would there be more fighting?

God had promised that one day his descendants would be a great people. But as yet Abram did not have even one descendant, and both he and his wife Sarai were getting old.

One day while Abram was thinking about these things, he heard God speak. "Fear not, Abram. I am your shield. I will protect you. I am your great reward."

Abram remembered that he had answered God's call so that he could come to know the One true God who ruled heaven and earth. He had obeyed God, and he was growing in his knowledge of God.

Abram decided to talk about what was puzzling him most. "Lord God, to whom will this great reward be given? I am without a child. One born of my servants will have to be my heir."

If a chieftain had no son, his rule passed over to a servant's child. These servants were really slaves. They could not go and come as they pleased.

"Your heir will not be one born of your servants," God told Abram. "I will hand down this promise to a son who will be your own child."

God told Abram, the elderly childless man, to look up at the sky. "Look at the stars, Abram. Can you number them? Your descendants will be great in number like the stars."

Abram believed God. He was sure it would all happen.

But it was more difficult for Sarai to believe. It was ten years since they had left Haran. She often thought about it. "Perhaps it will be Abram's child but not mine," she said to herself. "If Abram should take another wife and have a son, I could count the son as my own."

Men often had more than one wife in those days. Sarai told her plan to Abram. "Why don't you take my servant Hagar as a second wife," she said. "It seems as though God does not want me to have children. Perhaps Hagar will give you a son."

Abram agreed to Sarai's plan. And so Hagar, a young Egyptian girl, became Abram's second wife. In a short while Hagar announced that she was going to have a baby.

When Hagar realized that she was going to have a child, she forgot that Sarai was still her mistress. She scorned Sarai and made it plain that she looked down on her. This made Sarai angry.

"Now Hagar hates me," Sarai complained to Abram.

Abram thought Sarai should be able to take care of this family problem. "You must correct her," he told Sarai.

Sarai spoke harshly to her servant and frightened Hagar so that she ran away, out into the desert. She had gone a long way when finally she sat down and cried.

There God spoke to her. "You should go back to your mistress, Sarai," He told her. "Don't be afraid for your child. He shall be father to a great people. You shall call him Ishmael."

Hagar felt better. She returned to the tents. But there were often quarrels between the two women.

Then Ishmael was born. As he grew, he was a disappointment to Abram. He seemed very headstrong and often disobeyed. He did not want to walk in the ways of God as Abram taught them to him.

The years passed by. Abram believed Ishmael was the heir through whom God would bless the world and make of his descendants a great nation.

But one day God spoke again about His plan. He had surprising news for Abram. First He reminded Abram of something. "I am God, the Almighty. Live, always remembering that I am with you. Do what is right."

Abram bowed down before God. This was what he always tried to do.

Then God said, "Abram, I am going to make an agreement with you and your many descendants. You will be the father of many nations. From now on you will have a different name—not just Abram (exalted father) but Abraham (father of a multitude). My agreement will pass on to your descendants, and I will always be with them. I will also give them this land of Canaan."

Then God had something to say about Sarai. "Your wife also shall have a new name—the name of Sarah (meaning princess). I will bless her and give her a son. She shall be a mother of nations and of kings."

But Abraham could not believe this. His wife had grown old. God must be talking about Ishmael. "I wish Ishmael would live in your ways," he said.

God explained again. "Sarah, your wife, will have a son. You will call his name Isaac, and I will continue My agreement with him and his children.

"Ishmael, too, will be blessed, and his descendants will be a great people; but Isaac is the son whom I promised you long ago. It is Isaac who will inherit My special promise."

Abraham found it hard to believe. But Abraham had always trusted in God, and God had not failed him. He would continue to walk in God's ways. Then he would be sure of God's blessing.

Genesis 15, 16, 17

9. A City Is Destroyed

One day as Abraham sat at the door of his tent he was surprised to see three men approach. If they had traveled far across the burning desert they were sure to be hot and tired.

Abraham hurried to meet them and to give them the hospitality nomads always tried to show to strangers.

"You are welcome," he said. "I will send for someone to bring water to wash your feet." The men wore open sandals and traveling made their feet hot and dirty.

"Make yourselves comfortable under this tree, and allow me to bring you something to eat."

"We would like that," the men said.

They washed their feet with the water a servant brought. They made themselves comfortable in the shade.

"We have visitors," Abraham said to Sarah. "Make some biscuits, and I will go and get some meat."

Soon the visitors were refreshing themselves with the biscuits, cooked meat, and milk. While they ate, Abraham stood by them and made sure they had everything they needed.

The men had a message from God. One of them told Abraham, "Sarah will have a son in the spring."

In the tent Sarah heard the message. She could not help laughing, because it seemed so impossible to her.

"Nothing is too hard for the Lord," said the messenger.

When they had been strengthened for their journey they made ready to go. "We are going to the city of Sodom," the men said. "Which is the best way?"

"I will go a little way with you and show you," Abraham offered.

On the way Abraham heard important news about Sodom. "The cry of those who are hurt in this city has come to Me," God said, "and I am thinking of bringing judgment on the people. If the city is indeed as wicked as men say, it must be destroyed."

Abraham was disturbed. Lot and his family lived in Sodom. There were many others who would also be destroyed if God's judgment should come. Perhaps there were as many as fifty righteous men in the city.

It did not seem right to destroy the righteous with the wicked. Abraham felt sure God always did what was right; so he talked to God about it.

"If there are fifty righteous people in the city will You still destroy it?" he asked God.

God told him, "If I find fifty righteous people in the city, I will spare the whole place for their sake."

Then Abraham got to thinking. Maybe there were not as many as fifty. Sodom had a reputation for violence. It was not safe for a stranger to enter.

"If there are five less," Abraham asked, "will You destroy the city for lack of five?"

"No," God promised. "If there are forty-five righteous people I will not destroy it."

Abraham was not satisfied. He kept talking to God about it. God agreed that even if there were only *ten* people living in the right way, the judgment would not come.

But events proved that there were not that many righteous people in the city. There was only Lot and his family. Lot often tried to tell his neighbors what was right. He often warned them that God judged the wicked, but they always laughed at him.

That same evening Lot saw two strangers coming to Sodom. He hurried to greet them because he knew they needed protection from the wicked men of the city.

"Come and spend the night with me and my family," he invited. "Wash your feet and have food with us."

The men accepted the invitation. After dinner they warned Lot of the coming judgment of God.

"You and your family must leave this city," they said. "God is going to destroy it. He has heard of the wrongdoing of its people. Only you, your wife, and your daughters have met God's test."

Lot did not doubt this message from God. He quickly found the men his daughters were soon to marry. "Come with us and save yourself from God's judgment. We must run away, for God is about to destroy this place."

But his sons-in-law thought Lot was joking. They would not take him seriously.

In the morning the family was still not

ready to leave. The messengers from God had to take Lot, his wife, and his two daughters by the hand and pull them out of their home.

"Flee for your life. Do not look back or stop anywhere in the valley. Hurry, or you too will perish with the city," the men warned.

Lot did hurry. There was a terrible shaking in the earth. Behind them buildings tumbled. The rumble got louder and louder, and by now the family was running as fast as they could.

While they were still in the valley Lot's wife lingered and looked back at the place where she had lived. It was a tragic mistake. The earthquake overtook her.

Rocks of salt were thrown up by the quake. The sulphur of the region caught on fire and soon everything was in flames. Lot hurried on with his two daughters. Just in time they escaped to safe ground.

In the hills Lot and his daughters made a home. The city that had once been so proud now lay in charred ruins. All of Lot's possessions, earned by years of toil, were gone.

Perhaps Lot remembered the time when he had taken what he thought was the best place to live. It had not turned out to be a good choice after all.

Genesis 18, 19

10. A Son Is Born

In the spring, Sarah had a son. As Abraham held the baby in his arms he remembered God's promise.

"My son will be called Isaac," (meaning "laughter") he said.

Sarah was very happy, and many of the servants were glad for her; but one woman was not happy. This was Hagar. Because there was a new son, her son Ishmael would have to share the inheritance.

Hagar spoke against her mistress whenever she could. The two women quarreled even more than they had before. This made Abraham sad, because he was a man of peace.

When Isaac was three years old Abraham gave a feast for his son. All the tribe celebrated. Ishmael was jealous because there was a new son and everyone was praising him.

Ishmael was an older boy now. In a few years he would marry. Often his mother had told him how Isaac was going to spoil things for him. She had heard it said that Isaac would be the future chieftain, not Ishmael.

Instead of praising Isaac, Ishmael made fun of him. He made the little boy cry. Sarah saw them together and became very angry.

As she often did, she complained to Abraham about Hagar.

"Send Hagar away," she insisted. "I don't want Hagar and Ishmael living with us any more. I don't want the son of a slave to share the inheritance with our son, Isaac."

Abraham tried to argue with Sarah, but it was no use. It did not seem right to send Hagar and her son away.

He talked to God about it. Once more God reminded Abraham of His plan. "It is through Isaac that My promise to you will come true. It is his descendants who will one day inherit the land of Canaan.

But do not despair about Ishmael. His descendants will become a great nation too, because he is your son."

As Abraham thought about it, he realized that Sarah and Hagar would only go on quarreling. There would never be peace in the tribe with the others taking one side or the other.

"Yes, it is best that Hagar and Ishmael go," he said.

Early the next morning Abraham got up and said good-by to Hagar and Ishmael. He gave them food and water for their journey. Hagar carried the water in the skin of a goat. All the openings were sewn up to keep the water inside until they needed a drink.

Sadly Hagar and Ishmael left the camp and began the journey across the desert to Egypt. All their bright dreams for the future were gone. They had not wanted to share the inheritance, but now it looked as though they were to receive no inheritance at all.

Hagar did not remember how once before God had spoken to her and promised her that Ishmael would be the father of a great people. She was discouraged and tired.

It did not take long to drink the water, and when it was all gone Hagar sat down on the desert sand. She went away from Ishmael to cry. She did not like seeing her son thirsty when there was no way she could help.

Then God spoke to comfort Hagar. "Don't be afraid, Hagar. Take your son and continue your journey. I will make a great nation from his descendants."

Hagar felt better. Even though Abraham had forsaken her; God had not. She took Ishmael's hand, and they walked on.

"Look, there is a well," cried Hagar. Now they could get the refreshing water they needed.

As she gave Ishmael a drink, Hagar was grateful for God's help and for the promise He had given.

Hagar had come from Egypt. She and Ishmael went back to the land by the Nile, and Hagar found a wife for Ishmael among the Egyptians. They started a family of their own, but they did not stay in Egypt. They went back to the wild desert.

God was with Ishmael. He became a great hunter. He had many children. Today, the Arabs count Abraham and Ishmael as their ancestors. Some Arabs still roam the desert and live in tents.

Back in Canaan, among the southern hills, Isaac grew up. Abraham loved Isaac, but he loved God even more. He trusted God so completely that later Abraham was called "the friend of God."

God renewed His promise to Abraham, saying, "I will indeed bless you, and your descendants will be as the stars of the sky or the sand by the seashore. Because you have obeyed My voice I will continue to bless you."

Genesis 21

11. A Bride for Isaac

Abraham was very old. His wife, Sarah, had died.

"There is one thing I must be sure to do before I die," Abraham thought. "I must see that Isaac has a good wife. God will hand down the promise through his family."

Abraham called his head servant to him. "I want you to promise me something," he told the servant. "I do not want Isaac to marry any of the women of this land. They do not worship the one true God. I want you to go back to my kindred in Mesopotamia and find a wife for Isaac among my relatives."

The servant realized that this was a very important mission. He wondered if a young woman from the city would be willing to come across the desert to this hill country and marry a man she had never seen.

"But supposing I can't find one of your relatives who is willing to come?" he asked. "Then should I take Isaac back to Mesopotamia?"

"No," said Abraham. "Never take Isaac back there."

Abraham remembered that God had told him to leave Mesopotamia. Their future was here in Canaan. This was where God's promise was going to be fulfilled.

"God has promised that my descendants will own this land," said Abraham. "God will go with you and will help you find a bride for Isaac. But if you cannot find a woman from my relatives who is willing to come, then you are free from your promise. Only be sure that you never take Isaac, my son, back there to live."

The servant promised. Then he made ready for the long journey. A few other servants went with him. They took ten camels. Most of the camels were loaded with choice gifts for the bride and her family.

The servant crossed the desert and came to the land where Abraham had been born. He went to the city of Haran, because he knew some of his master's relatives lived there.

Outside the city was the well from which everyone drew water. After the heat of the day a woman from every household would come to get water from the well. It was evening when the servant and his caravan arrived. They were all tired and hot and thirsty, and so were the camels.

The servant made his camels kneel down to rest, and then he asked God to direct him and help him find a good wife for Isaac.

The servant determined on a test. He wanted a girl who was kind and thoughtful and courteous. "O God," he prayed, "I shall ask one of the women for water. If she not only gives me a drink but also offers to give the camels water, then I will know that she is your choice and would be a good wife."

The servant saw a beautiful girl come up to the well. She looked like a good person. She carried her clay water jar on her shoulder.

The servant watched as the girl let her jar down into the cool depths of the well. It came up brimming with refreshing water.

Then the servant ran over to her and bowed low. "Please," he said. "Give me a little water to drink from your jar?"

The girl did not hesitate. "Drink, my lord," she said politely. She took the filled jar from her shoulder and gave him a drink.

When he had refreshed himself she said, "Wait, I will also get some water for your camels."

It was not too much trouble for her at all. Again and again she let the jar down into the well to get water for the thirsty camels.

The servant looked at her in wonder. It was all happening just as he had hoped and prayed it would. Could it be possible that this was a relative of Abraham, his master?

When everyone had had enough water, the servant took a gift for the woman from his treasures, a ring and two gold bracelets.

"Whose daughter are you?" he asked the girl. "Is there room in your father's house for us to stay overnight?"

She answered. "I am Rebekah. My father's name is Bethuel. My grandfather is Nahor and my grandmother, Milcah. I'm sure there is room at our house for you to stay, and we can take care of your animals, too."

Then the servant thanked God. He knew that Nahor was Abraham's brother. "Blessed be God," he said. "He has continued to show kindness to my master. He has indeed led me to my master's family."

Rebekah was puzzled. This stranger seemed to know her family. She ran ahead to tell her mother what had happened.

Rebekah's brother, Laban, was one of the first to hear the news that company was coming. He looked at the costly gifts Rebekah had received. She told him all that had happened at the well.

Laban was eager to greet these important people. "Come in," he urged them. "Why do you stand outside? A room in the house is ready for you, and we will provide a place for your camels."

As the men came into the house, a servant washed their dusty feet. Laban hurried out and made sure the camels were given proper food and shelter. Rebekah's father also greeted them. Rebekah and her mother hurried to prepare food for them to eat. Servants brought the food to the guests.

But tired and hungry as Abraham's servant was, he said, "I will not eat until I have told you my mission. I am Abraham's servant."

Rebekah's family was very surprised. They had many questions about Abraham.

"My master has become very rich," he told them. "God has been good to him. But my mission concerns Isaac, the son of Abraham and Sarah. Abraham does not want Isaac to marry a woman of the Canaanites. He sent me here to find his relatives and to bring back a bride for Isaac. He promised that God would help me, and indeed He has."

The servant told Rebekah's father and brother how he had prayed and God had answered, and how kind and courteous Rebekah had been at the well.

"Will Rebekah come with me and marry my master's son?" he asked. "Please tell me quickly so that I may know whether or not I have failed in my mission."

In these days it was up to the father to decide such matters. Bethuel spoke briefly to Laban his son. Then they gave their decision.

"God has led you to us. It must be right for Rebekah to go with you and marry Isaac."

The servant again thanked God for His help. Now he could enjoy his dinner, knowing that he had been successful.

But before he ate, the servant brought out the costly gifts that Abraham had sent for the bride and her family. There were beautiful pieces of silver and gold jewelry and lovely fabrics from which clothes could be made.

Rebekah's family were glad to see that Abraham could give such things. It proved to them that Rebekah would be well taken care of, even if she did have to go so far away from home.

The next morning Abraham's servant wanted to start back to Abraham and Isaac. But Laban and Rebekah's mother objected. "Let Rebekah stay with us for at least ten more days," they said.

"Please do not delay me," said the servant. He knew how anxious Abraham and Isaac were.

So Laban said, "Very well, we shall ask Rebekah."

Rebekah was very excited about the great adventure ahead. She was eager to get started. "I am ready to go," she said.

Rebekah's father, mother, and brother said good-by. "May you be happy and have many, many children," they said.

So once again the camels were made ready. Rebekah took some of her servants along to the new home. They rode on the camels which had carried the gifts.

The hot, dusty trip across the desert began.

Many days later they approached the campsite in Canaan where the servant had left his master. Outside in the open spaces around the camp, Isaac had come out to enjoy the evening breeze and to think about God and talk to Him.

Rebekah saw him, just as Isaac saw the approaching camels.

"Who is the man who now comes to greet us?" she asked the servant.

"It is Isaac," said the servant.

Rebekah quickly got off her camel and put a veil over her face. It was the proper way to meet her future husband.

Genesis 23, 24

12. A Divided Family

Isaac and Rebekah were married. Isaac was very proud of his young wife. She was beautiful, and she was kind and gracious. He loved her very much.

They prayed that they would have children. After many years God answered their prayers by bringing them twin sons. They were named Esau and Jacob.

Esau was born just before Jacob, and so he was considered the elder son. This was always a position of great honor and usually meant that this son would become head of the tribe.

From early childhood Jacob and Esau were very different. Often Isaac would tell the boys about their grandfather, Abraham, who was now dead, and how God called Abraham out from the country of idol-worshipers. He would tell them that God had promised that Abraham would be father to a great people who would have a special relationship with God.

Jacob loved to hear these stories but Esau was always restless. He was glad when his father stopped so that he could run out into the fields. Jacob often thought about God. He wished with all his heart that this wonderful promise could be his. But, no, by custom it went to the eldest son.

When they were grown men, Esau became a great hunter. No one could match his skill at finding and killing wild animals to eat. His father Isaac admired his skill and enjoyed the meat which Esau brought back from his hunting trips. Isaac showed in many little ways that he was more proud of Esau than he was of Jacob.

Jacob's feelings were hurt by this. He could never be a hunter like Esau. Besides, he was not interested. He stayed around the tent and spent a lot of time with his mother. He was interested in seeing that the flocks and herds were cared for and that the business of the tribe was done well.

Often Rebekah said, "Jacob is our best son. He is the best son any parent could have."

For parents to show preferences is not good, and in Isaac's family jealousy and quarrels resulted from this division.

As time went on, Jacob thought more and more about the birthright Esau possessed as the eldest son. But when he talked to Esau about it, Esau was indifferent.

"Doesn't it matter to you that God wants to create a people who love and serve only Him?" Jacob would ask.

Esau would just laugh carelessly. "I like to hunt," he would say. "Life is a lot of fun, Jacob. You take everything too seriously."

Jacob did take it seriously, and he thought Esau had the wrong attitude. A plan began to form in the back of his mind. Maybe he could find some way to get the birthright away from his brother.

The son who had the birthright would be head of the tribe. He would receive a double portion of the possessions inherited from his father. He would receive the special promise of God. He would represent the family to God and be a kind of spiritual leader.

One day Jacob found his opportunity. Jacob liked to cook and he had just made a kind of soup with lentils. As he stirred it over the open fire it smelled good.

Just then Esau came home from a hunting trip but this time he had caught nothing. He was tired and very hungry.

"That smells good," Esau cried as he sat down by his brother. "I'm starved. Let me have some, will you?"

Quickly Jacob replied, "Will you give me your birthright in exchange?"

Esau laughed. Jacob was always worried about that birthright. Well, let him have it.

"Very well," he said. "You can have the birthright. What good does it do me? Right now I'd rather have a quick meal."

"Promise me," said Jacob. He wanted to be sure Esau was serious.

Esau promised. Then Jacob made him a good meal with the soup, some bread and something to drink. As he served it he wondered, how Esau could think so little of God's promise that he would exchange it for a meal? *Well, he had the birthright now instead of Esau, and he would uphold it. God's promise would come true through him.*

As the years passed, Isaac traveled about Canaan much as his father had done. He used the same wells that Abraham had dug. Once he found that the Philistines who lived nearby had thrown dirt into his wells. Isaac could have made war, but he was a man of peace. So he only opened the wells again.

Another time the people of Gerar came and claimed the wells Isaac was using. Isaac moved on to other wells. This time Abimelech, the king of the Philistines, realized that Isaac did not want to fight. He went to Isaac and asked for a treaty of peace.

"Your tribe is so strong and rich that we were afraid of you," he confessed. "Now let us promise to be friends."

Isaac agreed.

God was pleased with Isaac. He repeated the promise of blessing to him. "I will bless you. To your descendants I will give all this land. Remember I am with you."

Isaac walked in God's ways and tried to teach his children to do the same. He did not know about Esau selling his birthright or he would have been very disappointed in him.

Then Esau disobeyed his father in another way. Both Abraham and Isaac had said it was wrong to marry the women of the land. They felt that God did not want this. But Esau disobeyed by marrying two women from the Hittites.

His wives were used to worshiping idols and they had other ways that Esau's parents did not like. They made life unhappy for Isaac and Rebekah.

Genesis 25, 26

13. A Stolen Blessing

Even though Esau had disobeyed by marrying heathen women, Isaac still thought he should become the head of the family and be the one to receive God's special blessing. He still showed more love to Esau than Jacob.

This made Rebekah angry. She was sure Jacob would be the best one to inherit the blessing. She decided one day to take matters into her own hands.

Isaac had grown very old. His eyesight was failing and he was sure that he did not have long to live. Rebekah overheard him talking to Esau.

"Esau," Isaac said. "I do not have much longer to live. I want you to do something for me. Go out to the fields and hunt game. Bring me back some of my favorite meat and cook it for me. Then I will give you a special blessing."

"Yes, Father," Esau said. He hurried to get his bow and arrow and was off to the fields.

Rebekah hurried to find Jacob. "We must act quickly," she said. "I just heard your father tell Esau to hunt game and cook him one of his favorite dishes, and your father promised to give Esau his blessing. You must get this blessing for yourself."

"How?" asked Jacob.

"Go to our own flocks, and take out two kids. I'll prepare the meat myself, and you shall take it to your father. Your father will think you are Esau, and you will get the blessing."

Jacob objected, not because it was wrong, but because he was afraid of getting caught.

"What if my father touches me? My skin is smooth, and Esau's skin is very hairy. Even though his eyesight is bad, he will be able to feel the difference. He will be angry if he finds out I have deceived him. Then instead of a blessing, he will predict bad things for me in the future."

"Go and do as I say," Rebekah insisted. "I'll take care of everything."

Jacob did as his mother suggested. He watched as his mother cooked the meat. After it was ready, Rebekah took some of the kid's skin and gave it to Jacob.

"Put these on your hands and around your neck," she said. "If your father touches you, he will feel this rough hairy skin and think it is Esau. Wait, I'll bring you some of Esau's clothes to put on as well."

The mother and son worked hard to trick the father. Rebekah waited anxiously as Jacob went in to where his father was resting.

"Father," Jacob called.

"Here I am," said Isaac. "Which son calls me?"

"I am Esau," Jacob lied. "I have done as you told me. Now sit up and eat of my game. Then you can bless me as you promised."

Isaac was puzzled. "How is it that you found game so quickly?" he asked.

Now Jacob had to lie again. "The Lord helped me," he said.

Isaac suspected something. "Come closer so that I can touch you."

Jacob came close. Isaac touched the kid's skin on Jacob's hand. "You sound like Jacob," said Isaac, "but these are Esau's hands. Are you really Esau?"

"Yes," Jacob lied again.

"Bring me the food," said Isaac, "and then I will give you the blessing."

After eating the good food, Isaac asked his son to kiss him. Jacob did.

"Your clothes smell of the fresh out-of-doors," said Isaac. "May the rich harvests of the earth be yours. May you have the needed rain. Let other tribes and people serve you, even your own people."

Now Jacob had the blessing he had wanted so much. His father had said in the blessing that he would be head of the family.

Jacob went back and told his mother. Soon they saw Esau returning from the fields with the result of his hunting. Quickly Esau prepared the meat and brought it into his father.

"Sit up, Father," said Esau as he came to Isaac. "I have brought the food and am ready for your blessing."

"Which son are you?" asked Isaac.

"Esau, your eldest son."

Isaac trembled with anger and grief. He had let Jacob trick him. Now he had no more great words of blessing left.

"Your brother came in with food, and I gave him the blessing instead," Isaac told his son.

When Esau heard that Jacob had been made head of the tribe he was very angry. "He has tricked me again," he shouted. "He tricked me into selling the birthright, and now he has the blessing you meant for me."

Isaac was unhappy, but he did not recall his blessing of Jacob. "Your brother will be blessed," he said. Perhaps Isaac realized at last that Jacob was the best son to receive the promise.

"But don't you have any blessing for me?" asked Esau.

Isaac tried to think of some good promises for Esau which he had not already given to Jacob.

"You will live in the wilderness," he said. "You shall live by fighting. For a time your descendants will serve your brother's descendants, but one day your descendants will break away and be free."

Esau had been cheated. He was unhappy and angry. But Isaac's words came true many years later. The descendants of Esau were known as Edomites. As a nation they became enemies of the descendants of Jacob.

"I'll get even with Jacob," Esau said. "After my father dies I will kill my brother."

Some of the servants heard this boast and reported it to Rebekah.

She hurried again to Jacob. "Your brother is very angry and threatens to kill you. You had better go. Visit my brother Laban in Haran. When Esau gets over his anger I'll send for you."

As a result of her trickery Rebekah had caused an even wider rift in the family. Now Jacob had to leave—and she would never see him again.

Genesis 27

14. Jacob Meets God

Secretly Jacob made ready to leave Canaan. He dared not stay around his angry brother. Meanwhile his mother went to Isaac.

"As you know," she said, "the Hittite women Esau married have always been a trouble to me. I don't want Jacob to marry any of the women from these countries. I want him to marry one of the daughters of my brother Laban.

Isaac agreed. He called Jacob to him. "You shall not marry any of the women from Canaan," he said. "Go back to Haran and take one of Laban's daughters for a wife."

Jacob hated the idea of leaving home and going out into the dangerous wilderness, but he dared not stay. "Yes, Father," he said. "I will leave right away."

Isaac seemed more resigned to the fact that Jacob would be head of the family. He had to admit that Jacob cared more about God's promise than Esau had. Isaac disapproved of Jacob's way of getting the promise, but he had a kind farewell for his son.

"God Almighty bless you and make you a great nation. May God give you the blessing He gave to Abraham. May your descendants take possession of this land."

Jacob said good-by to his father and his mother but not to Esau. He did not want to see the brother whom he had tricked. He was anxious to get started and took no servants with him.

As he started out on the long journey to Mesopotamia, Jacob was afraid. It was dangerous for a man to be alone in the hills. Robbers might kill him. Wild beasts might attack him.

As the sun began to set, Jacob looked around for a place to spend the night. By now he had traveled many miles. He stopped by a rocky hillside and ate some of his food and water.

It was a lonely spot, but the limestone rocks would give him some shelter for the night. They looked something like steps climbing the hills.

"I am so alone," thought Jacob as he took one of the rocks and rested against it.

Jacob believed God was back at the camp with his family. He did not understand that God is everywhere. He had left God behind, he thought, and could not call on Him for help.

Jacob thought of the wrong he had done. He recalled his brother's angry promise. He remembered his mother's tears as they said good-by. He knew the sorrow that doing wrong brings.

At last Jacob fell asleep on the cold, hard ground with a rock for a pillow. But in his sleep he had a dream—a wonderful dream.

A staircase reached up to heaven and he was at the bottom looking up. Angels were going up and down the steps. At the top God spoke to Jacob, saying, "I am the Lord, the God of Abraham and Isaac. I will give to you and your descendants the land on which you lie. Your descendants will be many and will be a blessing to many."

This was the promise Jacob had wanted so much. And now God Himself was giving it to Jacob. God also knew about Jacob's immediate troubles. Even though Jacob had done wrong, God still loved him. God knew Jacob's heart, and He

knew that in time Jacob would learn better how to walk in His ways.

"I am with you," God said. "I will keep you wherever you go, and I will bring you back to this land."

Jacob woke from his dream. How real it had seemed. "I didn't realize God was here," Jacob marveled to himself. It frightened him, even though God had given him words of comfort. "This is the house of God. This is the gate of heaven," he declared.

Jacob slept again. Early in the morning he got up to continue his trip to Haran. But first of all he made a marker of the rock he had been leaning on, so that he would always remember this place. He poured oil over the rock. It was a way of making it a holy place where God is worshiped.

Jacob called the name of this place where he had spent his first night away from home, Bethel. In his language this meant, "The house of God."

Before he left, Jacob made a promise to God. "If God will be with me and will keep me in this journey, if He will provide food and other things necessary for life, if He does indeed bring me back home in peace, then the Lord shall be my God. I will always worship only God. I will make of this place where I put the rock a place of worship to God. And of all the good things God gives me I will give back ten percent to God."

As Jacob continued his journey, he was not lonely any more. Now he knew that God was with him.

Genesis 28

15. Jacob Is Tricked

Jacob continued his journey into the land of Mesopotamia. Just outside of Haran, he came across some shepherds in the fields. Their flocks were lying on the grass, making a circle around a well. A large, heavy stone covered the well.

Jacob greeted them. "Where is your home?" he asked.

"We are from Haran," they told him.

"Do you know Laban, the grandson of Nahor?" Jacob hoped these shepherds could direct him to his uncle's house.

"Yes, we do," said the shepherds.

"Is he well?"

"Yes, he is well. Look, here comes his daughter, Rachel."

Jacob looked up and saw a pretty girl coming down the road with a flock of sheep. When Jacob saw Rachel come up to the well, he hurried to take off the stone so that her sheep could have water.

Rachel was surprised at Jacob's strength, because usually it took several men to do this.

Then Jacob introduced himself. "I am the son of Rebekah, your father's sister. My father is Isaac."

Rachel was surprised. Of course she had heard about Isaac and Rebekah, her relatives who lived in Canaan.

She led Jacob to her home. She was excited as she ran in to tell her father who had come.

Laban came out and greeted Jacob warmly. "You are welcome," he said. "We are glad to have Rebekah's son with us."

Jacob met Rachel's older sister, Leah, and Uncle Laban's sons. He went to work at once helping his uncle in every way he could. Laban discovered that Jacob was very good at taking care of the flocks and herds. Jacob did not mind working hard.

After a month had gone by, Laban called Jacob to him. "You have worked hard for me, Jacob," he said. "Just because we are relatives does not mean you have to work for nothing. Tell me, what do you want for your wages?"

Jacob knew right away. He loved Rachel and wanted to marry her. He had no expensive gifts to bring for a bride

as Isaac had sent for Rebekah. He would have to work for his uncle instead.

"I will serve you for seven years if you will give me your younger daughter, Rachel," Jacob promised.

Laban was pleased. "I would rather she marry one of our own family than anyone else," he said. He agreed to the terms.

Jacob was happy. He worked even harder for his uncle. He thought about the happy day when Rachel would be his wife, and he did not mind the work. The time passed quickly.

When seven years were up, Jacob reminded his uncle of his promise. Laban announced a big wedding feast. Many guests came. The bride was given to Jacob.

But after the ceremony, Jacob had an unpleasant surprise. Women of that day, especially at the wedding ceremony, wore veils that covered nearly all their face and their hair. Jacob discovered that Laban had given him Leah as a bride instead of Rachel.

It was not a mistake. Laban had tricked Jacob into marrying Rachel's sister. There was nothing he could do about it.

Jacob was hurt and angry. "I served you for Rachel," he said. "Why have you deceived me?" Now he knew how it felt to be tricked.

"It is not our custom to give the younger daughter in marriage before the older daughter is married," Laban told him.

Then Laban had another plan. He liked the work Jacob did, and he was determined to keep his nephew's cheap labor as long as he could.

"In a week we will have another wedding," he said, "and then you can have Rachel for your bride. Only you must promise to serve me for another seven years."

It was a lot to ask of Jacob, because this would be all he would receive; but Jacob did not complain. He was learning to be patient.

"Very well," Jacob promised. "If you will give me Rachel as well, I will work for another seven years."

At the end of the week Jacob was given Rachel as a bride. Now he had two wives, but he owed Uncle Laban seven years of service.

This time the years passed more slowly. Jacob was working hard, but he was not getting richer. Then there was trouble in the family. Leah and Rachel were jealous of each other.

Leah was jealous of Rachel because she knew Jacob had never intended to marry anyone but Rachel. She knew Jacob loved Rachel best.

Rachel was jealous because before long Leah had a baby son. It was very important to have many children in those days. Large families had many hands to help with the work, and by working together they could grow wealthy.

Leah gave Jacob several sons. Then Jacob took two more wives, the maids of Leah and Rachel. They had sons; but still Rachel had none. She was very unhappy as sons and daughters were born to Jacob.

Finally the day came when she too had a baby boy. She called him Joseph.

Then Jacob decided to take his large family and go back to Canaan.

Genesis 29; 30:1-25

16. Jacob Grows Rich

Jacob went to his Uncle Laban to ask permission to leave. "I have given you good service," he reminded his uncle. "Now I would like to take my family back to my own land, the land of Canaan."

Because of Jacob's good management, Laban had grown very rich during the fourteen years Jacob had worked for him. He hated to let him go.

"What would you like in return for your continued service?" he asked Jacob. "Name your wages, and I will give it to you."

Jacob knew his uncle was not the generous man he was pretending to be.

"You yourself know how I have served you," said Jacob. "You had little before I came, but since then your herds and flocks have increased greatly. Now I need to provide for my own family, your daughters and the children they have given me."

Jacob had no flocks or herds of his own. He wondered that Laban did not mind that his daughters were poor.

Instead of offering Jacob a good share of his fortune, Laban again asked, "What shall I give you?"

Jacob made his request. "I would like to own all the sheep which are black or spotted. In addition I would like to have any spotted goats. Under these terms I will work for you a little longer."

Laban was pleased. "Good," he said. Most of the sheep were white and most of the goats were solid black or brown. He knew that Jacob would not receive most of the animals this way, but he wanted to be sure Jacob got very little in return for his work. He wanted to keep for himself the riches Jacob had brought.

To make it even more sure, Laban immediately took out all his spotted animals and black sheep and put them in a separate flock to be kept a good distance away from the others. He told his own sons to tend these animals. In this way Laban thought he would prevent many spotted animals from being born.

Then he told Jacob he had to care for the other animals—the solid-colored ones that belonged to Laban.

Jacob did not argue with his uncle, and he carefully tended the animals that were not his. But as each spotted animal was born he put it apart as his own. This was the agreement.

Because many spotted animals were born in spite of Laban's plan, Jacob's flocks grew in size. Before long, Jacob was wealthy.

Laban's sons were jealous of Jacob. "He gained all this wealth from our father," they grumbled. They forgot how hard Jacob had worked and that he was their brother-in-law.

Laban, too, began to complain.

"My uncle does not look with favor on me any more," Jacob told his wives. "Perhaps it is time to return to Canaan."

Then God spoke to Jacob. "Return to the land of your fathers and to your family," He said. "I will be with you."

Jacob told Leah and Rachel what God had said. "Your father has often tried to cheat me," he told them, "and yet God has prospered me. In spite of the harsh restrictions your father has given me, we are rich."

His wives agreed. "Our father treats

us like strangers. You deserve the wealth you have. It belongs to us and our children."

Still, they were afraid Laban might not let them go away, so they decided to leave secretly when Laban was not at home. One day when Laban was off to a far-away pasture, Jacob and his family left with their flocks and herds.

Three days later Laban came home and discovered that they had gone. He and some of his relatives pursued Jacob across the desert.

When they caught up, the uncle and the nephew had harsh things to say to one another. Jacob reminded Laban of the twenty years of service given him and how many times Laban had changed his agreement about wages.

"It is only because God has helped me that I am rich," Jacob said.

Laban realized that God was with Jacob. "Let us be friends," he said. "Let us promise to do no harm to each other."

Jacob agreed. He had no desire to make an enemy of his uncle. He took some stones and made a small pile. It was to mark the place of their agreement.

"God is a witness that we have made this agreement of peace," said Laban.

Then the relatives ate together and made camp for the night. In the morning Laban and his group went back to Haran.

Jacob watched them go. He was glad to be at peace with his uncle. God had helped him in every way; but there was a big hurdle to come.

Jacob still had to meet his brother Esau. Would Esau still be angry and want to kill him?

Genesis 30:25-43; 31

17. Jacob Meets Esau

Jacob recalled God's promise that God would always be with him and would bring him back home in peace. Once they crossed the Jordan River they would be in Canaan.

"Soon I must meet Esau," Jacob thought. "How can I show my brother that I have changed and that I want to be his friend? How can I show him that I no longer covet what is his and that I have wealth of my own?"

Jacob decided on a plan. He would send some of his servants on ahead as messengers to meet Esau.

Jacob gave the messengers instructions. "Go ahead of us into Seir," he said. "There you will find my brother Esau. Greet him with respect and tell him, 'Jacob sends you a message. He has gained much wealth during his stay with Laban. He hopes to find favor in your sight.' "

The messengers went on ahead, but before long they returned with startling news. "We came upon your brother Esau, and he is coming to meet you. Four hundred men are with him."

Then Jacob was afraid. He felt sure Esau was coming to make war on them. He divided his tribe into two parts, the one traveling some distance behind the other. In this way if one group were captured, the other group might be able to escape.

Jacob remembered how God had helped him when he had fled to Bethel away from his brother's anger. God had helped him as he served Laban in Haran. So Jacob turned now to God.

Jacob no longer demanded things of God. He prayed with humility.

"God of my father: O Lord, You told me to return to my country, and I have obeyed You. I am not worthy of all the love You have shown me. You have blessed me greatly since I left home. Now deliver me, please, from my brother's anger. I am afraid he is going to kill us all—even the mothers and children."

Jacob reminded God of His promise, "You said You would make my descendants be many and that You would continue to help me."

Then Jacob thought of another plan to make friends with Esau. He would send servants ahead with many gifts for his brother. This would convince Esau that he was coming in peace. It would show his brother that he wanted to make up for the way he had cheated him.

So Jacob took many animals from his flocks and herds. He put them in separate droves and had a servant to take care of each drove. The servants were to greet Esau with respect and tell him, "These are a present from Jacob and Jacob is behind us."

That night they made camp in a deep valley. High mountains were around them, and the Jabbok River made its twisting way through the canyon to join the Jordan River.

Jacob was still worried and could not sleep. As he was out alone by the shallow tumbling river he thought about God. He struggled between faith and doubt.

During the night a Stranger came to Jacob. He refused to give His name. The two wrestled together all night by the river, and Jacob wrestled so hard the Stranger could not beat him. Then the Stranger gave Jacob a message. He said, "Your name will no longer be Jacob but Israel—Perseverer with God. God is pleased with you. You have grown in good ways and are more worthy of God's promise."

As the sun rose in the morning, the Stranger was gone. But Jacob crossed the river no longer afraid because God had blessed him. Across the river he looked up and saw a large company coming. It was Esau and his four hundred men.

Quickly Jacob put his wives and children behind him so that they would have better protection. Then he went on ahead to greet his brother.

He bowed politely before Esau.

When Esau saw his brother, he ran to meet Jacob and embraced him. The two brothers were so glad to see each other again they could not help crying.

Esau was surprised to see Jacob's large family. "Who are these?" he asked.

"These are the children God has graciously given to me," said Jacob.

The wives and children also greeted Esau with politeness.

"What did you mean by sending all these presents ahead of yourself?" asked Esau.

"I wanted to find favor with you," Jacob told him. "I want us to be friends."

"Presents are not necessary," said Esau. "I have all I need, brother. Keep your flocks and herds for yourself."

But Jacob wanted his brother to have them. "If I have found favor in your sight, please accept the gifts," he said. "God has been good to me, and I want to share with you."

So Esau accepted the gifts. He wanted Jacob to travel with him, but the groups were too large to travel together. Esau

and his company went back to their own home. Jacob traveled more slowly to the south.

When they were back in Canaan, God reminded Jacob of his promise to worship at Bethel when God brought him back to his homeland.

"Let us go to Bethel," he told his people. "I want to make an altar there to God who answered me in the day of my trouble, and who has been with me wherever I have gone since."

At Bethel God renewed His promise to Jacob, saying, "I am God Almighty; have children and become a great nation. The land which I promised to Abraham and Isaac I promise to you and to your children."

Genesis 32, 33

18. A Brother Who Was Hated

Jacob and his tribe lived much as Abraham and Isaac had, going from campsite to campsite in southern Canaan. They stopped at many of the same places his father and grandfather did and used the same wells and springs.

In those days wealth was measured in terms of animals rather than money. Jacob's flocks and herds continued to grow.

Jacob had twelve sons. Reuben was the eldest. The youngest was Benjamin, who was born after they returned to Canaan. Benjamin and his older brother, Joseph, had Rachel for a mother (but Rachel died soon after Benjamin's birth). The ten older brothers were much older than Rachel's boys.

Jacob had been so glad when Rachel had a son that he made Joseph a favorite. When Joseph became a young man, Jacob was very proud of him. He was handsome, and a very bright boy.

Jacob generally kept Joseph nearby and gave him duties around the camp. The older brothers often had to go with the flocks far from the main camp in order to find good pasture. They would camp out in the hills for days at a time. Sometimes Joseph would bring them messages from their father.

The older brothers often got into trouble. They were always ready for a fight with strangers. Jacob warned them to be more careful because another tribe might make war on them.

Once when his brothers got into trouble, Joseph reported it to his father. This made the brothers angry. They were already jealous of Joseph, because the father always gave him easy work and showed favor to him.

On two different occasions Joseph had dreams indicating that one day he would rule over the rest of his family—they would all bow before him. People of that day believed that dreams often foretold the future.

The dreams made the older brothers angry and envious. They thought Joseph was conceited. They were also afraid the dreams might come true.

Then Jacob gave Joseph a present which made the brothers so angry that they no longer even pretended to be on good terms with Joseph. They would not even speak to him in a nice way.

The present was a coat with long

sleeves. It was the kind of coat that a gentleman wore and came down to the ankles. The brothers wore coats which were easy to work in. They had no sleeves and came down only to the knees.

One day when the main camp was in Hebron, Jacob told Joseph, "I want you to go to your brothers who have taken the flock to Shechem. See if it is well with your brothers and the flock."

"Yes, Father," said Joseph.

He put on his fine coat and started out, traveling north to the pasture land near Shechem. But although he looked all around, he could not find his brothers.

Then he noticed a man coming towards him. "What are you looking for?" the man asked.

"My brothers," Joseph said. "Do you know where they are pasturing the flock?"

The man remembered seeing the shepherds. "They have gone away," he said. "I heard them say they were going north to Dothan."

Dothan was twenty miles away, but Joseph made the trip. Sure enough, he could see the camp as he approached Dothan.

The brothers saw Joseph coming. "Here comes the dreamer," they laughed.

"This is our chance," one said. "Let's kill him."

Another agreed. "Then his dreams will never come true."

Reuben was surprised that his brothers would be that cruel. Reuben had often fought with strangers, but Joseph was their own brother. Even if Reuben did not like him, he did not believe in killing one of his own family.

"Let us not kill him," he said. "Just throw him into this empty well."

Of course Joseph would not last long left in an old well in this desolate place, but Reuben meant to come back and rescue Joseph.

The brothers agreed to Reuben's plan. When Joseph came up with the customary words of greeting all ready upon his lips, they grabbed him. He was amazed when they tore off his lovely coat and pushed him into the well.

It didn't matter to the cruel brothers when Joseph called for help. Reuben had business a little way off, and the other brothers sat down to have their lunch.

While they were eating Judah noticed a caravan approaching. (Dothan was on a caravan route between Syria and Egypt.) It gave him an idea.

"Instead of killing Joseph we could sell him as a slave to this caravan going to Egypt," he said.

When the traders, who were taking spices down to Egypt, passed by, the brothers took Joseph out of the well.

"Here is a fine young man," said Judah. "What will you give us for him?"

The men agreed on twenty shekels of silver. In spite of Joseph's plea to his brothers they would not relent. They allowed the men to take their brother away.

When Reuben returned, he was upset by what had happened. "What shall we tell our father?" he cried.

But the other brothers had this figured out. They still had Joseph's coat. They killed a goat from the flock and dipped the coat in its blood. When they returned home to the camp at Hebron they showed Jacob the coat.

"We found this," they lied. "Is it Joseph's coat?"

"Yes," cried Jacob when he had examined the coat. "I sent him to you to see how you were. He must have been killed by a wild animal."

Jacob mourned for his young son who had shown such promise, and the brothers kept their guilty secret.

Genesis 34, 35, 37

19. Joseph the Slave

"What is going to happen to me?" Joseph asked himself as the caravan made its way south. His father owned slaves, and he knew it was not a happy lot, even if one had a just master like Jacob.

Sometimes it was possible for a slave to be promoted to a good job with some authority over others. The best thing he could do was to work as hard and as well as he could.

Joseph wondered about God. Why had God allowed this to happen to him? He had always tried to do what he thought God wanted. What made his brothers do this to him?

Joseph was young, and he did not have all the answers to his questions. But as he entered the land of Egypt he felt sure of one thing—he would continue to trust God and would try to do His will. Surely God would help him, even in this strange land.

It had been a hard journey, but now they were in the land of the Nile. How different everything was! Joseph was used to the rugged hills and open plains. Here they passed through noisy, busy cities. He saw horses and chariots. He saw the green banks of the canals that controlled the yearly overflow of the river. He saw the pyramids and the elaborate temples to the different Egyptian gods.

When the caravan stopped to trade its wares, Joseph was sold to an Egyptian named Potiphar who was captain of the Pharaoh's body guard. (The Pharaoh was the king of Egypt.)

Egypt was an old and civilized land. There were many men of learning—sculptors, painters, poets, and mathematicians. But most of the people were poor. Many of them were slaves. In fact all the beautiful buildings had been built by slaves.

The most important people were the scribes (men who wrote Egypt's picture language in beautiful books), the priests of the Egyptian religion, and the military officers. As an officer, Potiphar was an important person and lived in a beautiful home.

Joseph worked hard as he served in Potiphar's house. He wasted no time feeling sorry for himself. As he worked, God helped him in every way.

Joseph believed that God was with him, even in this land of idol-worshipers. He determined to do what he believed right and to continue to worship God, whom his father and grandfather had worshiped.

Potiphar was pleased with Joseph. He was young and handsome, he worked hard, and he was a bright person who was quick to understand his job. He could organize and oversee the work of others, and Potiphar soon gave him opportunity to use these skills.

Joseph received more and more responsibility. Finally, as his chief servant, Potiphar let Joseph handle all his affairs.

But then trouble came to Joseph. Potiphar's wife accused Joseph of something he did not do. Because of her lie, Potiphar had Joseph put into prison.

Joseph was discouraged; but he was not sorry that he had done what was right. Because he was innocent he was sure God would help him.

Joseph was in a part of the prison

reserved for those who in some way were connected with the royal house. The keeper of the prison came to realize that he could trust Joseph. He gave Joseph special work to do, and Joseph did it well.

In time the keeper trusted other prisoners to Joseph's care. While Joseph was in charge, the cupbearer or butler to the Pharaoh and his chief cook were put into prison. They might have been accused of attempting to poison the ruler.

The keeper of the prison told Joseph to take special care of these important men. One morning Joseph noticed that they both seemed very troubled.

"Why do you look so sad today?" he asked.

"We have had dreams," they told Joseph, "and there are no interpreters here in prison."

The Egyptians believed dreams held important messages, and some men made a business of giving the special meaning of a dream.

Joseph was still interested in dreams. "God helps us to understand dreams," he said. "Will you tell me your dreams? Perhaps I can help you."

"Very well," said the cupbearer. "In my dream I saw a vine with three branches. I watched it bud, blossom and produce grapes. Pharaoh's cup was in my hand, and I took the grapes and pressed them into Pharaoh's cup. Then I gave Pharaoh the cup, just as I used to do."

Joseph thought for a while. "This is the interpretation," he said. "In three days Pharaoh will restore you to your office, and you shall again give Pharaoh his cup as you used to do."

The cupbearer was happy. "I hope it comes true as you have said."

"When you are restored," said Joseph, "will you put in a good word for me with the Pharaoh? Ask him to release me. I was stolen from my own home and made a slave. Since I have been in Egypt I have done nothing to deserve being put in prison."

When the cook heard the good news the cupbearer received, he wanted Joseph to interpret his dream.

"This was my dream," said the cook. "I was carrying three baskets on my head. In the top basket were sweet cakes for Pharaoh. Then birds came by and started to eat the cakes."

Joseph frowned over this dream. He thought about it, and then he had to give the cook bad news.

"Your dream means that in three days you will be put to death by Pharaoh's orders."

Three days later Pharaoh celebrated his birthday with a large feast. He had thought over the case of his cupbearer and cook. He had decided that the cupbearer was innocent but the cook was guilty.

Pharaoh sent to the prison and had the cook and cupbearer brought out. He told the cupbearer he could have his old post back and attend the feast. But he told the cook he was to be put to death.

Joseph hoped that the cupbearer, who saw so much of the Pharaoh, would speak for him. But the cupbearer forgot all about Joseph in his joy at being free.

Two years went by, and Joseph was still in prison. But he continued to believe that God would help him.

Genesis 39, 40

20. The Dream That Was a Warning

The Pharaoh at the time Joseph was in Egypt might have been one of a family of Pharaohs who came from Asia. They were called the Hyksos or Shepherd Kings. When these outsiders conquered Egypt, they put their own people on the throne and gave them the most important positions in the government.

The Egyptian people, though, hated outsiders, and they had special dislike for shepherds. They were farming people and did not like having land used for grazing sheep.

One night the Pharaoh had a dream that seemed very important. He was sure there was a message in his dream. The next morning, he called in his scribes.

Besides writing in books, these learned

men gave interpretations to dreams and performed magical acts. They were official advisors to the ruler in all his decisions.

"I had a dream," Pharaoh told his scribes. "I was standing by the Nile. I looked, and out of the river came seven sleek, fat cows and they ate the reed grass. Then seven more cows came up out of the Nile, but these were bony and thin. The thin cows ate up the fat cows. Then I woke up.

"I went back to sleep and had another dream. I looked and saw that seven ears of plump grain grew on one stalk. Afterwards seven thin, withered ears sprouted. The withered ears swallowed up the full ears of grain. Then I woke up."

After the Pharaoh had finished his account, the scribes all looked from one to another. They shook their heads. They were puzzled as to what this dream could mean. No one had an interpretation which satisfied the Pharaoh.

The cupbearer was standing nearby ready to serve the Pharaoh. Suddenly he remembered the young man in prison who had correctly interpreted his dream, for whom he had promised to speak. But he had forgotten.

Now the cupbearer spoke up. "Pharaoh, when you had the cook and me put in prison, we both had strange dreams the same night. A young Hebrew in the prison called Joseph interpreted our dreams. He said mine meant that I would be restored to favor. He told the cook that his dream meant that he would be put to death. And this is exactly what happened."

The Pharaoh was interested. "Have this young Hebrew, Joseph, brought to me," he commanded.

When the keeper of the prison received the message he released Joseph at once. "The Pharaoh wants to see you," he told Joseph. "To appear before the Pharaoh you must shave your head."

The Hebrews always liked beards, but no Egyptian wore hair on his head or face, Joseph was also given good clothes to wear before the ruler.

So Joseph came before Pharaoh, and bowed down before this powerful ruler.

"I have had a dream," Pharaoh told him, "and no one can interpret it for me. I have heard that when you hear a dream you can interpret it."

Joseph said, "It is not my power. God will give us an answer."

While Pharaoh told his two dreams to Joseph, Joseph asked God to help him. As he listened, Joseph believed that God had indeed given Pharaoh an important message—a warning about the future.

"Both the dreams have one meaning," Joseph told the ruler. "God has revealed something to you. There will come seven years of great plenty throughout all the land of Egypt, but afterwards there will come seven years of famine. The famine will be so great that everyone will forget the good years."

The dreams held both good and bad news. The Egyptian people depended on the overflowing of the Nile every year because it made the ground rich. Little rainfall during any year would produce little overflow, and the harvest of that year would be poor.

While he was before Pharaoh, a plan had come to Joseph's quick mind.

"During the seven good years let Pharaoh appoint overseers throughout the land," he said, "to take from every farmer a fifth of his harvest. Store it away under your authority. Then when the famine comes, there will be grain for use during these lean years, and the people will not perish from hunger."

In those days rulers had great power. Often a person who found favor was immediately given honor and riches; or a person who found disfavor was quickly put to death. This time Pharaoh was impressed. He talked over Joseph's plan with his advisors. "Joseph is wise," he concluded. "Can we find anyone better than he to take charge of this plan?"

So Pharaoh again spoke to Joseph. "Since God has shown you all this, there must be none so wise as you. You will be second to me and will have charge over all the people and help me rule this land."

To seal his agreement, Pharaoh gave Joseph a ring showing his authority, a chain on which was a special Egyptian emblem, and royal garments of fine linen to wear.

So Joseph became a high official, responsible only to the Pharaoh. It was truly a great honor and a great change for Joseph, the Hebrew slave.

There was a parade, and Joseph rode in the second chariot, directly behind Pharaoh. Servants ran ahead of Joseph's chariot crying, "Bow the knee."

As Joseph looked around at the crowd, he marveled at the way everything had turned out. Truly God had been with him and had helped him. Now besides honor and riches, he had been given an important task to do and a chance to help others.

Genesis 41

21. A Test for Ten Brothers

The famine had come. There had been seven years of plenty in Egypt and the surrounding countries. The needed rain and the Nile's overflow had brought good harvests. But now the rainfall was small and the river did not have enough overflow to enrich the ground.

Because of the warning God had sent through Joseph's interpretation, the Egyptians had saved part of the harvests from their years of plenty. When the people needed food they came to Joseph, as representative of Pharaoh, and bought what they needed.

The famine had come to all the surrounding countries, including Canaan where Jacob and his other sons still lived. The caravans that traded back and forth between Syria and Egypt brought Jacob's tribe the news: "There is grain for sale in Egypt."

They told others the same good news, and many people went to Egypt to buy grain.

One day Jacob said to his older sons, "There is grain in Egypt. Go down and buy grain for us so that we may have food."

The ten older brothers made ready. They took servants and asses and provisions, including money, with them.

"Benjamin will stay here," said Jacob. Jacob was afraid some harm might come to his youngest son.

When the brothers entered Egypt they asked from whom they could buy grain. They were told where to go and who to see. The official who gave out the grain was none other than Joseph. But he had been given an Egyptian name and everyone considered him an Egyptian.

The brothers were brought into the chamber of this important person, second only to Pharaoh. They saw a clean-shaven Egyptian, dressed in the official Egyptian dress. They did not recognize the brother they had hated.

But Joseph recognized them! They were older, but they looked much the same. They came and bowed low before him.

Then Joseph remembered the dreams he had dreamt while still a child. He also remembered the way his brothers had acted toward him. Another man in Joseph's place would have had his brothers put to death; but Joseph had no hatred for his brothers.

He thought quickly. He wanted to know about his father and his younger brother. He wanted them here if possible. Joseph also wanted to know if his brothers had changed. Were they still cruel, self-seeking men? Joseph decided to test them to see.

When they asked to buy grain, he spoke harshly to them. "You didn't come here to buy grain at all. You are spies. You want to see if Egypt is open to attack."

Egypt, as a land of wealth, was a temptation to armies from Asia. The Egyptians had built fortresses along their border to protect themselves.

The brothers protested. "No, my lord. We have come only to buy food."

Joseph continued to accuse them. "I don't believe you. You are spies."

"No, we are honest men. We are brothers of one family. We come from Canaan."

"Is your father still living?" asked Joseph. "Do you have any other brothers?"

"We have one younger brother," they told him. "He is with our father back in Canaan. We did have another younger brother, but he is dead."

"By this you shall be tested," said Joseph. "I will find out if you are telling the truth about yourself. One of you can return to Canaan, but he must bring your younger brother to me. Meanwhile the rest of you will be kept here in prison. If your younger brother comes, I will be able to check your story."

So the very frightened brothers were put into prison. How disastrously this trip had ended!

After three days Joseph had a different plan. He called the brothers to him.

"I fear God," he said to them. "I don't want to accuse you on suspicion only. I will sell you the grain you need, and you can take it back to your father.

"Only one of you needs to stay here in prison. The rest of you are released. But if you want to buy more grain, and if you want to release the brother who stays, you must return with your younger brother. If he is not with you, you will not see my face."

The brothers were dismayed. "We are being paid back for what we did to Joseph," they said to one another. "We would not listen when he begged us to have mercy on him."

Reuben said, "Didn't I tell you not to harm your own brother? Now God is punishing us for what we did then."

All this time an interpreter had translated Joseph's speech from the Egyptian language for the brothers. They did not know this important Egyptian ruler could understand their language.

Joseph felt sorry for his brothers, as he

listened to them. They did remember their sin against him, and now they were sorry. Joseph had to turn away because there were tears in his eyes. But the brothers did not notice. Then Joseph chose Simeon as the one to stay and dismissed the others.

"Give these men the grain they buy," he said to a servant, "but put the money they give you back into their sacks."

At last the brothers were on their way home. They were concerned about Simeon; but mostly they were concerned about what their father would say when they told him the ruler wanted to see Benjamin.

When they camped for the night, one of the brothers opened a sack to get grain for his ass.

"Look!" he cried, "here is the money I gave the Egyptians! Someone has put it back into the sack."

This frightened the brothers. Was it a trick? "God is judging us," they said again. For so many years they had lived with the guilt of having sold Joseph, and they had always been afraid that they would be paid back in some way.

When they got home it was hard to tell the story to Jacob. They told all that the ruler who sold them the grain had said to them. Then they opened their sacks to show their father the life-saving grain.

To their dismay they found that all the money they had given to the Egyptians had been returned.

"Now the Egyptians will accuse us of stealing," they wailed.

Jacob refused to allow Benjamin to go to Egypt. "Joseph is dead and Simeon is in prison. And now you want me to risk Benjamin's life also?" he asked. "Never."

But it did not take long for Jacob's tribe to eat the grain that had been bought in Egypt. Another family council was held.

Judah said, "We *must* take Benjamin to Egypt. The man warned us that we would get no grain if we came back without him. I promise you that we will bring Benjamin back unharmed."

After they talked some more Jacob finally agreed. He realized that they would all die if they could not buy food.

"Take presents to the ruler," he suggested, "some honey, spices, and nuts. And take back the money that was put into the sacks to show that you are honest."

Once more the brothers made the long trip and stood before Joseph. When he saw that his younger brother Benjamin was with them, he told his steward, "These men are going to have lunch with me."

So the steward brought the brothers to Joseph's house. They marveled at the beauty of the place. They spoke to the steward about the money in their sacks, but he told them to keep the money. Then he brought Simeon out from prison to join them.

When Joseph came in, the brothers again bowed low before him and gave him the presents they had brought from their father.

"Is your father alive and well?" Joseph asked his brothers through an interpreter.

They told him, "He is alive and well."

"Is this your younger brother?" Joseph smiled on Benjamin. "God be gracious to you, my son."

Joseph was overwhelmed with emotion as he spoke to his brother, and had to leave for a moment so they would not see

him weep. Then he returned, and the lunch started.

As an Egyptian, Joseph ate with his Egyptian officials. They could not eat with the men from Canaan; but he sent special dishes to their table. The brothers were surprised that Benjamin's portion was always larger than their own. They wondered why the ruler had taken such a liking to Benjamin.

Joseph did like Benjamin and wanted his younger brother to stay with him. He decided on a plan.

He would again put the money back into each brother's sack, but in Benjamin's sack he would also put his silver cup. He would send his steward after them to search them. Benjamin would be brought back.

This would tell him something else. Would the brothers try to protect Benjamin, or would they desert the young man as they had deserted Joseph? It would be a final test for his brothers.

Genesis 41:53-57
42, 43, 44:1-5

22. Good Out of Evil

After their grain sacks were filled the brothers started back home. They had gone but a short way when they saw an Egyptian official hurrying after them.

"What is wrong now?" they asked one another as they stopped and waited for the man.

"Why have you rewarded our kindness with theft?" Joseph's steward demanded. "Why have you stolen my master's silver cup?"

The brothers denied the charge. "My lord, why do you speak such words? We brought the money we found in our sacks back to you. Why would we steal from you afterwards?"

The brothers were so sure none of them had the cup that they said, "If you find the cup with one of us, let him die, and let the rest of us become your slaves."

The official said, "All right. The man who has the cup shall become a slave, but the rest of you shall be blameless."

So the official searched all the sacks. He began with the eldest. Sack after sack was opened, but no cup was found. Last of all Benjamin's sack was opened, and to the astonishment of all the brothers, the silver cup rolled out.

The brothers were distressed. Now they knew they were really in for trouble. Without resistance they loaded up their asses and went back with the steward to Joseph's house.

Joseph was waiting for them. "Why did you steal from me?" he demanded as the brothers bowed before him.

Judah spoke for them all. "What can we say? How can we clear ourselves? God has punished us, and we are ready to be your slaves."

Joseph was pleased that his brothers were willing to share the blame with Benjamin. But he said, "No, only the man in whose sack the cup was found shall be my slave. The rest of you may go in peace to your father."

But the brothers refused to take this way out and desert Benjamin.

Judah spoke again. He recalled all that had happened, how Jacob had at first refused to send Benjamin, but that he had promised his father that no harm would come to him.

"If we go back and the lad is not with us, our father will die," Judah said. "I am willing to stay and be your slave in Benjamin's place."

When Joseph saw how the brothers cared for their father and their brother, and that Judah was willing to sacrifice himself for Benjamin, he could keep his secret no longer. Now he knew that his brothers had indeed changed and were worthy of his help.

"Everyone leave but these men. I want to be alone with them," Joseph commanded his officials and servants.

The brothers wondered what could possibly happen next. But they were not prepared for what followed.

Joseph looked at his brothers and opened up his arms. "I am Joseph," he told them, and wept aloud.

The brothers could not answer. Now they understood why they had had so much trouble and why this ruler gave special attention to Benjamin. But they thought the end was near. Surely Joseph would have them put to death in revenge for what they had done to him.

But Joseph spoke kindly. "Come close to me. I am your brother Joseph, whom you sold into slavery. Don't be distressed or angry with yourselves because of what you did. God sent me to Egypt before you to save lives."

Joseph had thought many times about what had happened. He realized that God had been working in all these events. Because he had come to Egypt, he had been able to save his own family from starvation. He had also been able to save the Egyptians. Joseph had suffered, but now he realized that it had been for a good purpose, and he was content.

"Now hurry," he told his brothers. "Go back to my father in Canaan and give him the good news that I am alive and that God has made me a lord in Egypt. Bring my father and all his people and possessions here."

Joseph embraced Benjamin and his other brothers. They talked with each other and made peace.

Pharaoh heard about Joseph's brothers, and he was happy for Joseph. "Let them come to Egypt," he told Joseph. "Take wagons from Egypt for your brothers to bring back all their families without trouble. I will give you and your family and all their people good land to live in."

Joseph happily made plans to receive his family.

Meanwhile, the brothers brought the good news to Jacob. "Joseph is alive, and he is governor over all the land of Egypt," they told their father.

But Jacob could not believe them.

Then the brothers told him the whole story. They told their father that Joseph would make a home for them all in Egypt. And they showed him the Egyptian wagons.

Then Jacob believed. They made ready to move all the tribe to Egypt. The caravan began the long trip south.

On the way God spoke again to Jacob saying: "Do not be afraid to go down to Egypt; for I will make you a great nation while you are there. I will go with you into Egypt; and I will also bring you back to this land."

Jacob understood. The promise that his descendants would inherit Canaan

would still come true. One day his descendants would come back to Canaan.

In Egypt, Joseph embraced his father with great joy. "Now that I have seen your face and know that you are really alive, I am completely satisfied," said the happy father.

Joseph spoke for his people before Pharaoh. He had settled his family in the land of Goshen in the northeastern tip of Egypt. He wanted permission to stay there, because it was good grazing land. It would also give them a place to themselves away from the Egyptians who did not like shepherds.

Pharaoh gave his permission, and all was well with Jacob and his family. But Jacob did not live long in Egypt.

After his death, Joseph's brothers again wondered if now Joseph would take vengeance on them.

They sent a message to Joseph asking for his forgiveness. Joseph spoke to them. "Fear not. You meant evil against me; but God meant it for good. Because I came to Egypt many lives have been saved."

The brothers were comforted. It was true. What they did was wrong, but God had brought good out of their misdeeds. Now their children would be safe, and they would all prosper in this new land.

Genesis 44-48

PART TWO

THE PEOPLE OF GOD

For a little more than four hundred years the descendants of Jacob's sons lived in Egypt. They grew in number and spread out over Goshen, the northeastern section of Egypt.

Their flocks and herds had the food and water they needed. Life was ever so much easier than wandering from place to place in the desert or among the hills of Canaan.

The land of Egypt was a highly civilized country. From the Egyptians the Hebrews learned many things. But the Hebrews did not forget their own history.

Fathers and mothers told their children about Abraham, Isaac, Jacob and Joseph. Generally the people could trace their ancestry back to one of Jacob's sons, and they counted this their tribe.

"I am of the tribe of Judah," someone would say, or "we are of the tribe of Benjamin."

Later these Hebrew tribes came to be called the "children of Israel," which referred to Jacob's second name. Then they became known as the Israelites.

God had first chosen a man and a family. Now God had a nation of people. Only they were a nation living in a land which was not their own.

All went well while the Pharaohs were one of those who were friendly to the shepherds; but one day there was a change in government. A different family came to the throne of Egypt.

This new Pharaoh made many changes. He felt no gratitude to Joseph who had been a friend of the previous family. He counted the Hebrews as his enemies.

"These people are not Egyptians," he said. "How do we know that they would not side with the enemy if armies from Asia were to attack us? They have grown to be a large people. We had better do something to protect ourselves."

So this new Pharaoh made all the Hebrew people slaves. But God was watching over His people. The time had come in God's plan to move forward.

23. A Baby Is Saved

The new Pharaoh of Egypt had many monuments built. He wanted to be remembered as a great ruler. He collected much treasure and commanded that storehouses be built to hold it. For these constructions he used the forced labor of the Hebrews and other slaves.

As time went by the Hebrews were made to build cities on the frontier to be used as forts for defense. Many storehouses were built in these cities for provisions and arms. The Hebrews were also forced to work on the canals which was dangerous work. Many lost their lives.

But fear, suspicion, and hatred for the Hebrews had grown so that even this hard work was not enough. The Egyptians made their lives as hard as they could. The Pharaoh even wanted to kill all the male children, but the Egyptian women who helped the Hebrew women when they had babies refused.

"This is too cruel," they said. They made excuses to the ruler as the Hebrews grew in number.

In the tribe of Levi a man and his wife had a baby boy. The family was happy but very much afraid. How could they protect their baby from this wicked ruler who still said he wanted to destroy all the male children of the Hebrews?

"How strong and healthy he looks," said the father.

"He is a beautiful baby," said the mother.

"How could anyone hurt such a beautiful child," said the older sister, Miriam.

The little brother Aaron looked on, watching the baby smile in his sleep.

"We must hide our baby," said the mother.

It is hard to hide a baby who sometimes cries and soon wants to crawl around, but for three months no one knew that there was a baby in the house.

One day the mother said, "We must find a new place to hide the baby. I'll make a little boat and hide him in the river. Miriam, you stay close by and see that no harm comes to him."

The mother wove reeds together in the shape of a small boat just big enough to hold the baby. She plastered it with tar and pitch to make it watertight. She placed the baby inside. First they looked to make sure none of the soldiers of Pharaoh saw them. Then she and Miriam made their way to the Nile.

Near the bank they found a shallow place among the reeds. "Stay close by," said the mother to Miriam.

So Miriam hid herself and waited. It wasn't long before she heard approaching voices. She hoped it wasn't the soldiers. No, they were women's voices.

It was the Pharaoh's daughter and her maids-in-waiting. The Egyptians thought the Nile was a sacred river. It was part of their religious rituals to bathe in it.

"Here comes Pharaoh's daughter to bathe in the river," said Miriam to herself. "I hope she doesn't see my brother. She might tell her father."

The Egyptian princess walked along the river's bank with her maids. They looked down into the muddy water.

"Look," said the princess suddenly. "There's something among the reeds. It looks like a small boat."

The maids saw it too. "What could it be?" they wondered.

"Go into the water and bring it to me," the princess told one of her maids.

The girl waded out into the water. All the while Miriam was watching breathlessly nearby. The girl bent down and picked up the light boat.

"It's a baby," she exclaimed.

The maid carried the reed boat back to Pharaoh's daughter. Inside the baby began to cry.

As the princess looked in she too exclaimed, "It's a baby. How he cries! He must be one of the Hebrew children whose mother is trying to hide him from the terrible threats of my father."

Miriam scampered up the bank and ran to the group of women. She could see that the princess did not agree with her father's hatred for the Hebrews, and she was thankful.

Miriam bowed to the princess. "Shall I go and call you a nurse from the Hebrew women to nurse the child for you?" she asked.

The Pharaoh's daughter looked with love and pity on the little baby. "He will be my baby," she said.

To Miriam she said, "Yes, go and find a Hebrew nurse for me."

Miriam had a plan. She ran to her own mother and told her what happened.

"God is good to us," said the mother. "Our baby has been saved. He will have a good home as the adopted son of Pharaoh's daughter.

"You have done well, Miriam. Now I will go and offer myself as a nurse."

The mother and Miriam hurried back to the princess and her maids-in-waiting. There she was holding the baby in her arms.

The mother bowed. "May I serve you?" she asked.

"Yes," said the princess. "Take this baby home with you and nurse it for me. When he is a little older I want you to bring him to the palace. I will raise him as my own son. I will pay you for your work."

When the baby grew old enough, his mother brought him to the palace. The princess took him lovingly for her own son. To please her, the Pharaoh allowed the princess to keep him.

"This is my baby," she told everyone at the court. She showed him to the princes and other princesses.

"I have named him Moses," (meaning saved from the water.") she said.

Exodus 1; 2:1-10

24. An Unwanted Hero

Moses grew up in the Egyptian palace. He was given a good education and trained to be an official. A place of honor and importance was sure to be his.

But as Moses grew older he thought more and more about his own people. He knew he was a Hebrew. Yet he enjoyed the comforts and splendor of the court, while the rest of his people cried out under slavery.

One day when Moses had become a man he visited his own family in the land of Goshen where they lived with the rest of the Hebrews. He noticed how hard the gangs of slaves had to work. He saw the cruel taskmasters crack their whips over the bare backs.

"It is not right," he thought to himself. "I must find some way to help my own people."

As he watched, an Egyptian began to beat one of the Hebrews. Moses could stand it no longer. He looked around. No Egyptians were watching. He rushed to the Egyptian and struck him a blow that caused him to fall over dead.

Moses had not meant to kill him. Quickly he hid the body. The next day he was still in Goshen when he came upon two Hebrews having a fight.

Again Moses tried to help. It wasn't right that the Hebrews who were persecuted should also fight one another.

"Why do you strike your fellow Hebrew?" he asked one of the men.

The man did not want Moses to interfere. He laughed at him. "Who made you a judge over us?" he asked. "Are you going to kill me as you killed the Egyptian yesterday?"

Moses was afraid. *How many people knew about this?* he wondered. If word got back to Pharaoh what would happen? Then it might not be enough that he was the adopted son of Pharaoh's daughter.

The Pharaoh did hear about it. He was angry at Moses for taking sides against the Egyptians. "Now Moses must die," he announced.

Moses heard that his life was in danger and fled. The only place to go was out into the desert—away from the soldiers who bordered the frontier. Moses didn't stop running until he came to the land of Midian. Here he would have to make a new life for himself. He would never dare to go back to Egypt.

Moses was discouraged. He had wanted to help his people, but he had failed. He had done a foolish, rash thing in killing the Egyptian. He should have had a plan to help his people which was more thoroughly thought out. But even so, the Hebrews did not seem to want his help. They distrusted him.

Moses sat down to rest by a well. He watched seven girls give water to their sheep. They tried to work quickly, but they were not quick enough. Other shepherds came and pushed in ahead of them.

Once more Moses interfered. He made the men wait their turn while he helped the women get water for their flocks.

This time his help was appreciated. "We thank you," said the sisters.

When they got back home their father, Jethro, was surprised to see them. "You are early. Did the shepherds who sometimes trouble you fail to appear today?"

"They came," said the girls, "but a stranger helped us and made them wait. He even helped us water our flocks."

"Why didn't you invite the man to our tent?" asked the father. "Call him back and ask him to dinner."

The girls ran back to Moses and invited him to stay with them.

The Midians were nomad shepherds who lived in different places throughout the vast desert. Moses stayed with Jethro and his family many years. He became a shepherd and cared for Jethro's flocks. He married one of Jethro's daughters and had two sons.

Life was very different from that in the Egyptian court, but it was quiet and peaceful. Moses was content, but often he thought of Egypt and his people.

Back in Egypt the Hebrews were still suffering. The Pharaoh had died, but the son who ruled in his place continued to mistreat them. In time this son proved to be a weaker king than his father, and Egypt decreased in power.

The Hebrews still had to work under hard conditions. Finally they felt they could no longer bear their suffering and they cried to God for help.

God had not forgotten His people. He had a plan for their deliverance. Now the people were ready for a leader who would bring them out of slavery.

Exodus 2:11-25; 3:1

25. A Leader for God's People

For forty years Moses had been a shepherd, caring for Jethro's flocks. He was part of Jethro's family. One day Moses led the flocks into the Sinai Peninsula. They passed through a desert place where rugged mountains rose up on either side. Here there was little in the way of vegetation, and on this bright day the desert sun danced off the sand and rocks.

Suddenly Moses saw a strange sight. There was a bush on fire. Yet, as Moses looked closely, he saw that the bush was not burning away. God was using this way of attracting Moses' attention.

Moses went up the mountain side to look closer. "Why isn't the bush burnt up?" he asked himself.

Then God spoke to Moses, calling him by name. "Moses. Moses."

Moses was filled with wonder. "Here I am," he said.

"Do not come near," said God. "Take off your sandals, for the place on which you are standing is holy ground. I am the God of your fathers, Abraham, Isaac, and Jacob."

Moses hid his face from the holy fire. He was afraid. And yet it was a wonderful experience. Was it really God who was speaking to him? The God he had heard so much about from his Hebrew parents?

God continued his message. "I have seen the affliction of My people in Egypt and have heard their cry. I know the sufferings they endure at the hands of their taskmasters. I will deliver them out of the Egyptians' power. I will bring them out of the land of Egypt and take them to a good land, the land that I promised to Abraham, Isaac, and Jacob."

This was wonderful news. Moses knew about this long-ago promise. But God's next message frightened him.

"Come, I will send you to Pharaoh. You will bring My people out of Egypt."

Moses objected. "Who am I that I

should go to Pharaoh and bring the people out of Egypt?"

It was too hard a task. Moses had tried to help before and had failed.

"But I will be with you," God promised. "I will help you, and one day you and your people will come and worship Me on this very mountain."

Still Moses was afraid. He had many arguments about why he should not be the one to lead the people to freedom.

"They won't believe me," he protested.

"They will believe you," God promised. "Gather the elders together and tell them, 'The God of your fathers has promised to bring you out of the land of Egypt into the land of Canaan.'

"I will give you special signs to help convince the people that I have sent you. Throw your rod upon the ground."

When Moses threw the rod down it became a serpent. When he took up the serpent it became a rod again. God showed Moses how to perform other signs which would help convince the people.

God continued His instructions to Moses. "You and the elders must go to Pharaoh and say to him, 'The Lord, the God of the Hebrews, has met with us. We pray you, let us go a three days journey into the wilderness so that we may sacrifice to the Lord our God.' I know that Pharaoh will not let you go unless he is forced by a mighty power. After I have shown Egypt My power, Pharaoh will let you go."

Still Moses hesitated. "I am not a speaker who can arouse people to do great things. Send someone else."

But God insisted that Moses go. He spoke sternly. "It is My power that will enable you to do it. Your brother Aaron will help you. You must give him the message and then he can do the talking."

Moses realized that God had chosen him. He must obey. He went back to Jethro, his father-in-law.

"I would like to go back to visit my family in Egypt," Moses told him.

"Go in peace," said Jethro.

As Moses made his way back to Egypt, God spoke to Aaron who was also anxious to help his people.

When the two brothers met, Moses told him about his strange experience on the mountain.

"Come," said Aaron. "We must gather together all the elders of our people. They must hear your story."

When the representatives of the different tribes had assembled, Aaron told them what had happened, exactly as Moses had told it to him.

"God has promised to deliver us," he said. "The God of Abraham, Isaac, and Jacob is going to bring us out of this land of bondage."

Moses showed the people the rod which could become a serpent. He performed the other signs that God had shown him.

The people were happy. They believed the message. They bowed their heads and thanked God for his care for them.

"God has heard our cry," they shouted. "Soon we shall be free."

Exodus 3, 4

26. "Let My People Go"

Moses and Aaron were allowed to come before the Pharaoh. Moses had known him as a prince. He knew that this Pharaoh, like his father, hated the Hebrews.

The brothers made their request known. "The God of Israel says, 'Let My people go, that they may worship Me in the wilderness.' May we take this journey?"

Pharaoh scoffed. "I do not know this God. Why should I obey Him? I will not let your people go."

But Moses and Aaron persisted. "The God of the Hebrews has met with us. Let us go, we pray, a three days' journey into the wilderness and worship our God."

It was a little thing to ask, but the Pharaoh would not even consider it.

"You have been talking to the Hebrews," he said. "Lately they have not been working hard. They are becoming restless slaves."

When the brothers had gone the Pharaoh commanded his taskmasters, "You shall no longer give the slaves straw to make bricks. They will have to go out and gather their own straw. Still they must make as many bricks as they made before."

It was an impossible task. The bricks were made of Nile mud, baked in the sun. Chopped straw was added to the mud to make it hold together. Up to this time the chopped straw had been given to the slaves. Now they had to gather and chop it themselves, before they could even start making the bricks.

The Hebrews who had been so joyous and confident were now crushed. The Hebrew foremen were beaten, because the slaves were not able to produce the same number of bricks.

The foremen complained to Moses and Aaron. "Because of your request to go into the desert to worship God, Pharaoh is angry. He says we are idle and need to be given more work. He will surely kill us."

Moses was distressed. He prayed to God. "Lord, why did you send me? Now it is even harder on my people. You haven't delivered us."

But God said, "Wait. I am God. You and all of Egypt will see My power. Tell the people of Israel, 'I will deliver you from your bondage. I will take you for My people, and I will be your God. You shall know that I am the Lord, your God.' "

But the people were too unhappy to listen to these words of encouragement.

Moses and Aaron continued to pray to God for help. God told Moses to show Pharaoh the rod which could become a serpent. The two brothers went again to Pharaoh and made their request. They performed the sign but this did not impress Pharaoh. He still refused his permission.

Again Moses and Aaron turned to God for help. God promised His help. He told them to meet Pharaoh the next morning when the ruler went to the sacred Nile River to bathe.

The next morning when Pharaoh and his servants came down to the river's edge the brothers were waiting for them with a special message from God.

"The God of the Hebrews has said, 'Let My people go that they may serve Me in the wilderness, but you have not obeyed. By this you shall know that I am the Lord; I will turn the water of the Nile to blood, and the fish in the Nile shall die!' "

The Egyptians believed the Nile was a sacred river and that their gods would allow no one to harm it.

Then Moses told Aaron to strike the water with the rod in his hand and the water became red. The fish in the river died, and the people refused to drink the water. They dug in the ground about the Nile for better water.

Seven days later God told Moses to go and ask Pharaoh again. "Say to him that the Lord says, 'Let My people go that they may serve Me. If you refuse, your land will be infested with frogs.' "

Moses obeyed, but Pharaoh again refused, and God brought this second judgment upon the land. Frogs, too, were held sacred by the Egyptians. In this way God struck out at the false religion of the people.

Often frogs were a nuisance to the Egyptians, but this was the worst plague of frogs they had ever had. Frogs seemed to be everywhere. The Egyptians complained that they were all about their houses and even got into their food.

"Tell your God to take away the frogs, and I will let you all go and worship your God," the Pharaoh told Moses.

That night the frogs died. The people gathered them together and burned them. But now the Pharaoh changed his mind. He was afraid to let the slaves have such a good chance to escape.

"Back to work," he said to the Hebrews. "You may not leave."

God continued to show His power to the Egyptian ruler and people. There was a plague of gnats. Then swarms of flies covered the land. Both times Pharaoh promised that the people could go, but both times he changed his mind as soon as the plagues ended.

Then God caused a disease to come to many of the animals of the land. But, as with the flies, none of the people of Goshen were touched with the plague. Still Pharaoh would not believe in God's power.

More trouble came to the Egyptians. Many people and animals suffered from boils. Hail storms, such as Egypt had never seen, with thunder and lightning, rained down on the land.

Moses had warned the people that the hail was coming. All those Egyptians who believed in God's power ran for the shelter of their homes and brought their animals inside too, and so were not hurt. But in all of Goshen no hail fell.

Once more Pharaoh nearly let the people go, but when the terrible hail and lightning was over he said, "No, why should I?"

Pharaoh's servants pleaded with him, "Let these men go and serve their God."

Pharaoh said he would allow only the men of Israel to go.

"No," said Moses. "We must all go."

Then Moses told Pharaoh that God would send a plague of locusts to the land. Locusts had come to Egypt before, eating the growing grain, but never was there such a plague as this. They ate all the plants that had not been destroyed by the hail. And although Pharaoh said he'd let the people go, when the locusts left after Moses had prayed to God, Pharaoh again changed his mind.

This plague was followed by a time

of darkness in the land. The Egyptians, who worshiped the sun, were afraid.

The Pharaoh was stubborn. He did not seem to care how much his own people suffered. He did not want to lose this slave labor. He was sure that if he gave any people a chance to get away from his cruel dominion they would do so.

Now God spoke again to Moses. "One more plague will come," he said. "It will be so terrible that Pharaoh will relent, and will indeed let you go."

Exodus 5-10

27. The First Passover

"Get ready to go," Moses told the people. "You will have to leave in a hurry."

Then Moses warned Pharaoh of what was soon to come. "Tonight the eldest son of every family will die. All people will be included, from Pharaoh's family to the family of the lowest servant. Only the people of Israel will escape.

"By this, Pharaoh, you will know that it is Israel's God who is bringing this judgment on your land. There will be such a great cry in your land, that you and the rest of the people will push us out of Egypt."

Pharaoh did not believe God's power could do this. He refused to change his mind about letting the Hebrew slaves go to worship in the desert.

Moses had important instructions from God for the people of Israel.

"You will always remember this night," he told them. "God is going to deliver you from slavery tonight.

"Now you must take a lamb from your flocks and kill it. Make sure it is a lamb without spot or blemish. You will eat the meat roasted for your dinner. This will be a special dinner which you will remember and keep as a feast in years to come.

"With your meat eat unleavened bread and bitter herbs. Make sure you roast the lamb, and when you eat it, be ready to leave. Sandals should be on your feet and your walking staff in your hand. You will eat in a hurry.

"This evening when you kill the lamb, take some of the blood and put it in a basin. Then take a bunch of hyssop and dip it into the basin. Smear the blood on the door posts and lintel of your house.

"God is going to bring judgment on the Egyptians for their past cruelties. The eldest son in each home will die, but none of your sons will die. The blood on the door is a sign that you are one of God's people and have kept this special service to Him. The judgment will pass over you.

"In years to come, when you are living in the land of Canaan, and keep this service, your child will ask you, 'What is the meaning of this service?' Then you will say, 'It is the passover when God slew the Egyptians but spared us.' "

The people did as God had commanded. They made ready to leave the land of their sorrows. They ate their special meal in haste. They put the blood on the outside doorway.

Through the night they waited.

In the middle of the night a great cry was heard. In family after family sons were found dead. Pharaoh's son also died.

Pharaoh was roused from his bed. It had happened! The terrible judgment had come—just as Moses had said!

Everyone at the palace was up. Everyone pleaded with the ruler to at last let the Hebrews go.

Pharaoh called Moses and Aaron to him. "Rise up and go immediately," he told them. "Go into the desert and serve your God. Ask Him not to send any more plagues on us. Take your flocks, herds, and your families."

All the Egyptian people echoed the ruler's words. "Go and do as your God asks," they cried. "If you don't, we are all likely to be killed."

The people of Israel quickly gathered together. It was still dark. Many of them had dough in the house that was not leavened; but there was no time to put the leaven in and make it fluffy bread. They took the unleavened bread with them.

Some Egyptians who had married into Hebrew families went with them. Together they made a large group of thousands of people with many flocks and herds. They all journeyed south and east from Rameses to Succoth, a journey of two or three days.

Then Moses spoke to the people. "Remember this time as the day God brought you out of the land of Egypt, the land of your bondage. Remember that it was God's power that made you free.

"Every year we will celebrate this time of deliverance. The celebration will be seven days long. On the first day there will be a service of worship and another on the last day. During this time you will eat unleavened bread as a reminder of the way you left Egypt in haste."

The people of Israel did remember how God brought them out of slavery by an act of great judgment and power. Year after year they kept the Feast of the Passover. They had the special dinner. They gathered together to worship and thank God.

For seven days they ate the unleavened bread. They told their children, "It is because God brought us out of the land of slavery with a mighty hand."

Exodus 11-13

28. God's People Escape

The Hebrews did not stay at Succoth. They were determined to escape. The shortest way to Canaan was along the coast by the Mediterranean Sea. But soldiers guarding Egypt's frontiers barred the way. Also the people who lived there would have fought them off. The Hebrews were not ready for war.

Through their leader Moses, God led the people into the wilderness. They would go south towards Sinai, the place where God had called Moses to the task of delivering the people. But first they had to cross the Red Sea.

As God had shown His power to the Egyptians, He would now show His power to the Hebrews. He wanted to convince them that He was their God and much greater than any false gods the Egyptians worshiped.

A cloud of fiery light led the people by day and night. It was a sign to them that God Himself was leading them on to a home of their own.

Back in Egypt Pharaoh was told, "The Hebrews are escaping!"

"You see what we have done?" Pharaoh cried out in anger. "We have allowed all these slaves to escape. Now who will do all the work? Get ready. Our army will pursue the Hebrews and bring them back."

Pharaoh selected some of his best soldiers and finest chariots. The chariots were drawn by horses and carried two soldiers—one did the driving while one did the fighting. The soldiers were armed with the best weapons.

The Hebrews knew they must find a good spot to cross some part of the Red Sea. Moses led them to a place which might be shallow enough for them to drive their flocks and herds to the other side. Even though the water might come quite high, they could walk across. But it would take a long time.

Some believe the spot was a marshy place called the Sea of Reeds or the Bitter Lakes where high reeds grew in the water.

They had camped by the water for the night when in the distance they saw the Egyptian army coming towards them.

The people cried out in terror. "Now we are lost!"

Rugged hills rose on one side and water was before them. They complained to Moses. "You have brought us out here to die in the wilderness. Why didn't you leave us alone?"

They were so frightened that they lost their faith in the power of God. But Moses had not lost his faith. He believed God was greater than mighty Egypt and her trained soldiers.

He prayed and asked God to help them. God told Moses, "Stretch out your rod over the water and then command the people to go forward. I will show them My power and destroy the Egyptians."

"Stand firm and fear not," Moses told the people. "God will deliver us. God will fight for us. Come, let us go forward. We will cross the sea at once."

So the people made ready. Moses stretched his rod over the water. A strong east wind began to blow.

All night the strong east wind blew so hard that the waters were swept back, while the fiery cloud stayed between the Hebrews and the Egyptians.

In the morning the Hebrews started across the Sea.

"We are crossing on land," the people shouted in wonder and delight as they herded their animals across and made it safely to the other side. Meanwhile the Egyptians were getting closer and closer.

By the time they reached the Sea, the Hebrews were on the other side. The Egyptians started across but they were in for trouble. Their chariot wheels stuck in the mud.

Then God commanded Moses to stretch out his hand over the Sea. The strong wind stopped. A sudden rush of waters overflowed the chariots. Their horses and riders were swept away. All of the soldiers were drowned.

The people were amazed. They had finally escaped Egyptian tyranny. They were free now. A new land and a new life was before them.

Their God was great and powerful. They were confident again.

The people were so happy that they sang a song someone composed to mark the occasion. Miriam took a timbrel and with some of the other women led the people in a dancing march of joy.

The women sang the refrain of the song, answering the verses sung by the men.

These were some of the words:

> I will sing to the Lord, for he has triumphed gloriously.
> The horse and his rider he has thrown into the sea.
> The Lord is my strength and my song.
> He has become my deliverer.
> He is my God.
> O Lord you are glorious in power.
> You have overthrown those who rose up against you.
> Who is like to you, O Lord?
> Who is like to you, glorious in holiness, doing wonders?
> You, with your mercy, have led forth the people you have redeemed.
> The Lord shall reign for ever and ever."

The people had learned a valuable lesson. In later years when trouble came to the nation, they thought back to the time when God worked wonders to deliver them at the Red Sea. They often became discouraged and complained, but then someone would remember how back in their history God had delivered them. They would be encouraged to believe that God would do so again.

Exodus 13:17-22; 14, 15

29. God Cares for His People

God had enabled the Hebrews to escape from the cruel Egyptians. They were free people. But they found that freedom meant responsibility and discipline, as well as the right to plan their lives and do their own work.

Before them was a hard desert journey. It did not take long for the people to realize that the trip would involve more difficulties than they had thought.

After they crossed the Red Sea the people journeyed south into the Peninsula of Sinai. It was a vast desert of sand and rugged limestone rock. Very few trees and plants grew here. Water was scarce.

After the company was three days in the wilderness their water supply was used up and they found no more water anywhere.

Then they came to Marah and found water. But to their disappointment it was bitter. No one could drink it. Many of the people began to complain against their leader, Moses.

"What shall we drink?" they asked him.

Moses asked God to guide him, and God did help him. Moses found a plant which, when put into the water, would make it sweet.

Moses spoke to the people. "God wants us to trust Him during this journey," he said. "If you obey God, He will prove His love and care for you, by providing for your needs."

Their next stop was Elim. Every once in a while in the barren desert there are small spots of green grass, water and palm trees. They are called oases. Elim was such a place where the palm trees bent over the fresh running water. The people made their camp by the water.

But they could not stay here. They had to leave the comfortable spot and once more brave the barren desert. This time the people became hungry. The provisions which they had brought from Egypt were gone.

Now they were really afraid. They spoke against Moses for bringing them on this journey. They forgot the hardships of Egypt. All they could remember was that in Egypt they had enough to eat.

Some said, "Has Moses brought us out here for us to die of hunger? In Egypt we had all the bread we wanted."

Moses heard that the people were speaking against him. He asked God to help him know what to do.

God wanted the people to know of His care for them and to learn to trust Him. He told Moses, "I will give the people bread from heaven. Only they must obey my instructions. They must gather only what they need for that day. On the day before the Sabbath they must gather for two days, because none will appear on the Sabbath. The Sabbath is the day for you to rest."

God said, "Tell the people that I have heard their cries. In the evening they will find meat to eat, and in the morning they will find bread."

Moses told all this to the people. "God is going to provide for you even though you murmured against Him. When you complain against me, you are really complaining against God; because it is God

who brought you out of Egypt and set you on this journey."

That evening the people saw some quail migrating north. They were flying low and could easily be caught. Some were so exhausted they dropped to the ground. These birds made good food.

The next morning the people were in for another surprise. When the sun had dried the morning dew, they saw a white substance on the ground.

"Man na? What is it?" they asked each other. They had never tasted anything like it before. It was like a thin wafer and had a sweet taste. So they called it manna.

"This is the bread God promised to send from heaven," Moses told them. "Gather what you need for today. Tomorrow God will send us more."

When the sun grew hot it melted. But the next day more manna appeared. On the day before the Sabbath Moses reminded the people to gather twice what they needed. But some would not listen. On the Sabbath they went out to gather more but it was not there.

Moses scolded these people. "You must learn to listen to God's instructions," he told them.

Little by little the people learned to obey. But they expected God to make the journey easy for them. Whenever trouble came, they forgot to trust God. Their faith in God's love disappeared.

As they continued on their journey they came upon another long stretch of land where water was scarce. As their thirst grew, their murmurs against Moses grew.

"Why did you bring us out of Egypt? We are all going to die of thirst," they complained. Others said, "Is God among us or not?"

As they murmured their anger grew, and soon they were a violent mob.

"The people are ready to stone me," Moses cried to God. "What shall I do?"

God told Moses to go up the rocky mountainside and take the leaders of the people with him. While all the people watched, Moses was to strike a certain rock.

Moses did as God told him. When he struck the rock, water from a stream gushed out.

Once more the people discovered that God would not let them perish but would provide for their needs. Then a new kind of trouble met them.

An army of Amalekites, a tribe of desert people, came against them. The Hebrews had brought weapons with them, but they were not trained in war.

Joshua was one man who knew something about fighting a battle, so Moses made him a leader. "Choose men for the battle, for we must fight," he told Joshua. "While the battle is going on, I will pray to God for His help."

Joshua led the troop into battle while Moses prayed. The people of Israel fought hard, and chased the soldiers of Amalek away.

After the battle, Moses had an altar built. He led the people in giving thanks to God for His help and constant care.

Exodus 15:22-27; 16, 17

30. A Visit From Jethro

The people of Israel had come to the region of Sinai. At Mt. Sinai, a few days' journey from where they were camped, they were to meet God and worship Him in a special service. Soon after they made their camp in this region visitors came.

The men guarding the camp saw an old man with a woman and two boys approaching. "Who are you and what do you wish?" a guard asked them.

"I am Jethro," said the man. "I am Moses' father-in-law. This is Zipporah, my daughter, and these boys are the sons of Moses."

One man hurried to tell Moses that his father-in-law, his wife and his sons were here.

Moses ran out to meet them. He kissed them all warmly. "How are you?" he asked. He was glad they had found the camp so that his family could be with him again.

After Moses made sure his wife and sons were comfortable, the two men settled down in the tent for a long talk.

"God has been good to us," Moses told Jethro. "He delivered us from Pharaoh's rule with a mighty hand."

Moses told Jethro all about what God had done: about the plagues; that last night in Egypt when Pharaoh told him to go; the escape at the Red Sea; the way God had provided food and water for them on the hard journey through the desert.

Jethro listened with amazement. He rejoiced with Moses that things had gone as he had hoped. Jethro too was grateful to God.

"Blessed is the Lord who has delivered you out of the hand of the Egyptians," he said, "and brought you out of slavery. Now I know that your God is greater than all other gods."

As a sign of his thankfulness Jethro offered a sacrifice to God. Aaron and the elders of Israel were present. After the sacrifice they ate together.

The next day was a judgment or court day. Often as the people journeyed together there were disagreements. Sometimes people would quarrel over possessions, or about the pasture for their cattle, or other matters.

If they couldn't settle their arguments, they would come to Moses, and he would tell them what was right according to how God wanted them to live.

Always there was a long line of people waiting for Moses to hear their cases. Sometimes people waited from sunup to sundown.

Jethro saw the people waiting in the long line. He noticed how hard Moses was working, trying to do what God wanted and yet satisfy the people.

"What are you doing?" he asked Moses.

"The people bring me their problems and want me to settle their differences," said Moses. "They want me to tell them what God wants them to do."

"See how tired they are," said Jethro, "and you are wearing yourself out. It is too big a job for you to do alone."

Then Jethro gave some advice. "Teach the people God's way. Teach them His laws and commandments. Then when there are problems let them go to a judge.

"Appoint as judges good men who fear God, men who tell the truth and would not take a bribe. From these men make judges to oversee a smaller number of people.

"You could have a judge over every thousand; other judges could rule over a hundred people; some over fifty, and some over ten.

"If it were a very important matter it could be brought to you; otherwise one of these other judges could settle the difference."

Moses thought this was good advice. He remembered however to pray to God for His guidance. When he thought it was what God wanted, these judges were appointed.

Moses was glad for the visit of Jethro. He was not so proud a leader that he could not take good advice.

"Now I must return to Midian," said Jethro after a short time.

He said good-by to his daughter and grandsons. He said good-by to Moses and the other leaders. They watched him go.

Then Moses turned his face towards Mt. Sinai where he had promised that he and his people would meet and worship God.

Exodus 18

31. God Speaks From Sinai

At last the people of Israel were at Sinai. They made camp at the foot of the mountain. It had taken two months for the company to travel this far.

They would stay here for many months. Here they would learn from God how He wanted them to live, and how He wanted to be worshiped in the new land to which they were going.

The people looked around at the huge rugged mountains. The sheer cliffs rose thousands of feet into the sky. They found it easy to believe that God would speak to them here.

This was the Mountain where Moses saw the burning bush. Now Moses went up the mountain to worship God and seek His will for the people.

God gave Moses a message for them. When Moses came down he delivered it to the elders who represented all the tribes.

"This is what God says: 'You saw what I did in Egypt, and you know how I have kept you on this journey. Now if you will obey my commandments and worship me, you will be a special possession of mine. All the earth is mine, but I have chosen you from among all people to be my people. You will worship me and be a holy people to me.' "

The elders promised, "We will do whatever God wants. We will obey all the laws He gives you."

Moses went up the rocky mountain path to deliver this promise. When he came down again, he had more instructions for the people. There was going to be a special worship service.

"You must wash yourself and your clothes," Moses told them. "This is a sign that you are clean within and can come to God. You must all come to the mountain from which God speaks, but

you must not come up on the mountain or touch it, because it is holy. When you hear the trumpet sound, you will know it is time to assemble."

The people made themselves ready. Men put markers around the base of the mountain so that none of the worshipers would come too near by mistake. It was a way of showing that God is holy.

At the sound of the trumpet the people gathered. At the same time clouds swept over the mountain top and lightning flashed in the sky. Only Moses and Aaron were allowed to come up the mountainside. The people watched them disappear among the jagged rocks. Finally, way up high, they could see two small figures climbing.

On the mountaintop God spoke to Moses about the way He wanted to be worshiped and how He wanted the people to treat one another. There were many laws; some even about the care of animals. But most important were the laws we call the Ten Commandments.

God said, "I am the Lord your God who has brought you out of Egypt.
"You shall have no other gods before me.
"You shall not make an image for worship.
"You shall not take the name of God carelessly.
"Remember to keep the Sabbath day.
"Honor your father and mother.
"You shall not kill.
"You shall not commit adultery.
"You shall not steal.
"You shall not tell a lie.
"You shall not covet what belongs to others."

Several times Moses went up and down the mountain. Sometimes he was alone. Sometimes a few of the elders or judges went with him.

Moses repeated the laws of God to all the people waiting at the foot of the mountain.

Then the people answered. "We will do all that God has asked."

Moses wrote down the laws of God so that they would be sure to be remembered. Then God called Moses up to the mountaintop again. This time Moses took Joshua with him and left Aaron in charge of the people.

Moses was gone for forty long days. God had much to show him about the way He wanted to be worshiped; the special offerings to be made, and the special feast days to be held.

But the people in the camp became impatient. They remembered the big worship services the Egyptians held—the feasting and the good times that followed. If only Moses would come back, they could have a feast.

Then some said, "Let's have a feast without Moses."

Others said, "Maybe something has happened to Moses." Discontent grew. Finally a group came to Aaron.

"Make us a god to lead us," they demanded. "We don't know what happened to Moses, and the people need something they can see in order to worship."

The people forgot that they had promised God they would not make an image.

Aaron was afraid the people might revolt, and he might be killed, so he gave in to them. "All right," he said. "Collect all the golden jewelry you can find. We will melt it down and fashion an image to represent God."

Some of the men went to work. A young bull made of wood and covered with gold was put up before the people.

"This is the god who brought us up out of Egypt," the people cried.

The next morning the people had their feast. There was music and merry-making. Moses was just then coming down from the mountaintop with two tablets of stone in his hand. He and Joshua heard the music and shouting.

When they came to the camp they saw the golden bull. Moses was amazed at how quickly the people had sinned, doing exactly what God did not want. In his anger at them and at his brother for leading them into this disobedience, he threw down the tablets which contained some of God's laws. He seized the idol and destroyed it.

Aaron had excuses for what he had done and so did the people, but Moses would not accept them.

"You have committed a serious sin," Moses told them. "I don't know if God will still consider you His people, seeing you have disobeyed; but I will go up to the mountain again tomorrow and ask God to forgive you."

The next day Moses prayed for the people. "If you desert us now," he said "the Egyptians will say 'Their God could not take care of them and give them a new land.' Remember, we are your people."

The people too repented of the wrong they had done. They prayed for mercy. They promised that in the future they would keep God's laws.

God did forgive His people. He told Moses to bring up two tablets of stone to replace those which had been broken, and He would again give the laws.

On the mountaintop Moses was very close to God. He saw something of the great glory of God. He learned that God was great in mercy. Though He would always correct the wrongdoer, He would always forgive those who were truly sorry and wanted to do better.

When Moses again came down from the mountain, the people marveled. Because he had been so close to God, Moses' face shone with joy and holiness.

Exodus 19:34

32. A Traveling House of Worship

The people of Israel needed a place in which to worship God. It would help them to remember that God was with them and that they must worship God alone. It would be a beautiful place, because God deserved the best.

Moses spoke about it to the people. "God wants us to have a special place of worship, dedicated to Him. We are going to take an offering, because we need many things in order to build such a place. Those of you who are willing, bring of your possessions gold, silver, brass, cloth, linen, leather, wood."

The people were glad that they were still God's people. He had renewed His agreement with them. They wanted to build a very beautiful place.

They searched their tents and brought out bracelets and earrings and rings. These could be melted down. Others found that they had beautiful blue, purple, and scarlet cloth. Others took out the dried skins of animals.

The people stood in line presenting their gifts one by one. All the different items Moses had asked for were there.

But many of the items needed to be worked upon before they could be used. Some cloth needed to be dyed and embroidered. Furniture for the meeting place had to be made.

Because the people were traveling, they needed a house of worship which could be carried from place to place. It must be a tent.

All the furnishings had to be made with rings on the ends through which poles could be inserted. Then they could be carried from place to place.

As the people continued to give, the treasure mounted. Finally the men who had charge of gathering it told Moses, "Already we have more than enough. You had better tell the people to stop giving."

Moses spoke to the people and thanked them. "We have enough materials," he said. "But now we need workers."

Moses pointed out one man. "God has

given Bezaleel a great talent for carving beautiful designs. He is going to be in charge of the building."

Many men offered their services to Bezaleel. A large wooden frame was constructed to hold up the tent cover. Two altars of wood were built; one covered with brass, the other with gold. A table was needed and a seven-branched lampstand. Patterns of fruit were carved on the furniture.

The women spun cloth for the curtains at the entrance. Curtains also separated the special holy place at the back of the tent from the room in the front. They embroidered on the curtains. The tent itself was made of strips of linen covered with goatshair cloth and animal skins.

One special item in this tent of worship, which was called the Tabernacle, was the Ark of the Covenant. It was a wooden box covered with gold inside and out. The tablets of stone Moses brought from the mountain were kept in the ark.

The ark was placed at the back of the tent enclosed in the Most Holy place. Two guardian figures called cherubim were facing each other on either side of the ark. This was to be the very special place of God's meeting with His people.

While the tent was being made, special robes were made for the priests who would lead the people in their worship of God.

The people worked hard. There was something for everyone to do. Finally the day came when all was completed and the tent could go up.

It was not a large building. It was not made for many people. Only the priests would enter the tent itself, but the people would stand outside in the court. The large brass altar was in the court. The gold altar, and the table and lampstand were inside the tent, in the front room.

The court was enclosed by blue, purple and scarlet linen hangings attached to brass pillars which were driven into the ground.

God told Moses to make Aaron and his sons the priests. From then on all the priests came from the Levites, the tribe of Moses and Aaron.

Moses called all the people together. He called Aaron and his sons apart and put the new robes on them. He poured a little oil on each of their heads. It was a sign that their lives were given to God's service.

Then Moses offered a sacrifice for any wrongdoing they had committed. Even though they were priests they would sometimes do wrong and need forgiveness from God.

The day came when the first worship service would be held. The priests put on their robes. The people gathered in the court. They watched as Moses and Aaron presented an offering to God on the altar.

Then the glory of the Lord filled the place. The fiery cloud which had led the people came and settled over the tent.

It was God's way of showing that He accepted the sacrifices of possessions and labor which the people had made. It showed the people that this time they had done what was right. This was the way God wanted to be worshiped.

Exodus 35-40

33. At the Door of the Promised Land

While they were still in the wilderness of Sinai the people of Israel celebrated their second Passover. It was a year since God had delivered them from slavery in Egypt.

When it was time to travel, they carefully took down the Tabernacle and carried it piece by piece. The journey continued to be hard, and sometimes the people complained. They argued with Moses and questioned his leadership.

God was gracious to His people and continued to lead them. He provided for their needs, but sometimes He had to correct them.

At last they came to the border of Canaan. They camped at Kadesh-barnea, an oasis about forty miles south of Canaan.

Here Moses spoke to the people. "We are at the door of the land God is going to give us as a new home, the land He promised to Abraham. We must find out all about this land. One man from each tribe must go as a spy into Canaan."

So each tribe chose a leader. Joshua was one of them and a man called Caleb another.

Moses told them, "Travel through the land. Notice how many people live there and whether or not they are well-armed. We will need to know if there are many well-fortified cities. See if you can bring back some of the fruit of the land."

Moses and the people watched the men cross over the hills. *What news would the spies bring back?* They wondered.

They had to wait forty days. During this time the spies traveled throughout the land on their dangerous mission. They tried not to raise the suspicions of the inhabitants of Canaan. Before they made their way back to the camp, the men gathered grapes, pomegranates, and figs.

It was a rich land, they discovered, but most of the spies looked unhappy as they returned to the camp.

Eagerly the people gathered around to hear the news.

"Look at the huge cluster of grapes," cried one man. "It takes two men to carry it on a pole."

Moses and Aaron welcomed the spies. "Tell us what you have seen," they begged.

"It is a good land," the spies said. "The ground is rich and produces good crops. See the fruit we brought out?"

The people rejoiced; but the spies stopped them.

"Wait," they said. "All those who live in the land are strong. The cities are well fortified. The Canaanites are ready for war."

At this, the people of Israel began to talk with one another about the bad news. This wasn't a good report after all.

Then Caleb spoke up. "Don't be dismayed," he cried. "Let's go into Canaan at once. We are able to overcome these people."

Joshua agreed with Caleb, but the other spies said, "We can't win a war against these people. They are much stronger than we are. The men are so large and tall they are like giants, and by comparison, we are like tiny grasshoppers. How can we fight such people?"

In the argument that followed, only two of the spies—Joshua and Caleb—believed that God could help them win a victory against the people of Canaan.

Moses urged them to trust in God, but that night the people cried in their tents. They were disappointed. They believed they had endured all these hardships for nothing. They had lost their faith in God, and they were very much afraid.

The next day the people complained as they talked together. As usual, they blamed Moses.

Some angry men said, "Let's make a new captain and return to Egypt."

Moses and Aaron were amazed at this rebellion. So were Joshua and Caleb.

These two spies went everywhere among the crowds. "God will help us if we obey Him," they argued.

"God has not brought us out to this wilderness for us to be defeated and die. God has brought us this far, and He will not forsake us."

But the people chose to believe the other spies. Some became so angry at Caleb and Joshua that they threatened them with stones.

Moses prayed to God. He asked, "Do not be angry at these rebellious people, even though they have sinned against You by not trusting in Your help. If You desert us, the inhabitants of Canaan who have heard of Your greatness will not believe our God was able to bring us to a new land.

"Pardon the people according to Your great mercy, as You have pardoned them throughout this journey."

God forgave the people, but He said, "These people refuse to believe in Me even after seeing all My great works at the Red Sea and throughout the journey. Therefore they will not enter the land of promise."

In judgment of their sin, God said that of all the adults in the camp only Caleb and Joshua would enter Canaan. They must all stay in the wilderness now. When the parents would grow old and die, their children would become the leaders. These new leaders would successfully invade Canaan.

Moses brought this message to the people. They had done a lot of thinking.

"We have sinned," they admitted. "Now we will go into Canaan and fight."

"It is too late," said Moses. "The judgment has been given. God has decided that your children, and not you, will inherit the land."

But again the people did not listen. The warriors gathered together and went over into Canaan.

"Don't go," Moses warned, but they would not listen, and soon they came back in defeat. They had to accept God's judgment.

Because they had not trusted God, they could not enjoy the good land He had wanted to give them.

Numbers 13, 14

34. Moses Says Good-by

The people of Israel had to stay in the wilderness for forty years. It was difficult to find food and water and the people complained bitterly. Moses became tired of their complaining, and one time he became very angry with them. He was so angry he forgot that he was only a spokesman for God, and he did not follow God's instructions for getting water.

God told Moses "Another leader will go into the new land with the people."

Sometimes the people rebelled against Moses. God had to show them that Moses was the leader of His choice. God loved the people and continued to help them. He provided food and water.

When they sinned, God did not give them up. He corrected them, but He forgave them when they repented.

Miriam and Aaron both died during these years. Aaron's son, Eleazar, became head of the priests. As the fathers died, a new generation became leaders of the people. These men and women were stronger than their parents. The years in the desert had made them better able to bear hardship.

The time would soon be at hand to claim God's promise of victory and invade Canaan. This time they decided to start the invasion further north.

The Israelites wanted to go through Edom, but the Edomites refused to let them through. Neither would the people of Moab let them through. This made their journey to Canaan longer.

At last they came to Sihon which bordered the Jordan River. It was ruled by the Amorites. The people of Israel sent messages to the king of the Amorites. "We will not touch a thing in your land. We will not take food or water. Only let us march through."

The king refused and sent soldiers out to fight the Israelites. Israel fought and won the battle and so possessed this land east of the Jordan River. Now they had land of their own to live in, but it was not enough land for so many people.

The Israelites made their camp across the river from Jericho. Two of the tribes asked if they could make their homes on this east side of the Jordan. They promised to help with the fighting on the other side of the river.

Moses had grown very old. Since it was not God's will for him to lead the people into the land, a new, younger leader needed to be chosen.

Moses asked God's guidance in choosing a new leader. God said, "Take Joshua. He is a man who has God's Spirit within him."

So in front of all the people Moses called out Joshua. Joshua stood by Moses and Eleazar, the priest. Moses laid his hand on Joshua and said, "You are the one God has chosen to lead the people into the promised land. Do not fear. God will go with you. Be strong and have courage."

Moses had much to say to the people. He reminded them of all that had happened since their fathers had left Egypt.

He said, "Do not be afraid to go and possess the land God has promised to give you. Remember how God brought you out of Egypt by acts of great power. Remember how He provided for your needs throughout these many years in the wilderness.

"In this new land, remember to keep the laws of God. You have been chosen to be God's people, but if you forsake God and worship idols, God will punish you. As long as you obey God, you will dwell in the good land; but if you forsake God, your land will be taken away. God has shown His love for you in many ways, and He wants you to love and obey Him."

Moses urged the people to teach their children God's laws. Moses reminded them of the ten commandments which they had promised to keep. He reminded them that God loved them and had made an agreement with them.

Moses said, "Be faithful in keeping God's commandments. Do what is right and good in God's sight. Tell your children how God delivered you from Egypt and gave you a good land. In this land you will have plenty to eat, and water will be easy to find.

"Do not forget God, who gives you all these good things. Love the Lord your God with all your heart and with all your soul and with all your might.

"Do not turn away from God and worship idols. God is bringing judgment on the people of Canaan for their sins. If you are guilty of the same sins, you too will know God's judgment."

Moses was disappointed that he could not go into the land of Canaan; but he was glad the people would soon have a home of their own. He felt sure Joshua would lead the people in right ways.

One day God called Moses to come up to Mt. Nebo to talk with Him. From here Moses could look down on all the land of Canaan. He could imagine the people happily living here, their long journey ended.

He could see the green fertile fields, the Jordan Valley and the Dead Sea. He saw the rugged hills beyond and in the far distance, a silver streak of the Mediterranean Sea.

While he was up on the mountain, Moses died. The people mourned for their great leader. He had been a man who walked close to God, and now he had gone to be with God.

Numbers 20, 21, 27, 32, 33
Deuteronomy

35. A River to Cross

Joshua was the new leader. God commanded him, "Arise. Go over the Jordan. Possess the land which I promised to your fathers. Be strong and have good courage. As I was with Moses, I will be with you. I will not desert you."

Joshua obeyed God. He said to the people. "Get ready. In three days we will cross the river into Canaan."

Then he reminded the tribes which had already been given land that they had promised to fight with the others. "You can leave the rest of your families here," said Joshua. "Only the soldiers need to come across the river."

"We will do as you command," said the leaders of these tribes. "We will fight with our brothers until they all have their inheritance of land."

While the people made ready to go down into the valley, Joshua sent two spies on ahead.

"Find a way to get into the city of Jericho," Joshua told them. "Bring us back word about the defenses of the city."

Jericho was an important city in the center of Canaan. If they could capture it, they would divide the north of Canaan from the south.

There were many cities throughout the land, and each had its king. Seven different tribes of people lived in Canaan, and there was no one ruler. This was going to make it easier to conquer.

The spies made their way about the streets, posing as ordinary travelers. At night they found lodging in the house of a woman named Rahab. But the spies had been noticed.

Someone ran to the king of Jericho. "Two spies from Israel are in the city. They were seen going into Rahab's house."

The king of Jericho sent word to Rahab saying, "Bring out the men who are lodging with you, for they are spies."

But Rahab had seen the king's messengers coming. She told the spies to hide.

Then Rahab said to the king's messengers, "Two men came here, but they have left. Hurry and you may be able to catch them trying to leave the city through the gate."

Then Rahab went up to the roof where the men were hiding.

"I know God is going to give you this land," she said. "I believe in your God's power. Our people are very much afraid. They have heard how your God delivered you at the Red Sea. They know of the battle you won across the river.

"I have saved your lives. Please, remember me when your army comes here. Protect my family."

"We will do that," the men promised. "If you tell no one about us, we will make sure no harm comes to you or your family."

They went back into the house and Rahab got a strong rope. She tied the rope around each man and let him out of a window. Her house was built as part of the city wall, so that when the men reached the ground, they were outside the city.

Before the men said good-by they gave Rahab a scarlet cord. "Hang this from your window. Then our soldiers will know to pass by this house. Only warn your family to stay inside."

Rahab agreed. "Do not go right back to your camp," she advised. "The king's messengers are looking for you. Hide in the hills for three days and then go back."

The men did as she suggested. When they saw the king's messengers come back to Jericho empty-handed, they made their way back to their camp. There they told Joshua all that had happened, and how Rahab had befriended them.

"God is with us," they said. "We are sure to conquer Jericho and the rest of the land."

The next morning Joshua began the march. They would camp on this side of the Jordan and go over the river the next day.

Joshua's officers told the people, "When you see the ark of the covenant carried by the priests, follow it. The ark will go before us as we cross the river."

The ark helped the people to remember that God was with them.

Joshua told the people to be packed up and ready. "Tomorrow the Lord is going to show us wonders," he promised.

The next morning Joshua told the priests to take up the ark and start to cross the river. In the middle of the river they were to stand still. All the people had gathered, ready to cross.

It was springtime, and the Jordan had overflowed its banks. In the dry season it would be easy to cross, but not now.

God spoke to Joshua. "I will show you my power," He said. "I will assure the people that, as I was with Moses, so I will be with you."

Joshua told the people, "God is going to show us His power."

As the priests stepped into the swollen river, God caused the water to be dammed up so that they could walk across on the bed of the river. The priests stood still in the middle, and the tribes marched over as quickly as they could.

On the other side of the Jordan, Joshua selected twelve men, one from each tribe, to go back and make a pile of twelve rocks near where the priests were still standing. Each man was to bring another rock out with him.

The men did this. Then Joshua called to the priests, "Come out of the Jordan."

The priests made their way to the shore. As soon as they were safely out of the river, the water flowed freely again.

Now the people were sure that Joshua was the leader God wanted them to have. He would be led by God, and God would do great things for them.

That night they made camp at Gilgal. Here the families would stay while the men went out to fight. The flocks and herds were kept here too.

Joshua took the rocks which the men had brought out of the Jordan and set them up as a monument.

Joshua said, "In times to come your children will ask you what these rocks mean. Then you will tell them how God brought you safely across the Jordan into this land."

Joshua 1-4

36. "The Walls Came Tumbling Down"

All the kings of Canaan were frightened when they heard how Israel crossed the Jordan. They realized that these people had a God of great power helping them.

"We are lost," the Canaanites said.

Joshua was a brave and wise general. He mapped out a campaign. Jericho was the first city to be attacked. It divided the north and south of Canaan. With Jericho captured, they would not need to fear a united enemy.

While the Israelites were camped at Gilgal they kept another Passover. Again they thanked God for delivering them from slavery in Egypt.

The people in Jericho were afraid to leave the city. They wondered what would happen next.

Joshua rallied his army and spoke to his soldiers. God wanted the men to realize that it was only with His help that they would succeed; so God was going to help them win this city in a special way.

"Hear our instructions from God," said Joshua. "For the next six days we are to march around the city once a day. On the seventh day we will march around the city seven times."

Joshua showed them how to march. First of all came the armed men. Seven priests with trumpets made from rams' horns followed. Then came priests carrying the ark of the covenant. More armed men made up a rear guard.

The first day they paraded around the city walls. As they marched, the priests blew their trumpets. Joshua had commanded the soldiers not to speak a word. All that could be heard was their marching feet and the blast of the trumpets.

This happened for six days. On the seventh day Joshua told the people, "Today we will march around the city seven times. Do not speak a word until I give you the signal and then everyone shout as loud as you can."

Joshua had other instructions. Most soldiers took anything of value they might find when they attacked a city. But Joshua did not want his soldiers to do this.

"God is helping us win this battle, and you must not keep any treasure for yourselves," he said. "Any silver, gold, or vessels of brass and iron are to be used by the priests or for the worship of God."

That day the priests and soldiers marched around the city six times. On the seventh trip Joshua cried above the noise of the trumpets, "Shout, for the Lord has given you the city."

As the people shouted, the earth trembled and the walls started to crumble and then to fall. After the walls had come crashing down, the city had no defense. The Army of the Israelites could rush in to win the battle.

Joshua said to the two men who had been the spies, "Remember Rahab who befriended you."

The two men ran to Rahab's house where the scarlet cord hung out the window to rescue her and her family. Rahab and her people became one with the people of Israel and worshiped the Lord God.

After the battle the soldiers collected the vessels of gold, silver, brass and iron and brought them into God's service.

But unknown to the others, a man named Achan had not obeyed the instructions. He had taken a coat, some silver coins, and a bar of gold and brought them to his tent. He and his family buried them in the ground.

Next in Joshua's plan of conquest was the city of Ai, up in the hill country. First, spies went to the city. "We won't need our whole army," they said. "Only part of the army is needed to conquer this city."

So Joshua sent about three thousand men to fight against Ai. But this time the men were defeated. The soldiers of Ai chased them back.

The people of Israel were discouraged by the defeat and so was Joshua. He knew how important it was that Israel not be defeated even in a small battle, because then others would not be afraid of them.

Joshua prayed to God and asked Him why this had happened. God reminded Joshua of His instructions.

Joshua called all the people and spoke to them, "Someone has disobeyed God and taken treasure for himself. As long as we have stolen goods among us, God will not be with us."

Achan finally confessed that he had stolen and turned over the coat, the silver and the gold. After he had been punished, and the treasure put in its proper place, Joshua again planned an attack on Ai.

This time the whole army went. Joshua had a special plan.

At first they pretended they were turning back. The soldiers of Ai pursued them as they had done before. But other soldiers of Israel were waiting nearby. When they saw the soldiers of Ai leave the city undefended they entered the city and set it on fire.

This time Israel won the battle.

Joshua 5-8

37. A New Land for God's People

Joshua and his army moved south through the hills in the center of Canaan. Several of the kings of the south united to fight them.

One day when the army of Israel was back at Camp Gilgal, strangers approached. They were dressed in very old clothes as though they had come from a long journey.

They showed the bread they had brought with them. "We have come a long way," they said. "See, our bread is dry and moldy. We have heard about your victories and want to make a treaty of peace with you."

"We are at war with all the people of this country," said Joshua.

"But we have come from a faraway country," said the men.

Joshua and the other leaders agreed to make a treaty of peace with them. But they forgot to ask the advice of God.

Not long afterwards they discovered that they had been tricked. The men had only disguised themselves as travelers. Really they lived near at hand, in the city of Gibeon, north and west of Jericho.

"Why did you deceive us?" Joshua asked the men when the trick was discovered. "We will spare your lives, because we promised before God to do you no harm. But now you must work for us and be our servants."

The kings of the south were angry that Gibeon had made a treaty with Israel. They set out for the city armed for battle.

True to his promise, Joshua led his army in their defense. The armies of these kings were unable to stand before Israel and soon they were running away.

As a result, the people of Israel won more land for themselves. But the conquest of Canaan was not complete.

Next Joshua led the people north. Several of the kings of the north banded together to fight Israel. They made up a huge army and used horses and chariots —the most modern equipment.

The soldiers of Israel did not have such equipment, and yet they won these battles and took possession of the land they won because God helped them.

Now the people of Israel had a home of their own. They rested from war.

Joshua directed the dividing of the land. Each tribe was given a place to live. Two and a half tribes made their home on the east side of the Jordan River. The tribe of Levi was not given an inheritance of land, because they were the servants of God. They were given special cities to live in throughout the land.

Now the people of Israel could settle down with their families to raise crops and pasture their flocks and herds. Their wanderings were over.

The Tabernacle was set up at Shiloh. The ark was placed in its special room. The people could come here to worship and bring their sacrifices and offerings.

Years later when Joshua had grown old, he asked the leaders and people of the different tribes to come together so he could speak to them.

God had used Israel to bring judgment on the people of Canaan because of their many sins. Their worship of idols did not make the Canaanites better people;

in fact it made them worse—and displeasing to God. They continually did the kind of thing God said was wrong.

Now Israel had to live near these people. Joshua warned them that they must not be influenced to do wrong because their neighbors did.

"Do all that is written in the laws Moses gave you, and do not mingle with these nations that do wrong. God has enabled you to have this home of your own. Show your gratitude by obedience."

Joshua reminded the people of their past history. God had chosen Abraham and led him out of an idol-worshiping country with the promise that he would be father of a great people.

Moses had been used of God to free the people from Egyptian slavery. God had worked wonders to enable them to escape at the Red Sea. God had helped them have a home of their own.

"Now," said Joshua, "you need to decide. Choose whom you will serve.

"Are you going to serve the ancient gods your ancestors worshiped? Are you going to serve the gods of the people who live around you? Or are you going to serve the Lord who brought you out of Egypt?

"You must choose for yourself, but as for me and my family, we are going to serve the Lord."

"We will serve the Lord," the people answered.

"But," said Joshua, "you cannot serve the Lord and other gods as well. You must serve God alone."

"We will serve God," the people declared.

"You have made your decision," said Joshua, "and now any among you who carry about idols, get rid of them. Love God and serve Him only."

The people promised, "We will serve God and obey His laws."

Joshua 9, 10-12, 13-22, 23, 24

38. Warriors Who Helped the People

The people who had known Joshua remembered his words and their promise to worship only God. But new generations grew up, and they were careless about their worship of God. They were influenced by the practices of the neighboring farmers.

The Canaanites believed that their god Baal controlled the seasons and brought large harvests. They warned the people of Israel, "If you don't observe these ceremonies and kneel to the image of Baal as we do, you will not have good crops."

The people of Israel had been shepherds. They knew little about farming. Many of them gave in to the temptation to worship Baal along with their God.

But for the people of God there could only be one God, the Lord who delivered them from Egypt and led them across the wilderness.

The Israelites had been successful in conquering the hill country. But in the plains the Canaanites were stronger and better armed, and they kept their land. This meant that Israel had enemies nearby. The people of Moab and Ammon also threatened Israel. God used these enemies to correct His people and remind them of their promise to worship only Him.

After Joshua died, there was no one leader for God's people. Each tribe had its own leaders and carried on its own business.

Some of these leaders were men who believed in God. They not only helped to deliver the tribes from their enemies but helped the people back to the true worship of God. These men were called judges.

Othniel was a judge who delivered his tribe from a king of Mesopotamia.

Another judge was Ehud. During his time the king of Moab ruled part of Israel. Ehud went to Moab to visit the king and freed his people by killing the ruler. He escaped back to his own people and then he led the Israelites in battle against Moab.

When a strong judge was there to help them, the Israelites were true to God. But as soon as the judge was gone they went back to their old ways and bowed to the images of idols.

At one time different rulers of the Canaanites banded together against part of Israel, and for twenty years they ruled over them. When the Israelites suffered, they remembered how God had helped their ancestors cross the wilderness and conquer this land and they cried to God for help.

During this time Deborah lived. She was known as a woman who was close to God. People came to her for advice and asked her to settle their differences.

One day Deborah sent for a general called Barak. She told the general, "God wants you to fight those who oppress us. God has promised to deliver us. He will give you victory over Sisera, the captain of Jabin's army, even though Sisera boasts chariots and many soldiers." Jabin was the king of Canaan who lived in Hazor in the northern part of the country.

Barak promised to get an army together. "But you must come with me," he said.

Because Deborah was a woman of God, the general felt sure of God's help if she were there.

Deborah went with Barak to form the army and then went with the army to Mt. Tabor. They had heard that Sisera and his army were camped on the plains nearby. Sisera had heard about Barak's army and was ready for war.

On the day of battle, Deborah encouraged the soldiers. "This is the day the Lord is going to deliver us from our enemies," she cried.

Barak and his army rushed down the mountainside and charged. When Sisera saw that Israel would win he ran away from the battle on foot. But he did not run far. He went to a woman called Jael who he thought was a friend. But Jael was on Israel's side. She invited him into the tent and gave him some milk to drink. When he had fallen asleep she killed him.

After winning the battle, Deborah wrote a song as part of the celebration. The song recalled how God had helped His people in the past. It warned the people against serving the gods of the Canaanites. It praised the soldiers from the other tribes who had helped in the battle. Most of all, it praised God for remembering and delivering His people.

Once again God had proved His might and His care for them. The Israelites regained the control of their land and settled down to a time of peace.

Joshua 24:31; Judges 1-5

39. Gideon Answers a Call

More hard times came to the Israelites. The desert tribes called Midianites raided the land. They would leave the desert and cross the Jordan River. They would come down on a town to destroy or to take away anything of value. During the harvest they would raid at night and take away the fruit of the land. No one could protect his harvest.

The people of Israel cried to God for help. But a prophet from God told them, "God says, 'I brought you out of Egypt and gave you this good land. I told you not to worship the gods of this land, but you have disobeyed Me.' "

The people were again worshiping the Baals and depending on these idols to bring them good crops.

One day a young man named Gideon was beating the chaff from the wheat. He was hiding behind the wine press so that no Midianites could see him and take the grain away.

God sent a messenger to Gideon. "The Lord is with you, brave soldier."

Gideon was puzzled by this greeting. "If the Lord is with us, why are we having all this trouble? Where are all the wonders which God showed our ancestors? God is no longer with our people."

"God will send you to deliver your people," said the messenger.

"How can I deliver Israel?" cried Gideon. "I am a member of a small tribe and an unimportant family."

But God's angel insisted. "God will enable you to do it."

Gideon finally believed that he was chosen to help his people. He prayed to God for guidance.

God told Gideon he must destroy the idol which the people of the city had set up. Gideon's father, Joash was in charge of this place of worship to Baal.

Gideon was afraid. Even his own family would be against him, because they believed it was all right to have these nature idols. Still he found ten of his father's servants who would help him. They did it at night when no one was around.

In the morning the people of the town found the idol cast down and an altar to God in its place.

"Whoever did this shall die," they shouted.

Then they found out it was Gideon. "Bring out your son," they cried to Joash.

But Joash defended his son, "If Baal is really powerful, let him punish those who tore down his altar."

The people listened to Joash and no harm came to Gideon.

Gideon then urged his people to band together to fight the Midianites. He sent messages throughout all his tribe and many soldiers gathered together.

Still Gideon hesitated. Midianites had crossed the river and Gideon knew where they were camped. But would God really help them win? Gideon spent a lot of time praying to God until he felt sure of what God wanted him to do.

The next day Gideon led his army toward the camp of the Midianites. That night they camped by a spring. Then Gideon had a strange message from God.

"Your army is too large," God told him. "I want the people to realize that

I deliver them from their enemies. As it is now, they will credit their own strength."

So Gideon decreased his force. He addressed all the soldiers. "Any who are afraid may return home," he said.

The soldiers must have thought Gideon was foolish indeed. Different ones moved away. More and more deserted, until the army was about one third the size it had been.

Still Gideon had another test for the soldiers. He led them to the spring to get a drink.

Most of the soldiers knelt down on both knees to drink, picking up the water in both hands or else putting their face in the water. This was not good, because an enemy might attack from behind, and they would not be prepared to fight.

But a small group stood and bent over the water. They quickly took a drink with one hand, keeping watch around them. These were the best soldiers.

Gideon took these men aside. "With God's help you are going to defeat the Midianites," he said. He told the other soldiers to go home.

That night God said to Gideon, "Now you are ready. You will defeat the Midianites. But if you are still fearful, go down into the valley where the Midianites are camped and hear what they say to each other."

Gideon found his servant, Purah. "Come with me to spy on the Midian camp," he asked. Purah agreed to this dangerous mission.

It was dark and the rocks helped to hide them from the enemy as they went down into the valley. They managed to slip past a guard and to keep in the shadows, It was a large camp. The tents of the huge army were spread out under the bright stars. The large camels which the Midianites used so well in fighting were resting now.

Gideon and his servant listened as one soldier told another about a dream.

"I dreamt that a loaf of barley bread tumbled down into our camp and fell on a tent, crushing it completely."

The other soldier was frightened at this. "That must mean that Gideon will win this battle. Their God is going to deliver us into their hands."

Gideon's faith increased. He brought the good news to his army. "God is going to help us win," he told them. "Even the enemy is afraid of God's power."

Gideon knew his men were far outnumbered by the Midianites, but he planned to frighten them. He divided his army into three parts. Each man had a trumpet and a pitcher into which he put a lit torch. "Do what I do when we get to the camp," said Gideon.

They followed their leader. When the Israelites came to the outskirts of the camp the Midianites had just changed their watch. Gideon and his men divided into three groups and surrounded the camp. At the signal they all blew on their trumpets. Then they dashed the pitchers to the ground so that the lamps shone out brightly, and cried, "A sword for the Lord and for Gideon."

Many of the enemy were so frightened that they ran at once. Soon the Midianites were in full retreat.

Gideon's soldiers chased the raiders as they headed for home. On the way they called for help from other tribes of Israel. On the other side of the Jordan they continued the battle. The Midianites fled to the desert and did not come back. *Judges 6, 7*

40. Samson, the Strong

There were other judges who, in times of distress, led their tribes into battle, and in God's name delivered them. When the people were in trouble they turned to God, but afterwards they forgot about Him.

Then danger came to the tribes of Israel from another source, the plains by the Mediterranean Sea. The Philistines who lived there had come from across the sea. They proved to be Israel's most dangerous foe.

For many years the Philistines ruled over the people of Israel who lived nearby. Many Israelites had been captured and made slaves.

But God had not forgotten His people. He sent a messenger to a woman of the tribe of Dan.

The messenger said, "You will have a son. God will have special work for him to do, so you must obey these rules. You shall never cut his hair. Do not drink wine or eat anything which the law says is not called clean. This son of yours will begin to deliver the people of Israel from the Philistines."

The woman was amazed. She told the exciting news to her husband. "He was a wonderful man," she said. "But something about him frightened me."

Manoah prayed that he would have a chance to talk to God's messenger. So God's angel came again. He repeated the instructions.

Manoah was frightened; but his wife said, "God has blessed us. We must not be afraid, but we must be careful to do all that God says."

When his son was born Manoah called his name Samson. As he grew up, God was with him. Everyone noticed that Sampson was very strong.

One day when Samson was out in the hills, a lion attacked him. Samson felt special strength coming from God. Without a weapon he fought back and killed the lion.

Samson often thought about the way his people were being mistreated by the Philistines, and it made him angry. He spoke out against them. Whenever he fought with a band of Philistine soldiers he always won.

The Philistines realized that Samson was a dangerous rebel and a man of great strength. They vowed to rid themselves of this troublesome Israelite.

Samson was very strong physically; but he did not have that inner strength which enables a person to say "no" to temptation. He often disobeyed God's law, and he was known to keep company with rough people. Sometimes these friends were Philistines.

One Philistine friend of Samson's was called Delilah. He visited her often.

The leaders of the Philistines said to Delilah, "We want to know where Samson gets his great strength. There must be some secret. You must help us rid our people of this enemy. Besides, if you help us, we will give you a generous reward in silver."

Delilah agreed. She was not a true friend to Samson, but she pretended to be.

Soldiers of the Philistines were always nearby when Samson came to visit. She was to call them when she found out the secret.

One day Delilah said to Samson, "Tell me the secret of your great strength. Is there any way you could be bound and captured?"

Samson did not want to tell the secret; but when she kept on it annoyed him. He told her a lie.

"If I were bound with seven fresh bowstrings that have not been dried, I would have no more strength than any other man."

Delilah got bowstrings and bound Samson while he was asleep. Then she woke him. "The Philistines are coming," she shouted.

Samson snapped the bowstrings and was ready to fight. Delilah had soldiers hidden nearby, but they did not come out when they saw what happened.

"I was only testing you," said Delilah, "and now I see that you were fooling me. Please tell me the secret."

Many times Delilah begged, and each time Samson told her a different lie. He said that new rope would do it. Then he said that his strength would go if she gathered up his long hair and pinned it together. Delilah tried each way and always discovered that she had been fooled.

Then Delilah wept. "You say you love me, but you don't trust me," she argued.

Many days passed, and each time Samson visited Delilah she kept asking about the secret.

Finally Samson gave in and told her the secret. "My hair has never been cut," he explained. "It is part of a vow to God. If it is cut, my great strength from God will leave me."

This time Delilah could tell he was speaking the truth. The first chance she had she told the Philistine leaders. "I know the secret. Come and hide near my place, and tonight you will be able to capture Samson."

When Samson came, Delilah gave him a good dinner. She made him comfortable, and soon he was taking a nap.

She called to a man hidden nearby. "Come and cut his hair," she whispered.

The man knelt down and carefully took off all of Samson's hair. Then, as before, Delilah called out, "Wake up, Samson. Philistine soldiers are coming."

Samson jumped up. He rushed out of the house and the Philistine soldiers met him. This time Samson did not overcome them. His strength was gone. The soldiers captured him and put out his eyes.

The once-proud warrior was put in prison. He was chained and made to turn the wheel that ground the grain. He had plenty of time to think about the mistakes he had made. He should never have trusted one of the enemy. He should have kept God's laws about eating and drinking. Often he had disobeyed his special promise to God about these things. In time Samson's hair began to grow long again.

The Philistines rejoiced that their enemy was now helpless. They made a special feast to their god Dagon and bowed before the large idol. All the priests of their religion gathered. The people danced and sang songs of joy.

Then they shouted, "Bring Samson here to the temple."

The blind Samson was led into the crowd of loud, wild worshipers who laughed and made fun of him. He stood in the center of the temple between two pillars which held up the building.

Samson reached out and put a hand on each pillar. The worshipers of Dagon still laughed at him and at God.

Then Samson prayed, "Remember me, Lord and give me back my strength just this once. I will die here with the Philistines."

Samson pushed with all his might, and the two pillars fell over. The house came down, and all the people inside were killed.

Samson's relatives came for his body. They mourned him. Samson had done much to weaken the enemy's power, but he might have been a greater person if he had lived more as God wanted. Then he would have been strong in every way.

Judges 13-16

41. The Girl From Moab

Ruth was very sad. Her husband had died and she had no children to comfort her. Her mother-in-law, Naomi, had lost her husband, too, and wanted to leave the country of Moab and return to her old home in Judah.

So Ruth and her sister-in-law Orpah went part of the way with Naomi. Both Ruth and Orpah had lived all their lives in Moab, on the other side of the Jordan River from the Israelites.

Naomi and her family had left Judah years before because of a great famine. They had been happy in Moab and the sons had married Moabite girls. Then Naomi's husband and sons died.

When it came time to say good-by, both girls cried because they loved Naomi and Naomi cried too.

"You have been good to me," Naomi told them, "and you were both good wives to my sons.

"But there is nothing left for me in Moab, and I can do nothing more for you. It is best for you to return to your parents. Find other good men to marry. May you both find happiness and peace."

Orpah turned then and kissed her mother-in-law good-by. But Ruth would not leave Naomi.

"No," she said. "Don't make me leave you. I want to go with you to Judah. I want to live where you live and always be part of your family. Your people shall be my people, and your God, my God."

When Naomi saw that Ruth really wanted to leave her own people and come with her to a strange land she agreed.

"At least," thought Naomi, "there is one person in this world who cares about me."

Ruth did care about her mother-in-law. She did not want Naomi to be all alone in the world. She was old and would need someone to help her.

When they came to Bethlehem, in Judah, many of the people recognized Naomi. "But you have changed," they said.

Naomi nodded sadly. "I have lost those who were dearest to me."

Naomi was bitter. She wondered how she and Ruth would make a living for themselves. Before they left for Moab, Naomi and her husband had sold all the property they owned.

After Ruth and Naomi found a place to live, they talked about what they could do. It was time for the barley harvest.

"In this land it is the custom to leave some grain in the fields for the poor," said Naomi.

"Then let me go and see how much grain I can gather for us," Ruth offered.

Naomi was grateful. "See if you can find a place where the owner is generous."

The next day Ruth felt strange. It was a foreign country to her. As she made her way out of the city she was afraid some of the people would not be friendly. Up ahead wide fields were filled with ripe grain.

Ruth found a field in which many young men and women gathered the grain. Some had been hired just for the harvest. She went up to the man in charge of the reapers.

"May I gather the grain that is left in this field?" she asked.

The man recognized Ruth as the young woman Naomi had brought back from Moab. He spoke kindly to her.

All day Ruth worked, gathering the grain the reapers left behind. Then she heard someone say, "Here comes Boaz, the owner of these fields."

Ruth was afraid. Perhaps he would tell her to go because she was from Moab.

Boaz did notice Ruth. "Who is that young woman?" he asked the man in charge.

"That is Ruth, the daughter-in-law of Naomi. She has worked all day without rest."

"I have heard of her," said Boaz, and he went over to Ruth. "Do not go to any other field," he said. "We will see that you get enough here. If you need water, you may use ours."

Ruth bowed politely before Boaz. She was surprised at his kindness. "Why have I, a stranger to your land, found such favor?" she asked.

"Because I have heard how kind you are to Naomi, and how you were willing to leave your own people and your own land to come here. May God reward you for your goodness."

"You have comforted me," said Ruth. Now she was no longer feeling lonely and afraid.

When it was time to eat Boaz said, "Come here and eat with us."

After dinner Boaz said to his reapers, "Make sure you leave a lot of grain for Ruth to gather."

Ruth was happy as she gathered the barley. The kind Boaz had told her she could come and work in his fields as long as she wished—all during barley harvest and on through wheat harvest. The other reapers were pleasant to her too.

At the end of the day, Ruth beat out the grain. She had a good measure of barley to take home. Naomi was surprised that she had been able to gather so much.

"Who owns the field where you worked?" she asked. "God bless the man who was so good to you."

"A kind man called Boaz was the owner," Ruth told her.

Naomi was very excited at this news. "Boaz is a man of importance in this city. He is wise and generous, and he is a relative of my husband's. God has indeed been good to us. I believe all our troubles will soon be over."

Ruth 1, 2

42. Ruth Finds a New Home

For weeks Ruth continued to gather grain in the fields owned by Boaz. He was always kind to her.

One day Naomi explained to Ruth about certain laws of the Israelites. "Our law says that ownership of land should stay in one family as much as possible. My husband sold our land when we went to Moab, but a relative of my husband has the right to buy it back.

"There is one condition. Anyone who buys back the land has to marry you, because you are the widow of my son."

Ruth thought about the law. She wondered what her mother-in-law had planned. It must have something to do with Boaz.

"I want you to marry and have a home and family," said Naomi. "Boaz is my relative, and he could buy back the land. Here is my plan.

"Tonight after Boaz finishes his work in the fields and has his dinner, he will rest. I want you to put on your best dress and go to visit him. Tell him all that I have told you and that you are willing to do your part and be his wife."

Ruth put on her best dress for this important visit. She waited until Boaz had dinner and was resting alone. During the harvests, workers would often camp out all night in the fields.

Ruth came up to Boaz quietly. He was asleep. She waited patiently there until he woke up. He was surprised to see her.

Ruth told him all that Naomi had said about Boaz being able to buy back her husband's property. Of course Boaz knew about this law. He nodded as she spoke.

"I understand that I would marry the one who bought the property, and I am willing," she said.

Boaz smiled at Ruth. "You are being very kind to me," he said. "There are many young men whom you could marry. I am older than you by many years; but I will do what you ask. All people speak well of you."

Ruth was very happy. She loved Boaz for his gentle ways and wise thoughts.

"There is one problem," Boaz said. "There is another man who is related to Naomi's husband. He is a closer relative than I, and so he has first choice. If he wants to buy the property we must let him, but if not, then I can do it."

Ruth hoped that Boaz would be able to marry her, but she understood that the law must be obeyed.

Before she left, Boaz gave her a gift of grain to take home.

Naomi was very anxious to hear what had happened. When she heard what Boaz said she smiled happily. "I am sure Boaz will find out about this other relative right away."

She was right. The next day Boaz went into the city. Court was held by the city gate. Boaz often came here and helped to decide legal matters.

Now Boaz looked for Naomi's relative. "I have something important to discuss with you," he said.

Then he asked other men who were standing nearby to be witnesses to their discussion and agreement. When they all sat down, Boaz told his story.

"If you want to buy this land," he told the relative, "you have first choice. If not, I will buy it."

The man wanted to own more land, but he did not want to marry Ruth. "I will not be able to do it," he said.

In these days a man took off his sandal and gave it to the other to seal an agreement. So the relative said, "Buy it for yourself, Boaz." He took off his sandal and gave it to Boaz.

Boaz said to the others. "You are all witnesses of our agreement."

"Yes," they said, "And may God bless your marriage with Ruth and give you a fine family."

So Ruth and Boaz were married. In time a baby boy was born to them. They called him Obed.

Everyone was happy. Naomi, the grandmother, was among the happiest. As she looked at the little baby, all her bitterness was gone. God had helped them after all.

The other women said to her. "True, you have lost your husband and sons, but Ruth has been more than many sons to you. You have had her love, and now she has given birth to a baby who will make your last years happy."

Naomi tenderly took the baby in her arms. She hoped that he would grow up to be a fine man. She wondered what he would do and what his sons would do.

In the history of his people, Obed, the son of Ruth and Boaz, was remembered as the grandfather of David the king.

Ruth 2:23; 3; 4

43. A Boy Is Given to God

In Israel many families paid a yearly visit to Shiloh to bring offerings and to worship at the Tabernacle. One woman who came every year was Hannah.

Hannah was unhappy because she had no children. Her husband Elkanah tried to comfort her about this, but she could not understand why God did not give her a baby.

One day this family came to the Tabernacle and brought a sacrifice to God as the law of Moses told them. Part of the meat from the sacrifice was given to the priests for food and part was used by the family for a dinner.

After the sacrifice was given, Hannah sat down with the others, but she was too unhappy to eat.

"Why are you so upset?" asked Elkanah. "Even if you have no children, I still love you."

But Hannah could not stay at the dinner, which was a time of rejoicing. She went back to the Tabernacle to pray.

Eli the high priest sat by the door of the Tabernacle watching her as she prayed. He noticed how upset she was.

Hannah was bitter and unhappy. She wondered if God cared about her trouble. The tears ran down her cheeks.

Then Hannah made a promise to God, "O Lord," she said, "if you will give me a son, I will give him to the service of God."

She continued to pray from her heart and talk to God about her desire for a son. She told God how other women laughed at her because she had no child.

Then Eli came over to her. He wanted to find out what made this woman so unhappy.

Hannah told him her trouble and about her promise.

Eli encouraged her. He knew that Hannah had done right to bring her trouble and unhappiness to God, because God cared for each one of His people.

"Go in peace," he said as Hannah left. "May God give you what you desire."

Hannah felt much better. She was sure God was going to give her a son. She ate her dinner and smiled at everyone.

The next morning they again worshiped in the Tabernacle. Then they started on the journey home. During the next year Hannah and Elkanah had a baby boy. They called him Samuel.

When it came time to make the yearly trip to Shiloh, Hannah said, "I cannot go this year. I will stay home and care for Samuel. In a few years Samuel will be big enough, and I will bring him to Eli at the Tabernacle to live there and serve God."

When Samuel was old enough he went on the trip with his mother and father. He understood that he was going to live at Shiloh, in God's Tabernacle.

Hannah and Elkanah brought an expensive, large sacrifice to thank God for answering their prayers.

When Hannah saw Eli, she hurried over to him with Samuel.

"I prayed for this child," said Hannah. "The Lord gave me my desire. Now I am going to keep my promise. I want Samuel to stay here and train to be a helper in the Tabernacle. I know you will take good care of him."

Eli's face lit up with joy at the happy mother. He looked down at little Samuel. Here was a child who would grow up to love God and be a good, wise leader for the people. "God bless you my son," he said.

Then Hannah prayed and thanked God for His help. This was her song:

My heart praises God,
  for He has made me glad.
There is no one like God,
  He alone is holy.
He humbles the proud people,
  but He helps the humble ones who trust Him.
Riches and might are from the Lord,
  but He also brings honor to the good, even when they are poor.
The whole world is God's,
  and He controls it.

When his parents left, Samuel stayed behind. He would miss his parents, but he would be happy here. He would be trained to do important work. Eli gave him a special dress to show that he was learning to serve in the Tabernacle. During the first year he learned many things.

It came time for his mother and father to make their yearly sacrifice. He was very glad to see them.

"How you have grown!" cried Hannah. "Look, I have brought a coat for you to wear. It just fits. Next year I shall have to bring you another, larger one."

Eli spoke well of Samuel and thanked Hannah for the generous gift of her son to God's service.

In after years Hannah had other children, three sons and two daughters. Samuel saw them when they came to the Tabernacle to worship.

Samuel grew to be a fine boy. God was pleased with him. Everyone spoke well of him. He worked hard. He enjoyed serving God in His place of worship.

I Samuel 1, 2

44. A Call in the Night

At the Tabernacle Samuel was faithful in his many duties. He learned the rules about sacrifices and offerings, and he knew what ceremonies should be observed.

Others too helped in the Tabernacle. There were women who attended to certain things. They had helped care for Samuel when he was little. There was Eli, who as the high priest occupied a place of great honor. There were other priests who accepted the sacrifices of the people and offered them to God. Among these were two sons of Eli, Hophni and Phinehas.

Everyone spoke against these sons. They were not good men like their father. Young Samuel, along with the others, was shocked at the way they acted. When worshipers brought sacrifices, they demanded more than their share of the meat. They also refused to observe the ceremonies according to the law. The meat was supposed to be boiled, but they insisted on roasting it.

They cared nothing about the instructions in the law. By disregarding the sacredness of worship to God, they showed that they did not love Him. They broke other laws of God as well.

Eli spoke to them and scolded them, but they just laughed at their father. Still Eli did not take the honor of being a priest from them.

Once a prophet from God warned Eli, "God is not pleased with you. You honor your sons more than you honor God. God says, 'Because of the evil your sons have done and the way they have mocked at my worship, neither of them will ever be the high priest after you. The honor of being the family from which the high priest is chosen is taken from you. I will find men who will be faithful to Me!' "

Eli was saddened by this news. He did love God, but he hated to see his sons shamed before all the people. Perhaps, too, he hated to admit that he had been such a poor father.

Because of this, Eli still did not take his sons out of the service of the Tabernacle.

One night in the Tabernacle everything was very still. The flames in the seven-branched lampstand burned throughout the night. Behind closed curtains Samuel was fast asleep. Soon it would be morning. Then the lamp would be put out. Then Samuel would open the doors of the Tabernacle.

Suddenly Samuel woke up. He was sure someone had called him by name. It must be Eli.

Samuel got up and went into the place where the old man Eli slept. "Here I am," said Samuel. "I heard you call me."

"I didn't call you," said Eli, "go back to sleep."

Samuel obeyed; but he no sooner lay down than he heard it again. Eli must have thought of something he wanted to say.

Samuel hurried back to Eli, "Here I am. I heard you call."

"No," said Eli, "I didn't call."

Samuel went back to bed. Once more the call came, "Samuel. Samuel."

Samuel hurried in to the high priest. This time Eli sat up. He realized that God was speaking to Samuel.

"Go back to bed," said Eli, "If you again hear your name, it is God calling to you. Say, 'Speak, Lord, for your servant hears You.' "

Samuel went, wondering what would happen next. He lay back on his sleeping mat, but sleep was far from him.

Again God called to Samuel.

This time Samuel said, "Speak, for your servant hears You."

God spoke to Samuel. He had a message for Samuel to give to Eli. From now on Samuel would be a prophet, a messenger of God.

The message was not a happy one. Samuel was to remind Eli of what God's prophet had already told him. He was to say that God's judgment was soon to come on his sons.

Samuel went back to sleep. Soon the sun came up over the green hills. Samuel got up and opened the doors of the Tabernacle.

The day was bright and sunny, but Samuel's heart was heavy. He loved Eli and hated to bring this unhappy message to him.

Eli realized that he had done wrong, and that he had allowed his sons to do even greater wrong. He wanted to hear what God had told Samuel, so he sent for him. When Samuel entered the room he said, "Samuel, my son, come here."

"Here I am," said Samuel, just as he had the night before.

"What is the message God gave to you, Samuel?" asked Eli. "Do not keep it a secret from me. I want to hear all that God said."

So Samuel told him everything.

Eli was very quiet after Samuel finished speaking. Then he said, "God is just and right. I have sinned and so have my sons. It is important for the people to have priests who obey God and are a good example to others."

As day by day he worked in the Tabernacle, Samuel felt very close to God. The people who came to Shiloh realized that God was with him. They often went to Samuel with their problems and he advised them or judged between them. When Samuel spoke to them about God they realized that he was a prophet.

Samuel did not always stay in Shiloh after he grew up. He went throughout the different tribes teaching God's laws. Wherever he went, people came out to hear him. "Samuel speaks the words of God," they all agreed.

I Samuel 2:27-36; 3; 7:15

45. The Ark in the Hands of the Enemy

The Philistines were still the enemies of the Israelites. For years they had been gaining in strength and had conquered more and more land from God's people.

The Israelite soldiers were camped near Shiloh. They had fought this well-trained, better equipped army of the Philistines with courage, but the battle had gone against them. Then the leaders had an idea.

"Let someone go to Shiloh and bring back the ark of the covenant. We will take it into battle with us. Then God is sure to be with us, and we will win over the Philistines."

Messengers ran to Shiloh. Eli's sons, Hophni and Phinehas agreed to bring the ark to the camp and to carry it into the battle.

When the Israelite soldiers saw the priests bringing the ark of the covenant, they gave a great shout of joy.

The Philistines wondered what had happened. "What does the shouting in the camp of the Israelites mean?" they asked one another.

When they found out that the ark had been brought there, they were dismayed. "This is the God of the Israelites," they said. They did not understand, and thought the ark was like an idol. "We have heard what great wonders their God does," they moaned. "Now we are sure to lose the battle."

But their leaders shouted, "Be strong. Fight with all your skill and strength if you don't want to become slaves of the Israelites as we have made them slaves."

The Philistines did not understand that it was obedience to God which assured His people of His help, not the presence of the ark. And the Israelites had forgotten.

The Philistines fought hard. They killed many of the Israelites. Others fled away. Some soldiers of the Philistines saw a chance to win great glory for themselves. They killed Hophni and Phinehas and captured the ark of the covenant.

Back in Shiloh Eli sat trembling outside the Tabernacle. He was sure great judgment would come against the people. They had not been living in God's way and had no right to take the ark. Then Eli heard a great shout of dismay. Crowds in the street were spreading a message from one to another.

"What is it?" cried the old man, Eli. He was nearly blind, and it was hard for him to know what was going on.

A messenger from the camp came and told him of Israel's defeat. "Your sons have been slain," he said. Then he told the worst news of all. "The ark has been captured by the enemy."

At this, the old man fell over and died. All around people were mourning and weeping. Because the ark was captured, they believed that God was gone from them forever.

The Philistines took the ark back to their own country. They put it into their temple at Ashdod beside their idol, Dagon.

The Philistine soldiers continued the battle against the Israelites. Now they were very confident that one day they would make slaves of all Israel. They destroyed the town of Shiloh and burned the Tabernacle to the ground.

Back in Ashdod the Philistines received a surprise. Early in the morning the attendants of the temple discovered that their idol Dagon had fallen down.

They put the idol back in its proper place. The next morning it was down again. This time they were dismayed to find that the idol's head and hands had been cut off.

The priests of Dagon were very frightened. When many people of the city became ill with boils, they cried, "It is because we have this ark from Israel. Take it away from our city."

So the leaders of the Philistines took the ark to another city and put it in another temple to Dagon. But the people in this city became ill with boils.

Then the leaders took the ark to a city called Ekron, but the people of that city refused to let them bring it in. "Have you brought this holy object of Israel to our city to kill us?" they asked.

The leaders of the Philistines had a conference. "We must send the ark back to the people of Israel," they decided.

The priests of Dagon said, "We must also send an offering of gold so that the God of Israel will not be angry with us."

They put the ark on a newly built cart and journeyed to Beth-shemesh. Men out in the fields saw the ark coming and shouted with joy.

Levites came and took the ark and the offering. They led the people in giving thanks to God for its return.

From there the ark went to Kirjath-jearim, a town further inland. A man called Abinadab took the ark into his house. The priests consecrated his son, Eleazar, for the special task of keeping the ark safe.

I Samuel 4, 5, 6, 7:1

46. "Make Us a King"

Samuel became well known as a judge and a prophet of God. He could also perform the duties of a priest in sacrificing to God. He traveled all around Israel.

Samuel told the people, "The Lord will deliver you from the rule of the Philistines if you put away the idols you worship and serve Him alone."

Because of Samuel's message, many of the people got rid of their Baal idols and returned to God.

Often the leaders of the different tribes would ask him, "What can we do about the Philistines?"

Samuel decided that they should all get together and pray for God's help. He called for the leaders of the people to gather in Mizpah.

At this meeting the people admitted, "We are having this trouble because we have sinned against the Lord."

Samuel prayed for the people. He asked God to forgive them and to help them be a free people again.

The Philistines heard that many Israelites were gathered at Mizpah and they sent an army to attack them.

When the Israelites heard they were coming, they were very much afraid. "Continue to pray for us," the soldiers asked Samuel, as they made ready to fight.

When the army left, Samuel offered up sacrifice to God on an altar of rocks and prayed for the people.

Meanwhile the soldiers of Israel pursued the Philistines. That day they won a great victory over their enemies. "The Lord has helped us," said Samuel.

For years Samuel continued to judge the people. He made his home in Ramah; but he traveled throughout the land from Bethel, to Gilgal, to Mizpah and back home to Ramah.

Samuel made his two sons judges over Israel; but they were a disappointment to him. They were not as honest and just as Samuel. They even took money from men in return for giving the judgment the men desired.

One day some leaders of the people came to Samuel when he was at home in Ramah. They said, "Samuel, you are getting old, and your sons do not judge rightly as you have always done.

"We have talked about how we can successfully defend ourselves against the Philistines and be a stronger people. We need a king to rule over us. We want you, as God's prophet, to make us a king."

Samuel was surprised at their request. Was not God their king?

"The other nations around us have kings," said the leaders. "They are strong because they follow one man."

Samuel was not pleased. It did not seem right to him. He believed God alone should be king. But when he prayed to God about it, God said to him, "They have not rejected your rule but Mine. However, if they really want a king, they may have one. But warn them of some of the dangers."

So Samuel gathered the leaders of the people together. He reminded them of many things they could observe for themselves.

"Look around at these other nations,"

said Samuel. "Their kings live in wealth and splendor. The money for this comes from taxing the people. If you have a king, you too will have to pay taxes.

"You will find that many men and women are needed as servants and officials in order to maintain a king and his court. The king will demand the service of your sons and daughters. The crops you plant will not all be yours. Part will go to the king."

But the leaders were not convinced. "A king would lead our armies in battle against the Philistines," they argued.

Samuel agreed to the idea. He had done his part by warning the people of what could happen and pointing out some of the disadvantages of having a king.

"Go back now to your cities," said Samuel. "God will help us know who should be king. We will want a king who loves and obeys God. We will want a king who will lead our people in good ways; who will worship God alone and will uphold God's law."

I Samuel 7, 8

PART THREE
THREE RULERS

God's people had a home of their own; but they still had problems. They had always been shepherds, and learning how to farm had been difficult. Around them were enemy nations who raided their fields or tried to conquer their land. These troubles did one good thing. They helped the people to remember that their God was able to deliver them.

Sometimes the Israelites forgot their promise to worship God alone. They worshiped the idol Baal who was supposed to give them good crops. It would take many years before they would all be convinced that it was God who sent the sun and the rain and gave them good harvests.

Sometimes the different tribes would quarrel or one would refuse to help the others. They were not united into one nation.

Meanwhile the Philistines grew stronger and raided the land that belonged to the tribes of Israel. They took some Israelites captive and made them slaves.

"We need a king to lead us," the people decided. The prophet Samuel warned them that much trouble could come from a king who did not love and obey God.

The first king of Israel was Saul. After him came David and his son Solomon. These were great years for Israel. Under these three rulers the tribes were united and began to trade with other nations. They grew strong enough so that other nations were afraid to attack them. These were the golden years of Israel's history.

47. A King Is Found

Saul was a strong, good-looking young man. His father owned land and flocks and herds. They were a respected family, leaders in their tribe of Benjamin. People admired Saul and expected great things from him.

One day Kish, Saul's father, told him, "Some of our donkeys have wandered away. Take a servant with you and look all over the countryside. See if you can find them."

"Yes, Father," said Saul. He asked a servant to go with him.

The two men looked everywhere. They wandered further and further from home.

"It's no use," said Saul finally. "They are lost. We had better hurry back or my father will begin to worry over us. He will fear that we have been injured by bandits or killed by a wild animal."

"Just a minute," said the servant. "The prophet Samuel sometimes comes to this city we see up ahead. He is a great man of God. Let's go and ask him if he knows about the asses."

In those days people came to the prophets with many little problems as well as to ask for help in important decisions of right and wrong.

But Saul hesitated. "We have no gift for the prophet. We had better go home."

"I have a little money," said the servant. "I will give it to the prophet." He took out a coin to show Saul.

"All right then," said Saul. "Let's go and find this prophet."

On the way they met a group of girls who were carrying water jars. They were going out to the city well.

"Is the prophet in the city today?" asked Saul.

"Yes, he is about to go up to the hill where we offer sacrifice to God. The people have already gathered and are waiting for him to come and lead the worship."

The two men thanked the girls and went on. Down the road came Samuel on his way to the worship service.

Ever since the leaders had spoken to Samuel about a king, Samuel had been praying to God for guidance. Now as Samuel noticed Saul, God spoke to him. "Look, this is the man who will reign over My people."

Samuel looked closely at this young, handsome man.

The men had never seen Samuel before, and they asked, "Can you direct us to the prophet's house?"

"I am the prophet," said Samuel. "I know you are looking for your father's asses. They have returned home. Now I want you to come with me to the worship and take part in the feast. Then I want you to spend the night at my house. I have something important to tell you."

The young men were surprised, but they went with Samuel. At the feast Samuel made sure they had the best seats.

Saul was given the choicest part of the meat to eat.

Saul and his servant returned to Samuel's house. They slept out on the rooftop under the stars. In the morning Samuel called up to them. "It is time for you to be up and on your way home."

The men hurried to get ready. Saul knew his family would be anxious about them.

The prophet went with them through the city. As they came to the open countryside Samuel said to Saul, "Send your servant on ahead. I want to talk to you alone."

When they were alone Samuel took out a vial of oil he had brought with him. He poured a little on Saul's head, and told him.

"God has chosen you to be leader of His people. God is with you, and He will help you. Go home now. You will be hearing from me again."

As Saul left, he wondered at this strange turn of events. Had he really been chosen of God to be king? He felt close to God. He seemed to be a different person. What a wonderful experience he had just had!

When he returned home his family and friends noticed that something was different about him.

"What did the prophet say to you?" his uncle asked.

"He told us that the asses were found," said Saul.

Saul said nothing about being anointed by Samuel. He did not think that God wanted him to speak about his experience as yet.

A few days later Samuel called all the leaders of the people together and as many of the others as could come. They met at Mizpah. Excitement was in the air. Now the people felt sure they would find out whom God wanted to be king.

Samuel spoke to all those who had gathered. He reminded them how God had helped them in their past history.

"As you know," he said, "there has been a request for a king. Now we will cast lots and God will show us whom He wants for king."

This was a way the people often determined God's will. They prayed for God to show them and then they cast the special stones to get a "yes" or "no" answer.

First Samuel and the leaders cast the lots to see from which tribe the king would come. "It is the tribe of Benjamin," Samuel announced.

Then they threw down the stones to discover which family of Benjamin it would be. "It is the family of Matri," Samuel told them.

Everyone looked at the members of this family. The stones were cast again. Now they would find the name of the new king!

Samuel took up the deciding stone. "It is Saul, the son of Kish," he told the people.

Everyone looked around. "Where is he?" they shouted.

Someone ran to look for Saul and discovered him hiding among the baggage. The people ran and brought him up to the front. The new king was taller than most of the people. He looked strong and brave.

Samuel stood beside him. "See, this is the one God has chosen. Is he not the finest of all our men?"

The people agreed. They shouted their approval. "Long live the king," they cried. "Long live the king."

I Samuel 9, 10

48. Saul Wins for Israel

Now the tribes of Israel had a king. Before they could forget, Samuel reminded the people of what a king should do, and what he could expect from them. Samuel wrote these laws down and they were put away in a safe place.

Most of the people were happy with their new king, but a small group of people did not agree with the choice.

"How is this man going to save us from our enemies?" they asked. "He doesn't look like the kind of leader we need."

Many leaders from the different tribes sent gifts to Saul, but these people did not. Some of Saul's friends urged him to fight these men but Saul refused.

Shortly after Saul was made king, the people of Ammon attacked part of Israel. Even though the men of Jabesh pleaded, the Ammonites refused to make any kind of a peace treaty.

When Saul heard about this, he sent messengers throughout all the tribes of Israel. "Come together to fight our enemies," he commanded.

The people responded. Many soldiers came and under Saul's leadership the army fought well. They so scattered the enemy that no two soldiers were left together.

The people were delighted with their king. "He is a great soldier," they cried.

Then some of them said, "Bring out those who did not want Saul to be king. We will kill them."

"No," said King Saul. "None of them will be harmed. Today is a time to rejoice because God has given us victory."

Samuel led the people in giving thanks to God. They all accepted Saul as the king God had given the[illegible] happiness the people did [illegible] uel. They still believed Samuel [illegible] man of God.

Samuel said to them: "Both you and your king must serve the Lord with all your heart. I will continue to pray for you, and I will continue to teach you God's way. If you walk in God's way, God will continue to bless you."

When Saul was made king, the Israelites were still being forced to serve or to give money to the Philistines. They needed a strong military leader to deliver them from these foreign rulers. Saul promised to free his people from these men who had invaded their land. He began by an attack on one of the Philistine forts.

Immediately the Philistines sent an army to fight Israel. Thousands of soldiers rushed over the land. When the people of Israel saw the heavy chariots coming, they hid in the caves or anywhere they could.

Saul and his army were camped at Gilgal but they were not ready for such a big battle. They were not well trained, nor were they used to fighting as one army.

Saul knew the men were afraid. It looked as though his army was ready to desert him.

Samuel was soon to come to Gilgal to offer up a sacrifice and pray to God for their safety. He had told Saul, "Wait for me. I will be there in seven days."

But now it was the seventh day. Some of the soldiers had already run away, and still Samuel had not come.

"I can't wait for Samuel any longer," Saul told his officers. "Bring the sacrifice to the altar. I will offer it to God myself."

The soldiers gathered together before the altar. They watched as Saul offered the animal and prayed to God. Now they felt better.

But no sooner was Saul finished, than Samuel arrived at the camp. He was displeased with Saul because he had not waited.

"When I saw the soldiers deserting I had to do something," Saul explained. "The Philistines are ready to fight."

"I gave you orders that came from God," said Samuel. "You should not have disobeyed."

Samuel was disturbed. As a general Saul should have realized the importance of obedience. It looked as though Saul had already forgotten that God was their real Ruler.

"God will give the kingdom to another man and another family," Samuel warned. "He wants a king who will obey Him."

Then he left Saul.

King Saul continued to lead the army to victory, over the Philistines and over their other enemies. He and his son Jonathan proved to be good soldiers. The people were pleased; but Samuel, the prophet, was not pleased.

I Samuel 10:25-27; 11-14

49. A King Who Failed

The Philistines were not the only enemies of the Israelites. Sometimes other neighboring people caused trouble. One ancient enemy of Israel was the Amalekites. Saul gathered the army together to fight them.

Samuel, the prophet, had given the king a special message: "God will help you win the battle against this ancient enemy, but you must destroy them and all that they have. You may not bring treasure home for yourselves—even the animals must all be killed."

Saul agreed. He and his army camped in the valley near the city of Amalek.

The Kenites, a nomad tribe friendly to Israel, were also camped in the Amalekites' country. Saul sent a message to them, warning, "Depart from the Amalekites; for we are about to destroy them." The Kenites listened to the message and packed up and left.

Just as God had said, the battle was won by Saul and his men. But they took the king of the Amalekites prisoner and brought him back to their camp. They also brought back many sheep and oxen.

"Keep the best," Saul had said. "Destroy what is not good."

The day after the battle Samuel went to look for Saul. The army had already gone to a new camp, but Samuel followed them.

When Samuel arrived at the camp Saul greeted the prophet with great respect. "I have done as God commanded," he told the prophet.

Samuel was angry. He knew Saul had not obeyed. "If you did as God commanded, how is it that I can hear the bleating of sheep and the lowing of oxen? Did not God say you must destroy *all* the animals?"

Saul had an excuse. "We kept the best of the sheep and the oxen to sacrifice to the Lord. We destroyed the rest."

Samuel interrupted him, "Why did you disobey God?" he asked. "Was it not God who made you king?"

"I have obeyed," Saul insisted. "I only kept the best animals alive and I captured the king."

At first Saul had been a humble king, but as he grew in strength and power, he became proud. He thought he had the right to change God's command a little if he thought it best.

Then Saul tried to shift the blame to his soldiers. "They wanted to sacrifice the best of the animals to God," he told the prophet.

Samuel would not listen to this. King Saul did not need to fear his soldiers and should not have been swayed by them. After the sacrifice there would be a feast. Samuel wondered whether the men were concerned about giving something to God or with having a good time at the feast.

The prophet shook his head at the king he had once thought so promising. "To obey is better than to sacrifice," he said. "You have rejected God's command, and now God has rejected you from being king. He has chosen a better man than you to be king."

Samuel turned to leave.

Saul realized that Samuel had influence with the people. He did not want them to know about this quarrel.

"Please stay with me," he pleaded. "I am sorry I did wrong, but do not leave me now. Come with me, and we will talk to the people together. Worship with us here."

Samuel stayed and worshiped with the people as they thanked God for their victory. Then he went sadly back to his home in Ramah. He never again went to visit King Saul. He no longer had a message from God to Saul because God had rejected Saul as a king.

Samuel mourned over Saul as one mourns over one who has died. Saul could have been a good king if he had only understood that he must obey God, and that he ruled the people under God's guidance.

After many days God spoke to Samuel: "How long are you going to grieve over Saul? Fill your horn with the anointing oil. You will have the privilege of anointing a new king. Go to a man called Jesse who lives in Bethlehem. The new king will be one of his sons."

I Samuel 15:1-3

50. A Shepherd Is Chosen

Early one morning some shepherds led their sheep through the village of Bethlehem and into the hills. One of them was David, the son of Jesse. They each had a leather bag slung over their shoulders, with bread, cheese, and dried dates or figs for lunch. They each carried a club, a staff, and a slingshot to kill snakes or frighten off wild animals.

David also brought along his lyre, a small hand harp. While the sheep were eating green sweet grass or drinking from quiet pools they loved to hear his music. Sometimes David made up words to go with the tune.

God is my Shepherd;
  I won't lack anything.
He makes me lie down in green fields;
He leads me beside restful water;
  He revives me when I'm tired.
Yes, even though I walk through the
  valley of the shadow of death,
I won't fear any harm;
  for You are with me.
Your rod and staff comfort and help
  me.

. . . .

You have anointed my head with oil;
  my cup runs over.
Surely, goodness and unfailing love
  will follow me all the days of my life,
and I will live in God's house forever.

David's father, Jesse, owned this flock. The other shepherds had been hired or were servants of the family. David was young but he was a good shepherd. He loved the sheep and knew them all by their names. Several times he had killed an attacking bear or lion. David loved God, and he believed God helped him to face danger bravely.

This seemed like an ordinary bright, sunny day; but it was not. Something very exciting was going to happen.

While David was resting in the shade with the other shepherds, watching the sheep eat their fill, a very important visitor came to Bethlehem.

It was Samuel the prophet. Some of the people were a little afraid of Samuel. Had they done wrong? Had Samuel come to reprove them?

But the prophet set their minds at rest. "I have come to sacrifice to the Lord," he told them and pointed out the animal he had brought.

"Come share the sacrifice with me," he asked all the people.

Jesse and his sons came with the others. Samuel took special notice of this family. They were the ones he had come to Bethlehem to see.

Samuel looked at each of Jesse's sons. First he noticed Eliab. "Surely this is the one," he thought. "What a strong, handsome man."

But God said, "No, this isn't the one. Don't look for strength and beauty alone. Remember, 'Man looks on the outward appearance, but the Lord looks on the heart.' "

Samuel asked Jesse to introduce him to each one of his sons. None of them would do.

"Do you have another son?" he asked Jesse.

"Yes, there is my youngest son, David," Jesse told him. "He is in the hills, helping to care for the sheep."

Samuel said, "Send for him. We will wait. We will not have the feast until he comes."

Quickly Jesse found one of his servants. "Hurry to the hills and find David," he said. "Samuel, the prophet, wants to talk to him. Hurry. The prophet of God must not be kept waiting."

The servant ran off on his errand. He climbed a rocky path and went to a pasture he knew they often used. Yes, David was there with the others.

"You are wanted at home," the servant told David. "The prophet Samuel has come to the town. Even now the feast is ready. Your father says the prophet wants to speak to you."

David was surprised, but he left at once. He always enjoyed the worship service and the feast of joy and thankfulness to God which followed. He was especially excited about the prophet being there. He had no idea why such an important person would want to talk to a shepherd boy.

When they arrived at the place of sacrifice, Jesse took David by the hand and brought him to the prophet.

David looked up in admiration at Samuel, the man of God. Samuel looked at the young man. David was good looking, but there was something more about this young shepherd. He looked like a young man who loved God and who would grow up to be good and wise.

"Arise," God told Samuel, "anoint him; for this is he."

Samuel took the horn of sacred oil and poured it over David's head while his family and friends looked on. It was a sign that David had been chosen for some great work for God. They were amazed that this honor would be given to a young shepherd.

After the feast Samuel left Bethlehem. The next day David again helped lead the sheep into the steep hills and up onto a grassy plain.

God had chosen David to be the new king. Samuel was content. He knew that God would find a way to bring it all to pass.

I Samuel 16:1-13; 17:37;
Psalm 23, based on the Berkeley Version,
used by permission.

51. Music for the King

Saul was very unhappy. People had noticed that Samuel no longer came to see him. They realized that Samuel and the other prophets no longer supported his rule. The prophets said the king was disobedient to God and so was not worthy to lead God's people.

Saul felt guilty about his disobedience, and yet he did not repent and ask God to help him do better in the future.

Saul worried about what Samuel had told him. It made him angry to think that Jonathan, his son, would not be king after him. Who was this person who would start a new royal family? he wondered. Perhaps this someone was even now serving in his court. Saul began to be suspicious of everyone.

Often the officials of the king watched Saul sadly go off by himself. At other times King Saul would suddenly get very angry and shout and threaten everyone.

"Our king is not well," they said to one another. "Saul has shown himself to be a fine warrior. He has done good for our people. What can we do to help him?"

One had a suggestion. "I have heard that music helps those who act in such ways. Let's ask the king if he would like to have a good musician at the court."

One day when they were sure Saul was in a happy mood, the officials brought their suggestion to the king.

"Let us find a man who can play well on the lyre," they said. "When you feel unhappy such music will calm your spirits and help you to feel like yourself again."

The king thought it was a good idea. "Yes, send for a man who can play well. Do you have any idea where you can find a good musician?"

One of the young men of the court spoke up. "Once I visited Bethlehem and heard a young shepherd play on the lyre. He is David, the son of Jesse. He played beautifully. He was a handsome young man and everyone spoke well of him."

This sounded like the very one to be the court musician. "We will send for him," said Saul. "Perhaps music will help me."

King Saul sent messengers to Jesse. The father was surprised to hear what they had to say. "The king says, 'Send me David, your son. I want him to come and play on his lyre at the court.' "

Jesse called David. "My son, I have good news. The king has heard that you play well and wants you to come to the court to play on your lyre for him. You must go at once. I will prepare a gift for the king which you can take along with you."

David was excited. He wondered what the king's palace in Gibeah would look like. His soldier brothers had told him many tales about King Saul. Someday he wanted to be a soldier himself.

David said good-by to his parents and brothers. He took his lyre with him. His father gave him a gift of bread, a young goat, and wine for the king. It took one donkey to carry the gift of food.

Over the hills they went to Gibeah, the city where Saul held his court. It was not a wealthy, elaborate palace, but it thrilled David to be in the presence of the king, his officials and soldiers. Here all the important things were happening.

Saul liked the way David acted. He was strong and healthy looking. "What a fine young man," he thought.

Then David played the quiet melodies that the restless sheep had loved. The music spoke of the green hills, the wild flowers, and the tinkling of the mountain streams.

Saul could see the beautiful countryside as he listened. The wars with the Philistines, the troubles at the court, and his own fears seemed to melt away.

The officials were glad to see the king smile and speak calmly again.

"How beautiful your songs are," King Saul said to David. "Now I am indeed refreshed. You must stay here at the court and play for me often."

David was happy. He was glad the king had enjoyed the music. He wanted to stay here around all these important people.

The king sent a message back to Jesse which said, "Let David stay with me, for he has found favor with me."

I Samuel 16:14-23

52. A Slingshot and a Sword

David did not spend all his time at the court. Sometimes the king was not there. When David went home he again helped with the sheep. But he always looked forward to going back and playing his lyre before the king.

One day when David was with his father, Jesse said, "The army is camped nearby. Take this gift of roasted grain and bread to your brothers. And here are some fine cakes of cheese to give to their commander." Three of David's brothers were soldiers in Saul's army.

David was glad to go. He wanted to find out how the battle with the Philistines was going. When he came to the camp he found the battle was about to start. He heard soldiers shouting the war cry. His own brothers were lined up with the others. David ran to speak to them.

As they talked together everything suddenly became very still. "It is the champion of the Philistines," his brothers whispered. "Listen, does he have the same challenge to make?"

David watched as a fierce-looking giant soldier stepped out of the ranks of the Philistines. He was nearly ten feet tall, and his lips curled in scorn as he shouted boastfully.

"Why are you preparing for a battle? Choose one of your men to come out and fight me. If he is able to kill me, you have won the battle. These soldiers will be your slaves. But if I kill your chosen soldier, then you all must become our slaves. Why do you hesitate? Doesn't your God have anyone who will fight for Him?"

David grew angry at these words. "What is the matter?" he asked. "Why doesn't someone go out and fight him? He's defying the living God."

His brothers laughed. "Can't you see why? This man Goliath is a giant. Look at the size of his shield. See how his metal armor protects him from head to toe? And he is skillful in using that huge sword. None of our soldiers would have a chance with this man."

Many of the soldiers were so frightened by Goliath that they ran out of the ranks they had formed. Some soldiers standing near David said, "The king has promised great reward to anyone who will kill Goliath."

David said to the men, "Someone must answer this challenge. We must not let anyone insult our God and make fun of our people."

David's brothers thought he was making a pest of himself, but David would not be quiet. His words came to king Saul who sent for him.

"Let no one be afraid," said David when he came before the king. "I will fight the champion of the Philistines."

Saul shook his head. "You cannot fight this man. You are just a youth. You have not had the years of experience in battle that this man has had. You would only be killed."

But David insisted. "When I have been keeping my father's sheep I have often had to save them from a lion or a bear. I have killed both lions and bears. God has always helped me, and He will help me now."

This young man was so sure of God's help that Saul was convinced too. "Go, and the Lord be with you," he said. "But wait, I will lend you my own

armor to wear." Most of the Israelite soldiers did not have fine metal armor to wear.

David put on the breastplate and the helmet. He took the sword that was given to him. But he could hardly walk. "I can't fight this way," he said. "I'm not used to armor."

David took them off. He could move freely now. The other soldiers and the king watched as David quickly found five smooth stones in a nearby brook and put them in his shepherd's bag. With his staff and his sling shot, he walked bravely through the ranks and out into the open. There he faced the huge challenger who had come down from the hillside.

Goliath looked down at David. His face clouded over with rage. The crowds behind him were also angry. They all thought the Israelites were making fun of them by sending out a young soldier who was not even clothed in armor and carried no sword.

"Do you think that I am just a dog who can be frightened away with a stick?" shouted Goliath. "I will show you and your God what I can do."

"You have a great sword," said David, "but I come to you in the name of our God whom you have defied. Today you Philistines will know that our God has the power. Battles are not always won by those who have the best weapons."

Goliath stepped closer and raised his sword. David took out a stone from his bag and put it in his slingshot. As he ran towards Goliath he aimed the slingshot he used so well. The stone sped through the air and landed squarely in the forehead of Goliath. The challenger fell to the ground face down.

Then David ran to the Philistine soldier. Out of Goliath's sheath at his side, he pulled the giant's own huge sword, and with it cut off his head. At this, the Philistine soldiers forgot the promise Goliath had made and ran away. The soldiers of the Israelites pursued them and won the battle.

David returned to King Saul. The king was grateful for the way David had saved his people. The prince, Jonathan, was nearby. He too spoke his thanks to David. Jonathan admired this young man and decided right then and there that they must always be friends.

Saul wanted David to be with him always. "You must not return to your father's house." he said. "From now on you will be part of our court."

I Samuel 17, 18:1-5

53. David in Danger

David enjoyed living at the court of Saul. He became armor bearer for the king. In time he took on the duties of a soldier himself. Everyone remarked about how quickly he learned and how eager he was to succeed.

But more than all this, David found a true friend at the court, the prince Jonathan. David admired Jonathan, not because he was a prince, but because he was kind and brave. Jonathan, too, loved David.

Often the two young men talked together. They enjoyed each others' company because they liked the same things and thought alike. It seemed to them that they were alike, more brothers than friends.

To show how deeply he cared for David, Jonathan gave him a present. He took off his own coat and gave it to David. Then he gave David his armor, his sword, and his bow. This was a way of saying, "I give you part of myself," or "I promise to always be faithful and loyal to you."

David took the gift. He told Jonathan how much he thought of him as a friend and that his friendship had brought him happiness.

King Saul recognized David as a good soldier. He promoted him and made him an officer over other soldiers. It was a promotion with which every one agreed.

As the years passed, David's fame as a soldier and a man of the court grew.

Whenever the Israelite army came home from battle, the women and children and older people would come out to meet them. Musicians would be there to play. The people would sing songs of praise to those who were helping to free their country from the Philistines.

Sometimes the words of the songs were made right then and there. One day as the army marched home, someone noticed David among the warriors. "There is the noble David," he shouted. "He has killed many of our enemies. He has killed more than ten thousand."

"David is the best of soldiers," others agreed.

Some women made up a song about this.

"Saul has slain his thousands,
and David his ten thousands,"

they chanted over and over, as the timbrels played a tune to go with the words.

The women did not mean disrespect for their king. They knew Saul was a great warrior and a good king; but they thought that David was the best soldier, even better than the king.

But King Saul was angry when he heard the song. He was jealous. "Why do they say ten thousands for David and thousands for me?" he asked himself. "They think more of David than their own king."

Then a thought sprang up in Saul's suspicious mind. He remembered what Samuel, the prophet, had told him.

"David is likely to be the next king," Saul realized. "David wants my throne. He is so popular with the people, that they are likely to give it to him."

Often when Saul was alone he thought about this. He watched David closely. He noticed how Jonathan and everyone else admired David. Once Saul had loved David, but now his love turned to hate.

David still played his lyre before the king, but now instead of calming Saul, it made him have a fit of raving. One day when Saul was in an angry mood he threw his spear at David. David jumped back just in time.

After this, Saul decided that he would keep David busy at the battlefront. But this only resulted in making David more famous, because he was always successful.

"I must get rid of David," Saul decided, "but I don't want to murder him. If the people know I am responsible for his death, they will hate me."

Then King Saul had an idea. Anyone would be pleased to marry one of the king's daughters.

One day Saul sent a servant to David

with a message: "The king is pleased with you David," the messenger said. "He wants you to marry his daughter Michal."

David protested. "I am not good enough to marry one of the king's daughters. What present could I give him in return? I am poor and come from a poor family."

This was what King Saul had hoped David would say. He told the servant, "Tell David that instead of a gift of money the king will accept a mighty deed done in battle."

The servant went out with the message. *Now,* Saul thought to himself, *David will get himself killed by the Philistines. No one will be able to blame me.*

David was glad to hear the words of the king. "If that is the case, I shall so fight that the king will give me his daughter," he promised.

David went out to battle and did as he had promised by winning a big victory over the Philistines. Even the king had to admit that David had won his daughter, Michal. The wedding was held. Michal was very happy, because she had liked David for a long time.

But Saul was not happy. He still wanted to be rid of David. There was no quiet way to do it, but it must be done.

He called his officials together, including all his sons. "I want David put to death," he shouted. "I will reward any of you who kill David."

I Samuel 18, 19:1

54. David Runs Away

Jonathan was surprised at the words of his father. He knew the king was jealous of David, but he had not thought Saul would order him killed, especially after David became his son-in-law.

The prince ran at once to the fields where he knew David could be found. He told David of his danger.

"My father plans to kill you, David," he said. "Don't go back to the palace but hide yourself nearby. Tomorrow morning I'll bring my father out here. I'll speak a word in your defense, and we shall see what he has to say. I'll do my best to change his mind."

David was puzzled. "I can't understand it," he said. "My music used to make the king feel better, but now it makes him worse. He has given me his daughter in marriage, and yet he wants to kill me."

That night David hid in some nearby caves. In the morning he was up early, looking toward the palace. Then he saw two figures approaching. It was Jonathan and his father.

They came near enough so David could hear. "My father, why are you seeking David's life?" Jonathan asked. "He is your servant. He has killed many of your enemies and the enemies of our country. He has never tried to do you harm."

The king said nothing.

"You rejoiced when David brought victory to our armies. It would be wrong for you to kill David without a cause."

The king was quiet. He was not in one

of his angry moods. He nodded slowly. "Yes, you are right. It would be wrong to harm David. I promise before God that he shall not be put to death."

They went away then, but soon Jonathan came hurrying back. "David, David," he called. David ran out to meet him.

"Did you hear what my father said?" asked Jonathan. "It was only one of his bad spells which made him threaten you. He wants you back in the palace."

David was glad. Jonathan, the prince, led him back into the court. King Saul greeted him warmly.

Not long afterwards the Philistines attacked the land. David was sent out to chase them back across their border. As before David brought victory to the Israelites. Everyone in the country was grateful to him.

But Saul was jealous. He wanted the battles to be won, but he was afraid of David's popularity. He thought about this one day as David knelt before him, playing the lyre.

In a fit of rage he threw his spear at David. *I will kill him,* thought Saul, but David again stepped aside just in time. The spear stuck in the wall.

David ran from the room, but Jonathan stayed. He wanted to see if King Saul would again order David killed. This time the king's anger did not cease. He took aside some trusted messengers. "I want you to watch outside David's house tonight,'" he told them. "When everyone is asleep, go in and bring David to me so that I can kill him."

But the king's plan became known to Michal, David's wife. When David came home she told him, "If you don't escape at once, they will kill you tomorrow."

David hated to leave Michal by herself; but she brought out a rope to let him down out of the window in case the messengers were already at the door.

David said good-by and ran away into the dark shadows. Michal took an image and put it on David's bed. She covered it with David's cloak. Then she found a piece of goat's hair cloth and made it look like a head.

"Good," she said as she viewed her work. "It looks just like a man sleeping on his bed. They will also recognize David's cloak."

Then there was a knock at the door. Michal let in the king's messengers.

"The king demands that David come before him," said the messengers.

Michal pointed towards the sleeping mat. "David is ill," she said.

The messengers brought this report to the king.

"If David is ill bring him to me on his bed," said King Saul. "Then I'll kill him."

The messengers went back. They started to take up the mattress on which they thought David lay and then discovered the image.

The messengers hurried back to tell the king how they had been tricked.

King Saul spoke sternly to his daughter. "Why have you let my enemy escape?"

Michal was afraid to tell the truth. "David threatened to kill me if I did not help him escape," she said.

Meanwhile David was running through the hill country. *I'll go to Samuel at Ramah,* he thought to himself.

I Samuel 19:1-18

55. Faithful Friends

For a while David stayed with Samuel and the other prophets. Then he decided to go back to the palace secretly and talk to his friend Jonathan.

When the two friends were face to face, David asked, "Jonathan, what have I done that your father is so angry with me? Why does your father want to kill me?'

"I am sure if my father still sought to kill you he would have told me," said Jonathan. "You know how these angry fits sometimes make him say things for which he is sorry."

"Your father knows you love me," argued David. "He says nothing to you because he knows it would grieve you. I am sure he means to kill me."

"What can I do?" asked Jonathan. "I will do anything I can to help you."

"I have a plan," said David. "Tomorrow is the feast of the new moon which lasts three days. The king will expect me to be there, but I will not come. I will be hiding. See if your father is angry at my absence.

"If your father questions you, say, 'David could not come because his family is having a yearly sacrifice, and he asks permission to go home for a few days.' If your father is not angry that will show that he means me no harm; but if he is angry, it means he still wants to kill me."

Jonathan nodded. It sounded good.

"Remember our covenant, our promise to always be friends," said David.

"I do remember," said Jonathan. "I will keep nothing from you. If I knew for sure now than my father really did want to harm you, I would tell you."

"How will you be able to tell me if your father is angry at my absence?" asked David.

"Come, let's go out into the fields where no one can overhear us," said Jonathan.

They walked out together. Jonathan promised David, "I will tell you how my father reacts to your absence. But first David, I realize that one day God wants you to be king. Remember that I am your friend. Promise me that no harm will come to me or my family."

"I will always remember the promise of friendship we made before God," said David. "I will never harm you or your family."

Then Jonathan outlined a plan. He pointed to a rocky place where it would be good for David to hide.

"Hide yourself there," he said. "When I find out how my father feels about you, I will come out here with my bow and arrows. A boy will be with me. I will shoot three arrows at a mark and then say to the boy, 'Bring back my arrows. They are on this side of you.' By this you will know that there is no danger to you, and you can come back to the palace.

"But, if after I shoot the arrows I say, 'The arrows are beyond you,' then you will know that your life is in danger and you must run away."

Then Jonathan returned to the palace. The next night the feast was made ready. Jonathan sat near his father. Nearby was David's empty place.

King Saul noticed that David was not there; but he said nothing. The next night he looked to see if David would come. When he did not, Saul became very angry.

"Why isn't David here?" he asked Jonathan.

Jonathan gave the excuse they had planned. "David asked permission to go home for a feast with his family."

Saul became excited. "You are always making excuses for David," he shouted. "You are a disloyal son. Everyone knows that you have chosen David, my enemy, for a friend. Now bring David to me that he may die."

"Why must David be put to death? What has he done?" argued Jonathan.

Suddenly Saul threw his spear at Jonathan but the prince got away in time. He was very angry at his father for his unjust attitude toward David.

The next morning Jonathan took a boy with him and went out into the fields. He carried his bow and arrows. David was hiding where Jonathan had told him.

David watched as the prince shot his arrows and the boy ran to bring them back.

"The arrows are beyond you," Jonathan called.

David's heart sank. The king did seek his life. No doubt he would never be welcomed at the palace again.

The boy brought the arrows back to Jonathan. The prince gave the bow and arrows back to him. "Take these back to the palace," he said. "I will be out here for a while."

When the boy was gone, David came out from behind the rocks. He was thankful to Jonathan for saving his life.

Sadly the two friends said good-by. "We are still friends," Jonathan told David. "May God be with us both."

David wept as he left his friend. Jonathan turned and made his way back to the court.

I Samuel 20

56. A Chance to Kill Saul

David had left in such a hurry that he had no provisions of food or water. He did not even have a sword. Saul, he was sure, would soon be looking for him.

The first place David stopped was a town just north of the king's court called Nob. Here he went to see Ahimelech, the priest.

"I need your help," he told the priest.

The priest was surprised. "Why are you alone?" he asked.

David did not want the priest to know that Saul was out to kill him. "I am on a special mission for the king," he said. "It is secret and requires great haste. Do you have some bread you could give me?"

"I have only the holy bread that is kept in the sanctuary," said the priest, "but you may have it."

The holy bread was put on the table in the place of worship to remind the people how God had fed them in the wilderness. Fresh bread was put there every Sabbath.

David gratefully took the bread. "I left in such a hurry I forgot my sword," David told him. "Do you have a weapon I can use?"

"There is only the sword of Goliath which has been kept here for safekeeping. You can have that."

"Fine," said David. "There is no better sword than that."

As the priest went to get the huge sword, David noticed Doeg, a servant of Saul, standing in the sanctuary. He must hurry away. Doeg would probably tell Saul that he had stopped here.

David took the sword and the food and went away. Soon everyone heard that David had fled the court and that King Saul was trying to kill him.

David found a hiding place in Adullam, southwest of Bethlehem, his home town. There were many caves in the hills around Adullam, and it would be hard for anyone to find him. David's family joined him in the caves. They knew they were not safe from Saul's anger.

Other men also joined David. They wanted to be part of his band and fight his cause. Altogether David had about four hundred followers.

David was concerned about his family. "Let us go to Moab and see if the king will shelter you," he told them. David's great-grandmother Ruth had come from Moab.

The king of Moab was friendly to them and promised to care for David's family. David and his men left them there and went back to Judah.

King Saul was not idle. He and his soldiers were looking everywhere for David. They followed rumor after rumor as David and his men changed camp.

One day David heard that the Philistines had raided Keilah, not too far from Adullam. They were robbing the people of that town of their harvest. "Let's go and fight the Philistines," said David.

But his men objected. "Then Saul will find out where we are and capture us."

David asked God for guidance. When he felt sure that God wanted them to fight for the people against the Philistine invaders he led his men to the town.

After David and his men chased away the raiders Saul did hear about it. He commanded all his soldiers to come with him to capture David. But David and his men escaped out of Keilah in time.

One day when David and his men were camping out in the hill country of Ziph, south of Bethlehem, they were surprised by a visit from Prince Jonathan. Jonathan spoke encouragingly to David.

"Don't be afraid. God is with you. You will one day be king over Israel, and I will gladly be second to you. My father knows this and so he seeks to kill you, but God will protect you."

David renewed his promise of friendship with the prince. Then Jonathan went back to the court.

But some men who lived nearby went to Saul. "We know where David is camped," they said. Saul pursued after David, but David heard about it in time and escaped.

It was difficult running from place to place, and hard to keep on believing that God was going to help them. God *was* with David, however, and protected him.

Once David found shelter in a large cave in the rocky wilderness of Engedi, near the Dead Sea. The men were sitting in the back of the cave when they heard approaching footsteps. They were very still.

Then a man stopped at the entrance of the cave. It was Saul himself!

"Look, David," whispered his men. "God has brought Saul here. Now is your chance to kill him and be king."

David said, "No. I don't believe that. It would not be right to kill the king, because he has been anointed of God."

Still David crept close to Saul. He cut off a part of the bottom of Saul's robe. Then David crept back into the back of the cave.

David's men were amazed. If David did not feel right about killing the king, they would do it for him. They jumped up with their knives ready, but David forced them to keep back.

"He is the Lord's anointed," David insisted. "We must not harm him."

Then King Saul left the cave. He hurried back to his soldiers and soon they could be heard riding away.

Before they disappeared David ran out of the cave and called to them. "King Saul," he cried. "My lord and king."

Saul looked back. He commanded his men to be still. He could hardly believe his eyes when he saw David.

David bowed to the king. "Why do you listen to those who tell you I mean to do you harm?" he asked. "I had a good chance to kill you when you stopped at the cave. My men were inside with me and wanted to kill you. But I would not allow them to hurt you.

"See, I have a piece of your robe which I cut off. This proves that I could have taken your life if I had desired; but I would not kill one anointed of God."

Saul was ashamed. "You are a more righteous man than I. You returned good for evil. I realize that God wants you to be king after me. Will you promise to spare my relatives when you become king?"

David promised Saul this, as he had promised it to Jonathan. Saul returned back to the palace; but David and his men remained in the hills.

I Samuel 21-24

57. Abigail Saves Her People

For safety David and his followers camped at different places. Sometimes they camped near the desert. This was the edge of civilization, where Arab nomads would come at times and rob the people of Israel who lived nearby.

One day shepherds from the town of Carmel near Hebron brought their flocks near David's camp. They worked for a rich man called Nabal. David and his followers were friendly to them and protected them from robbers.

David's band of men had increased in size and sometimes it was hard to get food and other things they needed. One day when their food supply was low, David called some of his young men to him.

"Go up to Carmel where Nabal is now shearing his sheep, and feasting. Greet him with words of peace and friendship. Tell him how we befriended his shepherds and helped protect his property. Then ask him for a gift—whatever he can spare."

The young men rode off. Everyone was expected to give hospitality to wanderers and to give gifts of appreciation at feast times. To refuse to do so was a great insult. The young men had no doubts in their minds but what they would receive a handsome gift from such a rich man.

They found Nabal and his men busy with the shearing. Nabal had three thousand sheep, besides goats, so there was

a lot of work to do. Shearing was a time of feasting and rejoicing. The people seemed happy, even though Nabal was known to be a hard master and a bad-tempered man.

The young men greeted Nabal with great courtesy and respect as David had told them to do. They reminded Nabal that David had helped his servants and they asked for a gift.

They waited while Nabal just looked at them. Then he spoke scornfully. He had heard about David's quarrel with Saul.

"Who is David?" he asked. "Why should I help him? He is just a servant escaped from his master. Why should I share with him?"

The young men went back and reported to David. All the followers of David were angry, and so was David.

"Sword on everyone!" he commanded. "How ungrateful this fellow is for all our help. We'll teach him a lesson."

Meanwhile one of Nabal's servants went to Nabal's wife, Abigail. She was a kind and wise person.

"We are in great danger," the servant told her. "David sent some of his men here to ask a gift of your husband. David and his men befriended our shepherds and helped them protect their flocks from robbers. But Nabal is so foolish. Instead of being polite to such men he spoke scornfully of David and sent them away empty-handed."

"That is terrible," agreed Abigail. "Do you think these soldiers will come to fight us?"

"Many of us are sure they will. It was a great insult," said the servant. "But no one dares to speak about it to Nabal, because he is so mean tempered."

"I know what I will do," said Abigail.

She hurried and got some food together. She had servants bring loaves of bread, skins of wine, meat ready to be cooked, roasted grain, raisins and figs. It took several donkeys to carry it all. Then she herself got on a donkey.

"Go on before me with the gift," she told several servants. "I will be directly behind you."

Quickly they all rode down the mountain toward the desert but Nabal knew nothing about it. He was enjoying a big dinner with his friends. As they came to the foot of the mountain, Abigail saw David and his men coming towards them.

The little party stopped and Abigail got down off her donkey and bowed before David.

"Please put all the blame for this on me," she said. "*Nabal* means 'fool' and he is well named for Nabal is a foolish man. I didn't see your men, or this would never have happened. I have brought you some things you may need, with the thanks of myself and all our people."

Abigail had heard much about David. "May God help you and protect you," she said. "You have fought the enemies of our people. You are a man who is brave and just. God will one day make you king of our people."

David's anger was gone as he beheld this beautiful and gracious woman.

"God bless you," he said. "I am so glad that you stopped us from making war on Nabal. By your wisdom and kindness you have spared the lives of many."

Then David accepted Abigail's gift. "Go in peace," he told Abigail and the servants. "You have nothing to fear."

David and his men went back to their

camp. Some time later David heard that Nabal had died. He was glad he hadn't taken vengeance on Nabal. Then he thought about the lovely Abigail. What a wonderful wife she would make, if only she would be willing to join him in his life as a fugitive.

David sent men to ask Abigail if she would marry him. Abigail was willing. She got herself ready as soon as she could.

David watched for the return of his messengers. He saw them coming. Behind them was Abigail and five of her women servants. He rejoiced that now he had someone to share his lonely life.

I Samuel 25

58. A Visit to the Camp of the Enemy

Soon after David and his men camped in the wilderness of Ziph they heard rumors that Saul was near. Some people had found out where David was hiding and had reported it to the king.

"We must be sure," David said. "We will send out spies."

When the spies came back, they told David the exact location of Saul's camp. The king had brought several thousand soldiers to capture David. General Abner was with them.

David went to the spot with some of his men. Yes, there they were camped on the hillside. David stood on a higher hill a safe distance away and looked down at Saul and his men.

David asked for a volunteer. "Who will come with me into the camp?" he asked.

"I will," said the faithful officer Abishai.

They waited until night. Then they crept down, keeping in the shadows. King Saul and General Abner lay in the center of the camp. Around them, wrapped in their cloaks, lay the other soldiers. They were all fast asleep.

David was surprised that no one was awake, protecting the king. Saul's spear was stuck in the ground near his head. A jar of water was also nearby.

"Come," said David. He and his officer crept among the sleeping men.

They came near to the king. "God has shown you how to get rid of Saul," whispered Abishai. "Give me permission, and I will use my spear to kill this king. I will do it with one blow."

"No," said David. "Don't do it. It would be wrong to kill a king, one anointed of God. We can trust God to bring judgment upon Saul for the wrong he has done. I am not going to take vengeance on him, because he is still my king."

Then David drew Saul's spear from the ground. He also took the water jar from its place.

"Now let us go," he whispered to Abishai. All the while not a soldier woke up.

The two men made it safely out of the camp. They again climbed the hill from which they had a good view of Saul's army.

Then David called out. Again and again his voice broke the stillness of the night.

"King Saul," David called out. "King Saul! General Abner!"

At last a few soldiers woke up. Abner stirred. "Who calls for the king?" he shouted. Now he was alarmed.

"You are a fine general and protector of the king," said David scornfully. "The king might easily have been killed tonight while you were fast asleep. Look now. Where is Saul's spear and the water jar?"

Abner looked all around. They were not there.

Now King Saul was awake. "Is that you, David?" he asked, recognizing the voice.

"It is David, your faithful servant," called David. "My king, why do you pursue me? Why do you continue to believe those who say I would do you harm?

"Tonight I have spared your life. I was down in the camp with another. See, I can prove it. Have a young man come to us, and we will return the king's spear and water jar."

The king looked around. David was telling the truth. How easily the king, the general, and many others might have been killed. David had surely proved his love for King Saul.

The king repented of his hatred for David. He felt guilty and ashamed. "I have done wrong," he confessed. "I will never try to harm you again. Come back to the court. Because you spared my life, I will spare yours. I have acted like a fool."

But David could no longer trust Saul's promises. He knew how easily Saul could change his mind once he returned to court.

"The Lord rewards those who are faithful to him," said David. "God knows I have not wronged you. I trust Him for my protection."

Saul did not urge David to return. "God's blessings be upon you, David," he said. "You will do many great things."

So David and Abishai gave the spear and the water jar to the young man from Saul's army. Then they disappeared into the shadows.

When morning came King Saul ordered his men back to the court.

I Samuel 26

59. Refuge in Ziklag

When David returned to his camp he spoke to all his followers. "As long as we are in Judah we are in danger," he said. "Saul will again change his mind and seek my life. The only thing we can do is to seek refuge in the land of the Philistines."

No one liked to do this, but they all were convinced that for a time it would be the best thing to do. So David and his men with all their families crossed the border into Gath. It was a large group that asked refuge of King Achish.

"We will serve you if you give us a place to live," David promised.

The king agreed. He sent David and his followers to a town called Ziklag.

There was only one thing which worried the men. If the Philistines again made war on Israel, they would be told to fight against their own people. This they would not be able to do.

After living in Ziklag a little more than a year, it happened. All the Philistine rulers decided to unite and go to war against Israel.

Achish told David and his men to assemble for the battle. They came, but when the other Philistine rulers saw them they said, "Don't be foolish. We can't trust David. He will turn on us. We will not allow them to take part in this battle."

David and his men were told to go back to Ziklag. Back at the town an unhappy surprise greeted them. The Amalekites had used the opportunity of their absence to raid the town.

Not only had all the buildings been burned with fire, but all the people, including David's family, had been taken away as captives. All the animals were gone, also.

Some of the men were angry at David. They thought he had not left proper protection for the people at home. They were distraught at losing their sons and daughters.

David asked God's guidance. Then he said, "We must go after these Amalekites and rescue our people."

David and his soldiers started out. But after they had traveled several miles, some of the men were too exhausted to go any further. They stayed behind, while David and the others kept going.

On the way they found a young Egyptian lad who was very ill. They treated him kindly and gave him food and water.

"Who are you?" they asked. "Where is your home?"

"I am a slave to one of the Amalekites. We raided many towns. Ziklag was one. Then when we started for home I became ill. My master left me to die."

"Will you take us to the camp of the Amalekites?" asked David.

"If you promise that you won't harm me or turn me over to my master."

David promised. "You are safe with us," he assured the boy.

The Egyptian led the way for miles across an open plain. At last they came to the place where the large army of the Amalekites was spread out. The sound of music and dancing could be heard. The Amalekites were celebrating their success with a big feast. They had stolen so many treasures in their raids that they could afford to make merry.

David and his soldiers waited until twilight. Then they descended on the unsuspecting Amalekites. They won the fight with the raiders and recovered all the treasures that had been taken from them and all the cattle that belonged to them. And most important of all, they rescued their wives and children. It was a happy group that returned to Ziklag. The men who had been left near home were glad to see the returning heroes and their families. But some of the soldiers did not want to be generous. "We did the fighting," they said. "These men should not get any of their possessions back. Only their wives and their children should be returned to them."

"No," said David. "Everyone must get back all that belongs to him. God has kept us safe and helped us. The soldiers who stayed behind to guard the baggage should share alike with those who did the fighting."

I Samuel 27; 28:1, 2; 29, 30

60. Long Live King David!

David, his men, and their families waited in Ziklag to hear word about the battle between the Philistines and the Israelites.

A few days later a messenger came to the town. He had run a long way. Crowds gathered around and David came out to meet him. They knew the man brought bad news because he had torn his clothes.

"From where have you come?" asked David.

"From the camp of the Israelites," said the messenger.

"How did the battle go?" David asked eagerly.

"The Israelites have fled from the Philistines," the man told him. "Many of Israel have died, including King Saul and Jonathan."

David and the men who had gathered around tore their clothes as a sign of mourning. They wept for their defeated people and for all those who had given their lives. They especially mourned King Saul and Prince Jonathan.

Now their country was weak indeed. It would be even harder to free themselves from Philistine oppression.

The rest of the day David's followers mourned the fallen king and his son. David made up a poem to express how he felt. It went something like this:

Israel is defeated.
How could mighty Israel be fallen?
Do not tell it to the Philistines.
They would only rejoice.
Saul and Jonathan were greatly loved.
In life and in death they were not divided
In battle they were swifter than eagles
And stronger than lions.
People of Israel, weep over Saul, your king.
Weep over Jonathan, my brother, whom I loved.
How the mighty are fallen!

David and his men went back to Judah. Judah was David's tribe and they immediately acknowledged him as king.

At first General Abner wanted a young son of Saul to be the next king of Israel. But after a few years Abner was won over and promised to serve David. The rest of the people in the north agreed.

The leaders of all the tribes came to where David was staying in Hebron. "We are all one family," they said to David. "We remember how great a soldier you were under King Saul, and now we want you for our leader.

"God has said, 'David will be a shepherd for My people.' And so we want you for our king."

David welcomed them. He promised to keep the rules God's people had made for the king when Samuel the prophet was living.

Then the leaders anointed David king over all Israel. "Long live the king," the people shouted. "Long live the king."

Many wondered where David would make his court. David had decided that the stronghold of Jerusalem should be taken. It was a piece of mountainous land that almost separated the north and south of Israel. It would make for a stronger country if Jerusalem belonged to them.

The people of Jerusalem were confident that no army could take their fort, because it was in the midst of a rocky ridge of hills.

"We could fight David and win even if we used only our lame and blind people," they boasted.

But David did conquer the fort of Jerusalem. His men got into the city by using a tunnel which sometimes brought water from a spring outside the walls. The fort and its people became a part of Israel.

Here David built a city which became known as Jerusalem, the city of David. For his growing family he built a palace made of cedar and composed of many different sections or houses. There were enclosed courtyards with beautiful trees and flowers.

The Philistines realized that David might become a strong king. They rallied their army against him. They wanted to defeat him before he had a chance to make himself and his people secure.

David, on the other hand, had promised himself and his people that he would rid the land once and for all of the Philistines.

The Philistines attacked Israel, but David led the army of Israel and drove them away. Through battle after battle David showed his skill as a man of war. The Philistines were driven back to a small piece of land along the coast. They never again became a strong power.

The people honored David as a great warrior. He had delivered them from their oppressors. Now there would be a time of peace, a time when they could grow, and learn, and find better ways to live.

II Samuel 1-5
I Chronicles 10, 11, 12

61. A King Who Loved God

David was not satisfied with being a military hero. He wanted to help and lead his people in every way.

One day David thought, *The ark of the covenant lies in a house in a small town. It should be here in Jerusalem. We will put it in a special tent where all the people can gather to worship.*

David made ready to bring the ark to Jerusalem. He wanted the city to become a center for the worship of God. He asked many priests to come and be a part of his court. He was concerned that his people love God and obey God's laws.

David himself went with a large group of priests to get the ark. It was a happy procession that made its way back to Jerusalem.

At the beginning of the march they offered sacrifice to God. David and the priests wore robes of fine linen. Some priests carried the ark. Others sang or played musical instruments. David joined in the marching and the dancing as the musicians played on lyres, tambourines, and castanets.

People from all the tribes lined the roads the procession traveled. They shouted for joy when they saw the ark.

When the procession came into the city of Jerusalem, the special tent was waiting for its prized possession. The priests reverently carried the ark into the tent and put it to rest in its central place.

David the king offered sacrifice to God

at the altar. Then he spoke to the people gathered in the court. "God bless you all and give you peace," he said.

Then David's servants handed out presents of food to the people. Each one had bread, meat, and raisins to take home.

Now that the ark was here, many people came to Jerusalem from all over the nation to worship at this tent. One day David had another plan. He sent for the prophet, Nathan.

"Nathan," said David. "I have been thinking. I have a beautiful palace to live in, and yet we put the ark of the covenant in a tent. Why not build a beautiful house, a temple, for it? Other nations have beautiful temples for their worship."

"It is a good idea," said Nathan. "Let us pray and ask for God's guidance."

Nathan went home. The next morning he came back to the court with a disappointing message for David.

"God says that you cannot build a house for Him," Nathan told the king. "You have been in too many battles. It is not for a man of war to build God's house."

David was disappointed, but he did not question the authority of God.

The prophet went on. "God has never had a house. He doesn't need one. All through our history our people have worshiped in the court of a tent. Nevertheless God knows that you want to build a temple to show your love for Him. He knows that people often want to build something beautiful to show that they want to give their best to God.

"God is going to allow your son, the one who will be king after you, to build a temple for Him."

David was glad to hear this. But Nathan had more to say.

"God has a message for you, David. He says, 'I took you from taking care of your sheep to be king over my people, Israel. I have been with you ever since I first chose you, and I will always be with your family. Your sons will always be kings over my people, and I will be with them. When they do wrong I will correct them, but I will always love them. You wanted to build Me a house. But I will build you a house—a kingdom which I will make sure forever.' "

David was very quiet. It was a wonderful message from God. When Nathan went home, David went away where he could be alone and prayed to God.

David thanked God for His continuing love. "Lord God, how great You are. Who am I that You should promise me a house and a kingdom? There is none so great as You, for You alone are God. You have saved us from our enemies. How happy are those who believe in You. Bless my house, O Lord. May it bring glory to You. May my sons, who will be kings of Your people, always be faithful to You."

Although David would have liked to build the temple, he did not question God's judgment. "I will make plans as to how it should be built," he decided, "and I will leave these plans with the son who will rule after me."

David also put aside some of his personal treasure, gold, silver, precious stones. "These will all be needed and more," David thought. "It will be a big project, but one day a beautiful temple will stand in Jerusalem, built for the glory of God."

II Samuel 6, 7; I Chronicles 13, 15, 16, 17; 22:14; 28:11-19; 29:1-5

62. A King Who Showed Kindness

David was a good and just king. He wanted to do what was right in the eyes of God.

One day he was thinking about Jonathan. He was remembering all the good times they had together before Saul became so jealous, and he remembered how Jonathan had saved his life. Then he remembered the promise he had made to Jonathan.

David had kept his promise. He had not taken revenge on Saul's family as other neighboring rulers would have done. Upon taking the throne, most kings killed anyone related to a rival.

David wondered, "Perhaps I have forgotten someone who was related to Saul and Jonathan. The wars have kept me busy. Perhaps there is something more I can do."

King David sent for a servant. "Is there anyone living of Saul's family to whom I could show some kindness?" he asked. "Is there someone who has been forgotten?"

The servant said, "We have a man at the court called Ziba. He was a servant of Saul. I think he can tell you about someone."

David sent for Ziba. "Do you know a relative of Saul to whom I can show a kindness?" asked the king.

"Yes, there is someone," said Ziba. "His name is Mephibosheth. He is a son of Jonathan."

David wondered why he had not heard about this son before. The servant told him a sad story. When word came that Saul and Jonathan had been killed in battle, a servant woman bundled up Mephibosheth and joined others who were escaping. They were all afraid that a change of government might mean that all of Saul's family would be killed.

But in her haste, the woman fell and dropped the little prince. As a result he was crippled. All his life Mephibosheth had never been able to walk unaided. He lived in a town across the Jordan River.

King David sent for Mephibosheth. In spite of the reassurances of Ziba, Mephibosheth was afraid. It was unusual for a king to show kindness to his rival's family. Mephibosheth did not understand the great love David and Jonathan had for each other.

As he was helped into the court room where David sat on his throne, Mephibosheth was trembling. He bowed before the king.

"Are you Mephibosheth?" asked David.

"Yes," said the man, "and I am your servant." He wanted King David to be assured that he was loyal to him.

David spoke kindly. "Do not be afraid. I brought you here so that I could help you for the sake of Jonathan, your father, who was my dear friend.

"You need never fear want and poverty again. I am going to give to you, and to your sons after you, the land that belonged to Saul, your grandfather. I want you to live here at the court and eat at my table."

Mephibosheth was overwhelmed at this kindness. People had always thought of him as a burden. His life had been made hard by pain and handicap.

"How is it that you do me such honor?" he asked the king.

David smiled as he remembered the brave unselfish prince. Jonathan had been willing to take second place because he had believed God wanted David to be king.

"It is because you are a son of Jonathan," said David. "Your father was a kind and brave man. He saved my life by telling me of Saul's plans to kill me. I am happy to be able to help his son."

The crippled man left in great joy. David spoke to Ziba. "I have given Mephibosheth land which belonged to Saul. I want you and your family to serve him. Your family and servants will see that the land is farmed and that Mephibosheth receives the results of the harvests."

Ziba bowed in agreement. "I will do all that the king commands. But where will Mephibosheth live?"

"He will live here at the court with me," said David. "He and his family. He will eat at my table." *II Samuel 9*

63. David Does Wrong

The Philistines were no longer a threat to Israel, but there were still battles to be fought. Other neighbors caused trouble. As Israel won these battles they extended the land over which they ruled.

They became a wealthier nation, and David made sure the army had the best equipment with which to fight.

King David did not always go to battle himself. Often affairs at home kept him at the palace. He had a good general, called Joab, who led the army.

David, like most kings of his time, had many wives. Another king would seal an agreement of friendship by having David marry one of his royal family. This made them relatives. The wives who belonged to the king made up his harem.

One warm spring day King David got up from rest, and walked on the flat rooftop. He thought about Joab and the army. "I wonder how the battle is going?" he asked himself.

Then he noticed someone on another rooftop, a very beautiful woman. The king admired her. He wished she were a part of his harem.

He went inside and asked different ones about the woman who lived in this house. Finally someone knew the family.

"That is Bathsheba. Her husband, Uriah, is a soldier. He is even now with Joab."

David sent for Bathsheba. After they had been together for a while, she returned home. But David continued to think about her.

One day he sent a message to Joab. He asked that Uriah be sent back to the palace to report on the battle.

When Uriah came, he reported to the king, but he did not go home to Bathsheba. "It would not be fair," he said. "Why should I enjoy the comforts of home when my comrades are out camping in the field?"

David allowed Uriah to go back to General Joab. He had a plan. David wanted Bathsheba to be his wife, and he was willing to kill Uriah in order to make it possible.

David gave Uriah a written message for Joab. In the note David told Joab to put Uriah in the front line of fighting. David wanted to make sure Uriah was killed in battle.

Uriah delivered the note to the general. Joab went along with the king's plan, even though he had no idea what the king had against the soldier.

When time came for the next battle, Joab gave the instructions: "We will come very near to the walls of this city. We must come close to the gates."

He assigned Uriah and some other soldiers to the most dangerous position.

As Joab expected, when they drew near the city archers shot at them from the walls. Many of the men in the front lines were killed. Uriah was one.

The battle went against Joab and his men. The general had to send a messenger back to King David with the news that they had been defeated.

"Be sure to tell the king which men were killed," Joab told the messenger. "Be sure you tell him Uriah was one of them."

The messenger hurried back to David's court in Jerusalem. He told the king the sad news, and he made sure David knew Uriah was dead.

"Tell Joab not to be discouraged," said David. "It is too bad you lost the battle and these fine soldiers were killed, but try again. Make a stronger attack on this city and overcome it."

David let Bathsheba know that her husband had been killed. After her time of mourning was over, David sent for her. She moved to the court and became one of David's wives.

Some of the people at the court whispered about this. They suspected that the king had Uriah killed so that he could marry Bathsheba. Most of the people did not think this was a serious wrong. Kings of other lands always took what they wanted, whether or not it belonged to someone else.

But Nathan, the prophet, thought it was very serious.

II Samuel 8, 10, 11
I Chronicles 18-20

64. A Prophet Rebukes a King

"God does not want His people to act like the heathen round about us," Nathan said to himself. "Our king should not be allowed to do anything he pleases. He should be a good example of one who obeys God's law. If the king acts this way, the people will also disobey God."

As he thought about this, God told Nathan that he must rebuke the king for doing wrong. But would David be like these neighboring kings who put a man to death for criticizing him?

Nathan must take that chance.

Nathan loved King David. He needed a way to give David the message so that he would realize that he had sinned, not only against Uriah, but against God, and so that he would repent and come back to God's way.

God gave Nathan the help he needed. Nathan made an appointment to see the king.

When Nathan came to the court he bowed before David. Then the prophet told a story. It went like this:

Once there were two men who lived in the same city. One man was rich. He owned many flocks. But the other man was poor. The prized possession of the poor man was a little pet lamb whom he loved very much.

One day a guest came to the house of the rich man. "We must have a special dinner," said the rich man; "but I don't

want to take from my own flock. This man is poor and helpless. No one will say anything if I take from him. I'll take the lamb he has. It will make a fine dinner for my guest."

The rich man did this. The poor man was robbed of the little he had.

David was filled with anger at this story. How could anyone be so selfish? If this was a true story the man must be punished.

"Who has done this?" the king cried out. "Such a man deserves to die. Tell me who the guilty one is, and I shall see that he is put to death."

Nathan looked at David. "You are the man," he said.

Then David realized that the prophet knew about Bathsheba and Uriah.

Nathan faced the king with courage. "God has a message for you David. God says, 'I made you king over my people. You have great wealth; yet you robbed and killed a man who was poor. You had Uriah killed so that Bathsheba could be your wife. By disobeying my law you have brought trouble upon your family, which will not go away. Trouble always comes from doing wrong.' "

David was not angry at the prophet. He knew what Nathan said was true. "I have sinned against God because I broke His law. Now I confess my guilt in the presence of my people," he said.

David went away where he could talk to God. He confessed his sin, and asked God to forgive him.

He prayed:

Have mercy on me, O God,
  in Your great love,
I know I have sinned,
  and sinned against you.
Make me truly clean from my sin.
You want me to be truthful.
So please make me a clean heart, O God,
  and put a new spirit in me.
I have been unhappy
  knowing that I have disobeyed You.
Give me back Your joy,
  And Your presence with me every day.

God did forgive David. Once more David walked close to God.

Bathsheba stayed at the court as one of David's wives. She had a son whom they called Solomon. God told David, "It is Solomon who will be the next king." *II Samuel 12; Psalm 51*

65. Trouble in David's Family

It wasn't long before Nathan's words began to come true.

King David had many wives and many children. Sometimes these boys and girls quarreled among themselves, especially as they grew older.

Usually those who had the same mother lived together in one house. Each household felt that the other stepbrothers and sisters were rivals.

The young men all wondered who their father would choose to be the next king. There was no law that said it had to be the eldest son.

David wanted his children to like each other. It made him feel bad to hear of bitter quarrels, but he was not a very strict parent. He did not like to punish his children, even when they did serious wrong.

One day King David heard that his son Absalom, and his daughter Tamar had a serious quarrel with their stepbrother Ammon.

Everyone agreed that Ammon had done wrong. David was angry at Ammon, but he only scolded him. He did not punish him.

This made Absalom very angry. "I'll get even with Ammon," he promised himself. "I'll wait my opportunity to kill him."

Absalom pretended to forgive Ammon. He was always friendly to him, but deep inside his heart there was hatred.

Two years later Absalom announced that he would hold a large feast. It was time for Absalom to shear his sheep and feasts were often held then. Absalom invited all his brothers and half brothers to the feast so that all the king's sons would be there.

Before the dinner Absalom said to his servants, "Watch Ammon. When he has had many glasses of wine and is not as alert as he usually is, strike and kill him. Watch for my signal."

It was a good dinner with many different kinds of food. The guests relaxed on comfortable cushions and ate at low tables.

Everyone was having a good time when Absalom gave the signal. A servant crept up in back of Ammon and struck him. At this all the other brothers ran off in fear of their lives.

Someone brought a message to King David, "All the sons of David have been killed by Absalom," said the distraught messenger.

David tore his robe to show mourning and so did the others nearby. But then a more correct report was brought. A brother of David came to the king.

"It is not true," he told David. "All of your sons have not been killed. But Absalom has killed your son, Ammon. I am afraid he has planned this for a long time."

It was the custom for families to stand or fall together. If one member had a quarrel, all the other members of his family must take his side against the other.

Absalom ran away. He was afraid of what King David might do; but he was also afraid of what Ammon's family might do to take revenge.

Absalom found refuge in the home of his grandfather at Geshur. Here he stayed for three years.

David mourned for Ammon who had been killed. David also mourned for Absalom. He loved all his sons and only wished that they would live in peace.

David was an old man now. It had been many years since he had become king. Often he wished that Absalom was back at the court. General Joab realized this. "I will help both Absalom and the king," he decided.

Joab worked out a plan. He found a woman who was willing to help him. "I want you to go to the king dressed as though you were mourning the dead," he told her. "I want you to tell him a story and ask for his help."

The general told the woman exactly what to say. When she was ready, she came to the king as one of his subjects asking help.

She bowed humbly before David.

"How can I help you?" asked David.

"I am a widow," said the woman. "I had two sons, but one son killed the other. Now the rest of the family think the remaining son must also die.

"I loved both my sons; but I do not want my son, who is all I have, to be killed. I want him to live and marry and have children so that our family will live on."

David made a decision. "You are right. I will protect your son."

Now the most difficult part of the woman's act was to come. She had to make the king think about Absalom.

"O King," she said, "you are one who loves and fears God. I know you want to do what is right. But in granting my request, do you not condemn yourself? What about your son, Absalom? Is he not as good as dead if he is banished from the court?"

Then David realized that this was a plan to put in a good word for Absalom. "Tell me," he asked, "are you speaking for General Joab? Did he ask you to come and tell me this so that I would bring my son home?"

"You are indeed wise, King David," said the woman. "Joab did send me to you with this story."

The king sent for Joab. He was not angry. "I am going to grant your request, Joab," he said. "You may go and bring my son, Absalom, back to Jerusalem."

Joab went to Geshur with the good news. Absalom, his wife and children all came back to the court.

But a disappointment waited for them. They were not allowed to go in to see the king.

"Absalom may dwell in his own house and be at peace here," said David, "but I still must punish him for murdering his brother. I must not accept him on the same basis as I do my other sons."

This made Absalom unhappy. Many of the people admired Absalom. He was strong and as good looking as David had been as a young man. Absalom knew this. He was proud of his good looks and especially of his long thick hair.

Absalom was also ambitious. *I must find a way to get my father to recognize and accept me fully,* he thought. *I want to be the next king.*

II Samuel 13, 14

66. David Fights for His Crown

It was two years since Absalom had returned to Jerusalem, but he had not yet talked to his father, the king. Absalom decided that something must be done.

"I will send for Joab," he said. "He will deliver a message from me to my father."

Twice Absalom sent for General Joab, but he would not come. Joab had pleaded for Absalom once. If he spoke for him again Joab was afraid he might make David angry.

Absalom was still the hot-headed man he had shown himself to be in his youth. He told his servants, "Look, Joab's barley field is next to mine. Set it afire. That will bring Joab here."

The servants obeyed. A very angry Joab came to visit Absalom. "I have been your friend," he shouted. "I brought you here to Jerusalem. Now you set my fields afire."

Absalom just laughed. "It was the only way to get you to pay some attention to me. I want you to go to my father and ask him to see me.

"Tell David, 'Absalom says I might as well be in Geshur if I am not allowed to come before the king. If my father believes I should die for my crime, let him kill me himself.' "

Joab was afraid this headstrong, cruel man might do worse things to him, so he agreed.

Joab told King David exactly what Absalom had said.

David thought for a while. "Very well," he said. "Absalom has been punished. Now I will see him and welcome him home."

Absalom came before the king. He bowed before his father. David greeted him warmly and kissed him. He forgave his son.

But Absalom had not forgiven his father. He was determined to be the next king. He planned to take the throne before his father died.

"I must make myself popular with the people," Absalom decided. So he made all the friends he could. Soon he had followers who were ready to take risks in order to help the young prince.

Absalom and his friends would ride around to different cities and talk to people who had complaints for the court. Absalom would always listen with great interest.

"You are right," he would say, "and yet the king has not sent anyone to hear your story. If only I were king. I would make sure that every man received justice."

The young prince deceived many of the people. "He is a good man," they would say. "He is humble too. David is old now. Absalom should be king."

Four years later, the day came for Absalom to act. He told his father. "I must go back to Hebron. When I was in exile I promised God that I would present an offering to Him in Hebron if ever I came back to court."

David gave him permission to go. But Absalom used this occasion to stir up rebellion against his father. He won Ahithophel, a trusted advisor to David, over to his side. More and more people kept joining him.

In a few days a messenger ran to the king. "Your son Absalom has started a rebellion. He has soldiers, and is even now marching against Jerusalem."

The news took David by surprise. He had trusted Absalom. But he acted swiftly.

David knew there was no time to form an army which could be trusted and make a stand here at Jerusalem. Neither did he want the city destroyed. So he decided to leave the city. He led his family and those who were loyal to him out into the hills toward the Jordan River. From here they would make a stand and fight for the crown.

Two priests, Abiathar and Zadok, came with David. They carried the ark of the covenant. David sent them back.

"The ark belongs in Jerusalem," he said. "God will help me. Or it may be that God is punishing me for wrongs I have done and does not want me to be king any longer. Whatever God wants is best."

So the priests returned to Jerusalem with the ark.

Later, David heard that Ahithophel was with Absalom. David asked his friend Hushai to go back to Jerusalem. "Pretend to be on Absalom's side," he said. "You can also try to oppose Ahithophel's advice. Then send me word as to what Absalom plans to do. The priests, Abiathar and Zadok, will work with you."

Hushai returned to the city just as the prince Absalom was being welcomed as the new king by his followers. Hushai pretended loyalty to Absalom.

"As I served David so I will now serve you," he promised. Absalom believed him.

"We must plan our next move," said Absalom. He turned to Ahithophel. "What do you advise?"

"Give me some men," said Ahithophel. "We will go and look for David immediately. He is at his weakest now, because your rebellion surprised him. We will try to kill only the king."

It sounded like a good plan; but Absalom also asked Hushai. "What do you think of this plan?"

"I do not agree," said Hushai. "David is famous as a man of war. We must not move too quickly. It would hurt our cause if we did not win the first battle. Let us wait and make ourselves stronger. Then you yourself will lead us into battle."

Absalom said, "This plan is better."

The other leaders of the rebellion agreed —all except Ahithophel. He could see that this was God's way of defeating Absalom's rebellion.

Then Hushai the spy went and told the two priests all that had occurred. They used other spies to relay the message to David and his followers in the hills. "It is best to camp even further away," they advised.

That night David took his followers across the Jordan River. The next day they made ready to fight Absalom and his forces.

David was too old to fight. He made the plans while Joab and two other generals led the army.

Before the army left for battle David said, "Be gentle with my son, Absalom. I do not want him to be killed."

David's army met the rebels and chased them into the forest. There were swamps and thick trees. Many soldiers died from accidents.

During the fighting a man brought Joab a message. "Absalom has been caught in the branches of a tree," he told the general. "He is hanging there by his long hair."

Joab hurried to the spot. Absalom had been caught in the fork of low-hanging branches as he rode by. The mule on which he had been riding had ran off, leaving him dangling.

Joab remembered how Absalom had returned his kindness by burning his field. Absalom was cruel and deceptive and would bring more trouble to the king and to himself. Joab disregarded the orders of David and killed him. His armor-bearers also struck at Absalom. Then Joab blew his trumpet to signal to all that the fighting was over. The rebel was dead.

Joab sent two messengers to David across the Jordan. Then he and his men took Absalom down from the tree and buried him under a pile of rocks in the forest. That way David wouldn't make a big fuss over burying Absalom in Jerusalem.

Back at the camp King David waited to hear news of the battle. A watchman sighted two messengers coming.

Each one bowed before the king. One said, "The battle has been won." But he did not want to tell the king that Absalom was dead.

The second messenger said, "God has delivered into our hands all of David's enemies."

"But what about Absalom? Is my son well?" David asked fearfully.

Then the messenger had to give the bad news. "Absalom is dead."

David tore his robe. He wept for his son.

"Absalom, Absalom! My son, my son!" David cried out. "Oh that I could have given my life for you! O Absalom, my son!"

David knew Absalom was not a good man, but he still loved him because Absalom was his son. Yet he grieved so much, he almost forgot that Absalom had tried to take the kingdom away from him. Joab finally had to remind David that he was king and that God had given his kingdom back to him.

So David came back to Jerusalem, to be king once more. There was a lot of work to be done to regain the people's confidence and undo the results of the rebellion.

II Samuel 14:28-33; 15-19

67. Long Live King Solomon!

David the king was old and ill. Many people were wondering who would be the next king. They waited for word from David.

Some people said, "I have heard that David wants his young son Solomon to be king." Other people said, "But Adonijah is an older son. Surely David will make him king."

Adonijah wanted to be king. He had important friends at court. General Joab and the priest Abiathar thought he should be king.

Adonijah decided to take matters into his own hands. He gathered all those who supported him. "We will have a large sacrifice and a feast," he said. "I will invite my brothers. Then you can declare me king."

Adonijah made his plans. He invited

many important people at the court. But he did not invite his young brother Solomon, or Nathan the prophet. Nathan believed God wanted Solomon to be the next king.

The feast was held. All the king's sons except Solomon were there. There was much food and everyone was happy. "Long live King Adonijah," the guests shouted.

Adonijah looked around with pleasure. In a short time he would be king of Israel.

But Nathan the prophet heard about the feast. He ran to Bathsheba, Solomon's mother.

"Have you heard how Adonijah is laying claim to the throne?" he asked. "Even now his followers are having a great feast and acknowledging him as their king. King David knows nothing of this. You must go and tell him. Your life and the life of your son will be in danger if Adonijah becomes king."

Bathsheba hurried to David. Nathan promised, "I will come to the king after you and speak on Solomon's behalf."

Servants told David, "Bathsheba wants to see you."

"Let her come in," said David.

Bathsheba came into the room where the king was resting. She bowed before him.

King David could see that she was upset. "What is it?" he asked. "What can I do for you?"

"My lord, you promised me that my son Solomon would reign after you; but Adonijah has claimed a right to the throne. He has made a great feast, and others have said he is to be king. All the people of our land are waiting for you to say who will be the next king. Have you forgotten the promise you made to me?"

Before David had a chance to answer, Nathan the prophet came hurrying in. He too bowed before the king.

"My lord, have you declared that Adonijah shall be the next ruler? He acts as though you had. Even now he is host at a great feast, and the guests are crying, 'Long live King Adonijah.' "

David realized that he must make his decision known. He told Bathsheba. "As I promised you before, Solomon your son shall be the next king. He shall sit upon my throne, and God will bless him."

David told Nathan the prophet to go with the priest Zadok and another leader called Benaiah, and take Solomon to the spring of Gihon. This was just outside the city walls.

"Take trusted servants with you," said the king. "Have Solomon ride on my own mule. Anoint him king, and then bring him back into Jerusalem and have him sit on my throne."

Solomon was brought to the spring of Gihon. He rode on David's mule. Crowds gathered and shouted their approval. Zadok took the horn of sacred oil and anointed Solomon king. Other priests blew on their trumpets.

"Long live King Solomon!" the crowds shouted.

They continued to shout and sing and play on musical instruments as they followed Solomon back into the city. People ran from their houses. "What has happened?" they asked.

"David has declared Solomon to be the next king," the others told them. "He has just been anointed by Zadok."

Then they joined the procession honoring the new king. When they came to the palace, Nathan and Zadok took Solomon to the throne room.

The guests at Adonijah's feast heard the shouting and rejoicing. General Joab jumped to his feet. "What does this mean?" he cried.

A friend of Adonijah burst into the room. "I have bad news," he said. "David has declared Solomon to be the next king. He has been anointed, and even now he sits on the throne."

The guests trembled with fear. They did not want to be found here with Adonijah now that they knew he would not be the next king. New kings often put to death anyone they thought would not be loyal to them. They ran from the room.

Adonijah saw all his supporters run away. "Now my brother Solomon will kill me," he cried.

He ran all the way to the altar outside the tent where the ark was kept. He took hold of the horns that jutted out on each side of the altar and would not move.

When others spoke to him, Adonijah said, "I will not leave this altar until King Solomon promises to spare my life."

Word was brought to Solomon. The young king did not want to be cruel and revengeful. "Tell my brother that if he is loyal to me no harm will come to him," Solomon promised.

So Adonijah left the altar and bowed before the new king.

I Kings 1
I Chronicles 23:1

68. A Young King's Desire

David knew that he did not have long to live. He called his son, Solomon, to him. He talked to him about what it meant to be king over God's people.

David said. "God has promised me that if my sons obey Him, there will always be one of my family on the throne. Therefore, Solomon, keep the laws of God which our people received through Moses.

"Remember to worship God and keep all His feast days. Remember to act towards others in the way God wants. All of this you will find in His law.

"Serve God with all your heart and mind, Solomon. If you truly seek God you will find Him. God will bring blessing on you if you always seek to do His will."

David told Solomon about the temple he had wanted to build for God. "But because I was a man of war, God left this task to you, my son," said David. "I have left plans for you to follow. Now it is up to you to build God's house."

David also spoke to the officials of the court and the leaders of the people throughout the land. He reminded them how he had wanted to build the temple but God had forbidden it.

"Now Solomon will build this place of worship," he said, "and I want you to help him. Solomon is young and will need your help."

David went on to tell them, "I have collected valuable material for this temple. Some of my own personal wealth has been given for this project. Now as many of you as are willing and able, give to this task."

Many of the leaders gave freely for this work. It made David happy to realize that others thought it was important to have a temple.

After the large offering was collected, David prayed his thankfulness to God. He said: "Yours, O Lord, is the greatness and the power and the glory and the victory. All that is in the universe is Yours. Yours is the kingdom, O Lord, and all the riches of the world are really Yours. Who are we, to be able to give willingly to you? For all things come from You, and we give back to You only a part of what You have given to us. O Lord, keep us always wanting to give to You and to worship You."

Soon after this David died. Solomon sat on the throne and reigned in the place of his father.

Solomon was still a young man. Now that his father was gone, he wondered if he would be able to do as good a job of leading the people as his father had done.

Solomon wanted to be a godly king like David. He went to Gibeon to sacrifice and worship God at the great altar which had been set up in this town. He wanted to ask for God's help and guidance.

While he was there, God spoke to Solomon in a dream. God asked him, "What shall I give to you? Name what you most desire."

Solomon had the answer ready. "O God," he said, "You showed continuing love for David my father, because he walked in Your ways. You have shown great honor to me by making me king over Your great people.

"But I am a young man, and I do not have the wisdom I need for this important job. Therefore give me, I pray, the help I need.

"Give me an understanding mind, O God. Help me to be able to determine what is right and wrong as I seek to judge between those who bring their cases to me. Who can govern Your people well, O Lord, without Your help?"

Then God spoke to Solomon. "You have asked for that which is best. I will give you the help you need. I will give you the ability to understand what is right. I will give you a mind so keen and wise that all men will marvel at your words. You will be known throughout the lands for your wisdom.

"It is good that you have asked for this rather than for wealth and power. But riches and honor will also be yours. My blessing will always be with you if you keep My commandments and walk in My ways."

Then Solomon woke up. He thought about his dream. He was sure now that God would help him and give him the wisdom he needed.

As soon as he got back to Jerusalem, Solomon worshiped before the tent which housed the ark of the covenant. He called on his officials to take part with him. He thanked God for the help He had promised.

Solomon soon became known as a very wise man who understood better than others what was true and what was false. He understood people and why they acted in certain ways. In time, even people in other countries came to know about Solomon and his wisdom. His many proverbs and songs were written down and became well known.

I Kings 2:1-12; 3, 4
I Chronicles 22, 28, 29
II Chronicles 1; 9:22, 23

69. A House for God

Solomon set to work at the task of building the Temple. He sent word about his plans to Hiram, king of Tyre, who had been a friend of his father.

Solomon made an agreement with Hiram to buy cedar wood from Lebanon. The logs were made into rafts and sent by sea. Solomon also hired workers from Hiram who were skilled at cutting timber. Hiram loaned Solomon a famous builder to oversee the work.

Thousands of workers were needed to build this place of worship. The people were not given a choice. King Solomon made it a law that so many men from throughout the country should give some of their time to the work.

These laborers had to spend one month out of every three on work for the king.

First the laborers cut huge stones from the mountains. They brought them, ready to put in place, to the hill in Jerusalem on which the Temple would stand. It was hard work, because there was no kind of modern machinery for them to use.

The plan for the Temple was similar to the Tabernacle, but it was twice as long and twice as wide, and three times as high. Around three sides of the Temple Solomon added rooms three stories high to be used by the priests. The top of the third story was half as high as the Temple. Stairways inside and out led up to the higher floors.

The Temple itself was long and narrow, like a hall. Inside it was divided into two sections: the Holy Place and the Most Holy Place.

The Most Holy Place was the room at the back of the building in which the Ark of the Covenant was kept. The people thought of the cover of the Ark of the Covenant as the throne of God, their real King.

On either side of the ark stood the guarding cherubim. These winged figures were made of wood, decorated with gold. The wings were so wide that they touched each other as they met over the ark.

The heavy curtains at the front of the Most Holy Place were made of blue, purple and crimson cloth on which cherubim figures had been embroidered.

The Holy Place was the larger part of the hall. The walls were lined with cedar. Narrow windows high up on the walls let in soft light.

Here stood the gold seven-branched lampstands. Here was the Table of Shewbread and the Altar of Incense which were made of cedar and decorated with gold carvings of fruit and flowers.

It took seven years to complete, but at last the Temple was ready for its first worship service. This would be a service of dedication.

People came from all over the land. They marveled as they gathered in the large walled court. All eyes were on the white limestone building which stood on a high platform.

They exclaimed over the doors of the Temple which were made of cypress and covered with gold. On the doors were carvings of cherubim, fruits and flowers. On either side of the door stood a richly decorated brass pillar.

A procession of priests brought the Ark of the Covenant out of the Tabernacle. As they carried it to its new home in the Temple, other priests sang or played musical instruments. They entered the court and walked up the ten wide steps that led to the Temple entrance.

There were two landings on the steps which made room for the musicians and singers to stand there. The priests who carried the ark went inside the Temple. The ark was put to rest in its special room.

King David had wanted music to be a large part of worship to God. He had written some psalms himself and collected others. Now the choir of priests sang from one of them: "The Lord is good. His love continues forever." Other priests blew on their trumpets or clashed their cymbals.

In front of the Temple was the large Altar of Burnt Offerings. Here the priests would offer sacrifices brought by the people. Now King Solomon stood before this altar and spoke to all those who had gathered for this special occasion.

The king reminded them that David had wanted to build the Temple, but that God had chosen him instead of his father to do this work.

"Now," said King Solomon, "we have built the Temple and the Ark of the Covenant is within."

Then King Solomon knelt and spread out his hands as he prayed to God.

"Lord God," he prayed, "there is no one like You in heaven or earth. We realize that You are in all the universe and will not be limited to one house. But we have built this Temple to show our belief that You are with us and that we are Your people.

"Lord, when Your people pray in this court, hear their prayers. Forgive their sins. When they come to You in trouble, help them."

Then the king offered a sacrifice of many animals to God. For two weeks the people celebrated. Then those who lived in other parts of the land went home.

God spoke to Solomon: "I have consecrated the Temple you built for me, and I will meet with the people there.

"As for you Solomon, if you will walk in My ways as your father did, your family will always rule over My people.

"But if you, or your sons, depart from My laws and serve other gods, then trouble will come to your family and to the people you lead. If you and your people forsake Me, then this Temple will become a heap of ruins."

I Kings 5-9
II Chronicles 2-7

70. A King Breaks His Promise

For twenty-five years the people of the land were forced to help with Solomon's building projects. The Temple was not the only building Solomon constructed. There was a large costly palace, many storehouses for royal treasures, houses for the king's wives, stables for the hundreds of horses and chariots he had bought from Egypt.

Fortifications were also needed to protect all this wealth from enemies.

Israel now traded with other nations. Solomon built a fleet of ships which brought foreign wonders like peacocks, apes, ivory and sandalwood to the court. Caravans from all parts of the world brought new ideas as well as new products to the land.

It was a time of peace and great prosperity. A few of the officials and leaders became wealthy, but most of the people had no share in the riches that came to the nation. Yet those who had little were still told to contribute by taxes to the wealth of the king and his officials.

Solomon had many more wives than King David. Often he gave them expensive gifts. Many of these wives came from foreign lands and worshiped foreign gods. Solomon had shrines built where they could worship.

King Solomon, and the luxury in which he lived, became known throughout many lands. Many leaders from other countries came to visit him and everyone brought expensive gifts. One day a famous queen, the Queen of Sheba, came to meet him.

Solomon gave a large feast for this Arabian queen. She had seen many courts, but she was amazed at the golden dishes, the large number of beautifully clothed servants, and the wonderful food Solomon provided.

The queen of Sheba had heard that King Solomon was very wise. She asked him many questions to see if he really did know many things. She was delighted at all the things Solomon told her.

She asked him several riddles, and she was impressed with the way Solomon solved each one.

The queen could think of no other way to test the king. There was no doubt about it. King Solomon was a remarkable man and his kingdom was all she had heard it to be.

She confessed to Solomon, "I didn't really believe all the wonderful things I heard about you and your court. But now I have seen it with my own eyes. Your court is more wonderful and your wisdom is greater than I was told."

Then the queen gave Solomon expensive gifts of gold, jewels and rare spices.

As the years went by Solomon continued to increase his wealth. He wanted more and more. He had a throne of ivory decorated with gold. Statues of lions lined the steps leading up to the throne, and a lion stood on each side of the chair. No other king had such a throne.

God had given much to Solomon. Yet as the years went by Solomon forgot to be thankful to God. He listened to his wives talk about their pagan worship. He began to take part in this worship himself.

Solomon loved them and wanted to

please them. Gradually he had less love for God.

Solomon had promised to obey God and to worship only Him. One day God spoke to Solomon about the promise he had broken.

"Because you have disobeyed, part of your kingdom will be taken from you," God told him.

Trouble and discontent were already in the land. There had always been jealousy between the north and south of Israel. Solomon had used most of his wealth to make his own court and the capital city of Jerusalem great places.

The further north one lived, the less one benefited from the prosperity of the day. Yet the people of the north had contributed their share of taxes and labor. They began to complain.

King Solomon had given to a man named Jeroboam the job of overseeing work being done in Jerusalem. Jeroboam was from Ephraim, one of the northern tribes. The workers were also from the north, and Jeroboam listened to their complaints. He agreed with them.

"We should all rebel," Jeroboam said. He began to stir up the anger many felt toward the king.

King Solomon heard about this and tried to kill Jeroboam, but Jeroboam escaped into Egypt. Before he left the country, Ahijah, a prophet of God, spoke to him.

They were alone in the open countryside. Ahijah took a piece of cloth and tore it into twelve pieces to represent the twelve tribes of Israel. Ten pieces he gave to Jeroboam.

"God is going to punish Solomon because he has worshiped other gods," said the prophet. "Some of the kingdom will be taken from him. Now take these ten pieces. These are the tribes of the north. One day you will be king over them.

"God says: 'If, when you are king over My people, you will walk in My ways and keep My laws, I will bless you and make your kingdom great. I will be with you as I was with King David."

Jeroboam lived in exile in Egypt for many years, but he remembered the words of the prophet.

I Kings 9-11
II Chronicles 8, 9

PART FOUR

KINGS AND PROPHETS

Under David and Solomon, Israel grew into a strong nation. After the Philistines were defeated and driven back to the coast, peace brought time to spend on growing better crops and raising better animals. Then Israel began to trade with other nations. Solomon built a fleet of ships so that there could be trade with lands across the sea.

Other nations paid more attention to Israel. A country often grows like a person, and now Israel was a "grown-up" country.

As a result of all this, some individuals became wealthy; but for the most part the common people did not benefit. At the same time they were made to pay high taxes, and were also forced to give time to the king's work.

The people remembered the old days they had heard about when the country was less wealthy but there was more freedom. They complained about the taxes and the forced labor.

Now the nation was at a turning point. Would the needs of all the people be recognized? Or would the king and his officials continue to take all the wealth and merely use the people as servants and take advantage of them?

Samuel's warning about kings had come true. Now the people of the north were talking about becoming a separate nation.

In the years to come there would be different kings over God's people. Some would love and obey God, but others would serve idols. In all these years God tried to bring the people back to Him. He warned them that trouble would come unless they repented.

God sent his message to the people through prophets. These fearless men spoke for God to king and people. They warned them when they did wrong, and guided them when they wanted to know what was right.

71. "We Don't Belong With David"

When Jeroboam heard that Solomon had died he came back to Israel. Solomon's son, Rehoboam, was to be made king. He would be crowned and anointed at Shechem in the north. The leaders from all the different tribes gathered in this ancient city.

There was discontent in the air. Many people wondered what would happen next. The people of Judah had pledged their loyalty to Rehoboam; but the tribes of the north had not.

Some leaders of the north talked openly of rebellion. Others said they wanted to give the new king a chance to correct the wrongs of Solomon.

Everyone took note that Jeroboam, who had spoken out against Solomon, was back.

The leaders of the north brought a special petition to Rehoboam. They said, "Your father Solomon forced us to contribute money and work on his famous buildings. We had to pay more than we could afford. We had to give our time to the king's work when it was needed on our own farms and in our own towns.

"We want to know: Are you going to continue in these ways? Are you going to build and expand and expect more and more from us? Or are you going to reduce the money we need to pay? Are you going to force your own subjects to work, or are you going to get the work done by slaves alone?

"If you will make things easier for us, we promise to serve you and be loyal to you, our king."

Rehoboam had heard that some of these leaders were not satisfied. He wanted their loyalty, but he was not sure about making it easier for the people. He did not want to have less wealth than his father. He was used to having everything he wanted.

"I must think this over," he told them. "Come back in three days, and I will give you my answer."

The leaders of the north left the king's presence. Then Rehoboam turned to his officials and advisors for help.

First he called in men who had been friends of his father. They would know what to do, because they had served in government many years.

"How shall I answer these people of the north?" he asked.

The men said, "Your father Solomon accomplished many wonderful things, but the burden on the people has been great. It would be wise for you now to relieve them of some of this burden. Stop building and expanding for a while.

"Promise the people that they will share in the good things. Then they will love you and serve you all your days, and you will keep our people united."

Rehoboam thought about what they said. He was not so sure. After all, he was used to luxury. Why should he share with anyone? If he were king, he deserved to always have the best.

Rehoboam had appointed some new officials, young men like himself. He called for them.

"What shall I say to these northerners who want me to ask less in taxes and service than my father did?" he asked.

"You are the king," they answered. "You can do anything you want. You must not let the people think they can tell you what to do. You should tell them: 'I will make you work harder than my father did. He put a heavy burden on you, but I will make it even heavier. I will show you that you must obey the king.' "

Rehoboam liked this advice much better. When the leaders of the north came back and stood before the king, Rehoboam spoke in a proud, haughty manner.

"It is true my father Solomon made your burdens heavy, but I will add to them. I am going to be harder on you than my father was."

The northern leaders were stronger than Rehoboam realized. They were not to be put down by a threat of punishment. They shouted, "To our homes, men of Israel. We have no part with David's son. We no longer want to be one nation with Judah. We will have a nation of our own."

So the northerners united. They met together to decide who should be king over them. All the leaders wanted Jeroboam to be king. They sent for him and asked him to reign over them.

Jeroboam accepted and they shouted, "Long live King Jeroboam."

Rehoboam had hurried back to his palace in Jerusalem. He called for soldiers. "Come, we must gather up an army to bring these rebels back into one kingdom under my rule," he said.

Many soldiers gathered, but they were stopped by a prophet of God. The prophet said, "God forbids you to fight against your brothers. Return home. God commands it."

The people were afraid of great punishment from God and they did not fight to retain the rebel tribes. God's people were never reunited. After this the northern tribes were called Israel. The south became known as Judah. They each had their own kings.

I Kings 12:1-24
II Chronicles 10, 11

72. A Bad Beginning

Jeroboam was now king over the largest portion of God's people. The words of God's prophet, Ahijah, had come true. Still Jeroboam did not have much faith in God.

Jeroboam wondered, "How long will our northern tribes want to be separate from Judah? Perhaps they will think about the beautiful temple there. Perhaps they will remember the great deeds of David. Then what will happen to me?"

The new king thought a lot about this. He must do something to make his kingdom sure. "We will have our own worship centers up here in the north," he told himself. "If the people return to Jerusalem to worship on special feast days they will regret their independence. They will want to become one nation again. They will swear loyalty to Rehoboam and kill me."

So Jeroboam told his officials, "We will build two shrines. One will be at Dan, the other at Bethel. This will make it easy for the people, because one will be at one end of our kingdom and the other at the opposite end."

The king and his officials talked together about what these shrines would be like. Some people still wanted an image to represent God, even though Moses had long before told them this was not what God wanted.

Jeroboam ordered craftsmen to make two images of bulls. They were made of wood and covered with gold. He put the bulls in place—one at each shrine.

The people gathered before the shines. The king spoke to them: "It is too far for you to go to Jerusalem to worship God. I have built these shrines. Come here to worship."

King Jeroboam needed priests to carry on the work at these shrines and to lead the people in worship. Some priests liked the king's shrines, but others refused to take part in the services at them. They went to Judah to live, and the people who wanted to worship at the Temple went with them. So many priests left that Jeroboam had to make priests from tribes other than that of Levi in order to have enough.

Some of the prophets agreed with the king, but many did not. Those who disagreed pointed out that the neighboring people used images in their worship.

"These bulls will influence the people to worship Baal, the Canaanite god," they said.

One prophet from Judah journeyed far in order to warn the king. He came upon Jeroboam as he was offering in-

cense at the Bethel shrine.

"God is going to punish you, Jeroboam," he warned. "You and your people will have trouble, because you have forsaken the true worship of God." But Jeroboam would not listen. The prophet was right, though. The bulls did have a bad influence on the people. It encouraged them to worship as their neighbors did. It made them forget that God was righteous and just and that He wanted His people to be righteous. By breaking the law about images, they were encouraged to break other laws of God.

In the history of God's people Jeroboam became known as one who led his people astray. Often later prophets would say, "It was Jeroboam who made the people of Israel sin."

Back in Judah King Rehoboam married and had children. At first he led the people of Judah in good ways. He built up the fortifications of the country against enemy attack. But when his kingdom was safe and secure he began to forsake the true worship of God.

Besides going to the Temple the people worshiped on the hilltops. Although no bull images were set up at these shrines they began to include pagan practices in their worship. Once again, as in the time of the judges, they were influenced by their pagan neighbors.

For a long while Egypt had not been a powerful country, but now there was a change of government and Egypt was growing strong again. Egyptians attacked the small country of Judah.

Soldiers raided the great city of Jerusalem and carried away much of the treasure that King Solomon had gathered. Solomon had made shields of gold but these were taken. Rehoboam had shields of bronze made to put in their place. The great days of prosperity were over.

One of the prophets from God came with a message to the king. "It is because you have forsaken the true worship of God," said the prophet. God says: 'You have forsaken me, and I brought this foreign ruler to punish you.' "

King Rehoboam and all the people realized that they had done wrong. They asked God to forgive them.

The prophet then told the king: "God sees that you humble yourself and admit your sin. Your nation has suffered loss, but it will not be destroyed."

I Kings 12:25-33; 13, 14; 15:24, 30, 34 etc.
II Chronicles 11, 12

73. Asa Destroys Idols

The people of Judah did not remain faithful to the Lord God. At the altars erected on the hilltops pagan practices were still part of the worship. Rehoboam's son, Abijah, allowed idols representing pagan gods to be brought into the land.

Abijah had a short reign filled with war and strife. After his death his son, Asa, took the throne of David.

Asa was different. He loved God and wanted the people to come back to the true worship of God.

"I want all idols destroyed," Asa commanded his soldiers. "Go to the hilltop shrines and throw down any pagan images."

One of his leaders said, "But King, even your own mother has an image of the goddess Asherah. Will you take that away?"

"Yes, it must be destroyed," the king commanded.

King Asa was sad that his mother believed in this pagan idol. He loved her, but he was afraid she would influence others to do wrong. To be queen mother at the court was an important office.

From ancient times the people of Israel had said children should honor mother and father; but Asa knew that it was even more important to honor God.

The king called for his mother. He told her: "Because you have worshiped this image and been unfaithful to God, you can no longer be queen mother. I want all those in authority at my court to be worshipers of God alone."

King Asa talked to the leaders and all the people. "Seek the Lord your God," he said. "Keep His laws and commandments."

The prophets of God were glad for this king. He would bring the people back to the right way and keep them from going further away from God as Israel was doing.

The prophet Azariah spoke to the king: "The Lord is with you while you are with Him. If you seek Him, you will find Him. Continue to trust God. The Lord will reward you for your good work."

Asa continued to encourage the people to obey God's laws. He destroyed pagan worship wherever he found it.

The people listened to the king and again turned their loyalty and love toward the God of their ancestors. There was a feast of dedication to God.

The people gathered at the Temple in Jerusalem. They promised: "We will seek the Lord, the God of our fathers, with all our heart and with all our soul."

The people shouted with joy when the promise was made. The priests blew on horns and trumpets.

In the north, though, the people did not give up their images. Instead they wandered further and further from God's way. There was trouble on every hand, including battles with Judah.

Jeroboam's family did not continue to be the royal family of Israel. His son, Nadab, was murdered by Baasha. The prophets of Israel had thought Baasha would be a better king, but they were disappointed. Baasha was not true to the worship of God.

During the reign of Baasha there was continual war with Asa of Judah. King Baasha started to build a fort within Judah on the main road to Jerusalem. This would cut off Judah from trading with other nations.

King Asa realized that this was a dangerous situation. His own army, which was much smaller than Israel's, had recently pushed back an invading army of Ethiopians. They were not ready for another battle.

"Let us ask Syria for help," King Asa suggested to his leaders. "If we give them treasures they might break their friendship with Israel and fight Baasha for us."

The king carried out his plan. The Syrians accepted the gifts, and agreed to help Judah. The Syrian army attacked the northern borders of Israel. Baasha's soldiers had to withdraw from Judah.

The Syrians won the battle and took territory from Israel. King Asa used the materials Baasha had left behind to build forts for Judah's defense.

The leaders congratulated themselves; but the prophets of God were not pleased. They could see danger in trusting in pagan nations.

The prophet Hanani reproved the king. "Trust God," he said, "not the pagan nation of Syria. You have helped Syria, who is not your real friend, to grow in power."

King Asa was angry and had the prophet put in prison. But the prophet was right. The time came when Syria was a strong enemy both to Israel and to Judah.

I Kings 15; II Chronicles 13, 14, 15

74. A Wicked Queen and a Good King

After King Baasha died, his son Elah ruled Israel for a short time. Then Elah was murdered by Zimri, a commander in his army. But instead of acknowledging Zimri king, the army declared its commander-in-chief, Omri, king.

Zimri hid in a palace. When he saw that Omri's forces had surrounded him, he set the palace on fire and died in the flames.

King Omri had ambitious plans for Israel. He made a new capital in Samaria. He made friends with the powerful trading cities of Tyre and Sidon. These cities were ports in Phoenicia, a land by the sea to the north of Israel.

King Omri made Israel a trading nation, and goods from many ports came into the land. Israel became wealthy and powerful, and yet a mistake was made at this time which brought much trouble in the future.

In order to seal his alliance with the Phoenician cities, Omri agreed for his son Ahab to marry Jezebel, a princess of Tyre.

When Jezebel came to Israel she wanted a shrine built for the Baal her people worshiped. Jezebel's father had been a priest, and she was very religious. She vowed to be faithful to her pagan worship.

Omri did not care about this. He thought the military and economic affairs of the country were most important. So a shrine to Baal was built in Samaria.

But this was not enough for Jezebel. She wanted all the people in Israel to worship her Baal. She asked that priests of Baal be allowed to come from her homeland. They were allowed to come, and were given a place at the court in Samaria.

After Omri's death, Ahab and Jezebel became king and queen of Israel. Queen Jezebel used her new power to advance her religion. The people soon discovered that this proud, beautiful woman could be very cruel. Whenever the prophets of God spoke out against her religion she had them put to death. She did not hesitate to destroy anyone who got in her way.

Ahab was a weak person. He was influenced by Jezebel in many ways. He joined her in her worship of Baal. He took her advice on matters of state.

Many of the people wanted to please the queen. They knew they could do this by worshiping her Baal. Jezebel influenced many to be untrue to God.

The people could see that their king and queen did not think it was important to worship only the one true God. They began to worship as their Canaanite neighbors did, and erected Baals of Canaan.

The people paid less and less attention to the God of their fathers. They forgot the way God had delivered them in the past. They forgot His good laws.

In Judah, Asa's son, Jehoshaphat ruled. Like his father, Jehoshaphat believed in the God of Israel and wanted the people to worship Him alone. He tried to live in God's way and would have nothing to do with foreign idols.

Jehoshaphat built up the fortifications of Judah and worked hard to make them safe. He made the nation so strong that other kings wanted to be sure to be friends and sent gifts.

King Ahab made offers of friendship with Jehoshaphat which were accepted. It was a time of peace and prosperity for both nations.

Jehoshaphat realized that in order to worship properly the people of the land needed instruction. They needed to understand why their religion was different from their neighbors. They needed to know that God had led their fathers through the wilderness and given them this land. It was because of this that they belonged to God.

King Jehoshaphat sent for the priests. "We must instruct the people in their faith," he said. "It is not enough to talk to them when they come to Jerusalem for Temple worship. We must send priests and other teachers throughout the land to instruct the people."

The priests agreed. Soon a band of priests and teachers made their way throughout Judah. They taught the people the laws of God. The people responded by being true to God.

Jehoshaphat was loved by his people because he himself was true to God and he cared about the faith of his people.

I Kings 16; II Chronicles 17; 18:1; 19; 21:31-33

75. A Prophet Who Did Wonders

In Israel Jezebel had put many of the prophets of the Lord to death. But not all of them were gone.

The prophet Elijah realized how seriously the people were disobeying God. The altars dedicated to God were in disuse. Sometimes Elijah thought he was the only one left who was willing to stand up for God and His truth.

Elijah knew it was dangerous to be a prophet, but he had to warn the people of what was to come if they did not repent.

Elijah had come from across the Jordan River where he had lived on the edge of the desert. Everyone noticed him because he was strong and rough-looking. His robe was made of a hairy cloth and he wore a leather girdle.

One day God spoke to Elijah. He gave Elijah a special message to the king. Elijah went to the court and faced King Ahab courageously.

"God says He is going to withhold the rain from the land because you worship idols," said the prophet.

Those who worshiped the Baals of different lands thought their pagan god sent rain. The prophet was about to prove that this was not so. The Lord God, the One True God, sent sun and rain. It was He who would bring His people good harvests.

"There will be no dew or rain except I say so," the prophet told the king.

Because of this announcement, Elijah's life was in danger. Jezebel hated him above all the prophets who were true to God. Often he had spoken out against her, but she had not been able to catch him and put him to death.

God told Elijah, "Hide yourself in the caves."

The prophet found a good spot close by a brook. As the prophet had warned, no rain fell. The crops began to wither and die. Food supplies were low as famine came and spread across the land. But while he stayed in this hiding place, Elijah was fed twice a day. Ravens flew over him and dropped food.

After some time, though, the brook outside Elijah's cave dried up. "What shall I do now?" Elijah wondered.

God told him, "Go to Zarephath. There you will find a widow who will feed you."

Elijah left his cave and fled out of the country to Zarephath. This city lay between Tyre and Sidon. Near the gate of the city he found a woman gathering firewood.

Elijah called to her, "Will you give me a drink of water?"

She nodded and went to get it. As she

turned, Elijah asked, "May I have some bread as well?"

The woman sighed. "We have very little in the house," she said. "There is a little meal in a jar and a little oil with which to bake it. I was just gathering this firewood to prepare the last meal I can make for my son and I. We will surely die if this famine lasts."

The prophet said, "Do not be afraid. I can help you, but first take a little of the meal and make a small cake for me."

The woman was willing to trust Elijah. She invited him to her house. She made him a small cake. Now there was just a small amount of meal and oil left.

Elijah looked at the jar of meal and the cruise of oil. "God says that he will cause the meal and oil to stay in their containers no matter how much you use. It is by God's power. This will happen until it rains, and the famine is over."

And that is how it happened. The woman used the meal and oil every day, but always there was the same amount left over after each meal. Elijah the prophet stayed with the woman and her son.

One day the woman's son became very ill. "He is not breathing," cried the mother.

"Give him to me," Elijah said. He took the boy to the upper room where he slept and laid him on his own bed.

"Help me to make this boy well again," he prayed. "Bring life back to him, O Lord."

Then the prophet breathed into the boy's mouth, and the boy stirred. Color came back to his cheeks.

"Can you get up?" asked Elijah. "Can you come down and show your mother that you are all right?"

"I think so," the boy said.

Elijah helped him down the stairs. His mother shouted for joy when she saw him.

"See, your son lives," said Elijah.

The woman said, "Now I know for sure that you are a man of God, because God has given you the power to work wonders."

I Kings 17; 19:10
II Kings 1:8

76. Contest at Mt. Carmel

Obadiah was an important official to King Ahab. But Obadiah loved God and did not want to take part in pagan worship. He was loyal to the worship of God and to the priests of the Lord.

When Jezebel had many of the Lord's priests killed, Obadiah had led one hundred priests to safety. They were now hid in a large cave in the hills. Every day Obadiah made sure they had bread and water.

One day King Ahab said to Obadiah, "The lack of rain has dried up all the pastures near the palace. We need to travel throughout the land to all the brooks and streams and see if there is any green grass. "Then we can take our animals there and keep them from dying. This famine will kill us all if it continues. Oh, how I hate this Elijah who keeps rain from us."

Obadiah and King Ahab went in different directions to look. On the road Obadiah met Elijah.

Obadiah fell down before the prophet of God. "Is it really you, Elijah?" he asked.

"Yes," said the prophet. "Now go tell Ahab that I am here and wish to speak to him."

But Obadiah was afraid. "King Ahab has been searching everywhere for you. He has looked throughout Israel and neighboring kingdoms as well. Now if I go to the king and tell him, 'I have found Elijah,' and I bring the king here and find you have gone, then the king will kill me."

"I promise before God that I will stay here and wait," said Elijah.

"Very well," said Obadiah, "but do not disappoint me. As you know I too love God and want to see our people be true to God."

Obadiah hurried back over the road and caught up with the king. He told the king the surprising news. Ahab hurried down the path where Obadiah told him Elijah would be waiting.

Yes, there he was up ahead. Ahab hurried faster. He would make Elijah bring rain.

"You troubler of Israel!" the king greeted him angrily.

But Elijah had an answer, "You are the one who has disobeyed God's commandments and worshiped Baal. By this you bring God's judgment on the land."

Elijah had a plan which he hoped would convince the people that it was the Lord who had the power, and that it was He who brought the rain and the sun.

"I want you to gather all the leaders of the people together on Mt. Carmel," Elijah told the king. "And I want all the prophets who are supported by Jezebel at the court to be there as well."

Ahab went back to the court and announced the coming meeting at Mt. Carmel. He told the prophets of Baal to be there. They all gathered together on the day Elijah said. They all hoped this would mean rain.

Elijah stood before the people and spoke to them. "Why can't you make up your mind?" he asked. "Either Baal or the Lord is God. You can't worship both."

But the people did not answer. For a while they thought one belief was true; then they would change and think the opposite.

"I am the only prophet of God here," said Elijah, "and there are four hundred and fifty prophets of Baal. Nevertheless we shall have a contest. Bring us two bulls. We will make the sacrifices ready, but we will not put fire on the altars."

The prophets of Baal agreed. They made their sacrifice ready. Then Elijah called to them, "Now ask Baal to send fire from heaven."

The prophets of Baal called aloud for fire, but no fire came. They went on praying for hours. "O Baal, hear us," they called. "Baal, answer us." But nothing happened. They danced and shouted around their altar. Noon came, and went. Still no answer. Elijah taunted them—maybe Baal had gone for a walk, or was sleeping. The prophets cried all the louder.

It was getting late in the afternoon. Finally Elijah said, "You have had your turn. Now it is my turn to pray to the Lord."

The people turned their attention to Elijah. The prophet repaired an ancient altar of stones dedicated to the Lord but long neglected by the people. Then he asked the people to fill four jars with water. While they were doing that he dug a trench around the altar. When the sacrifice was laid out on the stones, he had the four jars of water poured over the sacrifice, the wood, the altar, and into the trench. They did this three times until the trench was full.

At last everything was ready.

"O God of Abraham," Elijah prayed, "let Your people know that You are God. Let them know that I am Your prophet and that You have told me to do all of this. Bring fire on the altar, Lord, so that Your people will understand that You have the power and will return to worshiping You alone."

Suddenly Elijah's altar was ablaze with fire.

"God has sent fire from heaven," the people shouted. They knelt before this wondrous sight. They were frightened as they saw the fire burn up not only the offering but also the altar and all the water. "The Lord is God," many of them said over and over.

That day the prophets of Baal were killed.

Then Elijah turned to the king, "Listen, Ahab, do you hear the rushing of rain?" he asked. "God is going to send rain. Return to your palace before the rain stops you."

After Ahab left Elijah went to the top of Mt. Carmel and prayed for rain to come. "Tell me when the first cloud is in the sky," he told his servant.

The servant stood on a high place looking out over the Mediterranean Sea, but he could see nothing.

"Go look again" Elijah told him.

The servant looked, but there was still nothing. The seventh time he looked a little cloud appeared up out of the sea. In a short time the sky turned black with clouds. They could feel the wind now. And then came the first cool drops of rain. The shower grew in strength until all the earth was soaking up the rushing rain.

I Kings 18

77. A Man and His Vineyard

When Queen Jezebel heard what had happened at Mt. Carmel she was very angry. Now she was determined to have Elijah put to death.

She sent a message to him saying: "You have a short time to live. I swear by my god that I will take your life."

But Elijah escaped. He left his servant at Beersheba, and then he journeyed into the wilderness. He went all the way across the desert to Mt. Horeb, where God had spoken to Moses long ago. It was a long journey, but God gave him the strength he needed.

Elijah was very discouraged. In spite of the miracle many people had not forsaken their worship of Baal. Those who did wrong seemed to have the victory. He felt as though it was no use to serve God.

Elijah made himself a home in a large cave and stayed there many days. He wondered if God would speak to him and give him some special message.

One day as Elijah sat in the cave he heard a great wind rush past the rocks. An earthquake made the cave shake, and outside the cave there was fire. In all this

Elijah could find no message from God.

Then Elijah heard a great stillness. He went to the opening of the cave and there God spoke to him quietly out of the stillness.

"What are you doing here Elijah?" said the quiet voice.

Elijah wrapped his cloak over his face as he stood before God.

"I have worked very hard for You," he answered, "and for Your true worship in a country where Your prophets have been killed, and Your altars torn down. Now the queen wants to kill me."

God answered Elijah by giving him another job to do. His life would not be taken by Jezebel—there was work to be done for God. And God told him there were 7000 people in Israel who hadn't worshiped Baal.

Elijah realized that he must be more patient in his work for God.

Meanwhile King Ahab was too busy to even think about Elijah. The King of Syria sent his army to besiege the royal city of Samaria. But the army of Israel beat back the invaders.

The Syrians said, "Israel's God is powerful in the hills; but if we fight Israel on the plains we will win." But again Israel defeated the Syrians and won back territory across the Jordan River which they had lost.

Ahab was glad for these victories, but it did not make him walk in God's way. He refused to follow the laws of God which had been given through Moses.

One day Ahab noticed a vineyard near his palace grounds. "That would make a nice addition to my property," he said. "I will go and see Naboth about it."

The king went to Naboth, the owner of the vineyard. "I want this vineyard for a vegetable garden," he said. "I will give you a better vineyard in exchange, or I will give you its value in money."

"But I cannot do that," said Naboth. "God's law says that I may not sell the property given to me by my fathers. I do not want to break God's law."

King Ahab argued, but in vain. When he went back to the palace he was in a sullen mood. He stayed in his bedroom and refused to eat dinner.

The queen went to see what was the matter with Ahab. "Why are you angry? Why do you refuse to eat?" she asked.

King Ahab told her about their stubborn neighbor. "He won't sell it to me," he said, "and I want that vineyard for a garden."

Jezebel was disgusted with her husband. She thought he was a very weak king "Are you king or not?" she asked. "You should just take what you want."

Jezebel thought for a while. "I have a plan," she told Ahab. "I'll see to it that you get your vineyard."

Ahab was cheered. He knew his wife was wicked enough to do anything, and he was glad to give her the opportunity if it aided him.

Jezebel sat down and wrote some letters and sealed them with the special seal of the king. These leters were sent to the leaders of the town where Naboth lived. They ordered the leaders to get rid of Naboth and told them how to do it.

The leaders followed Jezebel's commands. They proclaimed a fast. "There is a traitor in our midst," they said. They arrested Naboth and brought him to trial.

They found two witnesses who would say that Naboth had cursed God and the

"God has sent fire from heaven," the people shouted.

king. The judges then passed the death penalty.

The leaders sent back a message to Jezebel saying, "Naboth is dead."

Jezebel was happy to hear that her plan had worked. She went to the king and told him what had happened.

The property of any man executed as a criminal was given to the king. "Now Naboth's vineyard is yours," she said. "Go and take possession of it."

King Ahab hurried to the vineyard, but on his way he met a very unwelcome prophet.

"God knows what you have done, Ahab," said Elijah. "You will be punished for your wrongdoing. You have murdered and stolen."

"Are you here again, my enemy?" asked the king.

"I only come because you keep on breaking God's laws," said the prophet. "Now I must give you God's message of judgment. The kingdom will be taken away from your family. You and Jezebel have done violence to others. You will both die violent deaths yourselves."

I Kings 19, 20, 21

78. The End of a Wicked King

In order to seal his friendship with Ahab, Jehoshaphat had promised that his son, Jehoram, would marry Athaliah, the daughter of Ahab and Jezebel.

Often King Ahab thought about the territory Syria had won from Israel. One city he particularly wanted to get back was Ramoth-gilead. One day Ahab said to his leaders, "Do you know that Ramoth-gilead really belongs to us? We have allowed Syria to keep this important city. Why don't we try to regain it?"

The leaders agreed that the army was in good shape and that they ought to be able to win this city back.

"I am going to ask King Jehoshaphat to help us," said Ahab. "We are friends now. I will invite him to come to Israel for a visit."

So the invitation was sent. King Jehoshaphat accepted and sent word that he was on his way.

King Ahab gave orders that the palace at Samaria must look its best. "We must show Jehoshaphat that our land is strong, wealthy, and powerful and that he is lucky to have us as friends."

When Jehoshaphat and his officials and servants arrived the king and queen made him feel at home. Ahab arranged for a fine feast to honor the king of the southern kingdom. There was much rich food and wine. All the important people of the kingdom were there.

During the visit King Ahab found time to talk to Jehoshaphat about making war with Syria. "It is not right that Syria keeps this city that once belonged to us. Will you go with me to this battle? Our combined armies are sure to defeat the Syrians."

Jehoshaphat was not quite sure it was a good idea, but he wanted to keep Ahab's friendship. "I am willing. We are brothers and what is mine is yours. But first we must ask God if we should do this. Are there not some prophets we can ask to find out if we will win against Syria?"

"Of course," said Ahab. "I'll call my prophets."

Ahab had many prophets; but he only kept those who always agreed with him and gave him the message he wanted to hear.

Four hundred prophets were called before the two kings. They all agreed, "Go to battle. God will give you the victory."

Jehoshaphat thought it a little strange that so many men would agree. He wondered if these prophets were true to the worship of the Lord.

"Is there any other prophet of the Lord who could help us?" he asked Ahab.

"There is another," said Ahab. "His name is Micaiah. I hate that man because he never tells me good news. But if you wish, I will call him."

A messenger went to Micaiah. "The king wishes to see you," he said. "He wants your advice about going to war against Syria. All the other prophets have said that the king should fight and that the Lord would help him win. You must say the same thing."

Micaiah frowned. "I will tell the king whatever message I receive from God," he said.

The prophet went with the messenger to the court. He was brought before the two kings. As he stood before them, the prophet could not help laughing at foolish King Ahab who paid people to say what he wanted to hear.

King Ahab asked Micaiah, "Shall we fight Syria or allow her to keep Ramoth-gilead?"

Micaiah said, "Go ahead and fight. You will win."

King Ahab could tell that Micaiah was making fun of him. He became angry. "Speak the truth to me. Speak the message you have from God."

"Very well," said Micaiah. "You will not have victory over Syria. Your army will be scattered throughout the hills like sheep without a shepherd. You will be killed in the battle."

"See, I told you he wouldn't bring good news," cried Ahab. He ordered soldiers, "Put this prophet in prison. Give him only bread and water until I come back."

"You will not be coming back," Micaiah warned.

Then Ahab turned to Jehoshaphat, "We will go against the Syrians," he declared. "We will be ruled by the words of the other prophets."

The two kings made preparations and set a date. The armies met and marched on the city.

"Are you going to take part in the battle yourself?" Jehoshaphat asked Ahab. "Aren't you afraid the prophet's word might come true?"

"I will take part," said Ahab, "but I am going to disguise myself so that no one will know I am the king."

But on the enemies' side, the king of Syria had told certain captains in his army, "I want one of you to be sure to kill King Ahab."

In the course of the battle these captains tried to find the king of Israel. "There is a man in kingly robes," cried one.

They rushed toward Jehoshaphat, but when they saw that it was the king of Judah, they stopped chasing him and turned away to look for Ahab.

"We can't find him," they said one to another. "He must not be fighting in this battle."

Then one man shot his arrow at a soldier in a chariot. He did not know it, but the soldier was Ahab.

The arrow pierced the armor of the king. "I am wounded," Ahab called to his driver. "Take me out of the battle."

The driver directed the horses to the sidelines. He helped Ahab to prop himself up in his chariot. Ahab's spirit sank as he watched his soldiers being badly beaten.

At sunset Ahab died. The Israelites realized that all was lost. They sounded a retreat. Everywhere the soldiers of Israel scattered as they headed back home.

Ahaziah, Ahab's son, became king of Israel. King Jehoshaphat and his army returned to Judah.

II Chronicles 18
I Kings 22

79. Elisha Sees the Chariot

For years Elisha had been training under the prophet Elijah. Elijah had taught other prophets too. They made up a school with Elijah as their head.

Elisha always remembered the day when Elijah called him to be a prophet. He had been out with the servants plowing his father's field. Elijah had come and thrown his robe across Elisha's shoulders.

This was a call to be a prophet, and Elisha stopped plowing and ran after Elijah. "Will you wait a little while?" he asked. "I want to say good-by to my parents. We will have a sacrifice and a large feast. Then I will follow you."

Elijah had agreed and stayed for the feast.

Elisha had come to love and respect the older prophet. Often Elisha said, "How I wish that one day I could be as great a prophet as Elijah."

Now Elijah was old. "I will not be with you much longer," he told his pupils.

The prophets whispered among themselves that God was going to take Elijah up to heaven in a chariot. Elisha was determined to stay close by Elijah and see this happen.

Elijah and Elisha were with the other prophets at Gilgal. "Wait here," said Elijah to him. "The Lord wants me to go to Bethel."

"But I want to stay with you," said Elisha.

The prophet allowed him to come. At Bethel the prophets said to Elisha. "It is today that God is going to take Elijah to heaven."

Then Elijah said, "Elisha, wait here. The Lord wants me to go to Jericho."

"But I want to stay with you," said Elisha.

Elijah agreed. At Jericho the prophets told Elisha, "It is today that the Lord will take our teacher to heaven."

Elijah told Elisha. "The Lord wants me now to go to the Jordan River. You had better wait here."

The prophet wanted to be sure Elisha really wanted to go.

"But I want to stay with you," said Elisha. "Please let me come."

Elijah agreed. Some of the other prophets went with them. When they came to the Jordan River these prophets kept watch on a hill; but Elisha went right down to the water's edge with Elijah.

Then Elijah took off his robe. He rolled it up and struck at the water. The water parted, and they crossed over the Jordan.

On the other side of the river Elijah turned to his faithful pupil. "I will soon be taken from you. What can I do for you?" he asked.

"I want to have a double share of your spirit and be a great prophet like yourself," said Elisha.

Elijah was thoughtful. The power and spirit came from God, but Elijah knew Elisha loved God and had the courage to stand for His truth.

"If you are able to see me leave, you will have this spirit," Elijah told him.

They went on along the edge of the water and talked about things of the past and the future. Suddenly a chariot and horses appeared in the sky, burning like fire. They came between Elisha and Elijah.

Elijah stepped into the chariot, and a whirling wind swept him up. Before it disappeared, Elisha called out to the prophet, "I see it! I see the chariot and the horsemen!

Then everything was quiet. Elisha was left alone. He had seen the vision, and so he should have God's special power; but he must be sure.

Elisha picked up the robe Elijah had left behind. He went back to where Elijah had parted the waters. He struck the waters with the robe the same way Elijah had. "Where is the God of Elijah?" he asked.

The answer came in the fact that the waters parted. Now Elisha knew that God had given him the power to work wonders which Elijah had used to help others believe in the true God.

The prophets on the other side of the river had not seen the chariot. They could see that Elijah had gone. They watched as the waters parted for Elisha.

They hurried down to the shore to greet Elisha as he came across the river. "The spirit of Elijah rests on Elisha," they cried.

The prophets bowed before Elisha. "You are our new leader," they said.

It soon became known in Israel that there was a new prophet with the same spirit of faithfulness to God which Elijah had shown.

I Kings 19:19-21
II Kings 2

80. An Army Led by Song

When King Ahaziah had ruled Israel for only two years he died as the result of an accident. Because Ahaziah had no children, his brother Jehoram took the throne.

In Judah King Jehoshaphat continued to lead his people in good ways. The teachers went throughout the land and taught God's laws.

King Jehoshaphat knew it was important to know and to keep the laws of God. Many of these laws had to do with being honest and just. It was necessary to have courts where those who were hurt by others could find help. King Jehoshaphat planned a system of courts for his people.

The king appointed judges to sit at

certain courts in all the important cities throughout the land. Before they took up their posts the king said to them: "Be careful in making decisions. When you judge between right and wrong you are doing the work of God, and God expects you to do it in His way.

"Do not prefer one person against another. Only be concerned with what is right and what is wrong, and make your decisions according to God's law. Do not take money as a bribe for deciding in the favor of one man against another."

The king realized that it was very important to have judges who would be fair. Without them evils would grow worse and worse.

The king also announced that there would be a central court in Jerusalem. To be a judge in this court a man needed to be a priest or a leader of the court. A leading priest would have charge of the religious cases and a leading official of the king would be in charge of dealing with government cases.

To this court would come the most important cases, and those which had not been settled in the smaller courts.

To these important people the king gave a charge. "Do your work, remembering that God sees you and expects you to do justly. Be faithful in your work, and serve God by doing it with all your heart."

Because of Jehoshaphat's work the people were living in ways that pleased God.

Some time later armies from Moab and Ammon came against Judah. They were joined by soldiers from Edom.

A messenger brought news to the king while the armies were on their way. "A huge army is coming from the direction of Edom, beyond the Dead Sea," he said.

King Jehoshaphat was afraid. It looked as though the time of peace was over. But Jehoshaphat did not lose his faith. "We must ask God for help," he said.

The king proclaimed that there would be a fast throughout Judah. He urged the people to pray for God's help.

Many people from all over Judah gathered in the court of the Temple. Jehoshaphat came and prayed before the people: "Lord God of our fathers, You are the true Ruler over all nations. You have the might and the power. You have given this land to us, and we have built a house for You where we may worship and pray to You.

"Now enemies have come to invade our land. They are many, and we do not have the military power to win over them. We do not know what to do: but we are counting on Your help."

The men and women and the boys and girls of all ages stood before God's altar with bowed heads. They asked God to keep them safe.

Then one of the priests spoke up: "God has told me 'Do not be afraid of this great army. The battle is not yours but God's.'

"Tomorrow go out to meet them. But you will not need to fight. Stand still in your positions, and see the Lord's victory for you. The Lord will be with you."

The people and king bowed low and prayed their thanks to God, and the choir of priests sang praise.

The next morning Jehoshaphat led the army out of the city. His parting words to the people were: "Believe in the Lord your God. Listen to His prophets. Trust in God's help, and you will find the help you need."

The king had appointed choirs to go before the army, singing praise to God.

Now these singers, dressed in their special robes, led the way.

"Give thanks to the Lord;
for His love continues forever."

Meanwhile in the enemy camp the armies of Moab and Ammon began to quarrel with one another. This grew into such an intense battle that there was no one left to attack Judah. By the time Jehoshaphat and his army arrived on the scene, anyone who had not been killed had run away.

The singers led the way back. Now their song of praise was even stronger. The danger was over, and not one of their soldiers had been harmed. When the army got back to Jerusalem there was a time of great rejoicing and thankfulness to God.

I Kings 22:41-53
II Kings 1, 3
II Chronicles 17, 19, 20

81. A Room for a Prophet

Throughout the reign of Jehoram, Elisha took up the work of Elijah. He preached about God's will for the nation. He warned the king and the people about pagan worship. He helped others in distress.

Often when Elisha and his servant Gehazi were going to Shunem, a town in the northern part of Israel on the way to the Sea of Galilee, they would stop at the home of a man and woman who were friendly to them and who liked having the prophet to dinner.

One day this woman said to her husband, "Elisha is a holy man of God. Let us do something for him. He often stops to eat with us, but he needs a place to sleep on his journeys. Let us make a special room for him."

In these lands the roofs were all flat. Often there were steps on the outside leading up to the roof. On top of the roof people sometimes built a small room for guests.

The woman and her husband built such a room. In it they put a bed, a table, a chair and a lampstand. The woman looked around the room. "How pleased Elisha will be," she thought.

The next time Elisha and Gehazi visited they had a good surprise waiting for them. The woman took them up the stairs. She opened the door of the room.

"This is for you," she said to Elisha.

Elisha looked around the room. "You are very kind and thoughtful to us," he said.

Elisha and his servant made themselves comfortable. "I wish we could do something for this woman who is so kind to us," said the prophet to Gehazi. "Ask her to come up and see us."

Gehazi went down to the woman's house. "Can you come and talk to the prophet?" he asked.

The woman followed him up the stairs. When she came into the room Elisha asked, "What can I do to show my appreciation?"

"We have all we need," said the woman.

"But I want to help you in some way," said the prophet.

"These people have no son," said Gehazi. The servant had mentioned something that the woman wanted.

"But we are old now. It isn't likely we would have a child," said the woman.

"I shall pray to God and ask Him to send you a son," Elisha promised.

When springtime came a boy was born to the woman and her husband. And for several years after that Elisha continued to stop by. He enjoyed talking to the boy and watching him grow.

When the boy became old enough, he helped his father in the fields. One day when he was out in the fields he began to feel ill.

"My head hurts terribly," he complained.

The father told a servant, "Carry him home to his mother."

The servant brought the sick boy home. His mother held him on her lap. How she hoped he would get well soon.

But the boy did not get well. While his mother was holding him he died. She sadly took him up and laid him on the bed in the room which the prophet used. But she had not given up hope. She still believed the prophet of God might be able to help.

She said to her husband. "Tell a servant to get a donkey for me to travel on. I must go to see Elisha."

Her husband told a servant to go with her.

"We must hurry," she told the servant.

They galloped across the countryside to Mt. Carmel where many of the prophets stayed. Elisha and his servant Gehazi saw her coming.

When the woman got to the prophet

she bowed before him. She told him what had happened to her son.

Elisha assured the woman he would help. He sent Gehazi on ahead. "Do not stop to talk to anyone," he said. "Hurry to the house, and put this staff of mine on the face of the child."

The servant hurried away with the staff. Elisha, the mother, and her servant came behind. When they got to the house Gehazi came out to meet them.

"I did as you said," he told Elisha, "but the child did not wake up."

This was sad news. The mother was crying. Elisha went up into the room and shut the door, he prayed and asked God to make the child well.

Then Elisha bent over the boy lying on the bed. He breathed into his mouth. The body became warm and Elisha got up. In a few minutes the prophet tried again. This time the boy moved and sneezed.

Elisha was glad. God had again shown His power to heal. "Call the boy's mother," he told Gehazi.

Soon the mother came running up the stairs.

"He is well," said Elisha. "Now you can take him down with you."

The woman thanked Elisha and thanked God. She tenderly gathered up her son and went back to the house.

II Kings 4

82. A Foreigner Finds God

In the days of Elisha, Israel and Syria were often fighting. Syria sometimes made raids on Israel and brought back captives to their own land. One captive was a little girl who was told she must be a servant in the house of Naaman, a general of the army.

Naaman was a great man, and his king had given him many presents and much honor. But Naaman and his family were not happy. Naaman had a serious disease for which they knew no cure.

One day the little girl said to her mistress, "If my lord Naaman were with Elisha the prophet in Samaria, the prophet would cure him of his leprosy. Elisha has the power to heal. It is a gift from God."

Her mistress listened. She so wanted her husband to get well that she would try anything. When Naaman returned home that night she told him what her servant had said.

"If there is someone who can cure me in Israel I am willing to go there," Naaman said. "I shall speak about it to the king."

Naaman went to see his king. He told the king that a servant from Israel had said a man in Israel could cure him.

"You have permission to leave," said the king. "I will send a letter to the king of Israel telling him that he must take care of you."

Naaman got ready. He took provisions for the journey. Several servants went with him. They brought good presents for the one would make the general well.

Naaman went directly to the king of Israel. He handed over the letter. The king of Israel read:

"Here is my general Naaman. I have sent him to you so that you will cure him of his leprosy."

But the king of Israel became angry and frightened. "This is a trick," he shouted. "The king of Syria is trying to start a quarrel with me. He wants an excuse for war. Am I God? Only God can cure leprosy."

The incident was told around the court and Elisha heard about it. The prophet sent word to the king.

"Why are you upset?" was the message. "Send Naaman to me. He will discover that there is a prophet in Israel."

The king called for Naaman. "You must go to the house of Elisha the prophet," he told the general. "He promises to help you."

So Naaman and his servants again rode off with their horses and chariots to Elisha's house. They stopped outside the door.

"Go and tell the prophet I am here," said General Naaman to one of his servants.

One of Elisha's servants opened the door and took Naaman's request to the prophet. In reply, Elisha sent a messenger out to see the general.

The messenger told him: "My master says, 'Go and wash in the Jordan River seven times, and you will be cured.' "

Naaman was insulted at this message. He ordered his chariot turned around. "We are leaving," he told the messenger.

To his servants he said angrily, "What disrespect the prophet showed to me. Doesn't he know I am a famous general? I certainly thought he would come out himself to meet me, call on his God to cure me, and wave his hand over me.

"We have beautiful rivers in Syria. I did not have to come to Israel just to bathe in a muddy river."

Naaman told the driver to urge the horses forward.

They hadn't gone too far when a servant said, "My lord, let us wait a minute and think about this. If the prophet had told you to do some difficult thing, you would have done it. Then why not wash yourself in the Jordan? Try it, and see what happens."

Naaman calmed down. The advice did seem to be sensible. "Very well," he said. "We will go on to the Jordan River."

When they arrived at the river, Naaman waded out into the brown, muddy water. Up and down he went as the prophet had told him. The seventh time he came up, he looked at his skin in amazement. The leprosy was gone!

Naaman hurried out of the water. "Look! Look!" he cried to his servants. "Look at my skin. See how fresh and clean it looks?"

With great joy Naaman and his servants returned to Elisha's house. They spoke to the prophet.

"Now I know that your God has great power," Naaman said to Elisha. "Here are gifts of thanks to you, God's prophet."

Servants brought out gold, silver, and fine robes.

But Elisha shook his head. "The power is from God. It would not be right for me to take money or other gifts for using it."

Then Naaman thought of another way to show his gratitude. He would worship Elisha's God. Naaman believed any god must be worshiped in his own land. He asked, "Then may I take some soil from Israel? When I get back to Syria I will worship only the God of Israel."

Elisha was glad for this. It meant more to him than a gift.

But Gehazi thought his master was foolish. As they watched the general leave, Gehazi decided, "We could use the gold and silver and fine robes Naaman brought with him. I'm going to follow Naaman and ask for something."

After Elisha went back in the house, Gehazi ran after the horses and chariots. When he finally caught up, Naaman himself got out of his chariot and met him.

"Is all well?" he asked.

"Yes," said Gehazi. "Two young prophets have just come to us, and now my master wishes to know if you will give a little money and a robe for them."

Naaman was glad to give it. He gave Gehazi more than he asked. They said farewell, and Gehazi hurried back.

"I shall use these myself," Gehazi said. "No one will know."

But Elisha knew what his servant had done.

"I am disappointed in you," he told Gehazi. "Was it the time to receive presents? Was it not enough that Naaman had come to believe in the God of Israel? Your punishment will be that Naaman's disease will be yours."

II Kings 5

83. Trouble Comes to Judah

Jehoshaphat had seven sons. He had always tried to be a just and fair father. He did not want his sons to quarrel over the throne after he died. He had a plan which he thought would prevent this.

One day he called his family together. "Jehoram, my eldest son, will be king of Judah after my death," he told them.

Jehoram was pleased. He knew Athaliah, his wife, would be very pleased to be queen.

But Jehoshaphat had other words. "I have appointed fine gifts for each of the rest of you, my sons. After my death you will receive gold and silver and other possessions."

Jehoshaphat also realized that his sons wanted places of trust and honor. "I have also made arrangements so that after my death you will each be given certain important cities over which you will have charge."

The other sons were happy that their father showed confidence in them. But Jehoram was not happy about this, although he said nothing at the time.

Jehoram's wife, Athaliah, rejoiced over the fact that she would be queen. She did not understand why Jehoshaphat would give his other sons gifts and positions.

"The king should have all the power," she told Jehoram, "but never mind. When you become king you can easily fix that."

Athaliah was the daughter of Queen Jezebel of Israel, and very much like her mother. She believed in her mother's religion. She often thought, "I would like to see many altars and shrines to Baal in this country."

After Jehoshaphat died, he was buried with the other kings of Judah. The people mourned for him. As a way of showing honor they burned many spices at his funeral.

Jehoram and Athaliah became king and queen. Trouble came soon after they took the throne.

One day the people were shocked to hear that Jehoram had ordered all his brothers killed. Other leaders who might oppose this act had been slain.

"Jehoram is not going to be the great king his father was," many said. "He does not have the love for his people which Jehoshaphat had. And now he has committed this sin. The king wanted to be fair to all his family, but Jehoram cared nothing for fairness. He has murdered his brothers who were also of the family of David."

Then another surprise came to the people. The prophets and priests were upset to see images of Baal brought into the land. Athaliah was busy setting up the new worship.

Many who wanted to be friends with the queen offered sacrifice to Baal. The king also knelt before the images. He ordered shrines built on the hilltops near the towns and villages throughout the land.

"We are going in the ways of Ahab of Israel," the priests cried out in dismay.

Jehoram was king for only a few years, but much trouble came to the land because of his sin. Edom had belonged to Judah for many years, but under his rule it revolted and set up a king of its own.

Arabian tribes invaded the land and took away all the treasures in the palace.

They took as captives the king's wives and all but the youngest of Jehoram's sons. Only Ahaziah and his mother Athaliah were left.

It was soon after this that Jehoram became very ill. He suffered for two years with this disease before he died. The people did not mourn for him as they had for his father. They did not burn many spices at his funeral. No one was sorry he had gone.

The leaders among the priests and landowners said, "Because Jehoram is of David's family he must be buried in Jerusalem, but we do not want him buried in the tomb of the kings.

"He is not worthy to lie in the tomb of good kings like David, Asa, and Jehoshaphat. He murdered his brothers and turned away to pagan gods."

But Judah's troubles were not over with Jehoram's death. Athaliah had taught her children the religion of Baal.

Ahaziah, who was now king, believed in the religion of his mother and his grandmother, Jezebel. He too wanted to see pagan worship spread throughout Judah.

Ahaziah depended on his mother to help him make his decisions. He was very much influenced by her.

She told him, "Your Uncle Jehoram is king of Israel. Be sure to keep your friendship with him. He is a king of experience. He will be glad to give you advice whenever you need it. Your grandmother is also at the court in Israel. She still has much influence."

Ahaziah had been king for about a year when he went to visit King Jehoram in Israel. His uncle persuaded him to join him in battle against Syria. Again they were fighting over Ramoth-gilead.

Ahaziah and his army joined Jehoram and his forces, but they lost the battle. In the fighting King Jehoram was wounded.

The king of Israel decided to go to the town of Jezreel to rest and get well. While he was there, King Ahaziah and some of his soldiers journeyed from Jerusalem to visit him. Unknown to King Ahaziah, he was riding into revolution.

II Kings 8:16-29
II Chronicles 21, 22:1-7

84. Murder for a Throne

Many of the people of Israel were dissatisfied with the family of Ahab. Jehoram, his son, was following in Ahab's ways, and the wicked Jezebel was still alive.

Besides worshiping pagan gods, Ahab and Jehoram had allowed the rich people to oppress the poor.

The prophets were glad to see this spirit of rebellion rise among the people. They used this opportunity to try to put someone who was true to the worship of God on the throne.

Elisha, the prophet, had an important part in this revolution. He called for one of the student prophets.

"You have an important errand," said Elisha. "Take this flask of sacred oil. With it you will anoint Jehu, one of the commanders in the army, as king. You will find him with the other commanders of the army. Take him alone into a smaller room and anoint him."

The prophet found the commanders gathered together at Ramoth-gilead. He came into the room where they met and said to Jehu, "I have an errand for you, O commander."

Jehu followed the prophet into another room. Then the prophet poured the oil on Jehu's head, saying, "The God of Israel says, 'I anoint you king over the people of the Lord in Israel.' "

The prophet went on with his message: "Strike down the family of Ahab so that they are no longer rulers of our people."

Then the prophet turned and fled. Jehu wondered what he should do next. He wanted to be king, and he was glad for the prophets' support; but what about the other commanders?

When Jehu returned to the other commanders they wanted to know what the prophet had said. At first Jehu did not want to tell them. Finally he told the truth.

The commanders were glad. They wanted to get rid of King Jehoram. "We are with you," they shouted.

Someone blew a trumpet. "Jehu is king," they cried.

Jehu and the other commanders plotted how they would take over the government. "We must be careful," Jehu warned. "No one else must know of this."

The commanders wasted no time. That very night Jehu stepped into his chariot. He took soldiers with him. They were soon riding at top speed to Jezreel where Jehoram was staying.

In Jezreel the watchman in the tower on the town's walls was looking out for danger. When he saw a group of men coming with horses and chariots, he sent word to the king.

Jehoram was talking with King Ahaziah when the news came. "Send a man on horseback out to meet them and ask them if they come in peace," he commanded.

A man was sent out to meet them. "Do you come in peace?" the man asked Jehu.

Jehu invited the man to join the revolution. "Who is talking about peace? Ride behind us," he commanded.

The watchman again sent word to Jehoram. "The messenger reached these men, but he has not come back. The men are still riding towards us."

"Send out another man to meet them," the king said.

Another man greeted Jehu. "The king wants to know if you come in peace," he asked.

Jehu invited this man to join him, and he too accepted. Again the watchman was puzzled. What happened to the messengers? Then the watchman recognized the oncoming soldiers.

He reported to the king: "Soldiers are coming driving their horses furiously—like Jehu drives."

Then King Jehoram realized that there was trouble, and that he would have to defend his throne. He called the soldiers who guarded him. King Ahaziah and the men he had brought with him from Judah also made ready to fight. They all took their horses and chariots out to meet the rebel.

When they came near the advancing forces, Jehoram asked, "Is it peace, Jehu?" "How can it be peace," Jehu replied, "when you and your mother are disobeying God?"

When he heard Jehu's answer, Jehoram turned his chariot around to ride quickly away. But Jehu shot Jehoram with an arrow and the king sank down in his chariot.

Ahaziah and his men also tried to get away; but Jehu pursued them. Ahaziah was an ally of Jehoram. Jehu also realized that Ahaziah might claim the throne of Israel as nephew of Jehoram.

The arrows came thick and fast at the fleeing chariots. Ahaziah was wounded and died on the way back to Jerusalem.

Jehu took the throne of Israel. He ordered Jezebel and all the prophets of Baal killed. He murdered all of Ahab's sons and anyone he thought would be a threat to him. So Elijah's word about the violent deaths of both Ahab and Jezebel had finally come true.

Back in Judah there was panic. The king was dead, and all his sons were young.

When the Queen Mother Athaliah heard about the death of her son, her mother and her brother, she was very angry. Now she would not even be queen mother in Judah. She would have no authority.

But Athaliah saw a way to keep the family of Ahab a royal family. As queen she could promote her religion in Judah. Eventually she could get revenge on Jehu.

Athaliah ordered men who were loyal to her to kill all the sons of the royal family. It did not matter that they included her own grandchildren. The throne was more important to her.

II Kings 9, 10, 11:1
II Chronicles 22:7-10

85. A Prince Is Saved

Queen Athaliah was on the throne, but the people were unhappy. She was not of the family of David except by marriage. The priests of the Lord were angry when the queen built a house for the worship of Baal close to the palace and Temple. Athaliah had followers of her own, including priests, who tried to influence others to adopt her religion.

But the queen and her followers did not know an important secret. All of David's family had not been killed. Jehosheba, a sister of King Ahaziah who was married to the priest Jehoiada had saved one baby boy, named Joash.

Jehosheba took her little nephew and his nurse and hid them in a bedroom. Then she called her husband, the priest. Jehoiada took Joash to live with the priests.

"We must let no one know about Joash until he is a little older," Jehoiada told them. "Meanwhile we will help him to grow strong and wise. We will teach him God's ways and how to worship God truly."

For six years it was a well-kept secret. When Joash was seven years old Jehoiada said, "We can delay no longer. We must make Joash king. But we need the help of the army."

"What if the army is not with us?" asked other priests.

"We must trust in God. We must show the prince to the commanders of the army."

Jehoiada brought the captains together. He took them into a room and showed them the little boy.

He said, "This is Joash, son of Ahaziah, rightful heir to the throne."

The captains shouted their approval. They promised to help. Plans were made to crown Joash king.

"Soldiers must surround Joash at all times," ordered Jehoiada. "Some soldiers must stand guard at the Temple. Other soldiers must guard all the doors of the palace so that none of Athaliah's followers can come out."

The day came and everything was ready. The soldiers stood with their spears in their hands. The little king came out of the house where he had been hiding. Soldiers walked with him to the platform of the Temple.

Leaders of the people had been told to come. Many others from Jerusalem crowded the courts to see what was to happen.

Jehoiada was waiting at the entrance to the Temple. The choirs of singers were in their places. The priests who blew on the trumpets were ready.

Jehoiada anointed Joash with the sacred oil. Then he put the crown on the boy's head. The trumpets blew.

"Long live the king!" the people shouted.

The trumpets blew again. The choirs sang. When the news spread that a son of

David had been found and had been crowned king, more people came running.

Queen Athaliah heard the noise and rushed out to see what was happening. As she entered the court and looked up to the entrance of the Temple she understood only too well.

"Treason! Treason!" she shouted, but no one came to defend her. Instead, soldiers grabbed her and took her away. Jehoiada ordered her killed.

The people were glad to have a new king. They were glad the wicked queen was dead. They rejoiced that God had saved one from David's family to rule over them.

Jehoiada talked to the people. "This wicked Queen Athaliah brought a foreign god into our land. The Lord is our God. Are you willing now to worship the Lord?"

The people promised. "We will serve God and obey His laws." King Joash also made this promise.

Then the priest ordered the house Athaliah had built for foreign worship to be torn down. "All the altars and the images of Baal must be broken in pieces," he said.

Jehoiada turned to the new king. "Come, now you will go to the house that has always been yours, the king's house."

Joash was happy as he made his way with soldiers to guard him. They brought him into a room where a great chair waited. It was the throne of David.

Joash sat down on it. His aunt and uncle and all the others who had risked their lives to hide him were thankful to God. Now their land would have peace.

II Kings 11
II Chronicles 22:11, 12; 23

86. A King Who Forgot

Joash had learned many things from Jehoiada and the other priests. He loved God and wanted to be loyal to his worship.

When Joash grew up, he decided that something needed to be done about the Temple. It badly needed repair. Under the rule of Queen Athaliah the Temple had been neglected. She had used some of the sacred furnishings for herself and for her own worship.

Joash called the priest, Jehoiada, to him. "We have neglected God's house," he said. "Why haven't you been collecting the tax for the upkeep of the Temple?"

Jehoiada promised that something would be done right away. But time went on, and still there was no money for the work.

Joash spoke about it again. "The Temple needs repair," he said. "If God's worship is important, we must keep His house looking its best. I know it is hard to get the dues from the people. I know that the priests need money to live, but we must also repair the building."

"You are right," said Jehoiada. "We must convince the people that this is an important cause."

"I have an idea," said Joash. "Let us make a chest just for this purpose. Put it near the altar, close to the entrance of the Temple court. Here everyone will see it. Tell the people that all the money which is put into this chest will be used only to repair the Temple."

Jehoiada had the chest made. The carpenters bored a hole into the lid. It would be easy for the people to drop in their coins when they came for worship.

King Joash sent messengers throughout the land urging the people to give their money. From then on all the worshipers had some coins for the chest.

When it was full an officer of the king and a priest emptied it and used the money to hire workers. More money was needed, so the chest was left in its place. The people again filled the chest.

The workers soon had the Temple looking like new. Several times over the chest was filled with money. There was even enough to make new bowls and dishes of gold and silver to be used in the worship.

Jehoiada was a strong leader for the people. While he was around to guide them, both the people and the king were faithful to God.

Jehoiada lived a long time, but one day he went to be with God. The people mourned for him. The leaders of the land said that he should be buried with the kings of the past. This was a great honor.

Joash missed Jehoiada. He had depended on his advice.

There were leaders at the court who had never agreed with Jehoiada, but they had been silent for fear of their lives. Now they decided to try to bring back pagan worship.

They praised and flattered the king. When they got his trust they influenced Joash to allow pagan worship. Joash began to wonder if what Jehoiada had taught him was true after all. He began to lose his love for God and His law.

Jehoiada's son Zechariah was also a priest. He came to King Joash one day and spoke boldly to him. "You have disobeyed. You have forsaken the Lord God. God will bring judgment on you and on our nation, because you have been a bad example and influenced the people away from Him."

But Joash would not listen. The leaders who had influenced the king wanted to be rid of this prophet. They were afraid Zechariah might bring Joash back to God.

"Why don't you put this prophet to death?" they asked King Joash. Often they spoke against Zechariah. Finally Joash agreed to have him killed. He forgot how Zechariah's father and mother had saved his life.

After that trouble came to the land. An army from Syria marched against Jerusalem. It was not a large army, and yet they were able to force Joash to give up much treasure.

Some of the leaders were angry at Joash for killing Zechariah. Others were angry because he gave up the struggle and gave the Syrians the treasure they wanted.

Joash himself had been wounded and was ill. While he was in bed, servants who had been hired by others came into his room and killed him.

Joash had been a disappointment to most of the people, especially to the priests who had been his teachers. The leaders decreed that Joash was not to be buried beside the rest of the kings or Jehoiada his old teacher.

Amaziah, son of Joash, became king.

II Kings 12
II Chronicles 24

87. A Warning to the North

Up in Israel, Jehu had ordered all the foreign idols to be destroyed, but he and the people still worshiped God with the aid of the sacred bulls which Jeroboam, the first king of Israel, had made.

Because of King Jehu's murders, Israel had lost the friendship of Tyre, Sidon and Judah. There was war with Syria. Then Assyria, a land north of Israel, began to become a power.

King Jehu was glad to see the Assyrians attack Syria; but soon Jehu was forced to pay some tribute to the king of Assyria himself.

After Jehu's death his son Jehoahaz became king after him. In Jehoahaz' reign there was continual war with Syria; but when Jehoahaz' son Jehoash took the throne, he began to defeat the Syrians.

Jehoash also defeated Joash's son Amaziah who was then king of Judah. Amaziah had attacked Israel to get revenge on Jehu's family for murdering King Ahaziah.

After Jehoash, the next king of Israel was called Jeroboam, named for the first king of Israel. Around this time sixteen-year-old Uzziah, the son of Amaziah, took over the rule of Judah.

It was a time of peace and prosperity for both nations. The leaders grew in wealth, but the poor people suffered. The prophets thought of these times as evil, but the kings and their officials said they were good times.

In Israel the leaders enjoyed the greatest wealth the nation had ever known. The Syrians were busy fighting the Assyrians and so trade and industry could expand.

But these blessings did not lead the people closer to God. Instead the people of Israel did so many things that displeased God and broke so many of His laws, that the prophets had to give them severe warnings.

One prophet who spoke to Israel was Hosea. Hosea spoke out against Jeroboam, great grandson of Jehu. He said, "God is going to punish the family of Jehu because of all the murders Jehu committed. God is going to take the kingdom away from this family."

Hosea told the people: "God's judgment will come someday. How can He keep forgiving you, if you keep committing the same sins?"

Hosea spent long hours thinking about God and His people. Did God really care about His people? Did He still love them, even though they had forsaken Him? Would He soon lose patience with them and find a new people?

Hosea was a man who had many troubles. He loved his wife Gomer very much. He tried to give her all the things she wanted. But Hosea did not have much money, and his wife wanted many things.

They had three children, two sons and a daughter. Gomer was not a good wife and mother. One day she ran away from the home. Hosea had to take care of the children by himself.

Hosea was angry at Gomer. He looked for her but could not find her. Then Hosea realized that he missed Gomer, even though she had not kept the house well.

Hosea realized something that was

even stranger. When he thought about Gomer now, he was not so angry. He still loved Gomer, even though she had done so much that was wrong.

"If only I could find Gomer," Hosea thought, "I would bring her back into the house. I would not punish her or scold her. I would tell her that I forgive her.

"I would give her all I could to make the work easier for her. I would prove my love to her. Then surely she would love me back. Then she would become a good wife and mother."

One day Hosea found Gomer serving as a slave in a rich man's house. In order to bring her home, Hosea had to give the man money. Hosea was glad to do this in order to have Gomer back.

Through all this trouble Hosea learned something about God. The people of Israel had wandered far from God. They had taken over so many heathen practices that they were not really worshiping God but the heathen gods.

They had been unfaithful, as Gomer had been, but God still loved them. God loved his people and would forgive them, if only they would return to Him.

Hosea thought, "It may be that the people of Israel will have to live through many troubles as Gomer did, before they are willing to come back to God. If they do not come back soon, surely God's judgment will come.

"The Assyrians are growing powerful. They will expand their empire if they can. If our people do not repent God will use them to punish us."

So Hosea spoke to the people throughout the land. This was part of his message:

Hear the word of the Lord,
O people of Israel.
The Lord finds fault with
the people of this land.
There is no faithfulness
nor kindness
and no knowledge of God.
There is only swearing,
lying, killing and stealing.
You have forgotten the laws
of your God.

Israel's kings have not been
faithful to God.
They set up idols.
God rejects the bull at Bethel.
A workman made it;
it is not God.
It shall be broken to pieces
when judgment comes
to the land.

God says: "I loved Israel
as a father loves a child.
I brought my son out of Egypt.
In the wilderness
I taught him how to walk;
I protected my people.
But they have forgotten me.
They have forgotten my love
and kindness.

God does not want to punish
His people.
Ask God to help you
to return.
Ask Him to take away
your sin.
Do deeds of love and justice.
Trust in God, not in
alliances with Egypt
or Assyria.

God says: "I am the Lord
your God,
the God of your fathers.

There is no God but Me;
no one to save you
except Me.
If you do not return
to Me,
I will destroy your land;
but if you do return,
I will love you freely,
and your land will flourish
like a garden and have
peace."

O, Israel, God is the one
who looks after you,
not idols.
The ways of the Lord are
right and the upright
walk in them.

II Kings 13, 14, 15:1
II Chronicles 25, 26:1
Hosea

88. Amos' Message to a Neighbor

Amos was a poor farmer who lived in Judah at the time Uzziah was king. Every day Amos kept himself busy taking care of his fruit trees and watching over his flock of sheep.

Amos lived in a small village, but he was concerned about life in the cities throughout Judah and in other countries.

Amos loved God. He knew that the God of Israel loved righteousness and justice; but all around he saw just the opposite.

"God will have to punish us for the way we live," he thought. "Here in Judah and in Israel we say we are God's people, and yet we do not walk in His ways."

Amos had heard how the people of Israel used idols in their worship. He knew that Israel was in danger from the Assyrians.

One day God spoke to Amos, "I want you to go to Israel and warn the people that judgment is coming," He said.

"But," Amos thought, "if I go to Israel they will say, 'Get back to your own country where you belong.' "

Still, the message had come from God. "I must go," Amos decided.

Amos left his sheep and his trees in the hands of others and made the journey north. Once in Israel he talked on the highways and on the village streets. He talked to anyone who would listen.

First he told the people how God was going to punish the nations round about them for their sins. The people agreed that these heathen nations did much that was wrong. They deserved to be punished.

Then Amos admitted that his own nation of Judah often did what was not pleasing to God. Judah would be punished as well as the heathen.

Then Amos talked about the sins of Israel. "God's punishment is very near," he told them.

As a result of war and trade, Israel had increased its territory, and many of the nation's leaders had become wealthy. They had left the simple ways of living that their fathers had known.

They built large houses and ate expensive food. They wanted beautiful clothes and all kinds of beautiful objects of silver, gold, and ivory.

To keep living this way they needed more and more money. They got this

money by robbing the poor. When the poor brought their cases to court, the rich people bribed the judge to decide in their favor.

Amos spoke out against this: "Judgment will come to those who live in luxury, who eat lambs and calves, who spend their time feasting and singing. Your feasting will turn into mourning; because you trample on the poor, you take bribes, you turn aside the needy."

Then Amos went to Bethel, the religious center of Israel. Here at the shrine where the people worshiped Amos saw the golden bull. The people came often to keep the many feasts and to bring many sacrifices.

Because of this they thought they were very good. "God must protect us from our enemies," they said.

"God doesn't accept your worship and sacrifices," Amos told them. "God wants His worshipers to do righteous deeds. Even your worship is spoiled by wrongdoing."

Amaziah, the head priest at Bethel, heard Amos and he was angry. He went to King Jeroboam. "A prophet from Judah is upsetting everyone," he told the king. "He says God is going to punish us by destroying our nation. He says we will all be taken away as captives."

King Jeroboam did not interfere. He had no faith in what prophets said anyway.

Amaziah went to Amos. "You must leave," he said. "How dare you preach against our king and our nation here at Bethel, the king's shrine?"

Amos said, "It is God who sent me. I

must stay as long as He tells me. You will find out that I am speaking the truth when God's judgment comes and you are taken away to a strange land."

The priest was angry, but Amos went on with God's work.

"God has tried to win you back, but you have refused to come back," he preached. "God has given you many blessings, but you have not thanked Him. When God corrected you by allowing you to have trouble—drought, famine, sickness—this did not make you think of Him either. The end of Israel is coming."

But Amos' message was not all sad. The way was always open to repent and do what was right.

Amos told them:

Seek good and not evil,
  that you may live.
Then God will be with you.
Hate evil and love good,
  give true justice in the courts.
Let justice roll down like water,
  and let righteousness flow like a
  stream throughout the land.

Amos 1-9

89. A Rebellious Preacher

Jonah was another prophet who lived when Jeroboam II was king.

There was much work for God to do in Israel. Yet one day God told Jonah to take a trip. "Go to Nineveh," God said, "and warn the people that they are doing wrong and that God's judgment will come if they do not change."

Jonah was perplexed by this order. *These people are pagans,* he thought. *They are wicked and very cruel. Why does God care about them? I have work to do here.*

But God continued to speak to Jonah about the people of Nineveh.

To get to Nineveh one had to travel north and east from Israel. Jonah went to the port of Joppa on the Mediterranean Sea. He got passage on a ship sailing in the opposite direction. He wanted to get as far away as he could from God and His orders.

"I'll sail all the way to Tarshish," Jonah decided.

They set sail on a calm Mediterranean Sea with the sun sparkling on the blue waters. But by nightfall all was changed. A fierce wind sprang up and a storm broke. The ship was so tossed about on the ocean that the sailors were afraid. They had been in many storms, but this was the worst. They knew their small sailing ship was no match for such a storm. They took down the sails and used the oars.

The sailors came from many different countries. They all started to pray to their different gods.

"Come, we must throw the cargo into the sea," some said. "That will help to make the ship lighter."

They did this, but still the ship was in danger.

All this while Jonah was asleep below. Finally the captain went down to him. "How can you sleep in such a storm?" he asked, as he shook Jonah awake. "Come, we are in danger. Call on whatever god you worship. Perhaps your god can help us."

Jonah went up to the deck with the

captain. Here the sailors were casting lots.

"Someone here has done a wicked deed and his god is punishing him," the sailors said. "We are going to find out who is bringing this terrible storm on us."

The sailors threw the special stones. The lot came out to be Jonah.

The sailors all spoke at once. "Where do you come from? What wrong have you done? Who are you?"

Jonah hid nothing from them. "I am from Israel. I worship the Lord, the God of heaven, who made the earth and the sea."

The men were even more frightened. "What wrong did you do?" they asked.

"I am running from God," Jonah confessed. "He had sent me to Nineveh, but I did not want to go."

Meanwhile the storm grew worse. "What shall we do to stop this storm?" they asked Jonah.

The prophet believed the storm was God's judgment on him. He did not want to cause the death of these sailors.

"There is only one thing you can do," he said. "Throw me overboard. It is my sin that is causing this trouble. You will be all right if I am gone."

At first the sailors did not want to do this. "Row harder," they shouted. "See if we can get to land."

But nothing they did made any difference. The storm grew worse and the waves tossed higher. The sailors cried to Jonah's God for help. Then they took Jonah's advice and tossed him into the waves.

The storm ceased and the sea became quiet. The sailors were amazed. "It is Jonah's God," they said. "Let us pray and sacrifice to his God so that we will arrive at our port safely."

Meanwhile Jonah hadn't drowned. He had been swallowed by a huge sea creature. He found himself alive inside but very frightened.

He could not live in here for long. It was only a matter of time before his life would end. "Perhaps even though I disobeyed, God will still help me," Jonah thought.

Jonah prayed: "O Lord, You are able to deliver me. Bring me back home, so that I can again worship You in Your Temple."

God heard Jonah. The sea creature came out of the water and spit up Jonah on the beach. The prophet crawled up on the soft sand. He could hardly believe he was really safe.

Jonah thanked God for his deliverance. But God only repeated what He had said to Jonah at the beginning, "Go to Nineveh and preach to the people there. I have a message for them."

Jonah knew there was no way out. He was God's prophet. This time he traveled in the right direction.

When Jonah got to Nineveh he marveled at this large city with its beautiful trees and gardens and its many buildings. He began to preach. "You are doing wrong," he shouted. "God will bring His judgment on your city unless you change."

Jonah had thought none of these idol worshipers would pay attention, but they did. The people thought about their past doings.

"This preacher is right," they said.

The leaders of the people said, "Let us have a fast and wear sackcloth and pray. God may yet see and forgive us."

Even the king took part in the fast. "Let us all ask God to forgive us," he said.

But Jonah was not pleased that his preaching was successful. He left the city and went up on a mountainside where he could look down on Nineveh.

"I'll see if God is really going to forgive these people," he decided. He still did not think God should love and forgive anyone but His own people.

As he watched in the hot sun, Jonah was glad for the shelter of a tall plant which shaded him—but not for long. A worm began to eat at the plant and it shriveled up.

Jonah moaned unhappily, "Now I don't even have shade from the sun."

God spoke to Jonah. "You cared about the plant and were sorry to see it die, even though you didn't make it grow. Shouldn't I care about all these people whom I made and who have not known Me? They have repented, so no judgment will come to them." *II Kings 4:25*
Jonah

90. A Vision in the Temple

King Uzziah was a good king who was true to the worship of God. During his reign Judah grew in wealth, military might, and political power. Uzziah increased trade and helped develop better farms. It was the best time since Solomon.

In the last years of his reign Uzziah became ill with leprosy. He had to live in a separate house, because people believed this was a disease that spread from one to another.

Uzziah's son, Jotham, appeared for his father in public and helped him rule.

In the northern kingdom of Israel it was a time of conspiracy. Many people had not liked the royal family which had begun with Jehu. They took advantage of Jeroboam's death to plan an overthrow.

Six months after Jeroboam's son, Zechariah, took power he was murdered by Shallum. Only a month after Shallum took the throne he was murdered by Menahem.

Then King Uzziah died in Judah. At this time there was a man at the court in Jerusalem who was very troubled about his nation. Isaiah knew that God was not pleased with the way the people of Judah were disobeying His laws.

Now Jotham was the king. Would he help the people or lead them further away from God? Isaiah went to the Temple to pray and ask God's help for the people.

Often Isaiah stood and watched the people flock to the Temple. Outwardly they were loyal to God, but their hearts were far from Him. Their worship was just a matter of outward form. They did not really try to live in the way God commanded. The few people who had become wealthy took advantage of the poor. Instead of trying to help those in need, they were only concerned with getting more luxuries for themselves.

Some of the people had lost their faith in God. They sought help in magic or turned to idols.

As Isaiah prayed in the Temple, he had a vision of the glory of God. The vision filled all the Temple with its light.

There was the throne of God, and above it stood winged creatures. Their faces were covered with their wings.

Wings also covered their feet. They used another pair of wings to fly.

Isaiah could hardly look, the vision was so burning bright; but he heard the creatures call to one another:

"Holy, Holy, Holy is the Lord of hosts.
The whole earth is full of His glory."

The Temple shook at this song of praise. The smoke of incense filled the sanctuary.

Isaiah was frightened. He was not good enough to receive such a vision of God's holiness.

"I am lost," he cried. "I am only a man. I do and speak wrong, and I live among people who do wrong; and yet I am in God's presence."

Then one of the winged creatures flew to Isaiah carrying a coal of fire from the altar. He touched the mouth of the prophet.

"Now your guilt is taken away," the creature said. "Your sin is forgiven."

Then Isaiah heard God speak. He had a task for a man to do. "Who shall I send?" God asked. "Who will go for us?"

Isaiah spoke up. "Here I am. Send me."

God accepted Isaiah as His messenger; but He warned the prophet. "The people have wandered far from Me. Don't expect them to hear and understand. Your message will not be popular with the people.

"But I have not left My people. Even though My judgment will come, there will be some who will be saved. From these faithful ones I will make a new and better people."

Later when the way grew difficult Isaiah always remembered this vision. God had promised that there would always remain some who trusted Him and who would keep faith in Him alive.

So Isaiah went out and preached. He talked to many important people and to the crowds who thronged the city streets.

Some of his message went like this:

Hear, O heavens and earth;
for the Lord has spoken.
"The sons I reared have
rebelled against me.
An ox and ass know who
their master is;
But my people have forgotten
that they belong to Me.

"My people are sick
from their sins.
They bring Me offerings,
but I have no delight in them.
Those who bring the offerings
are guilty of breaking My law.

"Cease doing evil;
learn to do good.
Seek justice;
correct oppression.
Defend the fatherless
and the widow.

"Come, let us talk together:
Even though your sins are
very great,
this can be changed,
and you can be as clean
as pure snow.
If you are willing and obedient,
you will eat the good things
of the land;
But if you rebel against Me,
you will die by the sword,
for I have spoken."

II Kings 15
II Chronicles 26
Isaiah 1, 2, 3, 6

91. The Nation from the North

The Assyrians lived in northern Mesopotamia. For centuries they had dreamed of conquering many nations and forming a great empire. This nation from the north had developed the largest, best equipped and best trained army the world had known up to this time.

In battle they were cruel, and they often tortured their enemies.

The Assyrians took away much treasure from the lands they invaded. They made each conquered government pay a large yearly tribute. With this wealth they erected beautiful palaces and other buildings in their own capital, which was Nineveh at this time.

When the Assyrians completely conquered a nation they did something new. They took all the best of the people of the nation back to Assyria with them. They brought people from other conquered lands to live in their place. By mixing people in this way they destroyed the united spirit of each nation.

The great goal of the Assyrians was to conquer Egypt, but the nations of Israel, Judah, and Syria as well as their neighbors stood in the way. First these nations would have to be brought under Assyrian power. As people saw what Assyria planned to do, the dread of the mighty Assyrian warriors came on all the nations.

While Menahem was king of Israel Assyria came against them. Menahem reached an agreement with Tiglath-pileser, the king of Assyria, to take money rather than invade the land. He promised that more money would be paid each year.

This tribute came from the people by way of heavy taxes. Those who owned land had so much to pay that they could not afford the luxuries they wanted.

Some of the people of Israel wanted to be friends with Assyria, because they were fearful of her growing power.

Others thought it best to be friends with Egypt. They thought that they could fight off Assyria with Egypt's help. Then they would not have to pay such high taxes in order to raise tribute.

The prophets of God said that it would do no good to trust either of these powers. They should trust God alone.

The prophets, like Hosea and Isaiah, continued to warn the people of Israel that their nation would perish because of its wrongdoing. They saw Assyria as a nation who would bring God's judgment to pass.

After Menahem died, his son Pekahiah came to the throne. Pekahiah continued his father's friendship with Assyria. "We must pay this tribute," he warned the leaders of Israel.

But many important people did not agree. These people overthrew the government. Pekahiah and his sons were murdered. The leader of the party which was against paying tribute to Assyria was Pekah. Now he became king of Israel.

In Judah, Ahaz, the son of Jotham, became king. Jotham had been loyal to the worship of God, but Ahaz started to worship idols. Many of the people still mixed pagan practices with their worship of God.

Isaiah still preached to the people. He warned them that God was not pleased with them.

King Pekah and Rezin, the king of Syria, thought of a plan to drive the Assyrians back to their own borders.

"We must get Ahaz, the king of Judah, to unite with us," said Pekah. "Then we will all fight Assyria. If we do not, the Assyrians will swallow one nation after another."

"We will send special messengers to Ahaz," King Rezin agreed.

When Ahaz heard the plan he shook his head. "No, I do not believe it will work," he said.

He talked it over with his leaders. They all agreed that Judah would not join this war against Assyria.

Pekah and Rezin were angry. "We will put a man on the throne of Judah who will help us fight Assyria," they decided. They marched against Judah.

The army of Judah suffered a great defeat. Many people were killed. Thousands of others, including women and children, were taken captive and much treasure was lost to the enemy.

The Syrians took their captives to Damascus. The soldiers of Israel took their captives to Samaria. As they were marched into Samaria the captives were hungry and tired.

A prophet of God met the army. "It is wrong to make slaves out of your brothers," he said. "Send back these captives, or God will bring a great punishment on us. He is already angry at Israel for its sins."

Other leaders of the city spoke up. "It is not right to keep these men as slaves. They are our relatives."

The officers of the army agreed to let the captives go. Then the prophet and the leaders gave the captives food and water. They gave some who needed them clothes. Those who were ill from the journey they put on asses.

"We will go with you as far as Jericho," they promised.

The captives were returned, and the leaders who had wanted to spare their brothers went back to Israel.

II Kings 16:1-5; 17:24; II Chronicles 28
Isaiah 7, 8; Hosea 5:13, 14; 7:11-16

92. A Nation Falls

King Ahaz was afraid. "Syria and Israel will come back," he said. "Next time they will completely destroy us."

Ahaz thought of Assyria and its great army. He called in his leaders: "I think we should ask Assyria for protection. Of course we will need to offer them a large gift, but it will be worth it to save our nation from destruction."

The leaders agreed that a message should be sent to King Tiglath-pileser, asking for his help.

Isaiah heard about this plan. God sent him with a message to the king. The prophet found King Ahaz inspecting the city's water supply because he was worried about the defenses of Jerusalem. He wondered how long they could withstand a siege if it came.

Isaiah spoke words of comfort to the king. "God says, 'Do not fear.' In this time of crisis it is important to keep calm and trust in God.

"Syria and Israel are in the last days

of their power. Soon Assyria will destroy them. But do not ask Assyria for help. It is dangerous for us to make a treaty with such a strong pagan nation."

The king was not convinced. He would not change his mind.

Isaiah was greatly disappointed in King Ahaz. This king had no faith in God, and he had little wisdom in government.

"One day," Isaiah spoke out, "God will send a great King to His people. This King will bring God's truth to all."

Isaiah went on to describe this One who would come:

The people who walked in darkness
  have seen a great light.
God has made the nation rejoice.
For a child is born to us,
  a son is given to us.
The government will be upon his
  shoulder.
His name will be called
'Wonderful Counselor, Mighty God,
  Everlasting Father, Prince of Peace."
There will be no end to his government
  of peace.

Isaiah warned the leaders of the people about the danger of alliance with Assyria, but it did no good.

Ahaz sent a message to the king of Assyria. "We are your servants," it said. "Come and rescue us from Syria and Israel." With the letter Ahaz sent the gift.

The Assyrian king agreed. He sent his army into Syria. In exchange for its protection King Tiglath-pileser demanded yearly tribute. This meant that Judah was no longer a free and independent people. The price of protection was high.

King Ahaz was relieved of his worry about Syria and Israel; but he was very much afraid of Assyria and its king. "We must make sure Assyria is our friend," he told his leaders. "We must show our loyalty to this giant power."

In the nations which paid tribute to Assyria, the leaders would take up the worship of the gods of their conquerors. It was proof of their loyalty and friendship. It might mean advancement and power.

One thing Ahaz did to please the king of Assyria was to build an altar like those used in Assyria. He had this altar put in the place of the Altar of Burnt Offerings in front of the Temple. He had God's altar put to one side.

"Offer the sacrifices on this new altar," he commanded the priests.

The prophets and the people who wanted to remain true to the worship of God were very unhappy while Ahaz was king. "Our people should trust in God, not in the favor of Assyria," they said.

Isaiah went away with some of his followers. The prophet taught these followers the truths God had given to him. The messages were written down on scrolls.

"The time will come when the people will be more ready to hear God's truth," said Isaiah. "We must be sure to keep the teachings safe."

As Isaiah had predicted, the Assyrians defeated Syria. They destroyed the city of Damascus and other towns. They killed King Rezin and his noblemen. They took the other leading citizens captive.

King Tiglath-pileser conquered other nations to the north of Israel. Then the Assyrian army invaded Israel. Cities and towns to the north of Samaria fell. Other people were sent to live there to take the place of the captives the Assyrians took away.

Days of plenty such as those they enjoyed under Jeroboam the second were gone forever.

In the city of Samaria, Assyrian leaders helped a man called Hoshea to overthrow the government of Pekah and become king. From then on Samaria was expected to continue its payment of tribute to Assyria.

For some years Hoshea paid faithfully. Then King Tiglath-pileser died. The people who were suffering hardship because of the high taxes wanted to rebel. King Hoshea listened to them.

Spies sent by the new king, Shalmaneser, found out that Hoshea was making a treaty with Egypt against Assyria. Shalmaneser sent the mighty Assyrian army to Samaria.

Samaria was well fortified and stood on the flat top of a high hill. For three years it withstood the Assyrian army.

Under a new king, Sargon, the Assyrians broke down the high, thick walls of the city. They completely destroyed Samaria and took most of the people as captives into Assyria, about a thousand miles away.

The Assyrians sent people of other nations to live in Samaria along with the few Israelites who remained. Samaria became an Assyrian province, and Megiddo to the north became another province. King Sargon put governors of his choice over them.

These people became known as the Samaritans. Some who came from other countries started to worship the Lord God, but they also kept up the worship of their old gods.

This was the end of Israel. Never again was it a nation.

II Kings 16:5-20; 17; 18
II Chronicles 28:16-27
Isaiah 7, 8, 9

93. Hezekiah Calls the People Back to God

After Ahaz's son, Hezekiah, took the throne of Judah there were many changes. This new king let it be known that he trusted in the Lord God of Israel and meant to keep His commandments. He ordered all the idols and other symbols of foreign worship destroyed.

By this religious stand Hezekiah defied Assyria and her power, although he continued to pay the tribute.

Hezekiah told the people. "We must all return to the Lord. For myself I have promised God that I will serve Him faithfully all my days."

Hezekiah wanted the people to make the trip to the Temple to worship rather than to use the local shrines called high places.

These shrines were built on hills outside almost every town and village. Here the people came to worship God whenever they felt the need.

But the shrines were often spoiled by sacred pillars and other pagan symbols. Local priests were there to help; but they did not understand how God ought to be worshiped, or else they accepted the mixing of pagan rites with the worship of God.

Sometimes at these shrines there was a place to worship Baal and an image of this pagan god as well as a place to worship the God of Israel.

Hezekiah set about the work of destroying these shrines. "Come to the Temple and worship," the king told the people. "The priests will make sure you are worshiping God in the right way. We are God's people, and we must worship God alone."

Hezekiah told the priests: "The Temple must be the center of worship, and we must watch that the people worship God in the right way. We must make sure that God is worshiped here in accordance with His law.

"First we must cleanse the Temple of any pagan objects. My father shut up this house. Now go and open it again. Clean out all the dirt. Relight the lamps. Burn incense at the altar within the Temple.

Offer sacrifices to God on the altar in the court."

The priests did this gladly. They repaired the building. They brought out the pagan objects that had been added to the holy things within the sanctuary. They destroyed the Assyrian altar and put the original altar back in its place.

About two weeks later the priests came and told Hezekiah that the Temple was clean and ready. Then the king made preparations to offer a large sacrifice. The choirs of priests and the musicians practiced their songs for this special worship service.

When all was ready many people gathered in the Temple court to worship with the king. The singers and those who played musical instruments stood in their places.

As each offering of the king was presented the trumpets sounded; the choir sang a psalm. All those present bowed their heads. It was good to worship God together in the true way again.

Other people had offerings to bring.

"Now we have consecrated ourselves to God," said the king. "We have all promised to be truly His people."

Soon after this it was time for the Feast of the Passover.

"We will have a great feast this year," Hezekiah announced. "In these troubled days it is good for us to remember that God brought our people out of slavery.

"We will send word to our brothers in Israel, because they are also God's people. They too should keep this feast."

The king sent messengers with letters to the north urging the people who had not been taken captive by the Assyrians to come to Jerusalem to keep the feast.

"O people of Israel," the messenger read from the letter. "Return to the Lord your God. Come and keep the Feast of the Passover with us in Jerusalem. Remember with us how our fathers were delivered in their time of trouble.

"If you come back to the faithful worship of God, God will receive you. Do not be stubborn as your fathers were and refuse to turn from your wrongdoing. Confess your sins and turn from false gods. The Lord is gracious and merciful. He will forgive you."

The messengers went throughout the north. Most of the people who heard the message laughed and jeered.

"Why should we go to Jerusalem?" some laughed. "We can worship right here."

Others said, "God did not help us when the Assyrians came. Now we will worship the idols Assyria worships."

But some were glad to hear the message. "We will come," they promised.

These people from the north joined the many from Judah who traveled to Jerusalem to keep the feast. They thronged the court of the Temple at each worship service. They brought their sacrifices and asked for God's help and forgiveness.

All week the feast was kept as Moses had instructed so long ago. They observed the rule about unleavened bread. They had the special lamb dinner.

There had not been such a fine Passover for many, many years. And those who kept the Feast did not forget when it was over. They continued to make the trip to Jerusalem, bringing offerings and worshiping God in His Temple.

II Kings 18
II Chronicles 29, 30, 31

94. A Prophet from the Farm

After Hezekiah became king, the prophet Isaiah once more spoke to crowds of people. Many of his pupils spoke to the people as well.

Micah was another prophet who preached when Hezekiah was king. He was from a country village in Judah, near the border of the land of the Philistines.

Micah and his neighbors were farmers. They knew from experience how the wealthy men of the cities would buy up land from the poor people, taking advantage of their need. They did not care if the farmers who had to sell their land had no place to live.

When Micah came to Jerusalem he was shocked at all the wrong being done.

All of the people had not returned to the worship of God. Even those who had did not care if they disobeyed God's laws in connection with their business dealings. False measures were often used in trade. All kinds of cheating were common.

Even some of the priests and prophets hesitated to speak out against the sins of the wealthy.

But Micah did not hesitate. "One day God's judgment will come to you," he told them. "You robbed for the land you own. A foreign nation will come and take the land away from you."

The people who lived in Micah's village had seen the invading armies of Assyria march over Gath and Ashdod in the land of the Philistines. They knew what complete disaster the Assyrians had brought to these cities which had rebelled against them. Micah also remembered how Israel had been destroyed.

Some of the people had an angry reply to Micah's criticisms. "Don't preach such things to us. We bring our offerings to the Temple," they said. "We are true to the worship of God. We are God's people. He *has* to help us and deliver us from our enemies."

"But you do not keep God's laws," Micah told them. "The real people of God are those who obey Him in all their actions. It is not enough to be faithful in rituals of worship."

"We are not going to be punished," the people insisted.

Micah preached that judgment would come; but he also held out a hope for the people. "There will be some who will be faithful to God," he said. "These people will be delivered from their enemies. From these people God will bring about a new nation—one that will be faithful to Him."

Then Micah looked off into the future. He knew with sureness—just as though he could see it—that one day God's will would be done on earth.

He said: "Many nations will come and say: 'Let us go to the house of God; that He may teach us His ways, and we may walk in His paths.'

"God's Law will go out from Jerusalem to all people. They will not learn how to fight in war, because there will be no more wars. Nations will learn how to live at peace. They will take their swords and spears and make farming tools out of them. Everyone will live at peace in his own house. Tyrants will no longer make them afraid."

But most of the time Micah talked to the people around him about what they should be doing to please God there and then. He wanted them to show by their actions that they were God's people.

"What does God want us to do?" Micah asked. "Does He demand expensive offerings? Does He want to be worshiped in the way our pagan neighbors worship?

"I will tell you what God wants. God wants us to be just in our dealings with others. He wants us to love kindness. He wants us to walk in humility with Him. He wants us to be willing to learn from Him."

Micah agreed with Isaiah in many things. He too spoke of a coming King who would be a great Ruler of peace. He predicted where this great Ruler would be born in these words:

> You, O Bethlehem,
> who are a small town in Judah,
> from you will come
> the one who is to be Ruler
> in Israel,
> whose origin is from old times,
> from the ancient days.
> He will be like a shepherd
> to His people, and feed them
> in the strength of the Lord.
> They will live in security
> under His rule.
> And the rule of this King
> will last forever.
>
> *Micah*

95. A City Besieged

Hezekiah remained faithful to the worship of God, but trouble came which tested Hezekiah's faith.

The nations who had to pay tribute to Assyria often wanted to rebel and fight for their freedom. Sometimes a nation would rebel, but the soldiers of Assyria soon made them wish they had not.

There was a new king in Assyria. Sennacherib had taken the throne. Some nations under Assyrian rule decided to use this time of change of government to rebel by not paying the tribute.

A group of officials sent by the king of Babylon came to Jerusalem. They asked Hezekiah to unite with them in a fight for freedom. Egypt had already promised its help.

Hezekiah was impressed with their plan. He showed the officials all his treasures to assure them he was able to contribute his share of the expenses.

"Do not trust them," Isaiah warned. "Assyria is strong, and it is useless to try to free ourselves. Assyria is being used to judge our nation.

"The time will come when God's judgment will fall on Assyria too, but for now we must be patient and wait. One day, though, the king of Babylon will take away all you have shown the messengers of Babylon—nothing will be left."

The king and the leaders of the people would not listen. "We want to be free of Assyria," they said. "We can't afford to pay these taxes. This time many nations are banding together. We will be a strong force."

Hezekiah joined the rebellion, but it was not successful. Sennacherib had good control of his kingdom and sent his army to punish these nations.

First the Assyrian army defeated the king of Babylon. Then they moved west into Phoenicia and the land of the Philistines, destroying as they went. When the Assyrians came into Judah they took many cities in the northern hills. The Judeans living there were taken captive to Assyria.

Then Sennacherib continued to march toward Jerusalem. "There is much treasure for us to carry away from this city," he told his men.

King Hezekiah was frantic. His people were terrified, because the Assyrian soldiers were known for their cruel ways. They might all be tortured or killed.

Hezekiah sent a message to Sennacherib while they were fighting at Lachish. "We have done wrong," the message said. "Now tell us what tribute you want, and we will pay it."

The Assyrian king demanded a large tribute. In order to meet the amount Hezekiah had to order the gold leaf to be taken from the Temple doors. In spite of this, Sennacherib sent part of his army under the command of the

Rabshakeh to invade Jerusalem. They planned to march on into Egypt.

Hezekiah heard that the Assyrians were coming. "We must prepare for attack," he told his officials. "We must keep the Assyrians from using water from the spring of Gihon outside the walls of the city. We will need the water ourselves."

The people worked together and dug a tunnel that would bring the water of Gihon through the rock into a large pool called the Pool of Siloam, well within the city. They would be sure to have water, even if they had to stay within the walls for a long time.

The officials made an inspection of the city walls and ordered repairs made. The army commanders instructed the soldiers as to where they should stand on the wall. Even the civilians were told how they could help if fighting began.

Then the king spoke to the people. "Be strong and courageous. Do not fear when you see the Assyrians advance. They have military power, but we have God on our side."

The people took courage. "Our king is right," they said.

Then they heard the approaching army—the horses and the chariots. What a thunder they made!

The soldiers took their positions. The leaders and many of the citizens came out to the top of the city walls.

They saw the coming army racing towards the fast-shut gates. Then the enemy stopped. The leader of the Assyrians stepped forth.

"We will speak with your king," shouted Sennacherib's general.

Instead Hezekiah sent some of his officials. The Rabshakeh said to them: "Here is a message for Hezekiah. The great king of Assyria wants to know why you are preparing for battle? Do you still think Egypt may help you? Egypt has no more power.

"Or do you think your God will help you? Nothing can save your city."

The officials were afraid the people would believe the Rabshakeh and surrender without a fight. "Speak in the language all the officials understand. Do not speak in the language of the people of Jerusalem," they said.

The Rabshakeh laughed. "Why not? It is these people who are going to suffer." Then the Rabshakeh spoke directly to the people.

"Listen to me. Hezekiah cannot win this battle. Do not listen when your king tells you to trust your God. The other nations we defeated thought their gods could help them. They were larger nations than yours. How can the God of Judah help you?

"Now come out and surrender to us. We will treat you kindly. We will take you to a good land where you will live in peace."

But the people stood in silence. They refused to be disloyal. Hezekiah's officials turned from the wall and went to the king. They told him everything the Rabshakeh had said. They came with their clothes torn because now they were very frightened.

The king lost his courage. "I should never have rebelled," he cried. "I should have listened to Isaiah."

"Go to Isaiah," Hezekiah told his officials. "Ask him if God is going to deliver us."

Then Hezekiah went to the Temple to pray for God's help.

When the officials came to the prophet they heard good news. "Tell the king not to be afraid of the Rabshakeh," said

Isaiah. "God will protect the city because He loves Jerusalem, and because Hezekiah has sought to be faithful to Him. The officials of Sennacherib will hear a rumor and go back to their own land."

The next day the Rabshakeh heard that Sennacherib had left Lachish and he hurried back to his king. But the king and the Assyrian army were still at Lachish. While they were there news came of a rebellion in Ethiopia. The Assyrian king considered this more important than fighting for Jerusalem; so they left.

But Sennacherib sent a letter to Hezekiah. He warned him that he would return and conquer Jerusalem.

The letter upset Hezekiah, but his faith was stronger now. He took the letter to the Temple and spread it out before the altar.

Then Hezekiah prayed for God's help. "O God," he said. "You are God of the whole earth. Save us from the Assyrians."

Isaiah the prophet heard about the letter. He sent a message to the king. "The Assyrians only have their power because God permits it," he said. "Do not fear. They will never invade our city."

The Assyrians never did invade Jerusalem. A disease broke out in Sennacherib's army and many men died. The army went back to Assyria.

Years later Sennacherib was murdered by his sons who conspired against their father. Then his son, Esarhaddon, took over the Assyrian throne.

II Kings 18, 19, 20
II Chronicles 32
Isaiah 29, 37

96. Evil Days Return

After Hezekiah's death his son Manasseh ruled. Manasseh was a young boy, and he was influenced by those around him who urged him to restore the old idols.

Manasseh became very interested in pagan worship and in all the religious ideas of the nations round about.

He put up altars to pagan gods in the Temple court. He put an image in the Temple. He believed the worship of God could be combined with pagan worship.

The prophets spoke out against these practices. "God's judgment will come upon you," they said to the king.

Manasseh had many of the Lord's prophets put to death. But some still preached. They warned, "God will bring great judgment to Judah. The people of Judah do more wicked things than the Canaanites who used to live here before we came. God will drive us out of our land as He did them."

Other prophets said, "Remember what happened to Israel because of its sin."

But Manasseh went on with his false worship. He believed in magic, mysterious spells and fortune telling. He introduced the Assyrian practices of worshiping the sun, moon, and stars.

Manasseh knew this would please the Assyrian ruler. The Assyrian king, Esarhaddon, had continued his conquests into Egypt. He now ruled the largest empire that had ever been formed.

Manasseh allowed the people to rebuild all the high places which Hezekiah had destroyed. Once more pagan practices were combined with the worship of God on these hilltops.

Many of the people followed the king in his idol worship and Assyrian beliefs. They forgot all about God and His Law. It seemed as though all the good that Hezekiah had done was destroyed.

Then Manasseh got into trouble. He joined a rebellion against the king of Assyria.

Babylon was one of the most important places over which Assyria ruled. The king of Assyria had put one of his brothers in charge there; but this brother planned to betray the king. He persuaded some of the smaller nations to join him in rebellion.

The king of Assyria found out in time and stopped the rebellion. Because of his part in this, Manasseh was arrested by the Assyrian soldiers. They bound him in chains and brought him to Babylon.

In the Babylonian prison Manasseh had a lot of time to think. "I am in this trouble because I forsook the Lord God of my fathers," he decided. "Could I pray to God now?

"No, He probably would not listen to me after all the wrong I have done. My worship of these other gods was all in vain. Only the Lord is God."

Manasseh was truly sorry for what he had done.

"I will pray to God," he decided. "I do not deserve His help, but I must ask for it. Only God can help me."

So Manasseh prayed. "Please bring me back to Jerusalem again. From now on I will worship only You," he promised God.

God still had plans for His people in Judah. He was not ready to give them up. Besides God could see that Manasseh had really changed.

Before long Manasseh was brought to trial. The king of Assyria was gracious to him. He warned Manasseh against causing further trouble, but then he allowed him to go back to Judah. Manasseh promised that from then on he would faithfully pay the tribute.

When the king went back to Jerusalem he was true to his promise to God. "It is God who brought me back," Manasseh declared. "Now I know for sure that the Lord is God, and I will worship only Him."

Then Manasseh had the idols and the foreign altars he had installed torn down. He put the altar of God back in its place and offered sacrifices there.

He spoke to the people. "Serve the Lord God," he commanded.

But it is not always so easy to influence people in right ways. They had come to believe in these false gods and did not want to give them up. Many people continued their pagan worship.

Amon, Manasseh's son, kept his belief in idols. When he became king on his father's death, Amon brought back idols so that he could worship before them.

But Amon was not king for long. He had enemies at the court who murdered him. The land owners were angry at this and had the murderers put to death. The only one left to sit on the throne of David was little Josiah, a boy of eight.

II Kings 21
II Chronicles 33

97. God Chooses a Prophet

As Josiah grew up he listened to the priests and prophets who were true to the worship of God. The high priest, Hilkiah, was his special teacher.

Even as a child Josiah loved God and wanted to live in His way. But most of the people, including important leaders, still believed in the pagan ways Manasseh had once sponsored.

Assyria had been a strong power, but it was difficult to keep so many conquered people under control. After some two hundred years of rule, the Assyrian empire was beginning to topple.

Under a strong Pharoah, Egypt gained her independence. For some time Babylonia had been growing in strength and finally revolted. With the help of the Medes, the Babylonians completely destroyed Nineveh, the capital of Assyria.

Both Egypt and Babylonia hoped to be new world rulers. The small nations hoped for freedom. In these days of danger, God was looking for men who would faithfully preach His message.

Jeremiah always remembered the day he first realized that God wanted him to become one of His messengers. Although he was still a young man, Jeremiah had been concerned about his nation for a long time. He was distressed to see so many of his people turn from God to pagan worship.

God's call came to Jeremiah. God said, "Jeremiah, I have wanted you to be a messenger for Me since your birth."

At first Jeremiah was not so sure he was the right man for the job. "O Lord God," he said. "I am not good at speaking. Who will listen to me? I am still a young man."

But God said, "You will be a great prophet, Jeremiah. I will send you to many places and to many people with my message. Do not be afraid when you find yourself in trouble. I will deliver you."

It was not an easy thing to be a prophet in these days. Manasseh had put prophets to death. There were still many people in the land who practiced idol-worship.

Even some of the priests and prophets were saying it was all right to worship the Lord God and the gods of their neighbors as well.

Jeremiah knew his message would not be popular. He wondered, "How can I convince these people who are so determined to go in the wrong direction?"

God promised His help. "I will put my words in your mouth," He said. "Tell the people My message as you receive it from Me."

Jeremiah went up and down the streets of Jerusalem. "Hear the word of the Lord," he cried. The people gathered around.

Jeremiah began to preach. "God says, 'Why have you deserted Me? The nations who serve idols have been faithful to their false gods, and yet My people have forgotten the God of their fathers and turned to idols.'

"When trouble comes you will say to these idols, 'Arise, save us,' but they are only gods you made yourself and cannot help.

"Israel and Judah are sisters who have both been unfaithful and given their loyalty to idols, rather than to God. But the way is still open to come back.

"God says, 'If you truly return I will forgive you. I will give you teachers who will be good shepherds of My flock and will feed you with knowledge and understanding.' "

The people listened, but they did not change their ways. Even among the important leaders who ought to have known God's laws, Jeremiah found many turning from God to idols.

Then some important changes began to take place. King Josiah let his people know that he was faithful to the God of Israel and that he wanted them all to come back to God.

"I am going to destroy this false worship that has crept among our people," he announced. "Give up your idols. Worship God here in the Temple in the right way. Worship God alone and try to live by His laws."

II Kings 22:1, 2
II Chronicles 34:1-3
Jeremiah 1, 2, 3

98. A Message from a Long-Lost Book

Josiah carried out his warning. He started a program of reform. He commanded that all the altars to foreign gods be destroyed. His soldiers went throughout Jerusalem and Judah, tearing down altars and breaking idols and sacred pillars.

Josiah also cared about God's people who had been left in the north. He wanted them to come back to the true worship of God.

The king himself journeyed north into the Assyrian provinces of Megiddo and Samaria which had once been Israel. With his soldiers he destroyed all the idols they found.

As part of his reformation Josiah decided that the Temple should be repaired. He wanted it to be an attractive place for the people to worship God in the right way.

One day King Josiah called his official secretary Shaphan to him. "Go to the high priest, Hilkiah, and tell him the Temple must be repaired," Josiah ordered. "Ask him how much money for such work is now on hand."

Shaphan did as the king commanded, and brought back his report.

"Tell Hilkiah to start at once and use this money to hire workmen to repair God's house," the king said.

There was much to do to the Temple. Carpenters, men who worked with stone, and laborers who would dig and carry all worked together. The priests directed the work.

One day a worker came running to Hilkiah with something he had found. It was a scroll.

"Look!" he said breathlessly. "I found a book hidden among some ruins. Is it important?"

The high priest looked over the scroll carefully. "Indeed it is!" he exclaimed. "This is part of God's Law."

Hilkiah read the scroll carefully. When Shaphan came to see that the workers were paid, Hilkiah showed it to him.

"Look," the priest told him. "A worker found this book. It is part of the Law God gave to our fathers through Moses long ago."

"The king must see this," said Shaphan. "I am ready to go and report to the king on the progress of the work. I will take this along."

Shaphan came before King Josiah. "The work on the Temple is going very well," he told the king. "We have the necessary money, and the workers are making good time. The high priest just gave me this scroll. It was found by one of the workers."

Josiah looked with interest at the old manuscript. "What does it say?" he asked. "Read it to me."

Shaphan began to read. As he read his excitement grew. This was an important find. Here was a message from God telling them what to do—how to worship God—what feast days to hold—how to treat others. Many of the important truths it contained had never been heard by the secretary or the king before.

As he listened Josiah grew afraid. "How many of God's laws we have broken," he cried. "No wonder the prophets tell us His judgment is coming. Our fathers have not kept God's Law, and we have not kept it." And he tore his robe in dismay.

The king talked with Hilkiah and the other priests.

"Find out if this is truly God's Law," the king commanded.

The priests took the scroll and left. When they returned they told the king, "It is truly God's Law."

"Will God's judgment come as this Law declares?" King Josiah asked.

To answer this question the priests delivered a special message from the prophetess, Huldah: "God says, 'My judgment will come on Jerusalem.' But God is pleased with you, Josiah, because you have listened to God's Law and determined in your heart to keep it."

The the king made a proclamation. "I want all the leaders of our people gathered together. I want them all to hear these laws of God. Perhaps it is not too late to change."

The leaders came as the king commanded. They gathered in the court of the Temple. Many of the people of Jerusalem came too.

The king stood in front of the entrance to the Temple between the copper pillars and read from the long-lost book. The people listened as Josiah read the laws of God.

Then the king made a promise before God and all the people. "I am going to follow God's Law and worship Him alone. I am going to try with all my heart and soul to live as God wants."

The people responded with the same words. Many of the people meant their promise and lived differently from then on; but some were only pretending.

Josiah meant his promise. He continued his program to destroy any idols he found. He journeyed to Bethel and tore down the ancient altar that King Jeroboam had built. Many people from the north listened to Josiah and came back to the true worship of God.

II Kings 22, 23
II Chronicles 34

99. A Good King Dies

As part of his reformation Josiah destroyed all the high places, the shrines outside the villages and towns.

"Come to the Temple," he said. "God wants all His worship to be centered here."

The prophet, Jeremiah, supported the return to God's Law. He was glad to see pagan images and pillars destroyed. He understood that making the Temple the only place of worship was a good way to be sure the worship was correct.

Jeremiah preached: "Hear the words of God's agreement. Listen to His Law. God warned our ancestors when they came out of Egypt that judgment would come if they disobeyed.

"Our people did disobey. Idols were set up everywhere. But even now God is willing to accept you and forgive you if you come back to God and His Law."

Some of Jeremiah's relatives had been priests at the local places of worship which Josiah closed down. There were too many such priests for them all to serve at the Temple, so many of the local priests were out of a job.

These relatives were angry at Jeremiah

for giving support to Josiah's reformation.

When Jeremiah made a visit to his relatives at Anathoth he heard that his life was in danger.

Then some men of the town came and threatened him. "Give up preaching," they warned. "Stop agreeing with Josiah, or we will kill you."

But Jeremiah would not retract his message. He went back to his home in Jerusalem and continued to preach.

When it came time for the Passover, King Josiah said to the priests: "Make yourselves ready. Do exactly as the Law of God says to make ready for this feast.

"We will urge all the people to come to Jerusalem and worship God at this special time. As my share I will provide a fine sacrificial offering."

Josiah had great hopes for Judah. The people had returned to God and His Law. Assyria had lost its power. Now King Josiah hoped to enlarge his kingdom to include what had been Israel. Then the people of God would be united in one nation again.

But the troubles of Judah and the other small nations were not over. Both Egypt and Babylonia had ambitions to rule an empire.

Because the Egyptian Pharaoh, Necho, thought he could extend his rule, he marched north to challenge the Babylonians. He had to pass through the land that had been Israel.

Necho sent a message to Josiah which said: "I have no quarrel with you. I do not wish to fight you."

But Josiah did not trust Necho, and he did not want the Egyptians to rule what had once been Israel.

"We will fight," he told his army.

Josiah and his army marched north to fight the Egyptians. The battle took place on the plains of Megiddo.

King Josiah disguised himself and took part in the fighting but he was shot by an archer. His servants carried the wounded king back to Jerusalem, where he died.

All the people mourned the death of this good king. Jeremiah made up a lament, a poem of praise for one who has died. He spoke of the king's goodness and expressed the sadness that the people felt now that he was gone. It was a song that was sung for many years among God's people.

The leaders who owned land made a younger son of Josiah, Jehoahaz, king. Because the Egyptians had won the battle of Megiddo they now controlled Judah. They disagreed with this choice, because Jehoahaz was known to hate Egypt.

Jehoahaz was taken off the throne. He was taken as a captive to Egypt and put in prison. There he died.

The Egyptians made his older brother Eliakim king. He was friendly towards Egypt. They changed his name to Jehoiakim.

Now the people of Judah would have to pay yearly tribute to Egypt. Meanwhile the Egyptian army marched forth to meet the Babylonians at Carchemish.

II Kings 23
II Chronicles 35, 36
Jeremiah 7, 11

100. "Death to the Prophet"

King Jehoiakim was not faithful to the worship of God. He did not care about God's Law as his father Josiah had. He allowed idols and other pagan symbols in the Temple. Many people returned to pagan ways.

They said, "We let Josiah destroy the idols, and we promised to obey God, but God did not deliver us from our enemies. Now we serve Egypt."

They had expected God to destroy their enemies and immediately make things easy for them.

The prophets of God were truly discouraged. How quickly these people showed their little faith.

Even those who remained true to the worship of God did not live in the way God wanted. In their dealings with others they continued to lie, cheat, and steal. They took advantage of the poor who could not defend themselves.

Jeremiah went to the Temple with a warning. He stood at the entrance to the court and called to the people as they entered.

"God says: 'Change your ways, and I will let you remain in this city. Give true justice in your courts. Do not oppress the strangers, the orphans, and the widow. Do not worship other gods.' "

Jeremiah said, "You people do all these wrongs, and then you come here to worship God. You say, 'God will protect His Temple. This is the Temple of the Lord God.' Remember the ancient sanctuary at Shiloh in the days of Samuel?

"God destroyed the Tabernacle there because of the sins of the priests and the people. If you continue in doing wrong, God will also destroy this Temple."

Jeremiah thought it was fine that the people journeyed faithfully to the Temple, now that it was the only place of worship. But the people had come to think too much of the Temple. They thought that they could do anything, but that God would still protect the Temple.

Some angry people crowded around Jeremiah. "Do you hear what this man says?" they shouted to one another. "He says God will destroy our glorious Temple. He dares to speak against this place, right here in the court of the Lord."

Many gathered around as Jeremiah continued to preach. Some priests and prophets who did not agree with Jeremiah joined the crowd.

"God is going to destroy Jerusalem and the Temple," Jeremiah said, "unless you repent. God told me to come and warn you so that you will turn around and do what is right."

When Jeremiah finished speaking, the priests told him, "God will never destroy His Temple. You are not giving the true message from God."

"You shall die," shouted some of the people, and they rushed at Jeremiah. They all brought him before the judges.

The priests and prophets who had been at the Temple said, "This man deserves to die because he preached against this city."

But Jeremiah spoke up. "I delivered the message God gave to me. Change your ways, and the judgment which God has spoken against Jerusalem and the Temple will be changed. If you put me to death, you will have killed an innocent man who only brought you God's message."

The judges told the priests: "This man should not be put to death. He should be allowed to speak as God directs him."

One of the judges said, "Remember Micah the prophet? He told the people of his day that God would bring destruction upon the city of Jerusalem; but King Hezekiah did not have him put to death. Instead the king and people repented, and the city was saved."

Jeremiah was set free.

In spite of his narrow escape Jeremiah did not remain silent about God's message of judgment. He continued to preach.

"God says He is going to bring the judgment He has promised, because so far you have not repented," the prophet announced.

Often Jeremiah would hear people whispering about him. Sometimes they would make fun of his message of coming judgment. Some of the people who had been his friends began to avoid him.

One day the prophet became discouraged. He wished God had never made him a prophet. But Jeremiah did not run away from God. Even in his unhappiness he turned to God.

"Lord," he said. "Everyone makes fun of me. No one listens to Your message."

Then Jeremiah thought, "I won't give out God's message. I'll just be quiet."

But this did not work. In his heart Jeremiah knew the message was true. It was like a fire within.

"I must speak," the prophet said. "I must warn them. God has given me this task to do, and I must be faithful."

So once again Jeremiah went out to the people to bring them the unpopular message from God.

II Kings 23:36, 37
II Chronicles 36
Jeremiah 5, 6, 7, 20, 26

101. A Prophet on a Watchtower

King Jehoiakim continued to do much that was evil in God's sight. He had one of God's prophets put to death, because the prophet spoke against him.

Jehoiakim was not good to his people. He insisted on living in luxury no matter how heavy the taxes became. He forced some of the people to work at building fine palaces for himself.

He influenced the people to continue pagan worship. Both the king and the people worshiped idols. In many families little cakes were made and stamped with the image of Ishtar, a goddess worshiped in Assyria and Babylon.

Since coming to the throne, Jehoiakim had paid a large yearly tribute to Necho of Egypt. Then the Egyptians were defeated by the Babylonians at the battle of Carchemish. This was an important battle which determined who would be the next great ruler.

After this the Babylonian prince Nebuchadnezzar marched westward toward Judah and her neighbors. The Babylonians wanted to rule over all the land Assyria had once ruled and more.

The people of Judah were in the middle. Some people, including King Jehoiakim, continued to have faith in the power of Egypt to defeat the Babylonians. Others wanted to declare their loyalty to the Babylonians before they were invaded.

They all knew the Babylonians were as ruthless as the Assyrians had been. Might and power were their gods. It was a time of dread and fear for all people.

Many lost their faith in God, because they were so disappointed. They had thought that after the fall of Assyria they would become a free nation. But now an even stronger power was threatening them.

Even a faithful prophet like Habakkuk felt his faith wavering. Habakkuk was not even sure God heard him when he prayed. "Lord, how long will I cry for help and You will not hear?" he asked.

God had heard Habakkuk and cared about him. He helped Habakkuk to understand what was going on around him.

Habakkuk imagined himself on a high watchtower, looking out over the nations to see what would happen next.

Habakkuk saw much that was wrong. The people of Judah were disobeying God's Laws. The prophet saw the suffering of those who were hurt by the wicked. He looked far into the distance and saw the approaching Babylonian army.

"I can understand that God needs to punish His people," thought Habakkuk. "But the Babylonians are even more wicked than the people of Judah. Why should God use such a nation to punish us? Surely God can do no wrong. He is too righteous to overlook evil no matter where it is found."

God spoke to Habakkuk and helped him to better understand His ways. "Write this message plainly so that all may understand. The answer will come in time. Be patient and wait for Me to bring true judgment to all people.

"Those who are not upright will fail; but the righteous shall live by faith. Idols are nothing, and those who trust in them will be dismayed. But My people should trust in Me.

"One day My glory will be seen through all the earth. The earth will be filled with the knowledge of the Lord as the waters cover the sea."

Habakkuk thought he understood. "God's ways are beyond human understanding," he decided. "We need to have faith in God. We are to live by faith. We should believe in God's wisdom and goodness and be faithful in our worship of Him. Time will make God's purpose plain."

Many prophets of the day preached that all the wishes of the people for a free nation and a time of peace would come true. They said God would do this for them in the near future.

Habakkuk realized that these statements were just wishful hopes. Habakkuk wanted to be able to look at events as they really happened and still have faith in God.

Habakkuk believed that God still cared about them and would help them. He believed that a great day was coming for God's people, but it would not be soon. God's people had many important lessons to learn before they would be ready.

Now Habakkuk was strengthened in his faith. He knew that God had heard him and had given him a message of true hope for the people. God would bring them through all the troubles that would come if they kept their faith in God.

Habakkuk prayed: "O Lord, continue Your work in the world. Though You must judge wickedness, remember also Your great mercy."

Habakkuk wrote a song for the Temple choir to sing, a song of praise and trust in God.

> Even though the fig trees are
> all destroyed, and there is
> neither blossom left nor fruit;
> and though the olive crops all
> fail, and the fields lie barren;
> even if the flocks die in the fields
> and the cattle barns are
> empty,
> Yet I will rejoice in the Lord;
> I will be happy in the God
> of my salvation.

II Kings 24:7
Jeremiah 22, 26, 44, 46
Habakkuk

(Habakkuk 3:17, 18 from *Living Prophecies*,

102. A Book Is Burned

It was important that the messages God had for His people at this time be preserved. One day God spoke to Jeremiah: "Take a scroll and write down all the messages you have given to the people from the days when Josiah was king until now."

Jeremiah called his helper, Baruch, who was a scribe. Ever since he had been arrested in the court, Jeremiah had been forbidden by the priests to come to the Temple. Now the prophet had a plan to get God's message to the people there.

"Take down all that I tell you," Jeremiah said to Baruch. The scribe had the parchment, his pen, and the ink ready. Jeremiah dictated all the words he had preached about God's coming judgment.

"The judgment would mean destruction by the Babylonians," he said.

When the large task was finally done Jeremiah told Baruch. "I am not allowed to go to the Temple, but you can go, Baruch. Go and read from this scroll to the people who have come to worship."

Baruch gathered the scroll together.

"It may be that the people will listen this time and believe God's message," the prophet said hopefully. "It may be that they will turn from the evil they are doing."

Baruch went to the Temple as Jeremiah had directed and read to the people from the scroll. Because a special fast had been proclaimed, many people had come from the city and the surrounding countryside.

While Baruch was reading to them all the words of the scroll, an official of the king was listening. Micaiah was especially interested in what the prophet had to say about the Babylonians. Not all the officials agreed with the king's trust in Egypt.

"The king must hear about this," Micaiah decided and hurried away.

Micaiah went into the palace and spoke to the king's officials who were gathered at a meeting. He told them what Baruch was saying to the people.

The officials sent Jehudi, a scribe, to Baruch. "Come and bring this scroll," he said. "The officials of the king want to hear it."

Baruch followed Jehudi into the presence of these important leaders. He read all the words God had given to Jeremiah.

The message of coming judgment

frightened the officials. "We must tell the king about this," they said.

They asked Baruch, "Did Jeremiah give you these words?"

"I wrote them down exactly as he told me," said Baruch.

The officials said, "You and Jeremiah must go and hide, because the king is going to be angry. We will take this scroll to the king."

When the officials reported to Jehoiakim, the king wanted to hear the message. Jehudi read the scroll to the king.

It was a cold day and a fire was burning in a brazier in the room. Jehudi read and unrolled the scroll as he read.

Jehudi had read several columns when the king demanded the parchment. With a small knife he cut off what had been read and threw it into the fire.

As Jehudi read on, the king again cut off what had been read and threw it into the fire.

This went on until the whole scroll was burned in the brazier. All the prophet's work was destroyed.

Some of the officials tried to stop Jehoiakim, but the king laughed in scorn. "These words do not frighten me," he boasted.

Then Jehoiakim told his most important officials, "Go and find Baruch and Jeremiah. We will put them in prison for speaking against this city."

But the prophet and his scribe could not be found.

In their hiding place Jeremiah and Baruch heard how King Jehoiakim had burned the scroll. God spoke again to the prophet, "Take another scroll. Have Baruch write on it all the words of the first scroll which Jehoiakim burned."

So the work began again. Jeremiah dictated as Baruch wrote it out by hand. The prophet also had other messages to add.

Jeremiah sighed as the work was finished. "God's judgment will come, because God has said so. God is going to use the Babylonians to punish His people."

Jeremiah 36, 45

103. The Babylonians Come

The Babylonians forced the people of Judah to pay tribute. Prince Nebuchadnezzar was a fine general. He had added many small nations to his father's empire. Then the Babylonian king died. The throne went to Nebuchadnezzar. The prince had to leave his conquests and return to Babylon for a while.

As soon as Nebuchadnezzar could, he again led the army westward to invade Egypt. The Egyptian army fought on its border and drove the Babylonians back.

For three years King Jehoiakim had paid tribute to Nebuchadnezzar. But when Egypt won this war, he withheld the yearly tribute.

Nebuchadnezzar could not fight Jehoiakim right away, but in a few years he was ready. He led his army westward and invaded the land of Judah.

Jehoiakim was killed. His son, Jehoiachin, who was a young man, had been on the throne for only a few months when the Babylonians marched through the country and surrounded the walls of Jerusalem. They invaded the city and took away all the treasures of the Temple.

Jehoiachin and his queen mother were taken away as captives to Babylon with many other important leaders of the city. The nobles, the artists and musicians, the military officers were all taken.

It was a great loss to the nation of Judah, but at least Jerusalem and the Temple were still standing.

Nebuchadnezzar made Zedekiah, who was the youngest son of Josiah, king. Zedekiah promised to pay tribute and be loyal to Babylon.

Jeremiah urged the king, the officials, and the people who were left to cooperate with the Babylonians. They had proven themselves to be a strong people, and it was foolish to try for independence from them.

Jeremiah wrote a letter of comfort to those who had been taken captive to Babylon. He told them that though God had used Babylon as a means of punishing His people, God still cared for them and would be with them in the strange land to which they had gone.

The letter went like this:

"Build houses and gardens. Be good citizens of the land and pray God to bless it. The preachers are lying who say you will shortly return. It will not be for many years, but years from now God will bring your children back to this land.

God says, "I have good plans for you. There is hope in the future. When you seek Me with all your heart you will find Me. Then I will gather you from wherever you have been driven and bring you back to Jerusalem."

The best and wisest leaders had gone to Babylon. Some of Zedekiah's officials still urged the king to get Egypt's help and throw off the Babylonian rule.

The Egyptians always encouraged Judah and other smaller nations to rebel. They reasoned that if the Babylonians had trouble here they would leave Egypt alone.

Jeremiah continued to warn the people that they must not rebel. "It is God's judgment," he said, "and you would really be rebelling against God."

Jeremiah's message was not all gloomy. He said that God would bring back some of His people to start a new and better nation which would be true to God. This new nation would bring the knowledge of the true God to the pagan nations round about.

"God says that He will make a new agreement between Himself and the people of Israel," said Jeremiah. "God says, 'My laws will not just be laws written on paper, or even on stone. I will write My laws in men's hearts, so that they believe in Me and love My teachings and show that they are My people by their actions. I will be their God, and forgive their sin.' "

II Kings 24
II Chronicles 36:5-14
Jeremiah 21, 27, 28, 29, 32, 31

104. A Prophet in Prison

King Zedekiah wanted to do what was right, but he was a weak king. He could never quite make up his mind, and he did not have the courage to stand up against the officials who disagreed with him.

A strong military king came to Egypt's throne and promised to fight Babylon. This helped to persuade Zedekiah. He listened to the citizens who complained about the taxes, and he withheld the tribute from Nebuchadnezzar.

So again the army of Nebuchadnezzar marched into Judah and made camp near Jerusalem. But soon after Nebuchadnezzar's forces camped, they heard that the Egyptians were coming. They left Jerusalem in order to go and fight with them.

Many of the people remembered the story of how Jerusalem had been saved in the days of Hezekiah. They wondered if God was going to deliver them again, in spite of what Jeremiah had warned.

The king sent messengers to Jeremiah asking him to pray to God for their deliverance. But Jeremiah repeated the message he had given before.

"God is going to bring judgment on this city. The Babylonians will defeat Egypt. They will come back and destroy our city. You had your chance to repent. Now it is too late."

Because of Jeremiah's preaching like this, many people thought he was a traitor.

Around this time Jeremiah had some business to attend to outside the city, but he was stopped at the gate. The sentry recognized him.

"Where are you going, Jeremiah?" asked the sentry. "Why do you want to leave the city? I know, you are going to desert to the Babylonians. You are really on the side of the enemy. We all know that."

"It is not so," said Jeremiah. "I have some business with relatives in Anathoth. I have a chance to buy some property. I am not a deserter."

But the sentry took Jeremiah to his superiors. They beat Jeremiah and then put him in a dungeon.

King Zedekiah was sorry to hear the news about Jeremiah. He half believed Jeremiah really was from God and told God's truth. So he sent a trusted servant to secretly bring Jeremiah to him in his private rooms.

"Do you have any message from God?" the king asked the prophet.

"Yes," said Jeremiah. "It is the same message. It is God's judgment. You will be delivered into the hands of the Babylonians."

Then Jeremiah asked the king, "Why have you allowed me to be put in prison? What wrong have I done? The prophets who told you the king of Babylon would not come against this city have not been punished, even though you have found their words to be untrue."

The king had to admit that everything Jeremiah had said seemed to be coming true. Many of their people were already captives and many had died.

"Do not send me back to that dungeon," Jeremiah pleaded. "I would soon die there."

The king agreed. "You can stay here under guard in the royal court," he said. "And I will see that you have bread each day as long as we have bread in the city."

The people of the city were beginning to suffer from lack of food. Jeremiah spoke to any he could find, including the soldiers. "Surrender to the Babylonians before you die of starvation or by the sword."

The officials who had imprisoned Jeremiah before came to Zedekiah. "Now see what you have done?" they asked. "This prophet is discouraging the soldiers from fighting. He must be put to death."

The king did not know what to do. "I suppose you are right," he said. "Take Jeremiah away."

The officials took the prophet and put him into a worse place than before. They let Jeremiah down by rope into an empty cistern. When he reached the bottom he sank into the deep mud. Then they took up the ropes and left Jeremiah to die.

Jeremiah 21, 37, 38:1-6

105. A City Destroyed

A close servant to King Zedekiah heard what the officials had done to Jeremiah. He was Ebed-melech, a man from Ethiopia in Africa. "The king must be told," he said. "I am sure he does not want Jeremiah to die at their hands. They mean to leave him there with no food or water."

Ebed-melech hurried to the king and told him what had happened. "Jeremiah will die if he is left there," he said.

Zedekiah did not want to be responsible for Jeremiah's death, but he did not want to free him by royal order. "Take three men with you and find a way to lift Jeremiah out of the cistern," he commanded.

The servant and the three men went back to the king's palace. They found some old clothes and some ropes. "These will do," said Ebed-melech.

Carefully they avoided soldiers on duty. They crept up to the cistern. The prophet looked up and saw his rescuers.

"Put these clothes under your armpits so the ropes won't cut you," Ebed-melech called. They threw down the clothes to Jeremiah and the rope. When the prophet was ready they pulled him up—he was safe.

The king had given Jeremiah instructions to remain in the royal court. Soon he sent for the prophet.

"Tell me what I should do," said Zedekiah.

"If I tell you, you will have me put to death or you will deliver me to the officials again."

"No, I promise to protect you," said the king.

Jeremiah again told him God's message. "Surrender to the Babylonians. Your life will be spared. The lives of the people in the city will be spared. The city itself will be spared. But if you do not, many will die and the city will be burned with fire."

"I am afraid the others who have already deserted will torture me," the king confessed.

"You will not be turned over to them," the prophet assured him.

But Zedekiah could not decide. In the meantime the Babylonian army came back and besieged the city. For two years they tried to break down the city walls.

Many of the people inside died of hunger and disease, besides the many soldiers who died defending the walls.

Finally a break was made in the walls and the enemy rushed into the city. King Zedekiah and many of the soldiers fled out a back way. But the Babylonians saw them leaving and caught them.

The captured king and his men were taken to Nebuchadnezzar who ordered Zedekiah's eyes put out before he was put in prison. Zedekiah's officials who urged the rebellion were killed.

The Babylonian army rushed over the city of Jerusalem. They broke down the walls, burned the king's palace, robbed the homes of the wealthy landowners and set them afire.

All the treasures which had not already been taken from the Temple they carried away. The building was stripped of all of value and then it too was burned. The army left it a heap of ruins.

Many people young and old were killed in the fighting. After the surrender, the rest of the people were herded together and chained. They would have to walk all the way to Babylon, about one thousand miles.

Jeremiah was bound and lined up with many others. Then a captain of the Babylonian guard came to Jeremiah.

"We have had word that you are to go free," he said, "because you urged the people to surrender. You said that it was your God who was bringing judgment on this city, and your word has proven true.

"Now, if you want to come with us to Babylon we will give you a position of honor. But if you do not want to come, it is all right. You are free to go wherever you choose."

The Babylonians had left some of the people to stay in the city, but they had taken all the leaders and all the best of the people. Jeremiah wanted to help these poor ones who had to stay.

"I want to stay here with those of my people who remain," he said to the captain.

"Very well," said the captain. "King Nebuchadnezzar has appointed Gedaliah as governor over all the cities of Judah. Stay with him and you will be safe."

Jeremiah stayed in the ruined city and spoke encouragingly to those who went back to raising crops and repairing their homes.

He urged them to learn from the mistakes of others and to be faithful in their worship of God. It did not matter that the Temple was in ruins. True worship was a matter of the heart.

Jeremiah looked at the desolation all around him. He still believed that a part of God's people would return and that one day it would all be built again.

II Kings 25
II Chronicles 36:17-21
Jeremiah 38:7-28; 39, 52, 30, 31

PART FIVE

A NEW CHANCE FOR GOD'S PEOPLE

God's judgment had come to the northern and southern kingdoms. Their people had been taken away to a strange land; but God had not deserted them. The punishment was a way of bringing them back to God and showing them the important work He still wanted them to do.

The people of Israel who had been taken to Assyria married with the pagan people. Most of them forgot about God and did not stay together.

Some of the people from Judah adopted Babylonian ways and religion and married into Babylonian families. But most of the people of Judah were different.

In Babylon, and in other cities and towns to which they were sent, they stayed together. They met at certain times to worship God. They became known as the Jews.

The Jews discovered that they could worship God and keep their faith alive without a Temple or an altar. Even though the Babylonians worshiped idols, God was here.

The priests began to study God's Law and other writings of the past. They taught the people their past history. They taught them God's Law.

Some priests became scribes. They devoted all their time to collecting and studying these writings. Carefully they kept and made extra copies of the manuscripts.

Because of the instruction and encouragement of the scribes and other priests, the exiles were able to keep themselves from adopting the idol worship of those around them.

Babylon was the capital of a vast empire. A network of irrigating canals made the land good for farming. It was the center for trade, banking, and industry. Fleets of small boats sailed up and down the river Euphrates.

The Jews were not treated unkindly.

Those who had been slaves and servants were still slaves and servants. But those who were educated and skilled were given a chance to use their skills or learn new ones.

Many Jews went into different trades such as weaving, dyeing, or metal-working. They learned banking from the Babylonians and some went into business. Some were given important jobs with the government.

These people were allowed to build their own homes and have servants. Many grew wealthy.

The Babylonian rulers did not forbid them to practice their own religion. As the Jews gathered together on the Sabbath, their priests often spoke to them about Jerusalem. They reminded their congregations that the prophets had said that God would bring His people back to their own land.

The priests did not want the people to forget about Jerusalem. The priests and some others still hoped that one day they could again have their own nation.

The time came when the Jews did have an opportunity to go back to Jerusalem. God gave them a new chance to become a people especially devoted to Him.

Through years of exile the people learned many important lessons, but most important they came to realize that idols were nothing but man-made objects with no power. They turned away from the wrongs of pagan worship.

They also came to realize that God had a purpose for all mankind and that they were a part of this purpose.

106. A Prophet to the Exiles

Babylon, capital city of a great empire, was a strange but beautiful place. The Jews had never seen anything like it. All the buildings were larger and more costly than anything they had known, including the Temple at Jerusalem of which they had been so proud.

The city was built along the banks of the Euphrates River. Its many streets were spread out in even rows. A double wall surrounded all the city—so wide that four chariots could drive abreast on it.

The official buildings were in an enclosed section near the river. Many of these buildings were made of enameled brick with colored figures of bulls and dragons on them.

The north entrance to the city was called the Ishtar Gate, named after the mother-goddess of Babylonia. This gate was blue and gold. Figures of lions and dragons decorated the glazed tile. At night it and the other gates were closed by heavy bronze doors that came across the entrances.

The captives from many countries were marched through the Ishtar Gate and along Procession Street. They passed the palace where plants and trees grew on the roof. These were called the hanging gardens.

They crossed a canal that flowed through the center of the city and came to the high ziggurat temple which could be seen for miles across the flat land.

From here the street turned sharply and went over the sturdy bridge that crossed the river. On festivals the images

of the many Babylonian idols were carried on floats down this wide street.

When God's people had first been brought to this great city, they felt that God had deserted them. But that was not true. God still cared about them and wanted to help them. He called prophets and teachers to remind the exiles of His promises and to teach them His Law. One of the prophets God chose was a priest called Ezekiel.

Ezekiel had been taken captive at the same time King Jehoiakin and other nobles and leaders had been brought to Babylon.

It was five years since Ezekiel and his family had left Jerusalem. Now they were settled in their own house along with many other Jews in the town of Tel-abib near the Chebar canal, a short distance from Babylon. Often the leaders among the Jews of the town would come to Ezekiel's house.

One day Ezekiel received a vision of God's glory. In the vision Ezekiel saw a storm with dark clouds and blinding flashes of fire. There was a fast-moving chariot. On each side were four strange creatures with four different faces and four pairs of wings which were spread out and touched each other. Above the chariot was a platform and a throne surrounded by bright light.

Ezekiel realized that God was with him. He fell on his face in wonder and fright. Then Ezekiel heard a voice calling to him, "Son of man, stand up, and I will speak to you."

Ezekiel stood up and listened. He knew it was God speaking to him.

God told Ezekiel, "I am sending you to the people of Israel, although they have rebelled against Me. Whether they hear or not, they will know that I have sent a prophet to them.

"In the past they have not listened to My messages and that is why they find themselves in a strange land. Do not be afraid of them. Only be sure that you do not rebel against God as they have rebelled."

The vision left Ezekiel, but still he felt that God was very close to him. He went to speak to the other exiles at Tel-abib, but for several days he found himself unable to tell them all that was on his heart.

Then God spoke to Ezekiel. "Your job is to warn the people against disobeying My laws," he said. "If you refuse to warn them and judgment comes, it will be your fault."

So Ezekiel warned the people against breaking God's Law. He told them not to expect a quick return to Jerusalem. Because of the sins of that city, it would be destroyed.

Often Ezekiel acted out the messages he received from God. To tell the people that Jerusalem would fall he took a large clay brick and outlined on it the plan of the city of Jerusalem.

He built a wall around it and put battering rams against it. This was what soldiers used in battle for breaking down a wall. The people watched as Ezekiel acted out his play.

As another sign to the people, Ezekiel allowed himself a small amount of bread and water a day, just as though he were living in a besieged city.

Some of the people complained that they were being punished for the sins of their fathers.

"Not so," said Ezekiel. "You are being punished for your own sin. You have taken part in idol worship. You have broken God's laws. But God does not delight in punishing anyone. Return to Him. Keep His commandments, and He will give you blessing instead of judgment."

The time came when the exiles heard that King Nebuchadnezzar had begun his siege on the city of Jerusalem. As the months rolled by they all feared for their friends and relatives.

Early one morning a man who had escaped from the burning city came to Ezekiel. "Jerusalem has fallen," he told him. Soon the news spread throughout the exiles. The day came when additional captives from Jerusalem arrived in Babylon.

The people no longer believed in a speedy return. They were completely crushed. Many said, "Our nation is finished."

One day Ezekiel found a valley which was full of scattered dry bones. In a vision, Ezekiel saw the bones gather together and stand up, and be covered with flesh. Then they came to life—a big crowd of people. God spoke to Ezekiel through what he saw.

The people were so discouraged they had said, "We are like dry bones. Our hope is gone."

God told Ezekiel that He would bring new life back to the people. With God's power behind them they could become a nation again. Ezekiel delivered this message of hope to the captives.

Ezekiel also spoke out against the false prophets and wicked kings of the past. He compared them to shepherds who were careless with their sheep.

"God Himself will be your Shepherd," said Ezekiel. "He will bring you back to your old land and watch over you as a good shepherd."

Ezekiel often preached about the new day that was coming when God's people would go back and dwell in their own land. He also preached about a future Kingdom of God.

The prophet announced: "God says, 'The nations will know that I am God when I take you back to your own land. Then you will not worship idols. You will be a new people with a new heart and a new spirit. I will give you My Spirit.

"You will be faithful to My laws and walk in My ways. You will live in the land I gave your fathers. You will be My people, and I will be your God.' "

Psalm 137; Ezekiel 1-4; 24:1, 2; 33:21; 37:1-14; 34; 36:22-28

107. Loyal to the Law

Sometimes the captives throughout the Babylonian Empire were given important jobs. As long as they were loyal, the government wanted to use their skills and talents.

King Nebuchadnezzar had a school in which young men trained for positions at the court.

One day King Nebuchadnezzar told his official, Ashpenaz, "See if there are any young men among the captives from Jerusalem who could come to our school and learn our language and our knowledge. They must be handsome, intelligent, healthy, and skillful. We want only the best."

The official had young men from the best Jewish families brought to the school. Young men from other countries joined at the same time. They would all be educated for three years and then brought before the king. From the graduates the best would be chosen to serve at the court.

Four of the Jewish youths were Daniel, Hananiah, Mishael, and Azariah. Once they entered the school they were all given Babylonian names. Daniel's was Belteshazzar. The others were Shadrach, Meshach and Abednego. If at the end of the three years they passed the test they would become Chaldeans, a special group of wise men who could interpret dreams, perform magic, and give advice on many subjects.

The king wanted only the best for these future officials, and he ordered that they be given the same kind of food he ate.

But Daniel, Hananiah, Mishael, and Azariah were distressed when they saw the huge platters of food brought in. It looked good and smelled delicious, but there was a mixture of food in the dishes.

"Some meats which we are not allowed to eat are sure to be included," said Daniel to his Jewish friends. "And it is certain that some of the wine has been dedicated to idols."

Hananiah, Mishael, and Azariah agreed. "We would be disobeying the Law of God if we ate this."

The other Jewish boys did not care. They were not going to be hindered from success just because of some laws they learned way back in Jerusalem, a city that was now destroyed.

"I am not going to eat it," Daniel decided. "I am going to Ashpenaz and explain our laws."

Daniel went to Ashpenaz. "There are certain animals we may not use for food," he told him. "Our priests also teach us not to eat or drink anything which has been dedicated to idols."

Ashpenaz admired Daniel for wanting to do what he thought was right, even when others did not care.

"But I cannot help you," he said. "If you don't eat this food and don't look as healthy as the others, the king will blame me. He might even have me put to death."

Daniel did not want the official to get into trouble, but he did not want to disobey the Jewish law either. Daniel's three friends also decided that they would refuse the food.

Then Daniel had another idea. He talked to the steward who had charge of their particular group. He explained about God's Law of clean and unclean foods.

"Will you test us for ten days?" he asked. "Give us some vegetables to eat. They are sure to be clean to us. And for beverage we will use water."

"That would be a miserable diet," cried the steward. "Don't you want this fine roasted meat?"

"Just test us," said Daniel. "If after ten days we are not as healthy as the others, then decide what to do about us. We will go by your decision."

The steward agreed. He brought over some simply cooked vegetables and a pitcher of water.

At the end of ten days the steward had all the boys over which he had charge stand before him. He was amazed.

He had expected Daniel and his friends to look thin and pale, but instead they were rosy-cheeked and had not lost weight. They seemed more alert and vigorous than those who had enjoyed the rich food and wine.

"Very well," the steward said to Daniel. "You and your friends may continue to have vegetables and water."

Daniel and his friends studied hard. God helped them to learn from the many, many books the Babylonians had collected through the years. To Daniel God gave a special gift of understanding dreams and visions.

The day came when all the boys were tested by the king. Each one was questioned by Nebuchadnezzar himself. Some of the boys did not pass and were sent home. Others did well. But of them all Nebuchadnezzar said the best students were Daniel and his three friends.

"These boys know more than some of the older Chaldeans," Nebuchadnezzar said. "I want them to be among my personal attendants." *Daniel 1*

108. Daniel Is Promoted

Daniel enjoyed his work at the court. It was a beautiful place. Many interesting people with all kinds of skills lived there. The Chaldeans were admired as men who understood strange mysteries, and Daniel was proud to be one of them.

One night King Nebuchadnezzar had a bad dream. He woke up frightened and could not get back to sleep. Yet he could not remember what the dream was about.

The king and his people all thought dreams contained important messages and advice.

In the morning the king summoned all the Chaldeans who usually interpreted his dreams. "I had a terrible dream last night," he said. "I'm sure it was an important one, and I must know its meaning."

The wise men nodded gravely. "Great king, tell us what the dream was about. We will be able to tell you the important message it holds for you."

"I cannot remember," said Nebuchadnezzar. "I want you to tell me the dream and what it means."

"No one can do that," cried the Chaldeans. "We can interpret a dream, any dream, but we cannot tell you the interpretation if you cannot remember the dream. Now think hard, what was the dream about?"

The king became very angry. "Stop stalling for time," he shouted. "You will be put to death, all of you, if you do not tell me the dream. But if you tell me the dream and what it means, you will receive gifts and great honor as a reward."

King Nebuchadnezzar was the kind of king who would very easily give death sentences or very easily give great wealth. He had much power, and everyone was afraid of him.

"We can't do it," the wise men groaned, "and neither can anyone else. Only the gods can do what you ask, and we are human beings."

"All right," said the king. "You and all the other Chaldeans will be put to death.

Nebuchadnezzar sent the officials of his army to round up all the Chaldeans in the court.

A captain of the army came to arrest Daniel and his friends.

"What has happened?" Daniel asked the captain. "Why has the king given such a severe command?"

The captain told him about the dream.

"May I go to the king?" asked Daniel. "I want to try to do as the king has asked."

The captain led Daniel to King Nebuchadnezzar. "May I have a little time?" Daniel asked the king. "Then I will come and tell you what your dream was about."

"You have until tomorrow morning," said Nebuchadnezzar.

Daniel hurried to the house where he and his three friends lived. "We must all pray to God," Daniel told them. "Ask God to show me the dream so that we will not be put to death."

Daniel and his friends did pray. They asked God to have mercy on them. That night Daniel had a vision.

The next morning he hurried to King Nebuchadnezzar. He was sure God had shown him the king's dream.

On the way Daniel thanked God for helping him. "It is God who gives the wisdom to the wise and helps us to understand what is mysterious. Thank You, O God, for answering our prayer."

Daniel went to the captain. "I am ready to see the king now. Do not harm the wise men, because I have the answer the king desires."

The captain brought Daniel in before Nebuchadnezzar. "Are you able to tell me the dream and give me its interpretation?" the king asked Daniel.

Daniel said, "No wise men can show the king what he wants to know; but the God in heaven whom we worship has shown it to me. It is God who has spoken to Nebuchadnezzar in this dream. God has shown you a picture of the future."

Daniel went on to describe the king's dream. "You saw a huge image which frightened you. It was very bright as you looked at it. The head was of gold, the breast and arms were made of silver. The stomach and thighs were of bronze and the legs were of iron. The feet were part iron and part clay.

"In your dream a great rock came out of the mountain and struck the image on its feet. Then the whole image toppled and broke into tiny pieces. A wind blew the pieces away so that no trace remained. But the rock that came out of the mountain grew until it filled the whole earth."

The king grew excited. "Yes, that was it! Now I remember that great image. What does it mean?"

"This is the interpretation that God has told me," said Daniel. "God has allowed you to become king over a great empire and given you power and glory. You are represented by the head of gold. After your empire has gone other kingdoms and rulers will come after you, not as glorious, but perhaps more powerful.

"They will all one day perish. But the rock that came out of the mountain represents the Kingdom of God that will come to earth and last forever."

The king approved of this interpretation. "Your God truly reveals mysteries," he said.

Nebuchadnezzar insisted that Daniel receive gifts for his help. All the wise men were spared, and Daniel was made chief over them. The king wanted Daniel to stay near the court where he could get his advice at all times. He also put Daniel in charge of the province of Babylon.

Daniel asked that his three friends be given important jobs too. The king put them in charge of certain affairs throughout the empire. *Daniel 2*

109. In the Fiery Furnace

Nebuchadnezzar was pleased whenever he thought about his dream. In fact he became quite conceited about it. "I am truly a great ruler," he said. "All the world is mine."

So the king had a great image made—not just with a gold head, but all of gold. He set it up out on the open plain. Then he called all the leaders of the different provinces together to dedicate the image.

A herald of the king announced: "The king's musicians will give a signal, and whenever you hear this signal you must all bow down and worship the king's image. If any of you refuse, you will be cast into the fiery furnace."

The people shuddered. They had heard of this instrument of execution which the king used. At the musical signal given by an orchestra of horns, pipes, and harps all the people bowed before the image.

As the days went by the leaders of the different provinces watched to make sure those who heard the signal bowed and worshiped. They discovered that three other leaders ignored the signal. They were Daniel's three friends.

"Those men never worship any of our gods," the leaders said to one another, "and now they refuse to bow before Nebuchadnezzar's image."

"Good," said some who were jealous of their success. "Now we will have reason to accuse them before the king."

The leaders went before Nebuchadnezzar to speak against Daniel's three friends. They reminded the ruler of his edict.

"O king, you made a law that said everyone must bow before your image. You said anyone who did not bow down at the musical signal would be cast into the fiery furnace."

"That is right," said Nebuchadnezzar.

Then they accused Shadrach, Meshach, and Abednego, using their Babylonian names. "These men do not bow down," they said. "They ignore the word of the king. Neither do they acknowledge any of our gods."

Nebuchadnezzar was angry. These men were good leaders, but they had no right to disobey the king. Besides, it was insulting to him when they refused to worship the idols he worshiped.

Shadrach, Meshach and Abednego were brought before Nebuchadnezzar. The king was calmer now. He wanted to give them another chance.

"Is it true that you do not worship my gods or bow down to the golden image I have set up?" he asked them.

"Yes," they said. "We worship only our own God, and it is against His law to bow before any image."

"I will be lenient with you," said King Nebuchadnezzar. "From now on when you hear the musical signal bow down to my image. That is all you have to do. But if you refuse, you will be cast into the furnace. What god can help you then?"

The three friends did not need time to reconsider. "We have already decided that we will not bow to any image," they

said. "We know our God can deliver us. If we are delivered, we will be happy. But even if we knew that we would not escape death, we would still refuse to bow before the image."

Then Nebuchadnezzar became very angry. He had no more patience with the offenders. "Off with them," he shouted. "They will be put into the furnace at once. Heat it seven times hotter than usual. No one can defy me!"

The three friends were bound and led away, but the furnace was made so hot that the men who were throwing them in fell back dead from the terrible heat.

A little later Nebuchadnezzar was able to look in. He cried out in fear and astonishment. His officials who were there came to see what was the matter.

"Look! Look!" cried the king. "Didn't we cast three men into the furnace? There are four men down there, and they are all unharmed, walking in the fire! The appearance of the fourth is like a son of the gods."

Nebuchadnezzar then went to the door of the furnace and called: "Shadrach! Meshach! Abednego! Servants of the Most High God, come here! Come out of the furnace. You can go free."

The three Jewish youths came out to Nebuchadnezzar. How amazed everyone was to see that they had not been burned. The king examined them closely.

He declared: "God sent His angel to deliver these men because they were willing to give their lives rather than disobey Him. The God these men worship is the most powerful of all gods. I decree that no one in all the empire may speak against the God of Shadrach, Meshach, and Abednego."

Many years later, Nebuchadnezzar himself worshiped God as his own God.

Daniel 3, 4

110. A Message on the Wall

After Nebuchadnezzar's death the empire of Babylon grew weak. There was conspiracy and a change in the royal family.

Meanwhile the Medes and the Persians had grown stronger. The Medes had once helped the Babylonians destroy Nineveh, the capital of Assyria. As a result, the Medes, who at that time controlled Persia, had been given a large part of the old Assyrian Empire.

One night in Babylon King Belshazzar, who shared the throne with his father, Nabonidus, made a great feast. He was as proud and arrogant a king as Nebuchadnezzar had been. The poor were taxed heavily and suffered under his rule. Even the rich had to be constantly on guard. If they offended him, he would order them killed.

At the feast there was much food and wine. Belshazzar called a servant. "We need more vessels for our wine. Bring the vessels of gold and silver which Nebuchadnezzar brought from the temple in Jerusalem."

The sacred vessels were brought in and used. The king, his wives, and his guests drank from them and toasted their idols.

Suddenly a hand appeared and began to write on the wall! The king saw it first. He stared at it in disbelief. Then he shouted in alarm. He grew pale.

"Look, look at the wall!" he cried.

The guests turned. They were terribly frightened as they saw the hand write on. No one knew the meaning of the mysterious message—"Mene, Mene, Tekel, Parsin."

"Bring in the Chaldeans," cried Belshazzar. "They will be able to tell us what it says."

When the Chaldeans of the court came into the banquet room the king told them, "See that message written on the wall? What does it say? What does it mean? The man who can tell me will have great honor. He will be the third most important ruler in the kingdom."

The wise men examined the writing, but none of them could figure out the message.

Then the queen spoke up. "In Nebuchadnezzar's day there was a man called Daniel who had great power to understand mysteries. Why don't you call him?"

Belshazzer ordered his servants, "Find Daniel and bring him here."

Daniel was an old man now. He came before the king and bowed.

"Are you Daniel, the exile from Judah, who I hear can solve mysteries and give interpretations of dreams?"

"Yes," said Daniel.

"I have heard that you have much knowledge. If you can give me the meaning of that message on the wall I will give you great honor. I will put you over one third of the kingdom."

Daniel said, "I do not want your gifts, O King. I know what the message means."

Daniel did not approve of this king, and he knew that God's judgment was soon to come to him.

"O King," said Daniel. "You have heard how great a king Nebuchadnezzar was and how he ruled with great power. All men feared him. But Nebuchadnezzar grew proud. He thought he was a god.

"The God of heaven punished him by bringing sickness and disaster to him. You have learned nothing from this past history. You are as proud as he was.

"Even tonight you brought in the sacred vessels from God's temple for your feast. You toasted idols as you drank from them. You refuse to acknowledge the God who is really Lord of all.

"God sent this handwriting to you. The message is from Him.

Mene—God will soon bring an end to your kingdom.

Tekel—You have been weighed in the balances and found wanting.

Parsin—Your kingdom will be given to the Medes and the Persians."

Belshazzar insisted on giving Daniel the reward he promised, but it meant nothing because that night Belshazzar was murdered. The army of the Medes and the Persians entered the city and took it.

Daniel 5

111. From the Mouth of the Lions

When Darius the Mede ruled the empire he appointed three overseers. Daniel was one of the three.

Daniel did such a good job that Darius decided he should be given even more authority. The other two men became jealous. They talked with others who were jealous of Daniel's authority.

"We must find something wrong with Daniel and report him to the king," they said.

They watched Daniel, but he was a wise man. They could not catch him in a mistake or in doing wrong.

"He has a very different worship," said one. "His God has many strange laws. Maybe we can cause Daniel trouble in this connection."

They talked together and thought up a plan. First they made an appointment with King Darius.

"We have an idea that will bring honor and glory to you, our king," they said. "Give out a proclamation that no one can ask a petition of any man or god except the king for the next thirty days. Anyone who disobeys will be cast into the den of lions."

The king was flattered. He agreed. "I will write out the proclamation," he said.

"Be sure you make it a certain law by signing it according to the Medes and the Persians," said the leaders. "Then it cannot be changed."

The proclamation was made. The enemies of Daniel rejoiced. "Now," they said, "we will see if Daniel stands at his window and prays as he usually does three times a day."

They set up a watch outside Daniel's house. They did not need to wait long. Daniel knew that the document had been proclaimed and signed, but he would not obey this law.

As usual he went to the open window. Looking out in the direction of Jerusalem, he prayed to God.

The watchers waited. Others joined them later in the day. At the proper time Daniel again looked out toward

Jerusalem and lifted up his hands to God.

"Now let us go to the king," they said. "We will soon be rid of Daniel."

The men came before King Darius and reminded him of his edict. "Did you say that no one can petition any man or god except you during these thirty days?" they asked him.

"Yes," said the king. "It has been proclaimed according to the laws of the Medes and the Persians. It cannot be revoked."

Then they made their accusation. "You have made Daniel, the man from Judah, a great figure in your kingdom. Yet he has ignored your edict completely. He prays to his God three times a day."

Then Darius realized that this had been a trick to destroy Daniel. He sent the men away with no definite instructions. "Come back this evening," he said.

All afternoon King Darius tried to think of a way to save Daniel. When the sun went down the leaders came back to the king.

"The laws of the Medes and the Persians cannot be changed," they reminded him.

"Have Daniel brought in," Darius told a servant.

Daniel was brought to court. The leaders watched as guards took him down to the dungeons where the lions were kept in a den.

King Darius went with them. "I am sorry," he told Daniel. "May your God deliver you, because you have been faithful to Him."

Daniel entered the den without protest. A huge stone was put across the entrance, and the king put his seal on it. No one could get Daniel out without breaking the seal.

Darius had heard about the great power of Daniel's God. He hoped that Daniel would be delivered.

That night the king took no food, and he could not sleep. As soon as it was morning he hurried down to the lion's den. The stone was in its place and the seal unbroken.

Fearfully Darius called out: "Daniel! Daniel! Has your God been able to deliver you?"

Then Daniel's voice came from the other side of the rock. "Greetings, O King. Yes, my God has stopped the mouth of the lions. They have not tried to hurt me."

Darius was glad. He called to servants. "Come, I will break the seal, and you can roll back the rock. Daniel is safe inside."

The servants found this hard to believe, but when the entrance was clear Daniel climbed up.

"Now," said the king, "send for those leaders who conspired against Daniel, one of my most faithful servants. They will be cast into the lion's den."

King Darius wrote another decree. He said that all his subjects throughout the empire should acknowledge the God of Daniel. He praised God for His saving power.

Daniel continued to be an important man at the court until the time of Cyrus, the Persian ruler.

During his life Daniel had many visions. Through them God showed Daniel that God would have the victory over all the forces of evil in the world and that one day God's Kingdom would come.

Daniel 6, 7-12

112. A Chance to Return

A new empire began to form. Cyrus, the Persian, led a series of conquests. He conquered the Medes. He won a great battle with the Babylonian army. He was so feared that the city of Babylon surrendered to him without a fight.

Cyrus came to be ruler over the largest empire the world had seen up to that time.

The Babylonian ruler Nabonidus had offended the religious feelings of many of his people. He took some of the idols out of their cities and set them up in Babylon.

Cyrus was a more understanding ruler. He sent the idols back where they belonged. He let all his subjects know that he intended to treat them kindly. He allowed those who wished to return to their former countries to do so.

Through all this God was working to bring His people back to their own land as Jeremiah the prophet had promised.

Cyrus heard that some of the Jews desired to go back to Jerusalem and rebuild their temple to God. King Cyrus announced to the Jewish exiles: "Any of you who wish may return to Jerusalem and rebuild the house of the Lord, the God of Israel.

"You may take with you any presents your friends give you to help in this important work. You can resettle in your old city again."

The Jews were very happy at this news. But when they began to think about the hardships it would involve, many decided not to go.

Some said, "I was born in Babylon. We have our own Jewish community here and are happy."

Others said, "I was too small when I left Jerusalem to remember anything about it. This is our home now."

Some of the older people said, "How we would love to go back; but the journey is too long. We are not strong enough to build homes and plant fields again. We would just be in the way."

But some who could remember the city and some who had never seen it said: "Jerusalem is our real home. We must return and rebuild the Temple. It is only in Jerusalem that we can really worship God and live in the way He wants."

Some people whose families had lived in the northern kingdom of Israel joined the group who decided to return.

Many Jewish families in Babylon had become wealthy. They gave generous presents to the small band who were going to brave the trip. "We will help you all we can," they promised.

Before they left King Cyrus called the leaders together. "Here are the sacred vessels which Nebuchadnezzar took out of the Temple in Jerusalem. Now they are yours to take back to the house of your God."

There were many silver and gold vessels, bowls, dishes, censers. It was a rich treasure. The people were very happy to receive them, but they realized the danger it added to their trip. Bands of robbers roamed the desert ways they would have to pass through.

The main leaders of the group were Sheshbazzar, who had been appointed their governor, and his nephew, Zerubbabel. Sheshbazzar was a son of King Jehoiachin. Some important priests and scribes came with them. The scribes were men whose special duty was to study God's Law and keep safe the sacred writings of the past.

The journey was hard. The people walked, following a caravan route of about nine hundred miles. Animals carried supplies. They needed to use their provisions carefully so that they would last.

It was especially hard on the older people. They all prayed that one day their eyes would rest on the sacred city again.

After months of traveling they were rewarded. Their feet again stood on the ancient soil of their people. But some were disappointed. They had forgotten the destruction that war makes. The walls were broken down, ruins were everywhere, and the site of the Temple was just a scar on the ground.

The people who had stayed in Jerusalem had not tried to repair anything.

"We always heard this was a beautiful place," said some of the young people.

"It was," said the older ones tearfully, "but do not be disappointed. We will make it beautiful again."

The returned exiles set to work at once building houses and planting crops. But they also found time to gather together to worship.

During their time in Babylon they could not offer sacrifices to God as the Law demanded, because the Law called it an "unclean" land.

"Now we must build the Altar of Burnt Offerings," said the priests. "See, here was the courtyard, and this is the spot on which the altar stood."

The people set to work and built an altar to stand on the same spot as the old altar. Then they gathered before it. The priests offered up sacrifices of animals.

From that time on the priests obeyed the Law by offering up sacrifice morning and evening.

The next big task was to rebuild the Temple. Stones could be found nearby, but the cedar wood needed to be imported.

"We have a grant from King Cyrus which gives us permission to buy cedar from Tyre and Sidon," the leaders announced. "We will use some of the money our friends gave for this work to buy cedar and to pay stone masons and carpenters."

The people thanked God that they had this chance to begin again. Even though it was going to be hard, they knew God was with them.

II Chronicles 36:22-23
Ezra 1, 2, 3

113. "Work, for I am With You"

The returned exiles had many problems. They needed to provide food for their families. They needed to work on their houses. They were still under Persian rule and a part of the Empire. They would have to pay taxes and also support their local governor.

Still they started work on the large task of building a house of worship.

The Samaritans and other people who had lived in the surrounding areas during these past years were jealous because of the favor the Jews seemed to enjoy from King Cyrus. They disliked these intruders. They were afraid that if this city grew strong it would threaten them.

Some of these people were Jews who had married other nationalities. Others were children of those who had been brought from pagan nations to live in Israel. Many worshiped God, but they worshiped idols as well.

When the foundation of the Temple was laid, the Jews had a special worship service. The choirs of priests wore their special robes and sang: "Give thanks to the Lord for He is good. His love goes on forever."

The people shouted and praised the Lord. "It will be a beautiful Temple," the young people cried.

But the older people wept. They knew it would never look like the costly, beautiful place King Solomon had built.

Soon after this a group of Samaritans came to Zerubbabel. "We want to help build the Temple," they said. "We want to worship with you. We worship God."

"But you also worship idols," said Zerubbabel and the religious leaders. "Your worship is mixed with pagan practices. It was because of this sin that God judged our fathers. We want to worship God alone and strictly according to the Law of Moses."

"Besides," said another, "King Cyrus gave us this task to do, and we must do it alone."

The Samaritans were angry. "We will make trouble for these people who don't want to have anything to do with us," they said.

They began by making accusations against the Jews, threatening to tell the king that they were rebels building up their city so as to defend themselves.

This frightened the Jews and they hesitated to go on with the project. So for sixteen years work on the Temple was stopped. King Cyrus who had given them the order died. The next king, Cambyses, died soon after he became king.

After Cambyses, a man called Gautama pretended to have the right to the throne, but it was won by Darius.

The nations that formed the Persian Empire spoke of using this time of trouble to become independent. The Jews wondered if this might mean that their freedom was near at hand. But Darius became a strong king, and these wishes did not come true.

Meanwhile the Jews worked to make their houses more comfortable. They forgot about building the Temple, until two prophets from God reminded them.

Soon after Darius came to the throne Haggai spoke out to the people. "You have made your homes warm and comfortable and added luxuries, but the Temple stands in ruins. You have thought of yourself first and God last."

The people had been having a hard time. Besides all their other troubles, there had been a time of drought and the crops had failed.

"This isn't the time to build the house of the Lord," the people cried. "We are poor, and the people around us are unfriendly."

"You are poor because you have forgotten the most important thing, the worship of God," Haggai argued. "God has promised blessing to those who are faithful to Him, but you have not been faithful. You have neglected to build a place to worship Him. You show a lack of love for God."

Zerubbabel, who was now governor, the high priest, Joshua, and all the people listened to Haggai. His message reached their hearts. Within a few weeks they began to work. They cleared the stones away from the ruins. The building began to take shape.

The older people said, "It will look nothing like Solomon's Temple in glory." This discouraged the workers.

Haggai said to them. "Do not be discouraged. The Lord says, 'Work, for I am with you.' "

Haggai assured them that if they worked together and grew to be a strong people, this Temple could become even greater than Solomon's Temple.

The prophet, Zechariah, also spoke to the people. He encouraged them to build. "God is with us," he assured the people.

"God has told me, 'The work Zerubbabel began when he laid the foundations of My house he will finish. Those who despised the small beginning will have reason to rejoice because the work is done.'

"The Lord says, 'It is not by might or power but by My spirit.' "

The prophet told them: "God still loves Jerusalem. He has great plans for this city. Jerusalem will be known as the faithful city. Old men will sit outside thinking about the past. Boys and girls will play in the streets. It will be a city of peace. Other nations will hear about Israel's God and want to worship with us."

So they went on with the work. Then trouble came from another source. The unfriendly neighbors still accused the Jews of plotting rebellion. They spoke against them to any officials of the king they could.

One day the governor over all the empire west of the Euphrates River came with some other officials to the Jewish leaders. "Who gave you permission to build this Temple?" they asked. "We want the names of those who are working on it."

The Jewish leaders told them: "While we were exiles in Babylon King Cyrus gave us permission to return here and rebuild this house to our God. He also gave us the sacred vessels which Nebuchadnezzar had taken from the Temple that used to stand here."

The officials did not stop the work, but they sent a letter to King Darius. They told him about the building the Jews were doing, and the decree of Cyrus.

When Darius received the letter he told his officials who were in charge of documents to look and see if such a decree had been given. The officials looked among all the old records. They found it, and brought a copy of the decree to Darius.

Then Darius wrote to his governor. "I have found the decree of Cyrus bidding the Jews to do this work. Do not hinder them in any way. I am also sending money from my royal treasury to help with this work. Also see that the priests have the necessary animals to keep up the sacrifices at this Temple."

The governor obeyed the king. When the workers heard how Darius had endorsed their work they were overjoyed. In four years the Temple was finished.

It was very much like Solomon's Temple. Inside was a Holy Place and a Most Holy Place, which was empty because the Ark of the Covenant had been lost. Rooms for the priests were on each side. But now there was more than one court in front of it.

At the dedication service the people rejoiced. Once more they had a house of the Lord in which to worship the God who had brought them back to their own land in peace.

Ezra 3, 4, 5, 6;
Haggai; Zechariah 4, 8

114. A Queen for Ahasuerus

Most of the Jews lived in cities, towns, and villages throughout the Persian Empire. In these places many captives from different nations had been brought together. Some of these exiles had grown to be wealthy. Many had a part in the government at the king's court. Sometimes jealousies and hatreds would spring up among the different peoples.

After Darius died, Ahasuerus, known in Persian history as Xerxes, became king over the empire. To celebrate he proclaimed a festival that lasted for six months.

As a conclusion to this celebration he gave a banquet for all his important officials. It was held in the king's winter palace at Susa, north of the Persian Gulf. It was a warm night and they dined in the courtyard.

Around them were curtains of white and blue, the national colors of Persia. They were fastened to their marble pillars by purple linen cords and silver rings.

The guests made themselves comfortable while they ate. They settled back on the gold and silver couches which stood on a floor of a mosaic marble. They drank wine from golden goblets.

Only men were present at the king's banquet, but Queen Vashti was hostess at a banquet for the wives.

Ahasuerus and his guests were having a good time. The king had drank much wine. He was laughing aloud, telling all his friends what a beautiful queen he had.

Then King Ahasuerus commanded his servant: "Bring Queen Vashti here. Tell her to wear her crown and royal robes. I want everyone here to see how beautiful she is."

The servants went to the room where the woman's banquet was being held. They told the queen the king's command. "Come and show his guests your beauty," they said.

The queen did not think this was proper. "No, I will not come," she said. "Tell the king I refuse."

When the servants came back without the queen King Ahasuerus was very embarrassed and angry.

He said very little right then, but soon after the dinner, he called his royal advisors together. These men understood all the laws and traditions of the people.

"According to the law what should be done to Queen Vashti for disobeying me in front of all the important men of the empire?" he asked them.

One of the advisors said, "This matter is very serious. The other women heard the queen refuse to obey the king. No doubt the news is spread all over the empire by now.

"All your nobles and governors will be having trouble with their wives. All the wives in the empire will start disregarding the words of their husbands."

Everyone agreed that something must be done.

The advisor had a suggestion: "If you agree, King Ahasuerus, we will make a royal order saying that Queen Vashti has been expelled. Let the king give her place to another. We will put the decree among the laws of the Medes and the Persians so that it cannot be revoked."

The king and the other advisors agreed. Now they felt sure all women would have more respect for their husbands as the ruler of the house.

The king had the royal order proclaimed throughout the empire in all the different languages of the people.

Some time later King Ahasuerus got over his anger against Vashti, but a law of the Medes and the Persians could not be revoked.

The advisors had another plan. "Send officials throughout the empire who will bring us the most beautiful girls they find. The girls can stay here in the palace under the charge of Hegai. From these girls the king can choose a new queen."

All the beautiful unmarried girls were brought to the court. Some of them were proud and vain; others were sweet and natural.

One of the girls was called Esther. Everyone remarked at her beauty and sweetness. She never put on airs. She tried to be friendly to all. Hegai, who had been put in charge of all the girls, thought she was the best.

Esther's people had been brought as captives from Jerusalem. Her parents had died when she was small. She had been brought up by her cousin, Mordecai. Mordecai adopted Esther and raised her in good ways.

When Esther had been chosen to go to the palace Mordecai had warned her, "Do not tell anyone you are a Jew."

Mordecai worked at the court. He knew that some officials at the court disliked his people. Esther kept her promise.

For a year she stayed in the palace. The girls were given the best of food. They were given beauty treatments with ointments. They learned how to use cosmetics and perfumes.

At the end of the year each girl was to go alone before the king. "You may choose any clothes or jewelry we have," said Hegai. "I know you want to look your best. Unless you impress the king you will not see him again."

When it came Esther's turn she washed and put on a fine dress. "What do you desire in jewelry?" asked Hegai.

"I don't know," said Esther. "You choose what you think the king would like."

Hegai did this. Esther went before the king. Ahasuerus marveled at her loveliness. How like a queen she looked.

The decision was announced. Esther was to be the new queen. The king placed the royal crown on her head. A large banquet was held to celebrate.

In Esther's honor Ahasuerus sent many fine presents to his officials, and as a gift to the people he lowered certain taxes.

Ahasuerus soon grew to love Esther very much. Everyone spoke well of the new queen.

Esther enjoyed her life in the beautiful palace. She loved Ahasuerus and always tried to do what he asked. She had been taught to be humble and obedient.

Sometimes Mordecai had opportunity to talk to Esther. One day Mordecai told Esther some shocking news. "Two officials are seeking to kill the king," he said. Mordecai named the two men. "You must warn the king."

Esther told the king what Mordecai had said.

"We will investigate this," said Ahasuerus.

The king sent officials to spy on these two men. It was discovered that they were indeed planning to assassinate the king. They were arrested and sentenced to be hung.

King Ahasuerus said, "My queen told me that it was Mordecai who told her this. Let it be recorded in our official records that Mordecai saved the life of his king." *Esther 1, 2*

115. A Plot Against the Jews

One day King Ahasuerus made an important announcement. "Haman has been promoted over all my officials," he said. "You must all obey his commands, and when you see him, bow yourselves to the ground."

This made everyone afraid of Haman, and Haman grew proud. One day a servant came to Haman saying, "There is a man who works for the king called Mordecai who never bows when you go by.

"We have urged him to do so day after day, but he refuses. He says he is a Jew, and it is against their religion to bow down before any man as if he were a god."

"Is that right?" cried Haman. "Who is this man that dares to disobey the king and who shows me disrespect? I'll watch the next time I go out at the king's gate and see if he bows down."

The next time Haman passed where Mordecai worked at the palace gate he looked around. Yes, there was one man sitting at his place. All the others had prostrated themselves on the ground.

Haman was very angry. "I'll have my revenge," he shouted later. "I'll not only get rid of Mordecai but all the Jews."

Although Haman's quarrel was with Mordecai alone he plotted against all of Mordecai's people. First of all he went to his Magi friends, the wise men of Persia, and determined the best month for his revenge. Then he went to the king.

"There is a certain group of people in your kingdom who have different laws from anyone else, and they do not keep the laws of the king. If you will, O King, these people should be destroyed. Here is some money to put into the treasury to pay for this work."

The king agreed without further question. He trusted Haman's judgment. "Here is my signet ring," he told Haman. "This will make the decree impossible to revoke. We will destroy all these people. Take the money for yourself as a reward for getting rid of an enemy of the empire."

Haman was pleased that his plan for revenge was going so well. He called royal secretaries and dictated the decree that on a certain date all people should rise against the Jews. Their property and wealth would belong to any who killed them.

The message was copied in the many different languages of the people and messengers carried it throughout the empire.

Many people wondered at the cruelty of these measures. All the Jews were dismayed. They could not understand why the government had suddenly turned against them.

Mordecai, along with many other Jews, started a fast. They tore the upper part of their garments to show their grief, and put on sackcloth and sat in ashes. They prayed that somehow God would deliver them.

Then Mordecai thought about Queen Esther. He went in his clothes of mourning to the gate of the palace. He could not go inside because of his clothes.

Some of the queen's ladies-in-waiting noticed Mordecai at the gate. "Your father sits in mourning clothes at the gate," they told Esther.

Esther was disturbed. "I must find out what has happened," she said. She sent a servant with a robe for Mordecai to put over his clothes so that he could come in, but the servant returned with the robe.

"He refuses to put off his mourning," the servant told Esther.

Then Esther called Hathach, one of her man servants. "Go outside the palace gate and speak to the man in mourning," she said. "Find out why he mourns. He will have a message for me."

The servant obeyed. He spoke to Mordecai and Mordecai told him: "Tell the queen about the edict against the Jews. Here is a copy to show her. Tell her she must speak to the king for us."

Hathach brought back this message. Esther was greatly upset when she read the decree. Her relatives and friends were in great danger; but the queen did not see how she could help.

Esther sent Hathach out again with a message.

"Tell Mordecai that I have not been called to come into the king's presence for thirty days. I cannot enter his court without being called. Anyone who does so is put to death, unless the king holds out his golden scepter. I am afraid to take this chance."

Oriental rulers made sudden and cruel decisions, and Esther had reason to be afraid.

But Mordecai sent back another message. "You might die yourself when the decree is carried out," he said, "and it is certain all your friends and relatives will. Don't you care about us? God must have made you queen just for this purpose. You are the one who must save your people."

Esther thought about this. She was still afraid. "But it is true," she decided. "I must try to save us all. We will fast and pray to God for His help."

She sent another message to Mordecai. "I will go in to the king," she told him. "But I want all the Jews of this city to fast and pray to God for three days. My maids and I will fast also. Then I will go to the king, even though I may be killed."

Esther 3, 4

116. The Man the King Honored

The Jews of the city prayed to God for help. They prayed that Esther would find mercy before King Ahasuerus and that their lives would be spared.

On the third day Esther dressed in her royal robes. She made her way out of her own rooms and came into the king's court. Ahasuerus was sitting on his throne and saw Esther through the entrance to the throne room.

He was surprised. He had been too busy lately to see her. He realized he had missed her. He held out the golden scepter which was in his hand.

Thankfully Esther came into the throne room, touched the scepter, and bowed before the king.

Ahasuerus realized that Esther must have a special request to come in this way. "What is it you desire Queen Esther?" he asked. "I will give you anything you ask."

Esther did not want to state her request then. "If you will be so kind I would like you and Haman to come to a special dinner I have prepared."

"Go bring Haman here," the king commanded. "We will go with the Queen to dinner."

Haman was pleased to be invited. "What a sign of favor!" he said to his family.

Esther made sure they were served a fine meal. After it was over, the king again asked, "What is your request, Esther?"

But Esther lost her courage. "Will you and Haman come again tomorrow for dinner? I will ask my request then."

The king agreed. Haman was delighted. As he left the palace grounds he thought, "What an important person I have become. Even the queen favors me."

Then Haman went out the gate. There was Mordecai. Again this man ignored him and would not bow. Haman was angry, "Even now he is not afraid of me," he sputtered.

At home Haman called in all his friends. He told them how honored he was at the court. He told them about the banquet. "And tomorrow night the queen wants me to come again," he said.

"That is indeed wonderful," said his wife. His friends agreed.

"There is only one thing that destroys my happiness. One man refuses to bow before me, Mordecai, how I hate him."

His friends said, "Then why have him around? The king will do anything for you. Have a gallows made, and tomorrow tell the king that you want Mordecai hung."

"I'll do that," Haman promised.

That night King Ahasuerus could not sleep. Finally he got up and called some servants. "I can't sleep," he said. "Bring out some of the official records. I might as well get some work done."

The king had certain records read to him. One report told how Mordecai had saved the king's life.

"What reward was given to Mordecai?" asked the king.

"Nothing was done for him," the servants said.

"This is terrible," said the king. "He should have been promoted to a place of honor. What shall I do to make up for this mistake?"

Meanwhile Haman had come to the court early. He had already given instructions to workmen to build the gallows, and now he made ready to come before the king.

King Ahasuerus was still trying to decide how to honor Mordecai. Before Haman made his request the king asked him, "What shall be done for the man whom the king wants to honor?"

Haman thought *whom would the king want to honor more than me?* So he said to the king, "Why! such a man should be clothed in royal robes which the king has worn and ride on a horse which the king has ridden. He should be crowned and led through the streets by one of the king's nobles who cries out: 'This is a man whom the king honors.' "

"Fine!" said Ahasuerus. "That is just what we shall do for Mordecai. He saved my life, and so far nothing has been done for him.

"And you, Haman, may be the noble who leads Mordecai through the streets."

Haman was shocked. He had been sure the king was speaking of him. How could he know the king had wanted to honor his enemy? Now he had to show honor to the man he hated.

It was a terrible ordeal for Haman and when it was over he hurried home and told his wife all that had happened. This time his friends and advisors had no words of cheer for him. Then there was a knock at the door.

"We have come to take you to the queen's dinner," servants of the king announced.

"Yes, I shall come right away," said Haman. He went with the servants, but he was not as happy as he had been.

As before Esther provided a good dinner. As before the king asked, "What is your request, Esther?"

But this time Esther was ready. "My request is that you spare my life and the life of my people. It has been ordered that my people, the Jews, be destroyed."

"Who has done this?" cried the king.

The queen pointed to Haman. "This wicked man! Haman hates all the Jews and especially Mordecai who raised me from a young child."

Ahasuerus was so angry that he could not speak. He went out into the garden. When he came back he found Haman begging for his life before Queen Esther.

King Ahasuerus ordered nearby servants to seize Haman. One of the king's servants told Ahasuerus how Haman had planned to hang Mordecai. "He had the gallows built this morning," he said.

"Hang Haman on the same gallows," commanded the king.

After this King Ahasuerus made Mordecai an official second only to himself in the kingdom. Because Haman's decree had been sealed with the king's ring it could not be revoked, but the king gave the Jews permission to arm themselves against any who would attack them.

The Jews were happy to be spared. They were grateful to the queen who had risked her life for them. They were grateful for God's continuing love and deliverance. After this the Jews celebrated this deliverance every year at a special feast day called the Feast of Purim.

Esther 5-9

117. A Scribe Comes to Jerusalem

All was not well with the exiles who had returned to Jerusalem with such high hopes about sixty years before. The Temple had been rebuilt, but the walls of the city, so important for defense, were still in ruins.

More important, the people had lost their love for God. A prophet called Malachi, or "My Messenger," spoke God's message to the people.

"The Lord says, 'I have loved you,'" Malachi preached, "but you doubt God. You say, 'Has God really loved us?'"

Then Malachi turned to the priests. "A son honors his father, and a servant obeys his master; but you priests of the Lord have dishonored God."

The priests demanded: "How have we dishonored God?"

Malachi told them. "I have seen the animals you offer in sacrifice to God. They are the worst animals of the flock or herd—blind ones, lame ones, sick ones. You should give the best to God. And you are glad when the Sabbath is over. God knows that you find the rituals of His worship boring."

Malachi also rebuked the people for the cruel way they treated one another. "Has not one God created us?" he asked. "Do we not have one Father? Then why do we, God's children, hurt one another?

"God says, 'Return to Me and I will return to you.' Bring your gifts to the Temple so that its work can continue. Come to worship at the Temple regularly. Be faithful in keeping God's Law."

Some of the people had remained faithful to God. They spoke often together about God and His love and goodness. They thanked God for bringing them back to their own land.

"God knows these people," said the prophet. "He will not forget those who are faithful to Him. They are God's special possession."

Back in Babylon the Jews heard about the troubles of those who had returned to Palestine. Some of them got together to travel back to Jerusalem and make a new home there. The leader of this group was Ezra, a priest who was a scribe—that is a student of God's law.

Ezra said, "The people in Jerusalem need a good teacher to help them better understand God's Law. It is important that the true faith be kept in Jerusalem. The Temple is there, and there God is with His people in a special way.

Ezra went to King Artaxerxes who followed Xerxes as ruler over the Persian

Empire. He asked permission for this group to go to Jerusalem.

"My people need help in keeping God's Law," Ezra told the king. "The Jewish people here in Babylon keep the laws of our God better than they do."

King Artaxerxes thought it was important that law and order be maintained in Jerusalem. He thought this religious teacher would do a good job. He gave Ezra a letter of authority.

The letter gave Ezra and as many religious leaders and others who wished to return permission to go to Jerusalem. It gave Ezra the power to enforce God's Law and establish correct worship at the Temple. The king also gave Ezra a generous gift of money to help in this work.

King Artaxerxes said, "If you find you need more money there is a certain amount set aside in the royal treasury for you and your people."

Ezra thanked the king. He was very grateful for this help.

Ezra believed God was behind these happy events. "Thanks be to the Lord God of Israel who has put it into the king's heart to be kind to us," he said. "Now I am truly encouraged. God is really with me."

Ezra spoke to leading Jews about going to Jerusalem. He also persuaded singers and musicians to come along. He wanted the rituals of the Temple to be just right.

Other priests and scribes joined the group. More people came with them until there were several thousand in the group.

It was summer and the way was hard. The journey was about nine hundred miles. During the day the sun was too hot. Most of the time the caravan slept during the day and traveled over the deserts by the light of the moon.

There was danger from robbers on the way, but the people prayed that God would protect them. The journey took three and a half months. When they got to the city one of the first things they did was to have a large sacrifice and thank God for bringing them safely to Jerusalem.

Ezra showed the letter from King Artaxerxes to the governor and other Persian officials. They accepted his authority. Then Ezra talked to the Jewish leaders.

One thing upset Ezra. Many of the returned Jews had married women from pagan countries who worshiped idols. Some had married Samaritans who combined worship of God with pagan worship.

"Some of our most important leaders have done this," Ezra was told.

Ezra made a fast. He tore his clothes as a sign of mourning. At the evening worship time Ezra stood up in front of the people and prayed to God for them.

"We have sinned," he said. "We are Your people, but in all our history we have not been faithful to You."

Ezra spoke to the people. "God's Law says we must not marry anyone who does not worship God alone. It is this sin that brought trouble to our fathers. Those who worship idols influence our people to do the same."

Ezra wanted no idol worship in the land. He wanted this new city of Jerusalem and all Judah to be filled with those who wanted to worship God alone and obey His Law.

Malachi
Ezra 7, 8, 9, 10

118. A New Leader for God's People

A few years later another man became concerned about the people in Jerusalem. Nehemiah was an important person at the court of King Artaxerxes. He was with the king at his winter palace in Susa.

One day Nehemiah talked to Hanani and others who had come back from Jerusalem. "How are our brothers in Jerusalem?" Nehemiah asked.

He heard a sad story. The people still found it hard to earn a living. Their neighbors were still unfriendly. "Besides this," said Hanani, "the wall of the city has not been rebuilt."

Nehemiah wept as he heard about the troubles of his people. He prayed to God about it. "Lord God of heaven, we are Your people, and yet we have all sinned and broken Your Law. Be with the people in Jerusalem and help them."

Nehemiah wanted to go to Jerusalem and lead the people in rebuilding the wall so as to make the city safe. He planned to ask the king for permission.

He prayed, "Lord, help me to get the permission of the king."

King Artaxerxes noticed that Nehemiah was very sad. "What is wrong, Nehemiah?" he asked.

"I am worried about my people in Jerusalem," Nehemiah told him. "There is still much rebuilding to be done. The people need a strong leader to help them. The wall and the gates of the city lie in ruins. They have no protection from those who do not like them."

The king asked, "What is your request, Nehemiah?"

"O King, will you send me to the province of Judah? I want to help them to rebuild the city."

"Very well," said the king. "I will appoint you as the new governor."

Nehemiah was very happy. He was willing to leave his position at court and his life of comfort and wealth to help his people in Jerusalem.

"May I have letters to the governors of the provinces through which I must travel?" he asked. "And may I have a letter to Asaph, the man in charge of your forests, asking him to give me timber for the needed work?"

King Artaxerxes agreed to all of this. But he did not want Nehemiah, who was a trustworthy official, to leave his court permanently. "How long will this take?" he asked.

Nehemiah agreed that he would only give this work so many years. Soon all was ready for the long, dangerous trip. Officers of the army went with Nehemiah for protection.

As the new governor of Judah came through the provinces beyond the Euphrates River he handed his letters to the rulers appointed by the Persian king.

Sanballat, the governor of Samaria, and Tobiah, the governor of Ammon, looked with suspicion on Nehemiah. They were jealous that he enjoyed the favor of the king. They did not like the Jews, and they were angry to see an important Jew of the court at Jerusalem.

For a few days Nehemiah said nothing about the building program he planned to start. He noticed that the wall was completely broken down. This he decided was most important.

First he made a careful inspection of what needed to be done. Because the neighboring people were unfriendly, Nehemiah made his inspection by night.

He and a few of his men mounted donkeys and rode about the wall. There by the light of the moon they saw the ruined heap.

Hardly any stones were left on top of each other. In some places it was hard to see where the wall had been. They had to make their way carefully among the fallen stones.

Nehemiah sighed at this destruction. "Look, here is where one of the gates stood," he said at one spot and another. "They were burned with fire."

The next day Nehemiah called the Jewish leaders together.

Nehemiah told them how gracious King Artaxerxes had been. "God has blessed me in what I plan to do; but now we must all work together," he said.

"We are surrounded by enemies, and yet we have no protection. We need to rebuild the wall of our city. Let us start right now."

The people were glad for this new leader. He made them feel that something could be done. With his help they felt sure they could succeed.

"Let us start at once," they said. "We will rebuild the wall."

Nehemiah 1, 2

119. When the People Worked

The high priest and the other leaders all agreed with Nehemiah. They must lose no time in rebuilding the wall. The people started in on the project.

As soon as Sanballat, Tobiah, and Geshem the Arab saw what the Jews were doing they objected.

"What are you doing?" they asked Nehemiah. "Are you setting up the defenses of your city to fight King Artaxerxes?"

"No," said Nehemiah. "The king has given us permission to do this. I have heard how you have made trouble for our people in the past, but our God is with us. He will make our work prosper."

Every day as the workers sweated out in the hot sun these leaders poked fun at the work.

"Do they really think they can build this wall?" they laughed. "No amount of work can make the city what it was. How foolish of them to try."

"It will be such a weak wall," said Tobiah, "that if a fox jumps up on it the stones will all fall down."

So they laughed and jeered, but the people were determined to go on. Workers labored side by side all around the wall. Soon it was up to half its former size.

When their enemies saw that scorn and ridicule did not work they became very angry. They planned to attack the city, but Nehemiah heard about their plans.

"We must set guards about the wall day and night," said the governor.

Some of the people became discouraged. "The men do not have the strength to work at this pace," they said. "We will never be able to fix it in time. Our enemies will come in and fight us."

Nehemiah told some of the men. "Arm yourselves and stand behind the men who are working on the wall. Do not be afraid of these enemies. God will help us."

Sanballat and Tobiah realized that the Jews knew about their plans. They could see that the workers were ready for battle, so they did not attack.

Governor Nehemiah told his people. "From now on half the men will work on the wall while the other half stands behind them ready to fight."

So the workers kept on. Each worker had an armed man behind him. He also had a weapon for himself near at hand. They worked all day until the stars came out in the sky.

The day came when all the open spaces in the wall were closed. Strong and sturdy it stood; but the gates had not been put in place.

The enemies of the Jews were still determined to make trouble. Several times Sanballat and Tobiah asked Nehemiah to come to a conference they had called.

"I have important work to do," Nehemiah told them. "I cannot leave Jerusalem now."

Then Sanballat wrote a message to all the people. It was composed in the form of a letter to Nehemiah.

The letter said: "We have heard a report that you intend to build this wall as a defense against our rulers. You intend to rebel and become king. We will send this report on to King Artaxerxes unless you come and talk with us."

But Nehemiah did not trust these men. He would not leave the city until the wall was done. He sent a message to Sanballat saying: "We are not guilty of rebellion. You are making up this story."

"They only want to frighten us," Nehemiah told his leaders. "They want us to stop this work."

Nehemiah asked God for wisdom, guidance, and patience to go on. "Strengthen my hands, O God," he prayed.

Then Nehemiah found an enemy within his own people. One of the priests, Shemaiah, said to him: "Your life is in danger. This night they will come to kill you. Meet me in the sanctuary of the Temple, and we will hide there."

"But only the priests may go into the sanctuary," Nehemiah protested.

Then he thought, "Shemaiah knows this. He is trying to trick me. Sanballat and Tobiah must have hired him to betray me."

"No," said Nehemiah to the priest. "I will not hide or run away. I am going to see to it that the defenses of Jerusalem are strong."

Nehemiah kept his promise. When all the gates were in place, Nehemiah posted guards at them. He gave orders that the gates would be shut and barred as soon as sunset came. They would not be opened in the morning until the sun was hot. In this way no enemies could come into the city while some people were still asleep.

Jerusalem had once held many, many homes. By comparison the city was now half empty. Some of the Jews who had helped rebuild the wall lived outside the city. In time of danger they could now come within the city and be protected.

A service was held to dedicate the wall to God and thank Him for His help. There were two processions. One was led by Ezra, the scribe. The other was led by Nehemiah.

All the priests and Temple singers took part. All kinds of musical instruments helped them sing their praise to God as the processions marched one to the left, the other to the right, around the wall. They met at the same time in the court of the Temple.

The people sang and shouted and their joy was heard outside the city. The enemies had to admit that the work had been done in spite of their trouble-making and that God was with His people.

Nehemiah 4, 6, 7

120. An Agreement Is Renewed

Nehemiah and the religious leaders realized how important it was to know and keep God's Law.

They no longer had a king. Most of the land God had given to their ancestors so long ago was out of their control. From their own small portion they had to give part of the produce of the land to their foreign rulers.

But they were still God's people. God and His Law was all they had left which was really theirs.

A special day was announced for the reading of all of God's Law. The people crowded together in a large square before the Water Gate, near the spring of Gihon.

Ezra had been chosen to read. He stood at a wooden pulpit made especially for the purpose. Every so often he would stop and one of the other priests who were with him on the platform would explain what had been read. Ezra read from early in the morning until noon.

As the people heard God's Law they began to cry. They had not realized how many of God's laws they had broken. By the time Ezra finished, all the people were crying.

Nehemiah, Ezra, and the priests all said: "This is a day which is holy to God. Do not weep. God knows you are sorry for your sins. Now go and do better in the future.

"Begin now by having a fine feast. Rejoice that we again have a city of our own and that God is still with us. Rejoice that we have His Law which will show us how to live in God's way."

The people were cheered. They began to leave. The leaders said: "As you enjoy your feast, remember that some of our people are poor. Share with them. Send some of your dishes to them."

The people did this. They prepared fine meals, but they did not eat all the food themselves. They sent out gifts of fruit and cheese and dishes of cooked meat and vegetables. Everyone had enough.

In their study of the Law, the leaders found that it was time to celebrate the Feast of Booths. At this feast they remembered how their ancestors had lived in tents on the wilderness journey to Canaan.

The people made ready to celebrate. The booths they made were light shelters of branches and leaves. They constructed them on the flat roofs of their houses and slept up there under the stars.

Some of the children helped to make the booths attractive by hanging flowers and bunches of fruit around the opening of the booth.

Some people who had larger houses put the booth in their courtyard. There was a booth in the courtyard of the Temple, one in the square by the Water Gate, and one in the square by another gate.

For seven days they lived in the booths instead of their houses. Each day Ezra read from the Law. On the eighth day there was a special worship service. It was a festival of joy, and the people were happy.

But worship was not only rejoicing. The time came to confess sins to God. The priests called the people together and urged them to confess their sins to God and ask for His forgiveness. The people fasted and wore clothes of mourning.

Ezra stood up and prayed for the people. In his prayer he mentioned how God had cared for His people in the past. He thanked God for calling Abraham out of Ur of the Chaldees; for delivering them from Egypt; for helping them through the wilderness and giving them a land of their own.

He confessed that their nation had sinned greatly against God. He acknowledged that they deserved the punishment that had come. He thanked God for the prophets who had tried to warn them. He asked for forgiveness for not listening to them.

"You have been faithful, O God," Ezra prayed; "but we have been unfaithful. Yet You have not forsaken us. Now we want to renew the agreement our fathers had with You. We again want to promise to keep Your Law."

The priests and people made this promise. They remembered how long ago God had promised to be their God. He had promised blessing if they kept His Law.

"From now on," the people said, "we will truly keep God's Law. We will not worship idols or marry idol-worshipers. We will keep the Sabbath. We will keep the feasts of God. We will faithfully bring our offerings to the Temple."

The people kept this promise. They worshiped God alone. They taught His Law to their children. They walked in God's way.

Nehemiah 8, 9

121. What Happened Next

In the years that followed the return from exile the Jews began to build synagogues. Every village with as many as ten families had a synagogue.

The Temple was still the main place of worship. It was only at the Temple that they could offer sacrifice; but every Sabbath the people gathered to worship God in their synagogue.

Many Jews were scattered throughout other lands, but they still thought of themselves as Jews. These Jews also built synagogues in which they could gather. They formed communities of their own within the town or village in which they stayed.

God's people had come to realize that they could be true to God's Law and worship Him anywhere. These Jews kept their faith alive and practiced keeping the Law. When they could, they traveled to Jerusalem to keep a feast. They contributed money to keep up the Temple.

In this way more and more people heard about the One God. Some even became converts to the Jewish faith and traveled with them to Jerusalem to worship at the Temple.

After some two hundred years the Persian Empire began to weaken. During all this time the Jews living in Jerusalem and the surrounding area of Judah had been in a Persian province under Persian rule.

The story the Bible tells us in the Old Testament leaves the Jews under Persian rule. But we can learn what happened to them from Jewish books of history written during the next several hundred years, and from other historical records. After the fall of Persia, the Jews did not become independent. Another conqueror was leading armies to great victories.

Up to this time, all the great rulers had been from Asia. This new conqueror, Alexander the Great, was from Europe. He was only a young man when he conquered all of the Persian Empire and more. His Greek Empire became the largest the world had known.

Many of the Greek people were well educated. They had many books and teachers. They made beautiful sculpture and composed beautiful music and poetry. The people in all the lands they conquered copied Greek ways.

Even the Jews spoke Greek, read the Greek books and dressed as the Greeks. They attended the Greek athletic games. The time came when many Jews throughout the different lands in which they lived no longer understood the Hebrew language. So the Scriptures were translated into Greek.

Some of the Jews did not like this adopting of Greek ways, and gradually a party was formed to oppose Greek influences.

After the death of Alexander the Great, his generals divided the Empire between them. For many years the Jews were ruled by the same general who ruled Egypt. Then the Greek rulers of Syria took land away from Egypt and the Jews were ruled by them.

For a while it was pretty much the same. Taxes were high no matter who the ruler was. Then Antiochus Epiphanes took the throne of Syria. This meant that he also ruled over Judea, as it was now called.

Up to this time the Jews had been allowed to keep their own worship, but this ruler decided that they must worship the Greek gods.

The Jewish religion was outlawed. The Jews were told to bow before the Greek idols. A man could be put to death for observing the Sabbath or for possessing a copy of God's Law.

Antiochus Epiphanes took a pig, an unclean animal to the Jews, and put it on the sacred Altar of Burnt Offerings, sacrificing it to his pagan god. This made the entire Temple unclean and not fit for worship.

Altars to Greek gods were built throughout the land. When some Jews refused to worship idols they were put to death. Some went into the hills to hide.

There was one old priest called Mattathias who refused to sacrifice to the pagan gods. He killed the officer who tried to force him to do so. Then he and his sons escaped to the hills. One son, Judas Maccabee, became the leader in a rebellion against the Greeks.

Although his army was small, Judas Maccabee led them to victory and drove the Syrians and Greeks out of Jerusalem.

They were helped by the fact that Antiochus Epiphanes had taken most of the army east. When this ruler heard about the rebellion he marched home, but he died on the way.

The Temple was made clean. It was rededicated to God and could be worshiped in again. The people rejoiced and celebrated. They remembered the event ever after in the Feast of Dedication or Hanukkah.

Two brothers of Judas, Jonathan and then Simon, led the Jewish people until they won independence. They found favor with the Romans who were enemies of Syria.

When John Hyrcanus, the son of Simon, became ruler he strengthened the army by hiring soldiers from other nations. He made war on Samaria and destroyed its temple. He won wars with Idumaea and Galilee. Idumaea had once been Edom. Galilee was north of Samaria and had once been part of the northern kingdom of Israel. Some Jews returning from exile had settled there.

Syria tried to stop Simon, but that

nation had grown weaker and failed. Simon's sons continued his conquests into land on the other side of the Jordan.

For about one hundred years the Jews had the independence they had wanted for so long; but they were disappointed in their own rulers. The people did not want war. Some of the religious people, called the Pharisees, were dissatisfied with the religious views and the conduct of the family of John Hyracanus and other government officials.

Then trouble broke out in the royal family. Two grandsons of John Hyrcanus, Aristobulus and Hyrcanus, fought over the right to rule. They both promised tribute to the Roman General Pompey in exchange for military help in order to get the throne.

Rome had become a growing power in the world. General Pompey had just conquered Syria. He saw the opportunity to extend Roman control over more land and people, and he marched the Roman soldiers into Jerusalem. There the Roman general heard the case of each brother. As a result he decided that Rome should occupy and rule the country of Judea. The Roman soldiers quickly put down the resistance of the people.

Pompey allowed Hyrcanus to be high priest. He took his brother, Aristobulus, as a captive to Rome. From then on Rome was their ruler. Some time later, Antipater of Idumaea, who had helped to start the quarrel between the brothers, was appointed by Rome to be governor of Judea.

During all this time there were no prophets speaking God's word to the Jews. But a number of men wrote books to encourage their people. Gradually during these years a great hope sprang up for a deliverer, a king, the Messiah whom the ancient prophets had promised would come.

122. "Let Us Go to the House of the Lord"

When religious festivals came around, boys and girls who lived far away from Jerusalem eagerly looked forward to making a trip to the Temple. They liked traveling with other families and camping out overnight. The mothers and fathers enjoyed meeting old friends and relatives as other groups joined their caravan.

But it was a difficult, dangerous journey, and as they rode or walked the many miles they sang. One of the psalms they sang expressed their great joy at the thought that soon they would be at the Temple, the house of the Lord.

It went like this:

I was glad when they said to me,
"Let us go to the house of the Lord."
Our feet shall stand within your gates
O Jerusalem.

They sang of the walled city they were soon to see, the city where so much of their history had taken place. Jerusalem would be crowded with many pilgrims because of the feast. It would be exciting to be a part of it again.

The song went on to tell how they loved this city in which the Temple stood and how they prayed for its good.

Pray for the peace of Jerusalem.
Those who love you shall prosper.
Peace be within your walls.
Peace be with you.

When the travelers reached the city they stayed with relatives or friends. Or they had to pay to stay at an inn.

When it came time for the worship services, some families joined a procession to the Temple. During this walk to the Temple they sang. Some carried musical instruments, lyres and trumpets.

One procession began on a hill west of the Temple. From here they looked down on the gold-covered Temple and the other buildings within the court. This hill was higher than Mt. Moriah where the Temple stood.

One song they sang went:

How lovely are Your buildings
O Lord of hosts!
I long for the courts of the Lord.

The pilgrims traveled down the hill and through a valley. They passed the Pool of Siloam. Then they climbed up the hill on which the Temple stood, still singing. Sometimes birds made their nests within the Temple walls. Officials of the Temple lived in special buildings within the court. The song called them happy to always be in God's house.

The sparrow has found a house,
The swallow a nest for herself,
Where she may lay her young,
At Your Altar, O Lord of hosts.
Blessed are those who dwell in
Your house.
A day in Your courts is better than
a thousand elsewhere.

The psalm also praised God for His power and help. Then it closed by saying:

No good thing will He withhold
From those who walk in right ways.
O Lord of hosts,
Blessed is the man who trusts
in You.

At last the mothers, fathers, and boys and girls entered through a gate to the Temple court. It was a sacred place to them.

Within the court they stood with others of God's people. They sang praises to Him and prayed for His help. They brought their offerings and sacrifices to God.

There was much singing in the Temple worship. There were special Temple musicians and white-robed choirs of priests.

When the thank offering was presented a special psalm was used. It said that God was over all the earth, its Creator and Ruler.

Sing a joyful song to the Lord, all
the lands.
Serve the Lord with gladness.
Come before His presence with singing.
The Lord is God.
He made us.
We did not make ourselves.
We are His people, the sheep of His
pasture.
Enter His gates with thanksgiving.
Come into His courts with praise.
Be thankful to Him,
Bless His name.
For the Lord is good.
His mercy is everlasting.
His truth goes on forever.

Psalms 122, 84, 100

123. "Give Thanks to the Lord"

God's people did not only use the psalms in their Temple worship. They often quoted from them when they were home with their families.

They believed God was maker of heaven and earth, the sea and the land. They loved the world and its many different beauties. The psalms expressed their thanks to God for the world He made.

Most of the people lived in small one-roomed houses. The oven for baking was outside. The mother ground the grain outside. Often at night they climbed the stairs that led to the roof and sat out under the stars.

Sometimes the father would quote from the psalm that says:

The heavens tell the glory of God.
The stars are His handiwork.

Or he would recite these lines from another psalm that tells how God cares for His world:

He covers the sky with clouds.
He sends rain to the earth.
He makes the grass grow on the hills.
He supplies food for the wild animals.
He feeds the birds.

Few people were wealthy enough to own scrolls. But they had heard the Scriptures read over and over in the Temple and Synagogue and recited by their own parents. The words were in their minds.

Outside in the fields or on a journey they would pause to eat lunch. Then they would remember this psalm which thanks God for the world He made.

O give thanks to the Lord,
for He is good.
His love continues forever.
O give thanks to the Lord of lords,
To the One who does great wonders,
To the One who by His knowledge
made the heavens,
Who spread out the earth,
Who made the great lights,
The sun which rules over the day,
The moon and the stars which
rule over the night;
The One who gives food to all,
For His love continues forever.

Sometimes the world around them was not friendly. There would be an earthquake or a flood, or the crops would fail because of lack of rain. In times of trouble the people would remember psalms written by men who had known trouble and found help in God.

God is our refuge and strength,
Our help in time of trouble.
We will not fear though the earth
changes
And the mountains shake,
Though the waters roar and foam.

Troubles came from other sources. God's people often were in wars, or they had cruel rulers of their own or from foreign lands, or were oppressed by the wealthy.

People could pray to God in the words of psalms:

Defend my cause, O God.
Deliver me from deceitful and
unjust men,
For You are the God in whom
I take refuge.
Send out Your light and truth
to lead me.
Bring me to Yourself, for God
is my joy.
Why am I unhappy?
I shall hope for God's deliverance.
One day I shall praise God for
His help.

Sometimes these prayers for help turned into joyful psalms of thanksgiving:

I love the Lord because He heard
my prayer.
Therefore I will call on God as
long as I live.
I was distressed and in anguish,
Then I called on God;
"O Lord, save my life."
The Lord is gracious and merciful.
When I was in trouble He saved
me.

People then, as now, sometimes had to pray for forgiveness. One psalm writer told about his own experience:

Blessed is the man whose sin is
forgiven.
I confessed my sin to You, and no
longer hid my wrongdoing.
I said, "I will confess my sin to
the Lord."
Then You forgave me.
Be glad in the Lord and rejoice,
Shout for joy all you who love
God.

People always have needed God's help in order to live in God's way. Sometimes they prayed in these words from a psalm:

Teach me Your way, O Lord
that I may walk in Your truth.
I give thanks to You, O Lord
my God, with all my heart;
I will praise Your name forever,
For great is Your continuing love
to me.

Psalms 19, 147, 136, 46, 43, 116, 32, 86

124. "Remember Your Creator"

Every Sabbath the Jews would gather in their synagogues. They would listen to the reading of the Scriptures. They would sing psalms and pray.

But during the week the synagogue was not empty. It was used as a school. Only boys came to this school.

Every Jewish boy started when he was six years old and continued until he was thirteen. At the school he learned how to read and write. He also learned some arithmetic and music.

But most of his time was spent learning from the Scriptures. The Rabbis, as the teachers were called, were learned in the Law and the religious teachings of the fathers.

The boys would sit around the rabbi. Over and over they would hear God's laws until they were memorized. They memorized psalms and other portions of Scripture.

The boys soon learned that the keeping of God's Law was a very serious thing. They knew about the history of their people. They heard the stories about Abraham, Moses, Samuel, King David and the other kings and prophets. They knew that trouble had come to their people when God's Law had not been obeyed.

The girls stayed at home. They learned about keeping house from their mothers. The mother would tell them the stories of the past, and they would memorize parts of Scripture.

Sometimes at the synagogue the rabbi would quote from the proverbs of Solomon.

The fear of the Lord is the beginning of knowledge;
Only fools refuse instruction.

My son, do not forget my teaching.
Keep my commandments.
Be loyal and faithful.
Then you will find favor with God and man.

Trust in the Lord with all your heart
Do not depend on your own knowledge.
Trust in God and He will make it plain what you should do.

Do not be discouraged at God's discipline.
It is because God loves you that He wants you to walk in right ways.

Happy is the man who finds wisdom and understanding.
Wisdom is better than silver, gold or jewels.

With words such as these the rabbis helped the boys to grow up to be men who lived good lives.

The rabbi might read to them from Proverbs about seven things which God hates:

(1) haughty eyes;
(2) a lying tongue;
(3) hands that shed innocent blood;
(4) a heart that plans wicked deeds;
(5) feet that run to do evil;
(6) a false witness who lies;
(7) a man who starts quarrels among brothers.

Some proverbs seemed especially for children:

A wise son makes his father glad,
But a foolish son makes his mother sad.

A friend loves at all times.

Even a child makes himself known by his acts,
Whether he does what is pure and right.

Sometimes it was hard to study and memorize, especially in the springtime when all the flowers had bloomed on the hills. Spring came after months and months of rain. Suddenly the bright colored blooms were everywhere, but they would only last a few weeks.

The boys and girls liked to climb the hills, jump over the brooks, and sit for a while under the shade of a tree. Then they might remember part of a poem called the Song of Solomon:

The winter is past,
The rain is over and gone.
The flowers appear on the earth,
The time of singing has come,
The voice of the turtledove
Is heard in the land.
The fig tree puts forth its figs,
The vines are in blossom;
They give forth fragrance.

Back home again, sitting with their family in their one-roomed house, it would gradually grow dark. The oil lamp would be lit. Then the parents would have more sober words to recite from the Scriptures such as these from Ecclesiastes:

Remember your Creator in the days of your youth.
Fear God, and keep His commandments; for this is man's whole duty.

Proverbs 1, 3, 6, 10:1, 17:17, 20:11
Song of Solomon 2
Ecclesiastes 12

125. A Man Who Kept His Faith

There is a story which was told among God's people over and over for many generations. It was about a man called Job who lived in ancient times.

Job lived in the land of Uz, near Edom. He was known as a righteous man, one who loved God and who always found ways to be good to other people.

Job had a wife and seven sons and three daughters, all grown up. He was a rich man who had many flocks and herds.

God was pleased with Job. But Satan said, "Job does not serve God for nothing. He only loves God because of all the good things God has given him."

Then all on one day great trouble came to Job. A messenger brought him the first bad news. "I was with your other servants plowing out in the field. Arabians came and captured the oxen and asses. They killed all the others."

Another escaped servant came and cried, "There was terrible lightning from heaven. It destroyed the sheep and the servants who were caring for them."

Another servant had a story to tell. "Raiders have captured all our camels," he said. "They killed the servants who tried to stop them."

This was a terrible loss of servants and property to Job. He could no longer be called a rich man. But a worse tragedy was yet to come.

Job's sons and daughters were all having dinner in the home of the eldest son. While they were there a windstorm came and struck the house, and all of them were killed.

A servant came and told Job what had happened.

Job tore his robe to show mourning. He was greatly grieved; but he did not blame God.

"My possessions and my dear family were all gifts from God," said Job. "The Lord gave and the Lord took away. Blessed is the name of the Lord."

Some time passed. Job and his wife were sad because of their loss. Then Job became very ill. His skin broke out in boils.

Now Job was really discouraged. The boils would not go away. He sat down among the ashes of former campfires to rest and think.

Job's wife despaired and lost her faith in God. "Why don't you curse God?" she asked. "Why do you still believe God is good? Look what He has done to you."

But Job shook his head. "Do not be foolish," he said. "For many years I enjoyed health and many good things. These were gifts from God. Now I have trouble. It would not be right to love God only when everything goes well with me."

After this three friends came to visit Job. When they were some distance away they saw a man sitting among the ashes.

"That can't be Job," they said. They did not recognize him because he was so ill.

When they came up to Job they were so shocked and felt so sorry for him that for a long while they could not speak.

Then Job began to speak of his unhappiness. "I wish I had not been born," he admitted. "So much sorrow has come to me, and now I suffer pain."

Then the friends spoke up. All three of them agreed. "Job," they said, "you are suffering because you have done some wicked deed. Confess your guilt to God. Then He will forgive you and make you well and happy again."

"But I have done no wrong," insisted Job. "I have tried to think of some special sin which I have committed, but I can think of nothing."

"Confess, confess," the friends insisted.

"No," said Job. "It would be a lie; for I have done no wrong. Sometimes people suffer because of their sins, but not always."

"God must be just," said his friends. "He would not punish those who did not deserve it."

"God must be just," Job agreed. "I cannot understand what has happened to me. I wish I could know God better. I wish I could talk to God just as I am talking to you now."

Then another man who had been listening to the conversation came up to Job. He was a young man called Elihu.

"I waited for the older people to speak first," he said. "Now I want to speak.

You are wrong, Job, when you say you have not sinned. We all do wrong. But the trouble God sends is often of great help to us. It corrects us and helps us better understand what is right and wrong. The important thing is to continue to trust in God."

Job was too discouraged to answer. He was beginning to think that God did not run the world in right ways.

Job's friends and Elihu left him. As Job sat alone God spoke to him.

"Who is this who questions My wisdom and righteousness?" He asked Job.

Then God talked to Job about many things and asked him many questions. "Where were you when I made the earth? Could you have made the sea and control its tides? Can you bring the needed rain to the earth? Could you have made the animals, each so different, and continued to give them the food they need? Could you have planned all this wonderful world?"

Job realized that God was wiser than he was. He had been foolish to question God's rule over what God Himself had made.

"I know that You can do anything," Job told God. "I have asked some foolish questions. I am sorry. I didn't understand; but now that I have talked with You I realize how great You are. I know that I am only a man who often does wrong."

Job had learned much from talking to God. He knew now that there were signs of God's love and wisdom all over the world. He still did not understand why he had suffered, but he no longer expected to understand everything God did. He would have trust and faith in God. This was all he could do.

Some days later Job's three friends came back.

"God spoke to us," they said. "He told us we were wrong to blame you for sins because you were suffering. He said you would pray for us."

Job did pray for his friends. He asked God to forgive them for accusing him.

After this Job began to get well. He felt strong and healthy again. His relatives came and helped him by giving him money. Job bought and sold and one day he had herds and flocks again. He and his wife had children and Job enjoyed a happy family once more. He lived to be an old grandfather.

Job

THE NEW TESTAMENT

PART ONE

THE MESSIAH COMES

Pompey, the Roman general who had marched into Jerusalem, was defeated by the most famous of all Roman generals, Julius Caesar. Julius Caesar won great victories and new territory for Rome, but because some of the Roman senators believed he wanted to be an emperor he was murdered.

Civil war followed, and the final result was that Octavian, the nephew of Caesar, became emperor and called himself Caesar Augustus.

The Roman's appointed Antipater's son Herod as the ruler of much Roman territory including Judea. Herod married the granddaughter of Hyrcanus, the old Jewish royal family, but he took other wives as well.

These were troubled times, and men seeking power brought war and strife throughout the Roman empire. For the Jewish people these were unhappy days. The Jews resisted Roman rule and were sometimes cruelly punished. They would not accept the fact that they could do nothing against the power of Rome.

The Jews particularly hated Herod. He was not born a Jew and they knew he did not love their God or their Law. When Herod took power he had the Jewish leaders who had opposed him executed.

As time went by Herod became more and more suspicious and jealous. He had a younger brother of his Jewish wife murdered because he was popular with the people. He ordered the old priest, Hyrcanus, executed. These deeds made the Jews hate him more.

Through all of this the Jews remembered the words of their prophets about a great king who would come.

"We have suffered from these pagans," the Jewish people said. "Surely God is going to come to our aid. He will send His Messiah to take over the government of our nation and of the world. Then we will help the Messiah rule. It will be the Kingdom of God, and we will have an important place in it."

Meanwhile the Jews thought it was their right and their religious duty to resist the Romans whenever they could.

Although he was cruel and ruthless, Herod tried in some ways to be a good ruler. He thought he would win favor from the Jewish leaders by starting to rebuild the present Temple in Jerusalem. In a few years he redecorated and enlarged the main Temple building.

To help pay for this work Herod put special taxes on the people. He also took treasures from the tomb of King David.

Herod rebuilt Samaria and improved other cities over which he ruled. He built a seaport in honor of Caesar Augustus and a temple where Augustus was worshiped as a divine king.

Rome demanded two things of the people throughout their empire: taxes, and their share of soldiers for the army. They allowed the Jews to practice their own religion. With the approval of the appointed ruler the Jewish leaders could manage many of their own affairs.

But the Jews longed for the day when Roman soldiers would no longer patrol their streets, and Roman taxes would no longer keep them poor. They wanted to have their own small country left in peace. Their only comfort was the thought that the Messiah and the Kingdom of God were coming.

Many Gentile people throughout the Roman Empire had lost faith in their old gods and religion. They were looking for something better. Their teachers were thinking about what life meant, and pagan religion did not have answers which satisfied them.

In all of this God was working, making the world ready to receive new truth. New light was to come. God was ready to send His Son into the world.

1. "The Messenger Is Coming"

In the days when Herod was ruler, an old priest called Zechariah served in the Temple. By Herod's order the Temple was enlarged and made more beautiful. It was decorated with gold as Solomon's Temple had been. For many years, work on the nearby buildings within the court went on.

The priests were divided into groups which took turns leading the Temple worship. It was time for Zechariah's group to take charge.

Zechariah was known for his goodness and his faithfulness to God's Law. He had been chosen to perform a task which was a great honor. He was to take fire from the Altar of Burnt Offerings into the Temple to the Altar of Incense.

Sacrifice and prayers were made at the Temple every morning and evening. As many people as wished could come to the courts and take part in the worship.

On this day many had gathered in the court. The sacrifice was made. The people and the other priests watched as Zechariah took some of the fire and went alone into the Temple.

Outside the people prayed. They asked God to forgive them for sins they had committed.

Zechariah came to the golden Altar of Incense that stood in front of the heavy curtains which covered the entrance to the Most Holy Place. He lit the incense and the smoke rose. As he had many times before, Zechariah prayed that God would soon send the One who would bring deliverance to His people. He prayed that God's Kingdom would come.

Suddenly Zechariah was aware that someone was in front of him. He was supposed to be alone in the Temple for this special, holy moment. He was very frightened when he lifted his eyes and saw an angel standing to the right of the Altar of Incense.

The angel tried to quiet his fears. "Do not be afraid, Zechariah. God has heard your prayer. The One who has been promised by the prophets is soon to come.

"God knows that you and your wife Elizabeth have always wanted a child. God is going to give you a great honor. Your wife shall have a son. You must call him John. This son will prepare the way for the Messiah, the Anointed One.

"You will have joy and gladness. Many will rejoice because of His birth. He will help to prepare the people for the Messiah's coming.

"He will be filled with God's Spirit. He will live the life of a Nazarite and take no wine or strong drink. He will turn many people who have wandered from God's right ways back to loving and serving God."

In spite of the angel Zechariah found

this hard to believe. "Both my wife and I are old," he said. "Can you give me a sign that what you say will really happen?"

The angel said, "Zechariah, you should believe the angel of God who brings you God's message. The sign will be that you will be unable to speak until the promise has come true."

Outside the people and other priests began to wonder what had happened to Zechariah. Why did he not come out and give the benediction?

Then they saw him. Something had happened to the old priest. He seemed stunned. He lifted up his hands to say the prayer of benediction, but he could not speak. Over and over again he tried, but no words came. Another priest had to dismiss the people.

Everyone cried out in wonder. "The priest must have seen a vision in the Temple! How we wish Zechariah could tell us what happened!"

When it was time for Zechariah's group to finish serving he went back home. He still could not speak, but he wrote out for Elizabeth what had happened.

Elizabeth was overjoyed at the great promise. All her life she had wanted to have babies as her friends and relatives did. Their home had been lonely. Now God was going to give her a son who would be a prophet and do great work for God.

For many, many years there had been good priests and rabbis, but no great prophet had come to God's people.

"God has shown great love and mercy for me," said the older woman to her husband. "I am going to stay at home for five months. I will spend most of my time in prayer and thanksgiving. I want to be a good mother to this son who will be a prophet of the Lord."

Zechariah nodded. Now he believed that God's promise would come true. He waited with joy and gladness in his heart.

Luke 1:5-25

2. "Call His Name Jesus"

In a village in Galilee called Nazareth there lived a cousin of Elizabeth, a young Jewish girl called Mary. Everyone remarked at Mary's sweetness and gentleness. People loved her kind and thoughtful ways. They knew she loved God and walked close to Him.

Mary had always listened intently to the rabbis read and explain the Scriptures. She often thought about the Messiah who had been promised.

When the Messiah comes, she would think, *He will deliver our people from the proud, cruel men who rule over us. He will help those who are poor and in need. Righteousness and justice will be on the earth.*

Mary's family could trace their ancestry back to David the king, but they were poor in money and possessions. Their riches were found in their love for each other and for God.

There was a young man in the village called Joseph. He and his family were faithful Jews who kept the Law and attended the Temple on feast days. They believed that God's promise of a deliverer would one day come true. Joseph's family could also trace their ancestry back to David.

Mary had promised to marry Joseph. Plans and the wedding date had been set.

One day when Mary was alone in the house someone came in. As she hurried to find out who it was she saw an angel before her. Mary was frightened.

"Greetings, Mary. You are highly favored of God. God is with you."

Mary was puzzled. Why did this messenger from God treat her as though she were someone very special?

The angel continued: "Do not be afraid, Mary. You are favored of God. You will have a son. Call his name Jesus. He will be the Messiah and will be called the Son of God. He will rule over God's people as David did. But there will be no end to his kingdom."

Mary was even more surprised. It was the most wonderful news she had ever heard. She had prayed that the Messiah would come, but she had never dreamed she might be the mother of the Messiah.

The angel went on to tell her how special this birth would be. "God's Spirit will overshadow you," he said. "The child you will have will be holy, the Son of God."

Mary was overwhelmed. She did not feel she deserved this great honor. It was also a big responsibility. Supposing she failed? But if God had chosen her, she must simply trust in God and do her best.

The angel went on to tell Mary about Elizabeth. "Your cousin, Elizabeth, is soon to have a son. All her married days people said Elizabeth could not have a baby. Remember, with God all things are possible."

Mary told the angel, "I am willing to do whatever God wants. I am His servant."

Then the angel left. In the days that followed Mary thought about the angel's message. She was very happy, but she was a little frightened.

"Why has God chosen me?" she often wondered. Then she would remind herself that God always did what was best. *God will help me,* Mary thought. *Nothing is impossible with God.*

One day Mary remembered what the angel said about Elizabeth. Mary journeyed into the hill country of Judea where Zechariah and Elizabeth lived. As she came into their house God spoke to Elizabeth. He told her Mary would be the mother of the Messiah.

"You are the most blessed of all women," Elizabeth greeted the young girl. "I am honored that the mother of the Messiah should come to me. You are indeed blessed because you believed God's message. Your love for God and faith in His word is wonderful to see."

Mary was very happy, but she was not proud. "I am only a young girl from a poor family, but God has chosen me," she said. "My spirit rejoices in God. Because of this all generations of the future will call me blessed. God has done great things for me.

"God is holy and merciful. He will put down those who do wrong. The cruel rulers of the world will be deprived of their power. He will fill the hungry with good things. He will exalt those who are good."

Mary stayed with Elizabeth for about three months. Then she returned to Nazareth. Plans for her wedding soon got underway. But another person need-

"You are the most blessed of all women," Elizabeth greeted the young girl.

ed to be told about the birth of Jesus.

One night in a dream an angel from God spoke to Joseph. "Mary will have a son," the angel said. "You shall call his name Jesus. He shall save his people from their sins."

Soon after this Mary and Joseph were married. Often they talked together about the message of the angel and about the Child who was to come.

Luke 1:26-56; Matthew 1:18-25

3. The Messenger Is Born

The time came for Elizabeth to have her baby. The neighbors rejoiced with her when her baby boy was born. Elizabeth had not told them about the message of the angel.

Zechariah was happy when he saw his son. "The angel's message did come true," he thought to himself. "How I wish I could speak and tell everyone how happy I am."

Jewish boys were presented to God eight days after their birth as children of the covenant God had made with Abraham. At this time they were officially given their name.

At the ceremony for Elizabeth's baby, the priest wanted to know what name the baby would have. "I suppose you will call your son Zechariah after his father," he said to Elizabeth.

"No," said Elizabeth. "We are going to call him John."

Her friends and relatives were puzzled. "Why don't you name your only son after his father?" they asked. "You have no relatives called John."

Then they turned to Zechariah. "What name do you want the baby to have?" they asked.

Zechariah could not answer. Someone ran to get the writing tablet he had been using these past months. They handed it to the old priest.

Zechariah wrote in large letters: *His name is John.*

Everyone was surprised. And they

were even more surprised when Zechariah began to speak. "God has been good to us," he told them. "He has given us this child who will become a great servant of God."

The neighbors and friends were frightened. They remembered what they had heard about Zechariah seeing a vision in the Temple. They listened with wonder as Zechariah praised God and spoke about the future.

He said: "Blessed is God, for He has visited His people. He has brought redemption to us. He will send us the One from the family of David who will save us from our enemies. God has remembered His agreement with Abraham and our ancestors. God will deliver us from our enemies so that we can serve Him in holiness and righteousness all our lives."

Then Zechariah spoke to his baby son John.

"You will be called the prophet of the Most High. You will go before the Messiah to prepare the way, to help people repent of their sins and so be ready for Him.

"You will bring them the knowledge of salvation and proclaim the Messiah to them. You will show them the One who will be a light to those in darkness and who will guide us all into the way of peace."

The onlookers were amazed. They did not know if they dared believe such tidings. "Is the Messiah really to come soon?" they asked one another.

"Zechariah has had a message from God, that is certain," many people said.

The story of what had happened spread throughout all the hill country. Many said, "I wonder what kind of child John will be? We will watch closely as he grows up."

Back in Nazareth Mary and Joseph heard about the birth of Elizabeth's son. Mary remembered what Elizabeth had told her about the message in the Temple. She often thought about what Elizabeth had said to her, "You are the most blessed of all women."

Then Mary and Joseph heard some news that made them concerned. "There is going to be a census," neighbors said. "Caesar Augustus has announced that everyone in the empire must register."

"This means more taxes," grumbled many.

"It also means a long journey for some," said others. "Everyone must go back to the town where their family was born."

Joseph told Mary. "We will have to go to Bethlehem, the town of our ancestor David. It will be hard to go now because soon the baby will come."

"It is all right," said Mary. "God will help us."

They made ready to go. They packed their belongings. They made sure they had enough food and water for the journey. Joseph had a donkey upon which Mary could ride. He walked, as many people did on long journeys.

"Just think," said Mary, as they made their way over the winding path through the hills, "the baby will be born in Bethlehem, the city where David the king was born."

Luke 1:57-79; 2:1-5

4. Good News For All People

It was a three-day journey to Bethlehem. For safety Mary and Joseph traveled with others, but once the group came to the city they separated. Some of the people had friends to stay with, but Mary and Joseph knew no one in Bethlehem.

"How crowded the city is," said Mary. "Many have come to be enrolled."

"I am afraid we will have to go to the Inn and pay for our room," said Joseph. "We are not likely to find a stranger who is able to give us room when so many people are in the city."

As they approached the Inn they saw others being turned away. Crowds stood around the courtyard. "I have no more room," the innkeeper shouted at the doorway. "There is not another sleeping space. Already it is overcrowded with many in each room."

Mary and Joseph finally found a stable where they could stay.

At least it would be a roof over their heads, and there would be fresh straw to sleep on.

Mary and Joseph were grateful. They were not people who were used to luxuries and they could be comfortable here. How good it was to be safe and warm after the long journey.

There was food left for dinner. The donkeys, oxen, sheep and goats watched them eat.

"Now for a good night's sleep," said Joseph. "We are both very tired."

"It was a long trip," Mary agreed, "but I am glad to be here."

All was dark and still. The stars shone down on the white houses of the little city of Bethlehem. Then the stillness of the night was broken by a baby's cry. Jesus was born!

Mary and Joseph were happy as they looked at the newborn baby. The donkey, oxen, sheep and goats were quiet but they did not go back to sleep. Mary got out the swaddling cloths she had brought with her. Babies were wrapped around in these cloths.

There was a manger, a cut-out place in the rock where hay was put for the animals. "We can put Jesus in here," said Mary. "He will go to sleep on this soft hay."

It was still dark outside. On the hills surrounding the city, shepherds were out with their sheep. On warm nights they camped out in the hills rather than take the sheep back home to their fold. Some of the shepherds were sleeping. Others were watching the sheep.

Suddenly there was a bright light in the sky. The shepherds on watch fell back in amazement as an angel appeared before them. All around them the light of God's glory made the hills bright as day.

The sleepers woke up and staggered to their feet. They were half blinded, and very frightened.

"Don't be afraid," said the angel. "I bring you good news of joy which is for all people. This day the Messiah is born in the city of David."

The shepherds were amazed. They knew about the promises of a coming Messiah that had been made hundreds of years before. Was it really about to come to pass as the rabbis had told them it would?

The angel went on. "You will find this baby in Bethlehem. Look for a baby lying in a manger."

Then the sky was full of angels singing praises to God:

> Glory to God in the highest,
> And on earth peace and good will
> among men.

As they looked up, the light around them gradually faded. The song grew softer until it came from a great distance. Not one angel was left. Only the stars were there.

The shepherds shook themselves. They would have thought it was a dream if they had not all seen it.

"We must go to Bethlehem," they cried. "God has made a great happening known to us. We must find this baby."

Some shepherds stayed to mind the sheep but the rest hurried into the city to look for a baby in a manger.

Finally they found Mary and Joseph in the stable, bending over the manger. There, lying on the straw, was a baby!

Mary and Joseph were surprised when the shepherds knelt before the manger. The men looked in awe and wonder at the sleeping Jesus.

Then the shepherds got up and turned to Mary and Joseph. They told them about the angels. "We know that this is the One promised of old by the prophets," they said.

Mary marveled at this. God had made known to these shepherds that Jesus was the Messiah. She wondered who else was going to be told.

Mary thought about the words the angel had told the shepherds—"good news of joy for all people." Over and over she said the words of the song, "Glory to God in the highest, and on earth peace and good will among men."

As they left the house the shepherds rejoiced. On their way back through the city they told everyone about the Baby. "God has sent the Messiah," they said. "He was born tonight."

Luke 2:4-21

5. The News Spreads

When the Baby was eight days old He was presented to God as a child of the covenant and given His name Jesus.

Then when He was about a month and a half old, Mary and Joseph took Jesus to the Temple at Jerusalem (Jerusalem was just about six miles from Bethlehem.) The first boy of a Jewish family was dedicated to God in a special way forty days after he was born. Mary and Joseph wanted to do this at the Temple. They loved the Temple and were always glad to be in the courts of the Lord.

Before they left the Temple an old man came over to Mary and Joseph. He was Simeon, a religious leader who was known for his goodness and his faithfulness in the worship of God.

For many years Simeon had expected that the Messiah would soon come. God had told Simeon he would not die until he had seen the Messiah.

Now as Simeon looked at the Baby Jesus he knew that this was the Messiah. He took the Baby up in his arms and said, "Lord, now I am ready to die. My

eyes have seen the Messiah whom You have sent, the One who will bring the light of truth to the Gentiles and glory to Your people, Israel."

Mary and Joseph marveled at these words. God was working in such wonderful ways. He was showing many that Jesus was the Messiah.

"God bless you both," said Simeon to Mary and Joseph. "You will need God's help. This child will bring God's truth to His people, but all will not believe. Some will be against him. This will bring you sorrow, Mary."

Mary was puzzled. She had thought to be mother of the Messiah would bring only happiness.

Then a prophetess called Anna came over to look at the Baby. She was a widow, and very old. Through all her life she had been faithful in keeping God's Law and regular in her attendance at worship in the Temple.

She looked with awe and wonder at the Baby. "God be thanked," she said. "He has visited our people."

Anna did not keep the news to herself. She went to all her friends who believed as she did that the Messiah was soon to come. "The Messiah is here," she told them. "He has now been born, and his name is Jesus."

Mary and Joseph went back to Bethlehem. They found a house of their own to live in. Joseph was a carpenter, and he soon found work to do.

Other important people were looking for Jesus. On the night of Jesus' birth, in a country east of Palestine, wise men called Magi were studying the stars as they often did. One of them reported, "There is a new star in the heavens with special meaning for the Jewish people. Do you remember the ancient Jewish prophecy that one day a great king would be born to them? I believe this has happened."

The others looked where the one magi directed. These men thought the stars had much to do with events on earth. "It is a sign in the heavens," they said. "Let us go and pay our respects to this newborn king."

Several of them decided to take the long journey. Servants who went with them carried the gifts for the newborn king.

The wise men traveled over the deserts and rocky hills. They rode during the hot day and late into the night when the moon lit up the desert. The journey took a long time.

Each night during this time they searched the heavens for the special star. It led them on.

The magi traveled through the northern hills all the way down to Jerusalem. They thought that here in the capital city of the Jews everyone would know of the birth.

But they were surprised. No one seemed to know anything about it.

"Where is he who has been born king of the Jews?" they asked the people they met. "We have seen his star and have come to worship him."

But the people would look frightened and shake their heads. Not long before, Herod had killed many of the Pharisees, because he thought they were trying to take away his power. The people were frightened at the idea of anyone talking about a king of the Jews.

Some paid little attention to the wise men and laughed at their story. But when Herod heard what the visitors from the East were asking, he did not laugh. He took them very seriously.

Herod called a meeting of all the priests and scribes. He had heard the prophecy about the coming Messiah. Now he demanded of the religious leaders, "Where is the Messiah to be born?"

The leaders told him, "In Bethlehem of Judea." Then they quoted the ancient words of Micah the prophet where he said, "Out of Bethlehem will come a ruler who will govern my people Israel."

Herod said no more to the religious rulers. He now had the information he wanted. "Send these magi from the east to me," he told his officials.

They went to the magi. "Herod the king has heard your questions to the people and wants to see you."

When the magi appeared before this Roman-appointed ruler, he talked to them alone in a private room.

"I am very interested in this old prophecy," Herod told them, "and I am very sure magi like yourselves will uncover the truth or falsehood of this rumor. I have asked the Jewish priests and scribes, and they tell me that the king is to be born in Bethlehem. It is a town a short distance away."

"We are grateful for your help," said the magi. "We will go there."

"Now exactly when did you see this star in the sky?" asked Herod.

The magi told him.

"Go," said Herod, "search for the child. When you have found him, come back and tell me where he is. I want to go and pay worship to him also."

"Thank you," said the men. "We will do as you ask." The wise men did not know that Herod was a wicked ruler.

Once again the magi's procession was moving. This time it went out of the city and turned toward Bethlehem. "Now we will find the king," they said to one another.

Luke 2:21-36; Matthew 2:1-9

6. Escape to Egypt

It was night when the magi entered the town of Bethlehem. They searched the heavens for the special star. "There it is," they cried. "It is still leading us!"

As they urged the procession forward, they were full of joy. Then one cried, "Look, the star is directly over that small house."

The procession made its way down a narrow street. The richly robed men rode and the servants walked beside them. Suddenly they all stopped outside a little house squeezed in among many others.

At the door of the house they knocked. When Joseph opened the door they asked to come in. As they entered, they saw a young mother holding a little Child.

Joseph asked the men who they were, but before the magi answered, they fell down on their knees before the Child as people did to kings.

Mary and Joseph were surprised that these richly dressed foreigners would come to their humble home at all. And now they were kneeling before Jesus!

"We bow before the king of the Jews," they said "We know this is the One of whom the prophets spoke."

Mary was surprised. Since coming back to Bethlehem nothing unusual had happened. Now more strangers knew about Jesus.

The magi rose from their knees and spoke to their servants. "Bring in the gifts we have brought from the East for the one who will be king."

Then the magi presented their gifts to the Child. Mary and Joseph were amazed. They had never seen such costly treasures —gold, and sweet smelling ointments of frankincense and myrrh.

Before they left the next morning, one magi said, "Last night I had a strange dream. It seemed to say that we should not go back to Jerusalem."

"I had a dream too," said another magi. "God was warning us not to go to Herod."

The magi believed dreams were very important and gave advice.

"Then we will go back to our land by a different route," said another magi. "Herod might become jealous and try to kill a child who was said to become a great ruler. No doubt he wants his own sons to rule after him."

The wise men turned around and headed south. By nightfall many miles

were between them and Jerusalem.

In the little house in Bethlehem, Joseph and Mary again looked at the treasures which were given to their Son. "We must use them in some important way for Jesus," they said.

That night Joseph had a troubled dream. In the morning he said to Mary, "There has been much unrest in Jerusalem these last few years. Herod is suspicious and jealous. He does not hesitate to kill those who get in his way. We are not safe here."

"But where shall we go?" asked Mary, "back to Nazareth?"

"God has told me we must quickly get out of the country and go to Egypt," said Joseph. "We must protect Jesus at all cost. The treasures the magi brought will easily pay for such a trip."

"We must protect Jesus' life," Mary agreed.

"We will say nothing to our neighbors," said Joseph. "Tonight when it is dark we will saddle up the donkey and leave."

That night Mary, Joseph and Jesus left Bethlehem. They journeyed south to Hebron and then crossed to the trade route along the sea coast that led to Egypt.

Egypt was also ruled by Rome; but many Jews lived there. Mary and Joseph found refuge among them. They told no one about the prophecies concerning their Child.

Back in Jerusalem Herod waited for the magi. When they didn't come he was very angry. In a rage, he sent orders out to kill all boy babies in Bethlehem who were two years old or younger.

Not many months later Mary and Joseph heard that Herod had died. The Roman government had permitted him to divide his rule between three of his sons, Archelaus, Herod Antipas, and Philip, who each took control of sections of the territory over which their father had ruled.

God spoke to Joseph, telling him to go back to their own land.

"Now we can go back," said Joseph to Mary.

"Where shall we live?" asked Mary, "in Bethlehem?"

"No," said Joseph. "There is always trouble with the Romans in Judea. Let let us go north to our old home in Nazareth."

Matthew 2:9-23

7. The Boy of Nazareth

Mary and Joseph knew the people of Nazareth well. Many were relatives. It was good to come home to them. Joseph built a house with a carpenter's shop attached to it. Sometimes people brought work for Joseph to do, but often he went to their homes to do carpentry.

Many Gentiles lived in Galilee, but most of the people of Nazareth were Jewish, and they were strict in performing their religious duties.

Nazareth lay in a valley among the mountains in the lower part of Galilee. It was a small, little-known village, but much loved by the people who lived there.

Often the children climbed to the top of the hill. Below them the plains spread out for thirty miles. Far to the west another range of mountains stretched across the horizon, and beyond them they could just catch a glimpse of the Mediterranean Sea.

Often they would watch the traders with their caravans of donkeys or camels pass below them on the trade roads which went in many directions—to Jerusalem, to Samaria, the Jordan River, the Mediterranean Sea. They might be carrying anything to trade—fine woven and dyed cloth, heavy cloth for tents, grain, fruit, pottery, things made of many kinds of metal. The Romans had built fine roads and soldiers traveling throughout the empire helped to make them safe.

The flat-roofed houses of the village were made of white limestone, like those of the rest of the country. Most were one-room with a lower place for the animals to come in out of the cold. Most families owned at least a few sheep and goats, an ox and a donkey.

Outside the village was a well from which all the mothers drew water. Everyone had at least a small garden where they planted vegetables.

In this village Jesus grew in strength and wisdom. According to God's plan for life, Jesus grew stronger and taller in body. His mind grew in understanding and knowledge.

When Jesus was six years old He went to the synagogue with the other village boys. Here the boys were taught reading, writing, and some arithmetic and some music. But mostly they were taught from the Scriptures. They memorized prayers and psalms which were chanted in the synagogue service on the Sabbath.

Mary and Joseph were careful to always observe the Sabbath. They brought their family faithfully to the village synagogue. Often they spoke of God's love and care. As they sat around the reed mat spread on the floor Joseph thanked God for the food before they ate.

The family grew. Jesus had four brothers named James, Joseph, Simon and Judas, and He had several sisters. They had a happy home, because they loved God and showed love for each other.

In the morning and evening the family recited the Shema. These words from the Scriptures summed up the Jewish faith: They began:

> "Hear O Israel: The Lord our God
> is one Lord;
> and you shall love the Lord your
> God with all your heart, and with all
> your soul, and with all your might."

Mary and Joseph kept God's Law the best they could. They carefully taught it to their children. The children could see from their example what it meant to live in God's way.

God was with Jesus as the years went by. God was pleased with the way He was living the life of a boy. Jesus grew in favor with God.

Many people liked Jesus, because He was kind and thoughtful and fair and honest. He could be depended upon to do His share. The grownups liked this.

Jesus always kept His promises, and He did not insist on His own way when games were chosen. The other boys and girls liked this.

Boys and girls of Nazareth had many games they liked to play. Sometimes their games acted out what their parents did.

The children would pretend that someone had died. One boy would play a flute while the others made up a mournful procession.

Another time they would use the boy

and his flute to pretend there was a wedding. Then the tune would be merry and the procession would dance up the hilly pathway.

Sometimes there would be quarrels between the other children. Then Jesus would try to make peace. Whenever anyone wronged Him, Jesus was quick to forgive. Jesus grew in favor with men.

Sometimes Jesus liked to be alone. Then He would climb the hills and look out over the countryside. He would think about the past history of His people. He would think about the words of Isaiah, Jeremiah, Hosea and other great prophets. He felt very close to God. He knew that God had work for Him to do.

Often Jesus looked at the green tree-dotted hills and the fields of flowers around Him. They spoke to Him about God's goodness.

Jesus watched the farmer scattering his seed. He watched a shepherd care for a wounded sheep. He watched the men who gathered the harvest. He took part in the gay time when everyone helped shear the sheep. This wool would be made into yarn for clothing. All these things were part of God's plan for caring for people.

Jesus thought, "People should understand that God loves them as a good father loves his child."

Luke 2:39, 40, 52; 4:16; 7:32
Matthew 4:15; 5:9; 11:16, 17; 12:11, 12; 13:1-8, 55, 56; 6:9, 25-32
Deuteronomy 6:4, 5

8. A Visit to the Temple

The winter rains brought new life to the hills around Nazareth. The grain had been planted and now green shoots appeared. Springtime flowers scattered color throughout the fields. Fruit trees such as the pomegranate and the apricot were in blossom, and the fig trees bore fruit. The flocks of sheep and goats found the pastures full of new grass.

It was time for the Feast of the Passover. Mary and Joseph always made the trip to Jerusalem even though the journey meant camping out overnight. It was ninety-one miles from Nazareth to Jerusalem.

In recent years Jesus had watched them go with wistful eyes. "How I wish I could see the Temple," He would say.

Now Mary said, "Jesus is twelve. We should take Jesus with us."

"Yes," Joseph agreed. "He is old enough to make the journey. Some children even younger go with the company. We can depend on Jesus not to run off and get into trouble on a trip. Besides, he will soon be thirteen and a son of the Law."

So Joseph told Jesus. "Soon you will be thirteen and a son of the Law. Then you will be required to attend the Feast of the Passover every year; but we have decided to let you come this year."

Jesus was excited about going. He had heard so much about Jerusalem and the Temple. Sometimes rabbis from Jerusalem visited their synagogue. He felt sure the rabbis who sometimes taught on the great pillared porches of the Temple would be wonderful to hear.

That year a large party went to Jerusalem from Nazareth. The rabbis said all men must attend the Feast, but many women and some children went too.

Mary and Joseph had many close friends and relatives in the group. Sometimes Jesus walked along with cousins close to His own age.

They could take the route that followed the Jordan River or they could go south and then take the road from Joppa to Jerusalem. Robbers roamed the hills and so they kept close together when they were on the back roads. Some kept watch during different hours of the night while the rest slept out on the ground around the campfire. They had to carry their food and water with them.

During the third day when they were near the city they began to sing psalms about Jerusalem and the Temple. Jesus sang with the others:

> I will lift up my eyes to the hills.
> From where do I find help?
> My help comes from God who
> made heaven and earth.

The song encouraged the pilgrims who might be weary or afraid of robbers when it said:

> The Lord will keep you from all evil.
> He will keep your life.
> The Lord will be with you always,
> When you go and come,
> From this time on and forever.

Jesus loved the many words of the psalms that spoke of God's mercy and goodness. He knew them all.

At last Jesus would have His first look at the city of Jerusalem. How often He had questioned Mary and Joseph when they returned. Now He would see it for Himself.

The first thing He saw above the walls of the city was the Temple. Its white marble and gold decorations shone in the sun.

The large group entered the city through one of its gates. Jesus looked around eagerly. Merchants with wares to sell lined the narrow streets. Poor, ragged beggars stood about asking for money. Roman soldiers, who were sent to keep order during the feast, made their way through the jostling crowds.

It was time for the caravan from Nazareth to split up. Most people stayed with friends or relatives. Mary and Joseph had made such plans ahead of time. Now they went to their friends' house.

The next day Mary and Joseph took Jesus within the Temple courts. Herod had added courtyards, terraces and pillared porches or porticos all around the main part of the Temple. Jesus was eager for the worship service. He was happy as He listened to the music of the choirs of priests. He prayed with the others and sang the psalms. He was only sorry when it was over for the day.

Sometimes on the Sabbath and when there were special feast days the most famous rabbis of the land would take turns teaching in the Temple porticoes. Mary and Joseph took Jesus to hear these teachers.

Jesus listened with eager attention as a rabbi explained part of the Law. Another rabbi got up and preached from the message of one of the great prophets.

When the feast was ended Mary and Joseph talked with the leaders of their caravan about exactly when they would return. They arranged how they would meet.

Before the caravan got started there was much confusion. Finally they got

underway. Mary and Joseph thought Jesus was with some relatives, but He was not. He had gone to hear the rabbis for one last time.

When it came time to camp for the night Mary and Joseph searched throughout the caravan, but He was not there.

"We must go back to Jerusalem at once," said Joseph. "Jesus must still be there."

"I can't understand it," said Mary. "I thought Jesus would stay close by and come at the right time."

They searched throughout the city. They asked the friends with whom they had stayed. They asked many people if they had seen a lost boy. Finally they went to the Temple.

There they found Jesus among a group of people listening to the rabbis. They watched as Jesus asked the rabbis questions about God's Law and how it should be obeyed by their people.

The rabbis asked Jesus questions, and everyone was amazed at the wisdom He showed by how He answered it.

Here was a boy who loved God's Law and seemed to understand better than many adults how God wanted His people to live.

Then the crowd began to break up. Mary and Joseph went up to Jesus.

Mary said, "Son, why have you treated us in this way? Didn't you realize that we would be worried? We have searched everywhere for you. It is not like you to be so thoughtless."

"When I missed the caravan I came back here," said Jesus. "Didn't you know to look here first? Didn't you realize that I would be in My Father's house?"

"You must come at once," said Joseph. "We must find some other people with whom to travel home."

"Yes, I'll come," said Jesus. He was sorry He had worried them.

Mary and Joseph talked about it later. "What did Jesus mean by calling the Temple his Father's House?" they wondered. "We must remember what happened during this Feast."

Luke 2:41-51; Psalm 121

9. A Preacher From the Wilderness

John, the son of Elizabeth and Zechariah, grew up. He became a young man who was strong in body and mind. He was loyal and faithful to the worship of God. He wanted to give all his life to God and His work.

While he was still a young man John went to live in the desert places of Judea. He spent much time in thought and prayer.

He lived very simply and ate the locusts and wild honey which he found in the wilderness. He allowed himself no luxuries and no wine. He dressed in rough camels' hair cloth and a leather belt. He was a lot like the prophet Elijah.

Then one day John came out of the Wilderness of Judea. After years of waiting, God's message had come to him. He knew the work that God wanted him to do. He was to prepare the way for the Messiah, although he did not then know who the Messiah would be.

It was the time when Tiberius was

emperor. John preached along the banks of the Jordan River in Judea and across the river in Perea.

Herod Antipas, Herod's son, was ruler of Galilee and Perea. The son of Herod who had been given the rule over Judea had been exiled by the Romans. In his place they put a procurator, a direct representative of the emperor. At this time Pontius Pilate was the procurator.

Crowds of people came to hear John preach. Many came from the country towns of Judea and from the big city of Jerusalem. People journeying along the highways from Galilee to Judea stopped to listen.

John proclaimed that the Messiah was coming soon. The crowds grew excited with anticipation.

"We have waited for this," they said. "Now our enemies will be destroyed. Peace and righteousness will reign."

The news came to the religious leaders, the Pharisees and the Sadducees. "We must go out and hear this new prophet," they said. "We must be sure all he says agrees with the Law of Moses."

John preached, "Repent, for the Kingdom of Heaven is at hand. The Messiah is coming, and you must get ready for him. You are not ready. Our people are not really walking close to God. You must repent of your wrongdoing. Confess your sins to God and turn from wrongdoing. Then you will be ready to accept the Messiah."

Many people realized that what John said was true. "How can we show that we do repent?" they asked.

"Be baptized here in the Jordan River," John told them.

He took those who repented out into the water and baptized them in God's name.

Often he told the people: "The Messiah will bring judgment to Israel."

The religious leaders and the people were surprised. They had thought the Messiah's judgment would come only on those who worshiped idols, not the Jews.

Some of the religious leaders also came to be baptized. John knew that many of these men only pretended to be religious. They liked the praise they received from men, but they did not really care about God and His way. They were proud of their good deeds, and they were very proud of being Jews.

"Who has warned you to flee from God's judgment?" John asked them. "Have you really repented? God knows those who are true to Him. Soon it will become known who are really God's children. It is not enough to be descended from Abraham."

Many of the religious leaders were offended and refused to be baptized. "Anyway," they said. "It is for pagans who turn Jew to be baptized, not a man who is a child of Abraham."

Some of the people agreed with the religious rulers, but many saw their need to repent of past wrongdoing. They wanted to live closer to God.

They came and asked John how God wanted them to live. "What is it that God wants us to do?" they asked.

John knew that there were many things God wanted from His people. Mostly He wanted them to love God and others. But John thought of some very practical ways to show this.

He said, "If you have more than you need, share it with others. Share your extra clothes and your extra food. Give to others. Don't be selfish."

Some tax collectors were in the crowd. These men worked for the government and were unpopular with the people who disliked the government. "We want to be baptized," they said. "What should we do to show repentance?"

"Take no more money in taxes than what is fair," John told them.

There were soldiers who asked him the same question.

John told them, "Do not rob others by force or by falsely accusing them. Be content with your wages."

John spoke out against evil wherever it was found. He was not afraid to criticize religious and civil leaders who did wrong. He spoke out against the ruler, Herod Antipas, for marrying Herodias who was really his brother Philip's wife, while Philip was still living.

Herodias was very angry at this and wanted Herod to put John to death. But Herod was afraid to hurt John, because he was so popular with the people.

Many people wondered: "Is this man the Messiah? He sounds like it."

But John spoke out: "I am not the Messiah. I am preparing his way. The Messiah comes after me. He is much greater than I. I baptize you with water, but the Messiah will give you God's Spirit."

Luke 1:80; 3:1-20; John 1:6-8; Mark 1:2-8; Matthew 3:1-12

10. "This Is My Son"

Meanwhile in Nazareth Jesus had grown to be a man. Fathers always taught their sons their trade. Jesus and His brothers had learned how to make stools, chests, and farm tools.

Then news came to Nazareth about the preaching of John, the son of Elizabeth who was Mary's cousin.

"Great crowds have come out to hear our cousin John preach," they said. "They call him 'the baptizer,' because he baptizes those who will repent and prepare themselves for the Messiah."

Others said, "John says the Messiah will soon come."

Jesus knew it was time for Him to leave the little village of Nazareth. He would never come back to live this happy quiet life among the hills. He must declare Himself and start His great work for God. Now the way had been prepared. It was God's time.

Jesus had spent many years thinking about God and pondering over the Scriptures. He had spent much time in prayer. Now He prayed for God's continuing guidance.

Jesus told His family, "I am going to go down to the Jordan where John the baptizer is preaching."

Jesus journeyed down through the hills and countryside to the route that followed the muddy waters of the Jordan. Jesus had heard that John was preaching near Bethany which was on the east side of the Jordan. He crossed the river at a shallow spot and continued down a well-traveled road.

As He came near Bethany, Jesus saw a great crowd gathered on the river bank. John the baptizer was preaching.

Jesus listened as John said, "Repent, for the Kingdom of Heaven is at hand."

Many came out of the crowd. "We repent," they said to John. "We are sorry for the wrongs we have done. From now on we want to live good lives. We want to be ready when the Messiah comes."

John received them joyfully.

Then Jesus came out of the crowd and walked slowly over to the preacher. John had met his cousin, Jesus. He knew that Jesus walked close to God and kept His laws. As John looked at Jesus, God spoke to John's heart.

"This is He," God said. "This is the Messiah."

Jesus smiled and greeted John. "I want to be baptized," He said.

John was puzzled. Why should the Messiah be baptized? The Messiah would be righteous, not a sinner.

"No," said John. "That would not be right. I am not good enough to baptize you. I should have *you* baptize me."

"This is what God wants," said Jesus. "I must be a good example to others. I will show by this that I am dedicating My life to God and His work."

John knew that Jesus must know best. He led Jesus out in the water to be baptized.

When Jesus came up out of the water He stood praying to God. Then the clouds parted and God's Spirit came like a dove upon Jesus. A voice spoke to Him from heaven saying: "You are My beloved Son. I am perfectly pleased with You."

John was overjoyed. This was the sign that told him with certainty that Jesus was the Messiah.

But Jesus did not stay with John the baptizer. Jesus crossed the river and journeyed down into the desert places around the Dead Sea. It was the same Wilderness of Judea where John had spent many years alone with God.

Jesus had just had a wonderful experience with God. He was happy to have the Father's approval. Now He wanted time to think through just how His work for God should begin.

Jesus wanted to decide the best way to let people know that He was the Messiah. He wanted to review all the many things the people needed to know about God. Above all Jesus wanted to pray and be sure He was following His Father's will in all things.

John 1:6-34; Luke 3:21, 22; 4:1;
Matthew 3:13-17; 4:1; Mark 1:9-12

11. Jesus Wins a Victory

For forty days Jesus wandered throughout the rugged hills of the Wilderness of Judea. High in the cliffs, caves gave some shelter, but it was a lonely, forlorn place. Here and there were dried up bushes but there were no flowers or grass.

This was the home of wild animals. Sometimes Jesus saw the nimble wild asses and goats. Sometimes He caught a glimpse of a fox, a jackal, or a snake.

All this time Jesus had been fasting. He hadn't eaten anything and He began to be very hungry. Then Satan came to tempt Jesus.

God had proclaimed that Jesus was His Son. Satan said, "If you are the Son of God you do not need to go hungry. Command these stones to became loaves of bread."

Jesus shook His head. That would not be right. The divine power which God had given Him should not be used for selfish purposes. He answered the temptation with words of Scripture.

He said, "Man shall not live by bread alone, but by every word that comes from God."

Then Satan said, "If you are the Son of God throw yourself down from the top of the Temple. God has promised to take care of you. Then everyone will believe in you, and you will have all men following you."

Jesus knew He must do God's work in God's way. God did not want people to be forced by some great display of power to discover that He was the Messiah. God wanted the people to come to Jesus because they loved Him, and because they believed Jesus spoke the truth about God.

Jesus again answered by words of Scripture: "You shall not tempt the Lord your God," He said.

"All the kingdoms of the world are mine," said Satan. "I am the one they really follow. Come and worship me, and I will give these kingdoms to you."

Jesus jumped up. "Go away Satan," He cried. "It is written in the Law: 'You shall worship the Lord your God, and Him only shall you serve.' "

Satan left. He had failed to get Jesus to listen to him and do his will. Jesus had remained absolutely faithful to God and His will—He had won a victory over evil.

Now Jesus was exhausted and faint, but God sent angels to care for His needs.

Some days later Jesus went back to Bethany on the other side of the Jordan River and again joined the crowds who listened to John the baptizer.

The religious leaders of the Sanhedrin had sent priests and Levites to ask John, "Are you the Messiah?" (The Sanhedrin judged all religious matters.)

"No," John had said. "I am a voice crying in the wilderness, 'Prepare the way for the Lord.' One is even now among you who is greater than I."

When John the baptizer saw Jesus in the crowd he announced to all the people that the Messiah had come. John pointed out Jesus.

"This is the man I told you about," John said. "This is the One who is greater than I.

"At first I did not know that this was the Messiah, but God told me: 'The man on whom you see the Spirit descend and remain is the Messiah.' This happened. I saw it myself. This is the Son of God."

Many people were excited when they heard this. They looked with wonder on Jesus. Jesus accepted this witness of John, but Jesus did not begin just then to preach.

Jesus planned to have helpers. He felt it was not quite time to begin.

The next day John the baptizer was talking to Andrew and John, two of his followers, when he noticed Jesus walking along the river bank.

"Look," said the baptizer, "there is Jesus, the Lamb chosen of God."

"We would like to go and talk to Jesus," said Andrew.

"It is all right," said John the baptizer. "Go and see if you can find out where he is staying."

The two left John the baptizer, and followed Jesus. After they had walked a while Jesus turned around and saw them. "What do you seek?" He asked them.

They asked, "Rabbi, where are you staying?"

"Come and see," said Jesus. He brought Andrew and John to the house where He was staying.

Jesus invited them to come in and sit down with Him. They talked together for many long hours. Jesus' host brought food and still they talked on.

Jesus told them about the work God had for Him to do. He told them about God's Kingdom and how God wanted His people to live.

The men had many questions to ask. They talked about many things the Scriptures said. Finally John and Andrew had to say good-by for the time.

Andrew ran at once to his brother, Peter. "We have found the Messiah," he told Peter. "Come and visit him with me."

Andrew and Peter went back to the house where Jesus stayed. Jesus welcomed Peter warmly.

The next day Jesus talked to a man called Philip. He invited Philip to become one of His disciples, "Come and follow Me," He urged. Philip agreed.

"I want to tell my friend about this," Philip told Jesus, and went to find Nathanael. "We have found the One about whom Moses and the prophets spoke," said Philip. "His name is Jesus of Nazareth."

Nathaniel did not much care for the people of a little village like Nazareth. "Can anything good come from Nazareth?" he asked.

"Come and see," said Philip.

Nathanael agreed to go with his friend. After he met Jesus he changed his mind. Then he said to Jesus, "You are the king of Israel, the Son of God."

In this way Jesus found His first helpers.

Matthew 4:1-11; Mark 1:12, 13; Luke 4:1-13; John 1:19-51

PART TWO

GOD WAS WITH HIM

It was time for Jesus to begin His work for God. For about three years He would travel throughout the land proclaiming the Kingdom of God. Jesus wanted the people to understand that He was the Messiah whom God had promised through the prophets.

Ever since their return from exile the Jews had been waiting for this great Ruler from God. The prophets had said He would come and bring a reign of peace and righteousness.

After Ezra no great prophets had come to the people. The religious leaders spent their time studying and interpreting the Law and the prophets of the past.

Throughout the years the Jewish people often talked about the Messiah. Some men had claimed to be the Messiah, but their claims had proven to be false. More and more the Jewish people came to think of the Messiah as a political ruler.

Rome ruled the world and they believed the Messiah would first of all overthrow Rome. They thought of the Messiah as a general who would win battles for Israel as King David had once done.

Jesus knew these ideas were wrong. God's Kingdom was not to be one of war and force but of peace and love. Sometimes Jesus hesitated to use the word "Messiah," because the people had such wrong ideas about the Messiah. Instead He talked of God's Kingdom and what it would be like. He told men it was already here and invited them to join.

Many came out to hear Jesus. Most of them were poor, ordinary people, but some of them were leaders. The priests and Levites were important leaders who came. The priests led the services and offered the sacrifices at the Temple. The Levites were helpers to the priests and took charge of less important matters about the Temple.

Other religious leaders who came to hear Jesus were the Pharisees. These people had ordinary jobs, but they spent all their other hours studying and teaching the Law. They believed in the strictest keeping of the Law of Moses. They also thought that all the other Jewish laws which had been collected and added were just as important as the Law of Moses and must be kept exactly in order to please God. They were very much opposed to the pagan Romans.

The Sadducees were another religious party. Many of them were priests. They stressed sacrifice and Temple worship as most important. They were wealthy and wanted above all to keep on good terms with the Romans so that the Romans would not make war on them.

The Pharisees often were accompanied by Scribes, and some Pharisees were also Scribes. Scribes were like secretaries. They knew the Law and its interpretations well. People would look to them for the official interpretation of a law.

During Jesus' lifetime another party arose. They wanted to overthrow Roman rule immediately by force. They were called Zealots.

It was a time of great unrest and uncertainty. Jesus knew that what the people really needed was not the overthrow of Rome. Wicked rulers would come and go as they had in the past. The people needed to come back to God. They needed to know God as a good and loving Father.

They also needed to have their lives changed—to have the power to live as God wanted. But Jesus knew this would be possible only if He gave His life for them.

12. A Beginning of Miracles

Soon after Jesus found His new friends there was a marriage in Cana of Galilee, a town among the hills about two hour's walk from Nazareth.

It was an important wedding for Jesus. All His family would be there. Jesus' new friends had also been invited. Most of them were from Galilee. They all walked back to Galilee from Judea and got to Cana in time for the ceremonies.

Jesus and His friends stayed and enjoyed the feast which would last one or two weeks. His new friends met His family and other friends. They spoke to the bride and groom and their families. It was a happy time. Everyone was enjoying himself.

Then something went wrong. There was no more wine. The servants were upset.

"More people came than our master thought," they said. "It will be a terrible disgrace to have to tell the guests that the wine has been used up."

Mary, the mother of Jesus, heard about the trouble. The groom and his family were good friends of hers, and she wanted to help. Just then Jesus and His disciples came by.

Mary said to Jesus, "It is too bad. The servants say they are out of wine. Could you help them?"

Jesus told her, "It's not up to you or Me. I must use My power only as God directs Me."

Mary still felt sure that something special was going to happen. "If Jesus gives you any instructions," she told the servants, "be sure you obey him. Do exactly as he says."

Then she went on to be with other guests.

Jesus noticed six large empty stone jars which stood in the corner of the courtyard. These jars would be filled with water and used for the guests to wash their hands before eating.

"Fill these jars with water," Jesus called to the servants.

Without question the servants brought water to fill the jars. They each held about twenty or thirty gallons of water. Soon the water was up to the brim.

Jesus' disciples watched expectantly. They wondered, *Would Jesus show some great power which would prove to all that he was the Messiah?*

Then Jesus said to the servants, "Now draw some of the water out in a smaller vessel, and take it to the honored guest who has charge of the dinner."

One of the servants took a wine bottle and drew out some of the water. As he did, the water turned into wine.

The servant took the bottle to the honored guest. He told him nothing about what Jesus had said and done. He poured out a glass of wine for him.

"Will this wine be all right for the dinner?" he asked.

The guest tasted it. The servant watched. *Would it taste like wine?* he wondered.

"Send for the bridegroom," cried the guest.

The servant went to get him. He was worried for fear something had gone wrong.

"You are indeed a fine host," said the honored guest. "Most men first give out their best wine, and then after several dinners, they use their poorer wine. But you have saved the best wine until now."

The disciples heard what the guest said. They rejoiced that Jesus had shown this sign of His power. This miracle was the first of the signs which Jesus performed.

These signs or miracles were to teach truths and to show others that Jesus had been sent by God and had power given by God.

Through this miracle Jesus shows that times of joy and gladness are good for people and that all the good things of life are gifts from God.

John 2:1-11

13. A Caller Comes Secretly

It was spring and faithful Jews made ready for the journey to Jerusalem to keep the Feast of the Passover. Jesus and His new friends went with others from Galilee.

Jesus worshiped at the Temple as He had always done; but this time there was a difference. Now He had a message for the people there. Now they were about to see the power of God at work.

Many pilgrims were in the city. Jews and Gentiles who had been converted to the Jewish faith came from surrounding countries. It was a good time for Jesus to reach many of His people.

The first thing Jesus did to proclaim Himself to the people was to oppose something which had been going on in the Temple courts for many years. Jesus had often noticed how much noise the traders made.

Animals needed to be bought for sacrifice, and money needed to be exchanged from foreign currency to the only kind accepted in payment of the Temple tax. But instead of doing this outside the gates, the merchants were allowed in the courts.

The noise hindered the true worshiper who had come to pray and hear God speak to his heart. In addition to this, many of the traders were not honest. They cheated when they exchanged the money, or they overcharged for the sheep, oxen, and pigeons.

Jesus had often been saddened by this sight. Now He did something about it. He chased out the traders. He pointed to the animals and the tables of money. "Take these things away," He shouted. "You shall not make My Father's house a house of trade."

The men were frightened by Jesus. They recognized Him as a prophet. Those who had cheated were especially afraid.

The priests did not like what Jesus had done; but most of the people agreed with Him.

Then Jesus began to preach, "The Kingdom of God is at hand. Repent and believe the good news."

Jesus showed His power from God by healing many who were sick. He would place His hand on them or speak only a few words.

The crowds of people became excited. "This is a man of God," they said.

Many said, "This is the Messiah."

But Jesus knew that for most the belief was not a strong one. They were excited by the miracles, but to be a true follower of Jesus required more than this. Jesus wanted complete loyalty and love.

Most of the Sadducees and the Pharisees were angry at Jesus for criticizing their way of running the Temple. The miracles did not convince them that Jesus was the Messiah.

But a few of the religious rulers did marvel at Jesus. "This man must be from God," they reasoned. "How could anyone do such miracles unless God was with him?"

One Pharisee named Nicodemus thought a lot about Jesus. He was a member of the Sanhedrin.

I must see and talk to this new teacher, Nicodemus decided. *What if he really is*

the Messiah? It would be terrible if those of us who are to keep the faith true should fail to recognize the Messiah.

But, he thought, *many of the Pharisees are opposed to Jesus. I would hate for them to see me visit him. I'll go at night.*

Nicodemus found out where Jesus and His disciples were staying in Jerusalem. And one night he knocked on the door and asked for Jesus. The host took him to where Jesus was sitting on the rooftop in the cool of the evening.

Jesus greeted Nicodemus warmly. He was glad to talk to this man. He knew Nicodemus had spent years studying God's Law. He knew that Nicodemus loved God and wanted to lead his people well.

They talked about the things of God. Nicodemus asked Jesus about His work and what He expected to accomplish.

"Rabbi," Nicodemus said, "we know that you are a teacher who has come from God. No one can do these miracles unless God gives him the power. We know that God is with you."

Jesus had to tell Nicodemus that this was not enough to be a disciple. Jesus told him, "In order to be a part of God's Kingdom you must have a new birth. You must receive a new life from above."

"How can I?" asked Nicodemus. "I don't understand this at all. It isn't possible to become a baby again."

"As a teacher of Israel you should understand," said Jesus. "This new life comes from God through His Spirit. He gives it to you so that you can become a member of His kingdom and live in a new way. God loves all men, and has sent Me into the world to give men this new life. But you must believe in Me. Those who do not believe will be left out of the Kingdom."

Nicodemus did believe that Jesus was from God. As time went by he often thought about the words Jesus had spoken to him.

He went again to hear Jesus speak and saw Him work more wonders of healing in God's name. He began to love Jesus and believe in Him. He found the new life Jesus preached about.

But he said nothing to the Pharisees who did not like Jesus. *Perhaps,* he thought, *the time will come when I can do something special for Jesus.*

John 2:13-3:18; Matthew 4:17

14. John Is Arrested

After the Passover, Jesus and some of His disciples spent months traveling throughout the countryside of Judea. Jesus taught about God and healed the sick.

Jesus' disciples helped Him in many ways. Jesus had them baptize those who wanted to be a part of God's Kingdom. Many repented of their past wrongdoings and came to find the new life Jesus preached about.

In Judea and in Perea, on the other side of the Jordan, John the baptizer continued to baptize and preach. Some of John's disciples had become disciples of Jesus, but others had stayed with John. Some who stayed became jealous of Jesus.

They said to John, "Rabbi, remember

when you pointed out Jesus as the Messiah? Now all people are following him. Soon there will be no one for our own group."

John told them, "I have already said that I am not the Messiah. This is God's will. Jesus will become more important, and I will become less important. I can only rejoice that the Messiah has come. It seems strange to me that everyone has not believed in him."

John continued to preach and to speak out against evil everywhere. Many came to hear him and to be baptized.

Herod sent spies out to listen to John. Herod's wife, Herodias, was angry at John for speaking against their marriage, and wanted him killed. (Herod had taken Herodias away from her first husband, Philip, who was Herod's brother.) The spies told Herod that many people came to hear John.

Herod worried about this popularity. "John the baptizer might stir up people to rebel against my rule," Herod decided. "I shall put him in prison."

So he sent out soldiers to arrest John and bring him back to his fortress prison.

One day after John's arrest Jesus told His disciples, "There is much work to do. My message must go to all our people. It is time to travel back to Galilee."

There were two main routes they could take to Galilee, and there was another, shorter way through Samaria. But the Jews and Samaritans hated each other, and most Jews always used one of the longer routes. So Jesus' friends were surprised when Jesus said, "This time let's go through Samaria."

The disciples wondered at this. Jews who were strict in observing the Law never went through Samaria.

The Samaritans were descendants of those Jews who had married pagan people after the fall of the northern kingdom of Israel. By this time they had rid themselves of all idol worship. They kept the Sabbath and observed the Jewish feasts. They accepted the Law of Moses as holy Scripture but not the writings of the prophets or writings such as the psalms.

Even so, the Jews considered them out of God's family, because they would not join them in worship at the Temple in Jerusalem.

The disciples asked one another, "How is it that Jesus is willing to travel through Samaria?" But they felt that they ought not to question Jesus.

John 3:22-30; 4:14; Luke 3:18-20; Matthew 4:12; Mark 1:14

15. A Talk at Jacob's Well

Jesus and His disciples had been walking a whole day. It was getting on to noon the next day, and they were beginning to grow weary and hungry. Their food was gone, and Jesus was especially tired.

"Up ahead is the town of Sychar," said one of the disciples. "We can buy food there, and look, here is Jacob's well."

This was the same well that Jacob had dug and used a thousand years before. It stood outside the town in a field which was said to have been a gift from Jacob to his son Joseph.

One of the disciples said, "Rabbi,

wait here and rest. We will go into the town and buy food."

Jesus agreed, because He was very tired. He had worked very hard in Judea, and much preaching and healing were ahead for Him in Galilee.

Jesus watched the disciples disappear within the town's gates. Soon a woman came out. Jesus watched her come down the path carrying a waterpot.

Jesus was very thirsty, but He had nothing with which to draw water up from the well. When the woman approached He asked, "Will you give Me a drink?"

The woman was surprised. Generally Jews and Samaritans did not speak to each other unless it was absolutely necessary. Besides, most men would not speak to a woman in public. She did not know whether to be insulted or pleased.

"How is it that you ask a favor of me, a Samaritan?" she asked.

"If you knew who was talking to you today, you would have asked Him for fresh, living water," Jesus replied.

The woman was puzzled. "You don't have anything to get water with."

"I am not talking about well water," Jesus said. "You'll be thirsty again in just a little while after drinking this water. I'm talking about a kind of water that keeps springing up, that brings eternal life, and that keeps you from getting thirsty again."

The woman was even more puzzled at this and tried to change the subject. But Jesus talked to her about God and His will for people to have new lives. This new kind of life would be like spring water that would never grow stale.

The woman felt guilty. She knew she had committed some serious sins. The other women of Sychar looked down on her. They called her wicked and wouldn't have anything to do with her.

But Jesus cared about the woman. He knew she had done wrong, but He knew that God wanted to forgive her and help her to do better in the future.

The woman asked Jesus about worshiping God. "The Jews say we must come to Jerusalem to worship, but our fathers say God wanted the Temple built on Mt. Gerizim, one of our mountains."

Jesus told her that God had wanted the Temple built in Jerusalem. "But this is not the most important thing," Jesus said. "God cares more about how we worship. True worshipers worship the Father in spirit and truth.

"The Father seeks those who will worship Him in this sincere way. God is spirit, and those who worship Him must worship Him in spirit and truth."

The woman thought, *These are strange but wonderful words.*

She told Jesus, "I know that the Messiah will come. The Messiah will tell us all the truth about God."

Jesus told her, "I am the Messiah."

The woman was surprised indeed at Jesus' declaration. Just then the disciples returned with the food.

"Look," they said to one another as they approached. "Jesus talks with a woman—a Samaritan woman."

When they came to the well the woman hurriedly said good-by. In her haste she left her waterpot behind.

She hurried back into the town and told everyone about her talk with Jesus. "He told me marvelous things," she said. "Do you think this could be the Messiah?"

The other men and women said, "The Messiah? Is it possible? We must go out and talk to this man."

Meanwhile the disciples brought out the food they had bought. They ate eagerly, but Jesus did not seem interested in the good lunch.

"Rabbi," they asked, "Aren't you hungry anymore?"

"I forgot about food," Jesus told them. "I was so happy teaching that woman about God that I have My strength back. Doing what God wants Me to is like food for Me. Look, now others are coming from the town to hear."

It was true. Many men and women were coming out of Sychar to the well. They had not brought their waterpots. They had come out to hear Jesus.

Jesus taught them about God's Kingdom. He urged them to repent and become a part of this Kingdom.

They listened eagerly. Many said, "This is indeed the Messiah, the Saviour of the world. We believe in Him, not because of what the woman said, but because we heard Him for ourselves."

They invited Jesus to stay with them, and for two days He stayed and taught them. Then He and the disciples had to journey on.

John 4:5-42

16. A Sick Son

Back in Galilee the people welcomed Jesus and His friends warmly. They had heard of all the marvelous things He had done in Jerusalem. Many had been at the Feast and had seen the miracles for themselves.

Now crowds came out to see more miracles. As important as miracles were, it was also important that the people better understand God. Jesus wanted them to listen with all their hearts to His teaching and not just to come out to see something unusual.

One day in Cana a man came running up to Jesus. He was a Jew, an official of Herod Antipas, and a wealthy and important person. Now he was in great distress.

"My son is ill," he told Jesus. "I am afraid he is going to die. Please come home to Capernaum with me and heal him."

"Will you believe in Me only if you see miracles?" Jesus asked him.

The man asked again, "Please come. My child needs help."

Jesus had come to show God's love, and one good way was to heal the sick. Jesus wanted to see if the man really believed He could do this. When he continued to ask, Jesus knew that he did.

"Do not fear," said Jesus. "Your son will live. When you get home you will find him well."

The man hurried out of Cana and took the road leading to his town by the Sea of Galilee. He believed that what Jesus had said would be true.

"I'm sure Jesus has already healed my son," he said as he hurried up to his large house the next day.

Servants ran out of the courtyard, "Your son is much better," they cried.

The man was happy. After he had seen his son for himself he asked the servants, "When did my son start to get well?"

"Yesterday at the seventh hour his fever went away," they told him.

"That was when I was talking to Jesus," said the man. He told everyone he knew about Jesus. He and everyone in his family said, "We are sure Jesus is the Messiah."

People who heard stories like these brought their sick many miles in order that Jesus might heal them.

Jesus taught the people wherever they gathered; but on the Sabbath He went to different synagogues to preach. Although He had not attended the special schools for scribes and rabbis the people realized that Jesus was a good teacher. They called Him rabbi as a sign of esteem and respect.

Jesus told the crowds: "The time has come. The Kingdom of God is at hand. Repent and believe these good tidings from God."

John 4:43-54; Matthew 4:23-25; Mark 1:14, 15; Luke 4:14, 15

17. In the Hometown Synagogue

One Sabbath Jesus went again up the familiar steps of the synagogue in Nazareth. How often He had come here. First He had been carried as a baby by Mary. Then He had come as a boy to worship and to learn at the school.

Jesus had been well known to all the people of the village; but now He was known as a great teacher and miracle-worker throughout most of Judea and Galilee.

Everyone looked around as Jesus came in with His family. Men stood apart from the women, and so Jesus stood with His brothers. Jesus' new friends and followers had gone to their homes.

One of the leaders of the synagogue came over to Jesus. "Will you read for us today?" he asked.

Jesus was glad to be chosen. Often members of the congregation were given the opportunity to read the Scriptures. Every boy in school had his chance at one time. The people remembered when Jesus had done this as a boy.

They watched when, at the scheduled time, the attendant who had charge of the scrolls handed one to Jesus. The people had mixed thoughts that went like this:

Now Jesus has grown up to be a great teacher. Crowds flock to hear him. He has wonderful power from God to heal the sick. And yet this is a man we know well. We know Mary and we know Jesus' brothers and sisters.

Some doubted the stories they had heard. *How can it be that Jesus has the power others say he has? Isn't he a boy we have always known?*

It didn't seem possible to these people that Jesus could be the Messiah.

In the synagogue service it was right for the reader to stand while he read and then to sit down on a special chair to preach or explain the words of Scripture.

The attendant had handed Jesus the scroll of the prophet Isaiah. Jesus found a certain place and began to read:

The Spirit of the Lord is upon me.
He has anointed me to preach good news to the poor,
To proclaim release to those held captive,
To proclaim the year of the Lord."

Then Jesus closed the scroll and sat down. All eyes were upon Him. They wondered, *What will Jesus have to say about this Scripture?*

Some thought, *Jesus did many miracles in other places, but he has not done any such acts here. When will he heal our sick?*

Some had already said, "Unless we see Jesus do great miracles right here in Nazareth we will not believe."

Jesus spoke out: "Today this Scripture has come true. I have been sent from God to do these things.

"Now I know that you have wondered about Me, and you expect Me to perform great miracles. But in order for help and healing to come, you must believe. Most of you do not believe in Me. It is always hard for a prophet to find acceptance around those who have seen him grow up."

Jesus gave two examples of prophets who had not always been accepted in their own lands—Elijah and Elisha.

"You remember from the Scriptures that Elijah was sent to a widow of Zarephath to hide during the famine. There were many widows in Israel, but God chose this foreigner. In the same way there were many lepers in Israel at the time of Elisha. But the prophet healed Naaman the Syrian."

The people were angry when they heard this. Everyone began to talk at once. "Jesus has no right to compare himself to the prophets of old," some said.

Others said, "We are older than he is, and yet he rebukes us for lack of faith."

Others said, "Jesus talks as though God cares as much for pagans as for Jews who are loyal to His worship."

They became so angry that some started to crowd around Jesus and threaten Him. Soon the orderly congregation turned into an unthinking mob.

Some shouted that Jesus should be brought up on top of a nearby cliff and thrown down. The pushing, shoving crowd swept out of the synagogue and up the road.

But Jesus escaped out of the crowd. He knew the caves and narrow paths of the hills very well, and safely found His way outside the village.

Because of the lack of faith among His old friends and neighbors, Jesus had not been able to help many in Nazareth. A few sick people had believed. Jesus had laid His hands on them, and they recovered.

Jesus was sad that the people of Nazareth doubted His claims. It hurt Him to think that they were so jealous that they had wanted to kill Him.

The crowds had shouted that they wanted Jesus to leave Nazareth and never return. Jesus left the valley and made His way over the hills and down to the Sea of Galilee.

Mark 6:1-6; Luke 4:16-31; Matthew 13:53-58

18. "And They Left All"

The disciples who had become friends and helpers of Jesus had not spent all their time with Him. At different times some had returned to duties at home. Jesus made His trip back to Nazareth alone.

Now Jesus wanted men who would come with Him on special preaching tours. They would need to leave their ordinary way of earning a living and spend all their time with Him.

They would learn from Him so that they could teach others. They would help Him as He healed the sick and taught great crowds. They would share His poverty.

James, John, Andrew and Peter were all fishermen. Jesus went looking for them around the Sea of Galilee. This large lake was known for its good fishing.

The Sea of Galilee is thirteen miles long, eight miles wide and at its deepest two hundred feet deep. Around its shores in Jesus' day there were fishing towns and villages. Behind the beaches green hills surround the water. In the springtime they are covered with red anemones. On the east side the hills rise abruptly into mountains two thousand feet high.

As Jesus walked by the water the sun shown down brightly on the busy workers. Some were fishing, some were mending nets, some were packing fish for shipment. The water sparkled and the sand and rocks were warm under His feet.

Up ahead Peter and Andrew were standing in shallow water. They were fishing with the small castnet which required so much skill to use. How good these brothers were at their job!

Jesus greeted them. They were glad to see Jesus again. They stopped their fishing as Jesus talked to them about the preaching tour He was soon to start. He told them of His need for helpers who would be with Him continually.

"Come and follow Me," Jesus urged Peter and Andrew. "Then instead of catching fish, you will be catching men and bringing them into God's Kingdom."

"We will," Peter and Andrew cried. They put away their nets and walked with Jesus.

As they went further around the lake Jesus found James and John. These fishermen were in partnership with Andrew and Peter.

Now they were with their father, Zebedee, mending the large fishing net which had been damaged the night before. The fishermen often went out at night and brought their boats back in the morning, the nets filled with many kinds of fish.

James and John were glad to see Jesus. "Rabbi," they said. "It is good to see you again."

Jesus talked to them and their father. "I need good men to help Me," Jesus told Zebedee. "Your sons will make fine helpers. They will have a great part in bringing God's Kingdom to men."

He told James and John about the preaching tour. "I need men who are willing to leave all and follow Me," He said.

The fishermen had a good business. It would be a sacrifice. Zebedee was sad at the thought of losing his sons, but he did not try to stop them from working for God.

"We will come," said James and John. They left the fishing boat and the half-mended net.

Then Jesus began to preach to those who quickly gathered around. Some had heard Jesus before. They gathered around the shore. It was such a large crowd that some started to call out, "We can't hear."

"Peter," said Jesus, "the people would be able to hear if I got into a boat and put out a little from the shore. Then they could spread out on the bank."

"Please use one of our boats," cried Peter and ran to get it for Jesus. He rowed the boat with Jesus in it out a little way from the land.

Jesus preached to the people about God's Kingdom. When the talk was over, the people thoughtfully went away. Jesus' four fishermen friends stayed.

Then Jesus turned to Peter. "Let's take the boats out on the lake and get some fish," He suggested.

"It's no use," said Peter. "The fish aren't biting. We had a poor night last night."

"Come take the boats out," Jesus urged.

The four fishermen obeyed. When they were out in deep waters Jesus said, "Put down the nets."

When they did they found a large group of fish moving together, just waiting to be caught. Peter was awe struck as he helped bring in the nets. He called for James and John who were in the other boat to help. These brothers were also surprised. They were sure it was because Jesus had directed them that the catch was so large.

When the fishermen brought the boats to shore they told Jesus their decision. They would go with Him on the tour and stay with Him for as long as He wanted.

The fishing business could be handled by Zebedee and the hired fishermen. They left all to follow Jesus.

Matthew 4:18-22;
Mark 1:16-20; Luke 5:1-11

19. At Peter's House

Jesus and the four fishermen went to Capernaum. Peter's home was there and they stayed at his house. This town was chosen by Jesus as the center of His preaching tour around Galilee.

Capernaum was a busy town on the northwestern shore of the lake. The trade route from Damascus to Egypt went through here. Many Roman soldiers were stationed at the military post. They helped collect the taxes on goods going in and out of the country on the Roman highway.

On the Sabbath Jesus taught in the synagogue in Capernaum. Afterwards the people who had attended the service spoke with amazement.

"Jesus teaches with authority, just as though God Himself gave the message. Our religious rulers interpret the writings of the past; but Jesus has a message directly from God."

Jesus and the disciples went home with Peter. They were hungry and tired, but a good dinner would be waiting.

Peter's wife had dinner ready, but she

was upset. "My mother is ill," she told Jesus. "This morning she began to feel bad. Now she has a high fever."

"Can you help her?" asked Peter.

They led Jesus to the room where the mother lay on her mat. Jesus took up her hand, and at His touch the fever left her. She opened her eyes and sat up.

"Do you feel better now?" Jesus asked her.

"I feel fine," the mother said. "I must get up and help my daughter."

She insisted that she was able to help with the serving of dinner.

Others had heard that Jesus had power to heal. During the hot afternoon everyone rested, but at sunset when the Sabbath was over, Jesus and His friends heard talking outside. The noise grew louder and louder.

Peter looked out. All around the house people had gathered. Some were lame or blind. Some had been brought on sleeping mats. Children were in the arms of parents.

"We have come for healing," they called. "We need Jesus' help."

Jesus came to the door beside Peter. He went out to the crowd, touching some, speaking to others. At His command as many as had faith were healed of their sickness.

Jesus was glad to be able to help people in this way. He knew God wanted people to be well and strong and that God cared about those who suffered. It was one way Jesus showed the love of God.

Many people spread the word about Jesus. "He is a prophet who speaks for God," they said, "and he has power to heal all kinds of sickness."

The next morning while it was still dark, Jesus quietly left Peter's house. He went out into the hills where He could be alone with God. He prayed for God's help and guidance as they were to begin this preaching tour.

A little while later Peter again heard sounds outside his house. He opened the door, and once more he was greeted by a crowd who wanted to see Jesus.

"Just a moment," Peter told them. He went to find Jesus, but He was not in the house.

"Perhaps Jesus went off to pray," said one of the disciples. "He likes to pray in the hills alone."

The disciples and some of the people of the town went to look in the hills. There they found Jesus.

"Everyone is searching for you," Peter told Him.

"But we must go on to another town," said Jesus. "Everyone must hear the good news of God's love, and there are sick in other places who need help. Don't you remember the preaching tour I told you about?"

"Yes, that is right," said Peter. "We were to go to all the towns and villages around Galilee."

"We must go on to other places," John and James told the crowd.

"Please don't leave us," the people begged Jesus.

"I will come back," He promised, "but now I must go on. I was sent to preach the good news to all of God's people."

Matthew 4:13; 8:14-16; Mark 1:21-38; Luke 4:31-43

20. Jesus Forgives Sins

Jesus and His disciples went on and visited other towns and villages throughout Galilee. Large crowds came out to hear Him, and many people followed Him from place to place.

Some came from as far as Perea and Jerusalem just to see and hear Jesus. They were amazed at His teaching. "This is new teaching," they said.

They were amazed, too, at Jesus' power to heal.

One day a leper came to Jesus for healing. He had a disease of the skin, and because it was believed to be contagious he was not allowed to come near others.

Everyone moved away as the leper approached Jesus.

The poor diseased man fell on his knees before Jesus. "Lord," he cried, "if you will, you can make me well."

Jesus pitied the man. Because of his disease no one wanted him around. He was not permitted to live with his family. He had no way of earning a living and had to beg.

Jesus knew the man had faith in Him. The Lord put out His hand and touched the diseased skin. "I will," He said. "Be well."

The man's skin cleared up. The sores disappeared. The man was overjoyed. Now in order to return to his family and friends he would have to show the priest that he was cured.

"Go show yourself to the priest," said Jesus. "You are a leper no longer."

The man told everyone he met what a wonderful thing Jesus had done for him. As a result so many people came to hear Jesus that it was impossible to go into the market place of a town. The narrow streets could not hold the crowds.

Jesus and His disciples stayed outside in the fields or by the lake, and people came out of the towns and villages for miles around to hear Him.

Jesus kept traveling so that different people would hear His message. In time He came back to Capernaum. Within a few days the news was out that Jesus had returned, and a crowd of people gathered at Peter's house.

Peter had a fine home with many rooms surrounding a courtyard. There was a tile roof over part of the open courtyard. Jesus stood here in the shade and preached to the people.

Meanwhile some men who had brought a sick person tried to get up to the front of the crowd, but they couldn't. They carried the sick man on his mat, because he couldn't walk.

The men who brought him loved him so much that they carried the man up the outside stairs onto the roof of the house, above where Jesus stood, they took out some of the tiles of the roof and with ropes let the man down—sleeping mat and all.

Many people had gathered to hear Jesus that day, but all were not friendly. Some of the Pharisees from towns in Galilee and Judea had come to Capernaum to criticize Jesus and to convince themselves that He was wrong.

The Pharisees and their scribes did not approve of Jesus' teachings. He had never gone to their special schools to learn the Law, and He seemed to say things which contradicted the teachings of the rabbis of the past.

All were surprised when the mat appeared coming down from the roof. Then they saw the men on top and realized what was happening.

Jesus looked at the sick man. He was paralyzed, but Jesus realized something else. The man felt very guilty about the sins of his life. More than healing, he needed forgiveness of sins.

Jesus said to the man, "My son, be of good cheer. Your sins are forgiven."

The scribes and the Pharisees began to mutter to one another. "Jesus has no right to say that. Only God can forgive sins." They were shocked.

"Why do you question?" Jesus asked them. "Which do you think is easier to say—'Your sins are forgiven,' or, 'get up and walk'? To prove that I have the authority to forgive sins I will heal this man."

Then Jesus turned to the man. "Get up, take up your mat and walk," He told him.

Then the man, who had not been able to walk for a long while, got up on his feet and rolled up his mat. He was able to walk away with his friends.

Jesus wanted the religious leaders to believe in Him. This miracle of healing which could only come from God, should have convinced them that Jesus was telling the truth about being able to forgive sins.

But the rulers did not understand and did not believe. The people did not fully understand either, but they believed that Jesus had great power from God, and they rejoiced.

"We have never seen anything like this," they said. "Thank God for His mercy and love."

Matthew 4:23-25; 8:2-4; 9:2-8
Luke 4:44; 5:12-26
Mark 1:39-45; 2:1-12

21. Jesus Finds New Friends

Some of the religious rulers thought it was wrong to be friends with those who were not religious. Jesus showed love and friendship to all people. Often He sought out those He thought He could help. Jesus felt that even those who did serious wrong should be treated kindly and so helped to do better.

Jesus made friends with Matthew, a tax collector. Matthew had many questions about God. Jesus told him about the work God had given Him to do.

The tax collectors were hated by the Pharisees and the other religious rulers, because they worked for Rome or for Herod who was appointed by Rome.

The government demanded much in the way of taxes. There were taxes paid each year on lands, houses and persons. Other taxes were on certain goods.

Taxes were charged those who used the caravan routes which Rome had built. One of the places where people could pay these taxes was in Capernaum.

Every day Matthew sat at his booth in Capernaum. His job was to collect the charge from caravans of traders traveling from Egypt or Damascus. A soldier stood nearby. The tax collectors were so unpopular that a military guard was needed for their protection.

The religious rulers considered the tax collectors traitors and little better than robbers. Some tax collectors did cheat the people.

Because of this, the Jewish leaders would not accept the testimony of a tax collector at court, nor would they allow him to contribute money for the help of the poor.

One day Jesus stopped and talked to Matthew as he sat collecting the money for the government. Jesus asked Matthew to be a disciple.

"Come, follow Me," said Jesus. "Leave this job right now."

Matthew stood right up, even though crowds of people were standing in line, ready to pay their tax.

Matthew turned to the soldier. "Give this booth to another collector," he said. "From now on I follow Jesus."

The people were startled. They knew the religious rulers would criticize Jesus for accepting Matthew. They were also surprised that a tax collector would leave his job to follow Jesus.

Matthew was happy to be one of Jesus' disciples. "Rabbi," he said. "I want to hold a big feast in your honor. May I invite my other tax collector friends?"

Jesus was glad. He wanted to meet Matthew's friends.

The guests sat on couches in the courtyard of Matthew's house, in comfortable reclining positions. There were many fine dishes of meat and vegetables on the long, low table. There was plenty of bread, fruit and cheese. Jesus was there, and His disciples along with Matthew's friends.

People passing by looked in. Some began to gather outside where they could see into the partly open courtyard.

Some Pharisees and scribes stopped by. They entered the courtyard and stood looking with disdainful eyes. Finally they spoke to a few of the disciples. They hoped to take them away from following Jesus.

"Why does your master eat with tax collectors and other sinners?" they asked.

Jesus heard them. He spoke up. "A doctor comes not to the well people, but to those who are sick. I came to work with people who realize they often do wrong, and to help them repent and come back to God."

The Pharisees were strict in keeping the Law. Many of the things they did were good and right, but they were proud of their religious ways. In their pride they forgot to love others. They even thought it a sin to love those who did wrong.

Jesus reminded them of the words of a long-ago prophet. "Study what this means," He told them. "Through the prophet Hosea, God said, 'I desire mercy and not sacrifice.' "

Jesus wanted them to understand that showing love and mercy was more important to God than rituals and rules.

Matthew 9:9-13; Mark 2:12-17; Luke 5:27-32

22. At the Pool of Bethzatha

There were many different feast days in the Jewish religion. Three were most important: the Passover, Pentecost, and the Feast of Tabernacles.

It was time for one of these feasts and Jesus said to His disciples, "Let us take a trip to Jerusalem and keep the feast."

Once again they came to the city which was holy in Jewish history. As was always the case at special times great crowds pushed their way about the narrow streets of Jerusalem.

One day when Jesus was walking with His friends they came upon the pool of Bethzatha. This was a spring near the Temple. The pool was known to help sick people, and five pillared porches or porticoes had been built around it.

When the water moved, the sick people bathed in it. Many had reported that they had been helped by this, and so at feast times people came from other cities to try to find help for themselves. (There were no hospitals where they could get help.)

All kinds of sicknesses were there—invalids, the lame, and the blind. It made Jesus and His friends feel sad to watch.

One old man had been there for many years. When he was young, he was strong and healthy, but because he lived in wild ways and did much that was wrong, he became paralyzed.

The religious rulers would have condemned this man, but Jesus had mercy on him. He went over to where the man lay on his sleeping mat.

"Do you really want to be healed?" Jesus asked. Jesus knew that to get well a person needed to want to be cured.

"I don't have any friends to help me into the water," the man said.

Jesus did not help the man into the water. Instead He spoke His words of healing. "Rise and take up your mat. You will be able to walk."

The man felt strength come into his legs and his body. He got up. Yes, he could stand. He rolled up the mat and tried. Yes, he could walk.

By this time Jesus had moved away and was lost in the crowd. The man searched everywhere for Him.

Then some of the Pharisees saw the man. "What are you doing?" they asked him. "This is the Sabbath. You should not be carrying your mat. That is work."

The man was confused. "But you don't

understand," he said. "I have been paralyzed for years. Then today as I was lying by the pool this man came up to me. He spoke words of healing to me and made me well. He said, 'Take up your mat and walk.' "

"Who is this man?" the Pharisees demanded. "What is his name? Where is he?"

The man did not know. "I never saw him before," he said.

Later that day the man went to the Temple service. He thanked God for bringing someone to heal him. After the service Jesus came up to him. The man recognized Him and started to thank Him, but Jesus said, "Now you are well. Live a good life. Don't go into such sinful ways again, or else you will become ill again."

The man promised Jesus that he would not. He listened to others talk to Jesus and learned His name.

Then the man went to the Pharisees. He did not understand that these were the enemies of Jesus. He wanted Jesus to get the credit for performing this miracle.

"It was Jesus who healed me," he told them.

The Pharisees hurried over to Jesus. "Why have you healed on the Sabbath, and why did you tell that man to carry his mat? Don't you realize that you broke the Sabbath?"

Jesus did not believe this was breaking the Sabbath. "My Father does His good work for people every day," He told them. "Part of His work is healing the sick. I am doing God's work. It is God who sent Me."

The Pharisees were very angry. They thought it was terrible that a religious teacher should break God's laws, and they would not accept Jesus' explanation, especially because He called God His Father. They did not believe in Jesus.

Jesus warned them: "The Father loves the Son and tells Him what to do. Anyone who does not honor the Son does not honor the Father who sent Him. Those who believe in Me will have new life, but you refuse to come to Me."

John 5

23. "We Must Get Rid of Jesus"

Jesus and His disciples returned to Galilee and continued their preaching tour. Some of the Pharisees from Jerusalem followed them. They joined other scribes and Pharisees from Galilee who followed Jesus and His friends from town to town.

They did not believe in Jesus, and they tried to find people who would say things against Him in court. They wanted to bring Him to trial before the Sanhedrin for breaking the Sabbath. (The Sanhedrin had charge of judging all matters of religion among the Jews.)

Jesus and His friends knew the Pharisees were there, but they continued to do God's work as before. One Sabbath they went as they always did to the service in the synagogue.

The Jewish law said no one could eat

on the Sabbath until after the service. When it was over Jesus and His friends were very hungry.

"There is a field of grain," said one of the disciples. "Let's see if any grain has been left."

According to God's Law some grain was to be left after harvest especially for the poor or for hungry travelers.

The friends of Jesus were glad to find grain in the fields. They plucked the grain and rubbed out the kernels in their hands. It tasted good because they were hungry. They gave some to Jesus.

Some of the Pharisees saw them. "Look," they cried to the people around the synagogue. "Jesus and his friends are breaking the law of the Sabbath. By plucking that corn they are reaping a harvest."

In their interpretations and additions to the Law the Pharisees had made the laws defining work on the Sabbath very strict. It was wrong to help sick people when it meant others must work, they said. Only if it meant the difference between life and death could they be cared for. Jesus knew that much suffering resulted from these strict laws and that it was not what God wanted.

Jesus defended Himself and His friends. He reminded the Pharisees of a story about King David, when David was running away from Saul and had no food.

Jesus asked them, "Have you forgotten that David and his men once entered the Holy Place by permission of the high priest and ate the sacred loaves of bread that only the priests are supposed to eat? And this happened on the Sabbath."

The Pharisees listened, but they were not convinced.

"In the Temple the priests work on the Sabbath," Jesus reminded them. "Many helpers at the Temple also have work to do; but the rulers of the Temple permit this and say it is not breaking the Sabbath."

Then Jesus gave them a better interpretation of the Sabbath law. "The Sabbath was made for man," He said, "man was not made for the Sabbath. People and their needs are most important."

God had given this law because it was good for people to rest one day from ordinary labor. It gave them a chance to think about God and worship God together.

Jesus told them something else. "The Son of Man is Lord of the Sabbath." ("Son of Man" was a special name for the Messiah.) As the Messiah they should take His word for what was right and wrong.

But the Pharisees still were not convinced. They thought one had to always obey laws exactly, keeping every addition and interpretation strictly. "How can Jesus be the Messiah if he breaks the Sabbath?" they asked each other in scorn.

They followed Jesus and His friends back into the synagogue. As they watched, Jesus stopped before a man who had something wrong with his hand. The muscles would not work and the hand hung useless.

Jesus turned around to the religious rulers. They were waiting for Jesus to heal the man. This would be another sin with which to charge Him. This would be another time when He healed on the Sabbath.

Jesus asked the Pharisees, "Is it according to the Law to do good or evil on the Sabbath? Is it a day to save life or to kill? Don't you take care of your animals on the Sabbath? You even pull your donkey out of a ditch if it happens to fall in on the Sabbath."

A man was worth far more than a donkey. And this man needed his hand to do his work. Without a way to earn a living he could only care for his family by joining the hundreds of beggars who depended on a coin here or there.

The man needed help desperately, but this did not move the religious rulers. They would not give their approval to healing the man.

They refused to even answer Jesus. They stood there waiting to accuse Jesus if He did what they thought was wrong.

Jesus was both angry and sad. He felt sorry for these rulers who had such hard hearts. They kept themselves from ever learning God's way of love.

"Stretch out your hand," Jesus told the man.

Without hesitation the man obeyed. No one doubted but what Jesus could heal the man. Again it happened. When the man had faith enough to obey Jesus, the hand was healed. He could move it and work with it.

Now he could care for his family in the proper way. He was thankful and Jesus was happy that He could help him.

But the Pharisees were angry. They turned and left the synagogue. After this they often met together in secret. "How can we destroy Jesus?" they asked one another. "We must find a way. We must get rid of him. From now on we will have spies watching him all the time. We will find reasons to have him put to death."

Matthew 12:1-14; Mark 2:13-3:6; Luke 5:17; 6:1-11; John 5:18

24. Jesus Teaches in the Hills

Jesus knew these enemies were plotting His death. He left the towns and villages where they stayed and went out into the more open places. From then on Jesus taught more in the hills or along the sea shore rather than in the synagogues.

Many came to hear Him, some from a long distance–Judea, Idumea and from the other side of the Jordan. Some came from the ancient cities of Tyre and Sidon north of Galilee.

Jesus healed those who were sick. Some of these people were Gentiles. He asked them not to talk about it to others, because He knew His enemies wanted to catch Him.

Different disciples had followed Jesus from time to time. Many had come to believe in Him as the Messiah. But Jesus wanted a small group of leaders who would learn from Him and be able to teach others. Before making the choice of just who these would be, Jesus spent the night in prayer asking for God's guidance. He talked to God among the hills where He could be alone.

In the morning He called all His followers together. He chose twelve for this small group. These were: Peter, Andrew, James, John, Philip, Bartholomew (sometimes called Nathanael), Thomas, Matthew, James the son of Alphaeus, Thaddaeus, Simon and Judas Iscariot.

Jesus wanted these twelve men to know His teachings well. But it was not enough for them just to know God's way. Jesus wanted them to put these things into their own lives. As an example they could watch Jesus, for He always lived in the way He taught.

Jesus asked these twelve disciples to come up to the top of the hills where they could be alone. Then He taught them like this:

Happy are the humble, for they will find the Kingdom of God.
Happy are those who mourn about their sins, for they will be comforted by forgiveness.
Happy are the gentle, for they will inherit the earth.
Happy are those who want righteousness, for they will be satisfied.
Happy are the merciful, for they shall find mercy from God.
Happy are those who love God completely, for they shall come to know God.
Happy are the peacemakers, for they shall be called the sons of God.
Happy are those who are persecuted when they do right, for God will reward them with a place in His Kingdom.

Jesus wanted His disciples and all who believed in Him to understand the importance of the work to which they were called.

He said, "You are like salt to food. You are like a light in a dark world. Let your light shine. Then men will see your good deeds and give glory to God your Father in heaven."

The Jews all knew the commandments God had given through Moses; but Jesus said that to really obey the commandments meant more than outward actions.

Jesus said, "You have heard it said, 'Do not kill,' but I say, 'Don't get angry with your brother.' "

His listeners realized what Jesus meant. Anger sometimes led to murder.

Jesus said, "You have heard it said, 'Love your neighbor.' That is right, but you should also love your enemies. Forgive those who wrong you and pray for their good.

"It is not difficult to love those who love you, but My followers should love those who do not love them. God loves those who do not love Him. He sends His rain and sun to shine on all, the good and the wicked. Be like your Father in heaven.

"When you do good things for others don't make a show of it so that others will be sure to see you. When you pray to God, pray secretly, not where others will see you and praise your religious faith. Do these things for God and His praise, not for men and their praise."

Jesus knew that His disciples would have to give up much to follow Him. He knew that danger might come to those who believed in Him. He knew they would often worry about the necessities of life, such as food and clothing. So He said to them, "Don't be anxious about these things. Look at the birds and flowers around you. God has made the flowers beautiful with color. He has provided for their needs. He will also provide for you."

Jesus wanted His disciples to show kindness to others. He said, "Treat others in the way you want to be treated."

These were some of the teachings Jesus gave to His disciples that day and which He repeated many, many times to the great crowds of people who came out to hear them. He described for them what the Kingdom of God and its members would be like. He invited them to join.

Jesus knew it was not an easy life He was picturing. He compared the life He taught about to a narrow gate through which one must enter with care.

It would not be enough to call Jesus "Lord." A lord was someone to be obeyed. Jesus told those who listened, "Not everyone who says to me 'Lord, Lord' will enter the Kingdom of heaven, but only the one who does the will of My Father who is in heaven."

Jesus wanted His followers not only to call Him Lord but to obey Him as well.

Jesus told a story about people who listened to His teachings and obeyed them.

"Those who obey My words are like people who build houses on the rock. Their houses stand solid when storms come. The person who has obeyed My teaching has built the kind of life that will stand up under trouble. When troubles come they will have the strength and faith in God they need.

"But the person who doesn't obey is like someone who builds a house on sand. The house falls when the storms come because it isn't built on anything solid. So those who don't live in God's way lose all faith in God when troubles come."

The disciples and the crowds who came to hear Jesus were often surprised at His teachings. Jesus taught that it was best to be humble, gentle and loving—by living this way a person really obeyed God. This was just the opposite of what most people thought was important.

Some people went away from Jesus. "He doesn't talk about a kingdom of power and glory and might," they said. They were not interested.

But others said, "The life Jesus describes is wonderful. The world would indeed be the Kingdom of God if all people followed these teachings." They came out again and again to hear more.

Matthew 12:15, 16; 10:2-4; 5:1-16; Mark 3:7-9; Luke 6:12-49; 12:22-34

25. Questions From the Baptizer

Jesus often went back to Capernaum. On one visit an important officer in the Roman army came to him. Unlike many officers he was a good, kind man. He had many men under him and many personal servants, but he was fair with them.

The Jews liked him, because he had given them money with which to build a synagogue.

This officer had one servant whom he loved and trusted very much. Now this servant was so ill, many believed he would die.

The officer was a Gentile, but he had heard a lot about Jesus. He believed the stories of healing he had heard. He was sure Jesus could help his servant.

The officer came and told Jesus, "Lord, my servant is close to death."

"I will come and heal him," Jesus promised.

The officer knew that many Jews did not like to come into Gentile homes. He told Jesus, "You do not need to come yourself. I am not worthy to have you. Only speak the word, and I know my servant will get well.

"I am a man of authority. Others obey me. I know you too have authority and can command sickness to leave."

Jesus was happy. Here was one who really believed in Him. He said to those around Him, "Do you hear this man? He is a Gentile, and yet he has greater faith than I have found among My own people. There will be Gentiles in God's Kingdom, but some of the Jews will not be there."

Jesus said to the officer, "When you return home you will find your servant better. What you believed will happen."

The officer left. When he got home he found his servant well. He told all his friends what had happened.

The next day Jesus and His disciples went through the village of Nain. A crowd of people followed. As they entered the village they met a funeral procession. Jesus saw the poor, widowed mother whose son had died. He told her, "Don't weep."

Then Jesus went over and touched the open bier. "Young man, arise," He said.

The dead son came back to life. He got up and spoke. Everyone was frightened. The boy spoke to them all, and Jesus brought the son to the mother.

Everyone was amazed. They gave God the glory.

"Jesus is a prophet like no other," they said. They told everyone they knew about this miracle. Everyone in the surrounding towns and villages was talking about Jesus.

All this time, John the baptizer was still in prison, but his disciples were allowed to visit him from time to time.

John wanted to be sure that Jesus really was the Messiah. John had expected God's Kingdom to come right away. He had heard many wonderful stories about the work of Jesus, but the religious rulers had not accepted Him.

Some of John's disciples doubted Jesus. They often talked about it to John when they visited him. John told them to go

and see Jesus for themselves and to bring back a report from on the scene.

So a delegation traveled to Galilee where Jesus was preaching. They watched as Jesus healed many sick people. They listened to Him talk about God. Eventually they found opportunity to talk to Jesus alone.

"Are you the One who is to come or ought we to look for another?" the disciples of John asked Jesus.

Jesus told them, "Go back and tell John what you have seen today. Have you heard how the official's servant was healed? Have you heard about the boy who was raised from the dead?

"Tell John, 'The blind receive their sight and the lame walk, lepers are healed, the deaf hear, the dead are raised up and the poor have good news preached to them. Happy is the person who continues to believe in Me even when things are difficult.' "

The disciples left to tell John that Jesus had done these things, just as the prophets had said the Messiah would.

Then Jesus had many good things to say to the crowd about John the baptizer. "John was a great prophet," said Jesus. "Many came to hear him because he was a strong man. He did not speak to please and flatter men. He boldly spoke out God's truth. He was the one sent to prepare the way, as the prophets foretold."

Jesus added, "John only announced the coming Kingdom, but you have the chance to actually become members of the Kingdom."

Not long after this the disciples of John the baptizer came again to see Jesus. This time they had a sad story to tell Him.

"Herod had not planned to kill John," they said. "Sometimes he would ask John questions and listen to him teach about God. But Herodias hated John. Time after time she had urged that John be put to death.

"Then she got her daughter to help persuade Herod. On his last birthday Herod gave a party, and at that time, as a favor to them, he ordered that John be put to death."

Jesus was sorry to hear this. He spoke words of comfort to John's disciples. Then He went alone where He could think and talk to God about it.

Matthew 8:5-13; 11:2-15; 14:3-13; Mark 6:7-29; Luke 17:1-28

26. Stories About God's Kingdom

Soon after this Jesus and the disciples went on another preaching tour around Galilee. This time some of the women who believed in Jesus went with them. There was Mary Magdalene, Joanna, Susanna, and many others.

They helped to provide some of the necessary money, and they took care of womanly matters such as cooking and sewing.

Jesus had some good friends who believed in Him and were willing to work with Him; but some of Jesus' friends did not understand His work.

Jesus' own brothers did not believe in Him. They could not understand His teachings at all. They worried about Him when they heard He had made the Pharisees angry, but they refused to join His followers.

Jesus missed His family, but He found a new family in His friends and disciples. He said anyone could be in His family who did the will of God.

One day Jesus taught out by the shore of the Sea of Galilee. As usual, great crowds came to hear, so again Jesus got into a boat and sat down in it. The crowds gathered about on the shore. In this way Jesus' voice carried out over them and all could hear.

On this day Jesus used stories to explain the Kingdom of God. First of all He warned His followers that everyone would not believe the message He had from God.

"It is like a sower who scatters the grain in his field. Some grain falls on good soil and good plants grow from the seed. But some falls on the hard pathway, or among thorns, or in a rocky place, and the seed does not produce a good plant."

Jesus went on to tell other stories or parables to teach about God's Kingdom. He said the Kingdom of God was something that would grow.

He said, "A seed sprouts and grows. First comes the blade and then the ear. In time the grain is ripe and the farmer gathers the harvest.

"The Kingdom of God is small now, like the tiny mustard seed. But like the mustard seed, which grows into a large bush so that birds come and make nests in its branches, the Kingdom will grow to be great in size.

"God's Kingdom will grow like the leaven women put in bread before it is baked. Women will put a small amount of leaven in a loaf of bread, but this small amount makes the whole loaf larger and makes it fluffy, good tasting bread."

This was good news. It meant that Jesus and His teachings would one day be known and believed throughout the world.

Being in God's Kingdom might cost a person friends and might involve danger, but Jesus said it was worth it.

He said, "The Kingdom of God is like a chest of money someone buried in a field. A man found the treasure, but he did not own the field. So he went out and sold all that he had in order to buy this field and own the treasure.

"The Kingdom of God is like a merchant who buys and sells pearls. One day he finds a larger, more beautiful pearl than he has ever seen. It will bring a great price. He is willing to sell all he has in order to buy this pearl."

In Jesus' day many teachers taught with parables. They made people think and wonder and discover what is true for themselves.

Some of those who listened did not like the parables. They had already decided that Jesus was not the Messiah and these stories confused them.

But those whose minds and hearts were open found new truth in these stories. They also found encouragement that God was working in His world, and that good and not evil would have the final victory.

Luke 8; Matthew 13; Mark 4; John 7:5

27. The Lord of the Lake

Jesus and His friends loved sailing on the deep blue waters of Galilee, but it was a dangerous lake. Sudden storms often swept across it. Small boats would turn over in the fierce winds and mounting waves. Then, as suddenly as it had begun, the storm would be over. The sun would come out again on quiet gentle waves.

Even today such storms still come up suddenly. This happens because the lake is 680 feet lower than the Mediterranean Sea, and to the east of the lake high mountains rise. The cold winds rush down the mountains through ravines and gorges on to the warm air above the lake.

One day Jesus and His disciples taught all day on the shore of Galilee. Jesus healed many who were sick, but still the crowds came.

Some came who said they wanted to become followers of Jesus but not right away. They were not like the fishermen followers who had left all at once in order to follow Jesus.

One was a scribe. "I will follow you wherever you go," he told Jesus.

Many people around were impressed. Here was an important person with a good education who was willing to be a disciple.

But Jesus knew the young man had not given the matter much thought. As a scribe he was used to many comforts because of the good job he held.

Jesus told him following Him would be a very different kind of life. "Foxes have holes to live in and the birds have nests of their own; but I have no home. There is no house of My own where I can lay My head at night."

The scribe had nothing to say. He had not expected it to be this hard.

Another man said, "I'll be a follower someday. Right now my parents need me."

"Now is your chance to follow Me," Jesus told him. "The work needs to be done now."

The other disciples had families to care for and they had found ways to care for them as well as to be followers of Jesus.

Another man said, "I will follow you, Lord, but first I have to spend some time at home. They will give me a fine farewell feast."

Jesus could see this man was not eager enough. His first thought was of a party in his honor. Such a one could never stand the hard life of a disciple. At the first sign of trouble he would run away. He would not want to follow Jesus enough to continue to be true.

"If you were really ready to make this great decision you wouldn't be looking back to your old life. It is not a good beginning to a new life if you look back with regret at leaving the old life," Jesus told him.

By now it was growing late. The sun was going down behind the green hills surrounding the lake.

The people did not leave, but Jesus said, "We are very tired. We must go somewhere and rest."

"Let's go across the lake and find some quiet place," suggested one of the disciples.

Jesus agreed. The disciples got several small boats which belonged to Zebedee, the father of James and John. They said good-by to the crowds and started across.

All was still and peaceful out on the lake. Jesus had worked hard and He was exhausted. He curled up in the stern and put His head on a cushion. Soon the quiet lapping of the water put Him to sleep.

A brisk wind filled out the sails and

carried them across. When they got to the middle of the lake the disciples realized that the wind had grown stronger. It was dark now and a few drops of rain came.

Suddenly a storm was upon them. "It's a bad one," cried the fishermen. "Quick, bail as fast as you can."

Each boat was having trouble. The waves were so high that the boats were in danger of being turned over. In the boat where Jesus was sleeping the disciples were ready to despair.

"We're going to drown," they cried.

One shook Jesus, "Lord," he cried. "We're going to drown. Don't you care? Wake up!"

Jesus got up quickly. "Do not be so frightened," He said. "Keep your faith in God."

Then Jesus held His hands over the troubled waters. "Peace! Be still," He commanded.

As suddenly as it had come, the storm ceased. The waves quieted.

The disciples were amazed. The storm had been going full force, but at the words of Jesus everything was still.

The disciples looked with awe and wonder at Jesus. Those in the other boats had seen enough to know what had happened. They all talked about it among themselves. "Jesus is more than an ordinary man," some said. "Even the winds and the waves obey him."

Matthew 8:18-27; Mark 4:35-41; Luke 8:22-25; 9:57-62

28. Welcome Across the Sea

When Jesus and the disciples crossed back to the other side of the Sea of Galilee they found many eager to see and hear Jesus. Some had seen the boats coming and spread the word.

"Jesus is back," they told everyone in the market place. Many went to greet Him at the shore.

They gathered around as Jesus found a place by the sea to sit and teach. While He was telling the people about God's Kingdom and how God wanted them to live, a man came up to Jesus and knelt at His feet. It was Jairus, a man who was one of the rulers of a nearby synagogue.

"Please come and help us," he begged. "My daughter is dying."

Jesus got up to go with the man. He comforted him as they went. Many of the crowd went too. They pressed around Jesus, wanting to hear all that He had to say.

One woman pushed her way close to Jesus. For many years she had been ill. She had gone to many doctors, but instead of getting better she grew worse. But she believed Jesus could heal her.

"I haven't had a chance to talk to Jesus," she thought, "but I know that if only I could touch his cloak, I would be cured."

She shoved until she could reach out her hand and touch the tassle on the corner of Jesus' cloak. When she did she felt better. "My illness has been cured," she said to herself happily.

Then Jesus stopped and turned around. "Who touched Me?" He asked.

The people nearby were frightened. They thought Jesus was going to scold them. "It wasn't I," everyone said.

The disciples were surprised at Jesus' question. "Rabbi," they said, "so many people were near you, and pressing on you."

But Jesus knew that someone had touched Him for a special reason. He looked around the crowd.

Then the woman came forward. She was frightened now, but she knew she must tell the truth. She knelt before Jesus, "I have been ill for many years," she confessed, "and I knew you could heal me. I thought even touching your cloak would do, and when I touched your cloak I was healed."

Jesus smiled at the woman. "It's all right," He said. "It was your faith in Me that made you well. Go in peace."

This had caused a delay on the way to Jairus' house. Now a man came from the ruler's house with a sad message. "Your daughter has died," the man said.

But Jesus turned quickly to the ruler. "Do not fear. Believe in Me, and she shall be made well," He said.

The man continued to believe as they walked along the road to the village where Jairus lived. When they came to Jairus' house they found the mourners there. One man played a sad mournful tune on the flute. This was the custom when someone died.

Jesus told the mourners to be quiet. He asked everyone to leave but the father and mother and His disciples, Peter, James and John. With these He went into the house.

The mother showed Him where the little girl lay. Jesus bent over the still form. He took the small hand and then called to her saying, "Child, arise."

To the delight of the parents the little girl sat up. She started to get out of bed, because she felt so much better.

"Give her something to eat," Jesus directed.

The parents were very happy and grateful. Jesus too was happy to see her eating and walking about.

Jairus sent the hired mourners home. "You are not needed," he said. "My daughter lives."

Jesus came out of the house followed by Peter, James and John. The other disciples joined them, and many of the crowd followed as He left the village.

Jesus had made arrangements to stay at a friend's house, and the crowd followed Him up to the door. Two men from the crowd came in with the disciples. They were blind and wanted Jesus' help.

They asked Jesus, "Have mercy on us, Son of David."

Jesus asked them, "Do you believe that I am able to heal you?" To have faith was important.

"Yes, Lord, we believe," they both assured Him.

Jesus touched the eyes of each man saying, "Let it happen as you believe." Then their eyes were opened and they could see. They were very excited as they ran out and told everyone.

Many of the people who had seen the wonders of that day were excited. "There has never been anything like this before," they cried.

Some Pharisees had also seen the wonders, but they said, "We still do not believe in him."

Matthew 9:1, 18-28;
Mark 5:21-43; Luke 8:40-56

29. Sent Out to Help and Heal

Jesus continued to preach and teach in all the cities and villages of Galilee. Whenever He could He taught in the synagogues. At other times He taught out in the hills or by the sea. He healed the sick who were brought to Him.

Jesus loved the people who came to hear Him. He wanted to help them. Only He was sorry that they knew so little about God and did not have the joy that comes from walking close to God.

Jesus often thought, "They are like sheep who have no shepherd."

Jesus was glad to see that most of the people wanted to listen and learn. They were like a harvest field ready to be reaped.

"The harvest is ready," said Jesus to His disciples, but there are few laborers. Pray to God, the Lord of the harvest, that He will send out laborers in His work."

Jesus meant that though the people were ready to hear, there were few preachers.

One day Jesus called His twelve special disciples together. An important day had come. Now they were ready to go out on their own to teach and heal as Jesus did.

Jesus had a special message for His disciples before they separated.

He said, "For this trip go to the people of Israel, not to the Gentile cities."

Jesus knew it would be easier for the disciples to talk to their own people.

Then Jesus told them what they were to do on this trip. "Preach as you go from one town or village to another. Tell the people that the Kingdom of God is at hand.

"God will give you the power to heal the sick as I have done. This is a gift from God so don't charge for doing it. Take no reward from anyone.

"Don't take provisions along with you. Ask for food and lodging from those who wish to hear the teaching. Ask God to bless those who give you the food and shelter you need."

The disciples were thrilled to think that God would give them the power to heal as Jesus did. They were eager to give the message of God's Kingdom to others.

Jesus warned the disciples that some would not listen, and some might be unfriendly. "But remember," He said: "Anyone who receives you, receives Me, and anyone who receives Me, receives God who sent Me."

After the disciples went on their tour Jesus taught and healed in nearby towns.

Some people told Jesus, "Herod has been asking a lot of questions about you. When he heard about the miracles you perform, he told his servants, 'This must be John the Baptist risen from the dead.' "

Herod felt guilty about putting John to death. Now it frightened him to hear of Jesus' power. He decided that he ought to find a way to see and hear Jesus for himself.

In about a month the disciples returned from their preaching tour. When they again met with Jesus they had many stories to tell.

They rejoiced because people had listened to them preach about God's Kingdom. They had been able to heal many of the sick and had caused the lame to walk and the blind to see. The disciples were excited that they had been used of God in these great ways.

But others wanted to talk to Jesus too, and the disciples had little time to talk to Him alone.

Jesus knew it was important to discuss this tour, so He told the people, "My disciples and I must go away. We will be back."

To the disciples Jesus said, "Come, let's take a boat and go over the lake to a quiet place."

They found a boat large enough for them all to climb into, and pushed out from the shore. Soon the winds had filled their sails and they were making good time over sparkling water.

The disciples could talk of nothing but the preaching tour. They were eager to share it all with Jesus.

Matthew 9:35-38; 10; 11:1; 14:1-13; Mark 6:6-32; Luke 9:1-10; John 6:1

30. Dinner for Five Thousand

Jesus and His disciples landed at a deserted area on the northeast shore of the Sea of Galilee near the village of Bethsaida. A surprise awaited them. Many people had walked around the water and were there on the shore.

The disciples were disappointed. They could not be alone with Jesus after all.

Jesus welcomed the crowd. He was glad to teach any who wanted so much to hear about God's Kingdom that they took this long walk.

The hours passed as Jesus taught and preached. Many who were ill were brought to Him, and He healed them all. Some had come from the different towns around the lake. Some travelers on their way to Jerusalem to keep the Passover joined the crowd.

Thousands were gathered, and now it was late in the afternoon.

One disciple said to Jesus, "It's dinner time."

Another said, "You had better send the people away. They must be hungry, and we don't have food to feed this huge crowd. They had better go to the nearest village and buy something to eat."

"They don't need to go away," said Jesus. "You can give them something to eat."

"We don't have enough for this large crowd," one disciple protested. The others agreed.

"Well, then"—Jesus turned to Philip—"where shall we buy food for them?"

Philip said, "It would take a lot of money to buy food for these people—more than half a year's wages. There are about five thousand men here."

But Jesus knew what He was going to do. And He wanted His disciples to believe in Him.

Just then Andrew came up. He had found a boy who had food with him and was bringing the boy to Jesus. "This boy has five loaves of barley bread and two fish," Andrew said. "But what is this among so many people?"

Jesus smiled at the boy. The boy had meant to eat his bread and fish, but now he wanted to give them to Jesus.

"Rabbi, if it will help, it's all yours," he said.

Jesus thanked him. "Yes, you will see how much it helps," He said.

Jesus told His disciples. "Tell the people that we have food for them. They do not need to take a long walk while hungry. Have them sit down in rows."

The people made themselves comfortable on the green grass. Jesus took the basket of food and looked up to heaven. He asked God to bless the food.

One prayer of blessing often used went: "Blessed art Thou, Jehovah, our God, King of the world, who causes bread to come forth from the earth."

Jesus began to break the loaves of bread into pieces. He broke up the dried fish. The more He divided, the more there was. He handed some to each disciple who gave a portion to each person.

Up and down each row they went. Then they returned to get more bread and fish. Jesus was still dividing the food.

The boy who had given the bread and fish was astonished as he saw the original portion grow. He enjoyed his own share. The others around him were enjoying theirs.

When everyone was finished eating Jesus told the disciples to go and gather up what was left. They filled twelve baskets with leftover bread and fish.

Word spread throughout the vast crowd that Jesus had given them this dinner from just five loaves of bread and two fish. The people grew very excited.

"This is indeed the prophet who was promised," they cried. "Just think what a wonderful ruler Jesus would make. We would never need to go hungry again."

"We wouldn't even need to work," added some. "Jesus could make food for people by a miracle."

"Jesus must be made king. He will overthrow Rome," the people began to shout.

Jesus had tried to make the people understand that God's Kingdom was not an earthly, military rule.

The people wanted to accept Him, not because they loved Him and wanted to live in God's way, but because they wanted free food.

"Go at once to the boat," Jesus told His disciples.

Roman soldiers were always waiting to hear of rebellion. Jesus knew the situation would be dangerous if the people tried to force Him to be king. Many might be killed.

"Coast along the shore," Jesus told the disciples. "I'll join you later."

The crowd was angry because Jesus would not be made a king. Some of His enthusiastic followers went away saying that they would no longer come out to hear Him.

Matthew 14:13-22; Mark 6:32-46; Luke 9:10-17; John 6:1-15, 26-31, 66

31. A Visit to Pagan Places

Jesus left the crowds and went up in the hills to pray to God. He wanted God's guidance in finding ways to show people that He was the Messiah, without starting a rebellion. He also wanted the people to understand about the Kingdom of God and how it would grow in the world.

Jesus loved to talk to God. He found help and strength in prayer. Time went quickly, and the sun set. Then Jesus realized His disciples would be waiting for Him, and He hurried down to the shore.

In the boat the men were having trouble. A strong wind had blown them out to the middle of the sea. They were trying to row back to shore to pick up Jesus, but the more they struggled, the more the wind beat against them.

"I don't think we're going to make it," cried one disciple.

"We'll never get to shore," the others agreed.

They were about to give up when one shouted, "Look! Look! There's someone out on the water!"

It was dark, and they could just about make out a form coming towards them. "It's a ghost!" one cried. They were terrified.

The figure drew closer. Then Jesus spoke, "It is I. Don't be afraid."

The disciples recognized the voice of Jesus, but still they were afraid. They could not believe Jesus had the power to walk on water.

Peter decided to make a test. He said, "Lord if it is you, ask me to come to you on the water."

"Come," said Jesus.

Peter stepped out into the water. He looked at Jesus and took one step after another. He found himself walking, the water under his feet. But then the wind blew at his cloak, and he became frightened. He began to wonder, and then he began to sink.

"Lord, save me," he cried out, as he sank up to his knees.

Jesus reached out His hand and caught Peter. Then Peter could stand.

Jesus said, "You did not have enough faith, Peter. Why did you start to doubt?"

By this time they were both near the boat. The disciples reached out their hands to help Jesus and Peter into the boat.

When they were safely in the boat, the wind died down and the disciples rowed to shore. They headed for the fertile plains of Gennesaret on the west side of the lake.

Some people on the shore recognized Jesus. Throughout the nearby villages they spread the news that Jesus had come. The next day many came to hear Jesus and to bring their sick for healing. Some of the sick had to be brought on their sleeping mats. Jesus healed them all.

Jesus continued to travel north of the lake, up to the ancient cities of Tyre and Sidon. Near these cities He healed the daughter of a Phoenician woman who had heard about Jesus' power to heal.

Then Jesus journeyed down through the region of the Decapolis where there were many Greek cities. Here Jesus had a chance to preach to many people who were still idol worshipers.

Jesus used His healing power to help these people. One man was brought to Jesus who could not hear and who could not speak plainly. His friends begged Jesus to help him.

Jesus put His fingers to the man's ears and touched the man's tongue. Then He looked up to heaven, then again at the man. He said, "Be opened."

Suddenly the man could hear what the others around him said. He could speak plainly and thank Jesus.

The crowds were excited. "Jesus does all things well," they cried. "He even makes the deaf hear and the dumb speak."

For several days the crowds followed Jesus. The people brought food and bedding with them. But one day Jesus noticed that their food had run out.

"The people have no more food," Jesus told His disciples. "We must give to them. I do not want to send them away hungry. Some might faint on the way."

The disciples protested. They had forgotten how Jesus had fed the five thousand, or perhaps they thought Jesus would not do as much on foreign soil and for pagan people.

"There are about four thousand people here," they said. "How can we buy bread enough for them in this deserted place?"

"What do we have left from our own provisions?" asked Jesus.

One disciple counted. "There are seven loaves of bread," he told Jesus, "and a few small dried fish."

"That's enough," Jesus said. "Get the people to sit down for dinner before the meeting is over."

The people sat down on the ground, and Jesus stood in front of them with the food. Again Jesus thanked God for the food. Then He broke up the bread and fish.

As before, the small amount of food fed all the people. After the crowd had eaten, seven baskets of small pieces were gathered from the ground.

Then Jesus dismissed the crowd. They went away wondering at the power of God. They told everyone they knew about Jesus.

Matthew 14:23-56; 15:21-39;
Mark 6:46-56; 7:24-8:9; John 6:15-21

32. A Great Confession

After this miracle Jesus and His disciples went back to Galilee. Here they found the Pharisees and the Sadducees who usually quarreled with each other about religion united in opposing Jesus.

They were always criticizing Jesus in public and demanding why He did this or did not do that.

Jesus knew that the religious leaders in Judea and Galilee did not believe He was the Messiah. Many of the ordinary people were also beginning to doubt. They could not understand why He did not organize a revolt against Rome and start a kingdom on earth.

Jesus knew that He did not have much longer to do the work God had sent Him to do. He wanted to have an important talk with His disciples. He decided that they should go where they would not be disturbed by critics.

They needed a quiet place, away from crowds, in which they could begin to learn some new truths and be free from interruptions. North of the Sea of Galilee near the foot of Mt. Hermon was Caesarea Philippi. This was a Gentile city built by Herod's son, Philip. Few people would recognize them here.

When they found time to sit and talk together, Jesus asked the disciples an important question, "Who do people say I am? What do they call Me?"

The disciples told Him, "Some say you are John the Baptist, Elijah, Jeremiah, or another prophet of old times."

Some people thought that Jesus was like these great men, but others thought Jesus was one of these great men brought back to life.

Jesus had heard this from many different sources. He was mostly interested in what the disciples believed.

The disciples had called Jesus the Messiah. They had told others that He was the Messiah. But did they really believe it in their hearts? Were they sure that He was the One?

Jesus asked them, "What do you believe? Who do you say I am?"

Peter answered, "You are the Messiah, the Son of the living God."

Peter spoke for all the disciples in believing in Jesus as the Messiah. They had seen the miracles, the raising of the dead, the feeding of the crowds.

Peter had also been convinced of something more. He realized that Jesus was Son of God and had a special relationship to God, the Father.

Jesus was happy that Peter knew this. He said to Peter, "Peter, it is My Father in heaven who has revealed this to you. On this confession I will build My Church and nothing, no evil power, will be able to destroy it."

The disciples were happy. For the first time Jesus had wholeheartedly proclaimed Himself to be the Messiah. Now they felt sure He would announce this to the world. Now He would set up a kingdom on earth.

They did not realize, even now, that Jesus meant to establish a different kind of kingdom. They were really shocked when Jesus began to give them bad news.

"My work on earth is nearly done," Jesus said. "It is the Father's will that I go to Jerusalem. There I will suffer many things. I will be arrested by My enemies and put to death. But on the third day I will rise from the dead."

The disciples could not imagine anything like this happening to the Messiah. Peter was especially puzzled. *How could this happen to God's Son?* he wondered.

Peter spoke out: "God would not want this to happen."

Jesus rebuked him. "It *is* God's will for Me to die. You are not thinking like God but like a man. I want to do this, because it is the only way to bring men back to God."

Jesus warned His disciples that danger lay ahead for them also. He urged them to keep their faith in Him and in God.

"Remember," said Jesus, "you must be willing to risk your life for God's work. Because I want to give new life to others, I am glad to give My life for them. I want My followers to feel as I do."

From that time on Jesus warned His followers of what lay ahead. Jesus wanted them to understand that He was doing this freely and that death at the hands of His enemies would not be a surprise to Him.

Matthew 15:39; 16
Mark 8:10-13, 27-37
Luke 9:18-25

33. Up and Down the Mountain

A few days later Jesus invited Peter, James and John to go to Mt. Hermon with Him and spend some time praying.

They walked fifteen miles north of Caesarea Philippi and started the climb up this tall mountain whose peak glistened with snow the year around.

High up they found a good place to look out over the valley below and off into the distance, where the Jordan ran down to the Dead Sea. Here they stopped for awhile, to think and pray.

For a long time they prayed. Peter, James and John grew drowsy, but Jesus prayed on. He knew He needed much strength from God in order to face what lay ahead in Jerusalem.

Suddenly the three disciples were aware of a bright light. Now they were wide awake! There before them stood Jesus. His whole figure shone with God's glory. His face seemed to be filled with sunlight and His white clothes glistened.

Two men were talking with Him. The disciples realized that they were Moses and Elijah. They were talking to Jesus about what would happen at Jerusalem.

Then a cloud of light covered them all. The disciples were frightened. They listened as a voice spoke from the cloud saying: "This is My beloved Son, My Chosen, listen to Him."

Suddenly the light was gone. The disciples looked around. Moses and Elijah were gone. Only Jesus stood before them.

"Don't tell anyone about what you have seen," Jesus told them, "until after I have risen from the dead."

God had wanted these close friends of Jesus to see Jesus in all His glory as God's Son, so that they would be strengthened and still believe, even when Jesus would be taken by His enemies. But these close friends of Jesus did not understand God's purpose.

As Peter, James, and John came down from the mountain they were filled with wonder. They were sure now that everything was going to turn out in some wonderful way for God and His truth. They refused to think of Jesus dying. They had no idea what He meant by rising from the dead, and they were afraid to ask.

There had been power and glory at the top of the mountain, but below was confusion and lack of faith. The disciples had been trying to heal a boy who was epileptic, but they had failed.

Now the father of the boy ran over to Jesus. He knelt before Him crying, "Lord, have mercy on my son, for he suffers terribly. He is epileptic, and sometimes when he has a seizure he nearly falls into the fire or into nearby water. I took him to your disciples, but they could not heal him."

Jesus said, "Bring the boy to Me."

As several people took the boy and pushed him toward Jesus, the boy had a seizure. He fell on the ground and rolled about.

Jesus said to the father, "How long has your son been like this?"

"From childhood," said the father. "If you can do anything, please help him."

Jesus noticed that the man was not sure He could help. "You must believe that I can," He told the man.

"I do believe," said the man, "but help me to believe more strongly."

Jesus then spoke words of healing to the boy as he lay on the ground. The boy's body became very still. Some of the people nearby thought the boy was dead, but Jesus took him by the hand and lifted him up.

The boy got up and ran happily to his father. Everyone was astonished that Jesus had been able to do this.

As soon as they were alone the disciples asked Jesus, "Why were we unable to heal the boy?"

"Because your faith was weak," Jesus told them. "You must continue to pray and ask God's help in order to do God's work. You must really believe in God's power, and you must live in God's way yourself."

The time of rest was over. More work for God needed to be done.

"Let's go back to Galilee," Jesus said.

The disciples gathered the provisions together. They took the road that led to Galilee and Capernaum.

Matthew 17; Mark 9:1-30; Luke 9:28-43

34. Quarrels on the Way

On the way to Capernaum the disciples had a serious discussion which led to a quarrel; but they tried to hide the fact from Jesus.

Some disciples said that because only Peter, James, and John had been invited to the mountaintop with Jesus, these three would be the greatest in God's Kingdom.

Some argued over this choice. Others began to question which of the three would be the greatest of all, such as a prime minister is to a king. They all wanted an important place.

One would say why he was important. Another would laugh and contradict him. Jesus knew what it was they were quarreling about, but He said nothing at the time.

The disciples were eager for the future. They refused to think of what Jesus had said about death. They were sure that Jesus would soon set up God's Kingdom. They were only concerned that they be rewarded for their faithfulness with an important post.

When they got to where they were staying in Capernaum, Jesus asked the disciples, "What were you discussing on the way?"

The disciples were ashamed. Jesus had taught them to be humble, but they had been talking about pride and honor for themselves.

One was brave enough to ask the question. He hoped Jesus would be able to settle it once for all. "Lord, who will be the greatest in the Kingdom of God?" he asked.

Jesus was sorry to hear this question.

It showed that the disciples still did not understand what the Kingdom of God would be like. They were still thinking of an earthly kingdom with prime ministers and other officials. God's Kingdom was to be a growing band of people who loved and served God.

Jesus took one of the children standing near Him. He lovingly took the child in His arms. "Do you see this child?" He asked. "He isn't proud and ambitious.

"He knows there are many things he must learn, and he is eager to learn. Whoever is humble, like this little child, is the greatest in God's Kingdom."

Jesus told the disciples their thoughts were wrong. "You must change," He told them, "or you won't even be a part of God's Kingdom."

Jesus used this time to tell them some important truths which they remembered when they became leaders in the first churches.

He said, "Into God's Kingdom all the little children are welcome, and all who become like little children—all those who are unimportant in the world's eyes may come, the poor, the uneducated, those who fail, those who do wrong. You must accept all of these people who repent and come to God."

Jesus asked, "What do you think? What would a shepherd do who had a hundred sheep in his flock and one became lost?

"Would he say, 'I don't care. I still have ninety-nine sheep. I'll leave that one on the mountain. The simple little animal should not have wandered away'?"

The listeners knew no shepherd would do that. The shepherds were faithful to their task and loved their little charges.

"Or," asked Jesus, "would the shepherd leave the ninety-nine in the care of others and go back into the mountains and search for the lost sheep?"

The listeners agreed. This is what the shepherd would do.

"And," said Jesus, "when he finds this sheep he rejoices. He continues to love it. God loves all people. He wants all people to come to Him."

Jesus knew that sometimes His disciples quarreled about other things. Resentments grew and one disciple did not forgive the other.

Jesus said, "When someone wrongs you, go to him and try to make things right."

This made Peter feel uncomfortable. There was someone he had forgiven many times, and yet this person still did things to hurt him. He asked Jesus, "Lord, how often do I have to forgive one who wrongs me? Is seven times enough?"

The religious leaders had answers to this question. Some said seven times; others said three.

But Jesus said, "No, not seven times, but seventy times seven."

Peter realized that Jesus did not mean four hundred and ninety times. Jesus meant that he should keep on forgiving and not count the number of times.

Jesus told them all, "God has forgiven you. You ought to be willing to forgive one another."

Then Jesus told a story about a king who had many servants. One of them owed him a large sum of money. In those days a man could be put in prison for failing to pay a debt. When the king demanded the money the servant said,

"I don't have the money. Please wait a little longer. Right now I have nothing."

The king was sorry for the servant and

told him, "We will forget about the debt."

The servant was very happy. Now he wouldn't need to worry about going to prison and not being able to care for his family.

As he was going home with the good news he met another servant. He remembered that this man had borrowed money from him and had not paid it back.

"You owe me money," he said roughly. "Pay it back immediately."

But his fellow servant didn't have the money. "Please wait a little longer," he said. "Right now I have nothing."

"No," the first servant said. "I'm going to have you put in prison."

Another servant heard that this man had put his fellow servant in prison, and he went and told the king about it. The king called in the servant whose debt he had cancelled.

"I showed mercy to you," he said, "and yet you did not show mercy to your fellow servant. You are a wicked man and must pay back all your debt."

Matthew 18; Mark 9:30-37

35. At the Feast of Tabernacles

It was fall, the season of harvest, and time for the Feast of Tabernacles. This was the Feast when the Jews thanked God for the grain, oil, and wine which the fields brought forth. They remembered how God had provided food and water for His people in the ancient days in the wilderness.

"We will go to Jerusalem and keep the Feast," Jesus told His disciples.

The preaching tours in Galilee were over. Jesus had more friends in Galilee than anywhere else, but He could not stay around friends forever. He had work to do elsewhere. Now He would finish His work in Judea and on the other side of the Jordan River in Perea.

The road Jesus chose to take this trip to the big city lay between the boundaries of Galilee and Samaria. As Jesus and His disciples entered a village, they were met by ten lepers.

The disciples drew back in fear. They did not want to catch this dreaded disease. But the lepers did not get too close. They stood off a ways and shouted.

They had recognized Jesus. "Jesus, Jesus," they shouted. "Have mercy on us."

The disciples noticed that nine of the men were Jews, but one was a Samaritan. They wondered if Jesus would heal them all, or only the Jews.

Jesus spoke to them all as He went closer to them. "Go, show yourselves to the priest," He told them.

When a leper was rid of disease he had to show himself to a priest. If the priest agreed that the disease was gone, he was allowed to live and work with other people again.

There was no change in the men at these words of Jesus, but all ten of the men believed that they would be healed. They had enough faith to start out to see the priest.

Over the hill they went. The disciples watched them hurrying away. Some distance down the road the men looked at their hands and feet. They were healed!

As Jesus and His disciples walked along the narrow streets of the town they heard running feet behind them. It was one of the lepers, the Samaritan. He knelt before Jesus and the disciples noticed that his skin was clear. The sores of leprosy were gone.

"Thank you, Rabbi," cried the leper. "As I walked I was healed. Thank you for giving me back my life."

Jesus spoke kindly to the man. Then He asked His disciples, "Were not ten men healed? Only one found time to return and give thanks—and this was the Samaritan."

To the man He said, "Get up now and go your way. It was your faith in Me that healed you."

At Jerusalem many had come for the Feast. The religious rulers were looking for Jesus. "Does he dare to come?" they asked.

Many of the people were talking about Jesus.

"He is leading the people astray," some said.

But many of them were followers of Jesus. "No," they said, "he is a good man."

One day when the Feast was about half over Jesus stood up before the crowds. He preached in the Temple court. Everyone crowded around to listen to Jesus talk about God and His Kingdom.

Some of the people were puzzled. "Jesus understands the Scriptures," they said, "and yet he never studied in the schools of the rabbis. How is it that he is such a great Teacher?"

Jesus told them, "My teaching comes from God. If you sincerely want to know and do God's will, He will teach it to you."

Many people whispered, "Isn't this the man the rulers want to have put to death? Why don't they arrest him?" Some of the people became convinced that Jesus was the Messiah.

The Pharisees and the leading priests decided that something must be done. This Man was making Himself equal with God. They sent some of their officers to arrest Jesus, but the officers came back empty-handed.

"Why didn't you arrest Jesus?" the rulers asked them.

"We listened to Jesus preach," they told the rulers. "We will not arrest him. No one ever spoke like him."

The Pharisees were angry. "Do you believe in him too?" they asked. "You are being led astray."

Then Nicodemus, who was still one of the rulers, spoke up. "It is not right to judge any man without a trial," he said.

But the rulers paid no attention to Nicodemus. They continued to plot the death of Jesus.

John 7
Luke 17:11-19

36. A Man Born Blind

On the last day of the Feast Jesus talked seriously with the people. He used many ways to tell them that He was the One promised by the prophets.

He said, "I am the light of the world. The person who follows Me will not walk in darkness."

He told them, "The Father sent Me, and it is by His authority that I preach and heal. The Father is always with Me, because I always do what pleases the Father. All those who really love God will believe in Me."

The rulers were angry at this. They took up stones and started to throw them at Jesus. Jesus turned and escaped from them. The disciples were close behind as He left the Temple courts.

Outside the Temple Jesus stopped and and talked to a blind beggar who sat by the Temple gate. He used spittle and a little dust from the ground to make a clay. He put this on the man's eyes.

People gathered around to see what would happen next. The last day of the Feast of Tabernacles was observed as a Sabbath, and they knew the rulers would be very angry if Jesus healed anyone.

Jesus said to the beggar, "Go and wash your eyes in the Pool of Siloam."

The man used his walking stick to guide him as he always did. Some friends directed him to the pool. He knelt down and used his hands to wash his eyes.

Then he opened them. He could see the water, the trees, the bright blue sky, the curious faces of those around him. He had been born blind. This was the first time he had seen the beautiful world.

Now the man could make his way back unaided to the place near the Temple gate where he had sat each day and begged. When he got there, many people recognized him.

"Isn't this the blind beggar?" they asked.

Different ones agreed. "Yes, this is the same man," they said. "I wonder how he got his sight?"

Others said, "You are wrong. This man just looks like the beggar. That beggar was born blind. No one could cure him."

Then the beggar spoke up. "It is I," he said. "I am the man who used to beg here. Now I can see."

The people crowded around the beggar. "How were you made to see?" they asked.

"A man called Jesus came and talked to me," the beggar told them. "He made clay and put it on my eyes. Then he told me to wash it off in the Pool of Siloam. So I did, and when the clay came off I opened my eyes and saw for the very first time. That is how it happened!"

"Where is Jesus now?" one asked.

"I don't know," the man replied.

The people grew excited. "The Pharisees must hear about this," they cried.

They brought the man to the leaders of the Pharisees. Everyone began to talk at once.

One Pharisee said, "Be quiet. Let the man speak. You say it was Jesus who spoke to you? Now just how did you receive your sight?"

The man told them, "He put clay on my eyes, and I washed, and now I see."

The people all had different ideas about the miracle.

"Jesus can't be from God because he breaks the Sabbath by healing," said one.

But others said, "How could he do such miracles if he were not from God?"

Others said, "This man is probably not the same one as the blind beggar. Find his parents. See if they recognize him."

Some of the leaders went around the crowd and found the parents of the man. The parents were fearful as they were brought before these important judges. Some Sadducees and members of the Sanhedrin had joined the Pharisees.

"Is this your son?" the rulers asked the parents.

"Yes," said the parents.

"Was he born blind?"

"Yes," they said again.

"Then how can he see?" the rulers demanded.

The parents wouldn't say anything more. They had heard that Jesus had healed their son. But they knew that these rulers had said anyone who confessed belief in Jesus as the Messiah would be put out of membership in the synagogue.

"We don't know how he sees," they insisted. "He isn't a child. Ask him. He can speak for himself."

So the rulers questioned the man again. "Give God the praise for your healing," they said. "This man is a sinner."

The beggar spoke with courage. "I was blind and Jesus made me see. God doesn't give sinners such wonderful power.

"No one else has ever opened the eyes of anyone born blind, and yet you refuse to believe Jesus is from God. If Jesus weren't from God, he couldn't do these things."

The rulers were angry. "You are no longer part of the synagogue," they told him, and they chased him away.

Jesus and His disciples had left the area near the Temple, but they heard about the excitement, and they came back to look for the man and finally found him.

When Jesus spoke to the beggar, the man recognized Jesus' voice. Now he could see the One who had helped him.

"Do you believe in the Son of Man, the Messiah?" asked Jesus.

Jesus knew that the man had been cast out of the synagogue. Jesus wanted him to find new friends among His followers.

"Tell me who he is that I may believe on him," the man said.

"I am He," said Jesus.

The man knelt before Jesus. "Lord, I believe," he said. *John 7:37; 8, 9*

37. Seventy New Missionaries

When Jesus and His friends went to Jerusalem they often stayed in the nearby village of Bethany. Mary, Martha, and their brother Lazarus lived here. They were followers of Jesus and often helped Jesus and His disciples in any way they could.

One day Jesus visited the sisters alone. The sisters were surprised. Martha hurried around getting a big dinner ready. Mary sat and talked with Jesus. She had questions about the Scriptures she wanted Him to answer.

Martha served the dinner. They sat in

comfortable reclining positions to eat it. Martha kept offering Jesus more food, but Mary was very quiet and wanted only to hear Jesus speak of God's Kingdom.

Finally Martha lost her patience. "Lord, don't you care that my sister has left all the serving to me? Why don't you tell her to help me?"

Jesus said, "Martha, you didn't need to fuss with a big dinner. I came here to talk with My friends.

"Mary wants to hear about God's Kingdom. That is more important than all these many dishes of food. From now on give Me only one dish of food and take time to hear about God and His work."

Jesus and His disciples stayed near Jerusalem for the next two months. In the winter there was another important feast, the Feast of Dedication. This was the feast that celebrated the time when the Maccabees defeated Antiochus Epiphanes and rededicated the Temple for the worship of God.

During the Feast Jesus attended the Temple services. One day He walked in the portico on the east side of the Temple. It was called Solomon's portico.

The religious rulers gathered around Him. "How long will you keep us in suspense?" they asked Him. "If you are the Messiah, tell us so."

"I have told you," said Jesus, "but you refuse to believe what I say. The miracles I have performed are signs to help you believe, but you refuse to believe."

Then Jesus went on to talk about His work and about the Father who sent Him. Jesus told them He was God's Son.

As at other times they did not believe Jesus, and when He said this, they tried again to arrest Him, and took up stones to throw at Him.

But again Jesus escaped in the crowd and confusion. The disciples got away too.

When they all met together Jesus said, "We must leave here. It is too dangerous, and the Father has more work for Me to do. Let us go across the Jordan."

The disciples were glad. They took the trail that brought them down to the Jordan Valley. They crossed the river to Bethany on the east side of the Jordan. This was the place where John the baptizer had done much of his preaching.

Here the people were friendly to Jesus. They remembered that John had introduced Jesus. They came to hear Jesus preach and many believed in Him.

Jesus knew that there was not much more time to do God's work. He knew that He would need to turn this work over to others who believed in Him.

One day He called many of His followers together. From these He chose seventy to go as missionaries on a preaching tour. They would go in pairs to the surrounding towns of Perea. Later Jesus Himself would go and preach in each one of these towns.

The special twelve disciples would stay and work close by Jesus.

When the missionaries were assembled together Jesus gave them final instructions. They were similar to the instructions He had given the twelve when they went on their special tour in Galilee.

Jesus told them again, "The harvest is plentiful, but there are few laborers. Pray to the Lord of the harvest—ask God to send laborers into His harvest fields so that more people will hear of God's Kingdom.

Jesus wanted them to realize that prayer was an important part of God's work. Jesus always remembered to pray for God's guidance in doing God's work.

There were many who were waiting to hear the message of God's Kingdom, but it would take much prayer and many brave messengers to bring it to them. This tour would bring the message of God's Kingdom to the many Gentiles who lived in Perea.

Jesus said, "Go your way. Carry no provisions or money with you. Hurry, and spend all your time preaching and healing. Ask for food and lodging in the towns. Be thankful for anything which is offered to you.

"Preach to the people, 'The Kingdom of God has come near to you.' Heal the sick. God will give you the power."

The missionaries were excited. It was wonderful to be used of God. They couldn't wait to get started.

Jesus' parting words were, "He who hears you, hears Me; and he who hears Me, hears God who sent Me."

Jesus and His disciples did work nearby. Some weeks later the first missionaries returned with a report. More pairs returned. Finally they were all gathered together.

They were all excited and happy. "It was a wonderful tour," they told Jesus. "Many came out to hear us. God did give us the power to heal in your Name."

Jesus was happy too. By the power of preaching in the Name of Jesus evil would one day be completely conquered.

"You do have great power from God," Jesus told them, "but that is not the most important thing. It is more important that you have a place in God's Kingdom. That is your best reason to rejoice."

Jesus thanked God for helping these missionaries of His. "I thank You, Father, Lord of heaven and earth," He prayed. "I am glad that You have revealed Your truth to these followers of Mine."

Then Jesus said to all His followers, "You are really blessed of God. Many prophets and faithful Jews of the past have desired to see the things you have seen."

Luke 10; John 10

38. The Good Neighbor

Jesus spent several months traveling around Perea. He went to the different towns and villages where the missionaries had preached. Here the people were ready to listen to Him.

One day a scribe who had spent many years studying God's Law and other religious writings asked Jesus a question, "Teacher, what should I do in order to please God?"

Jesus asked him, "What does the Law say?"

The scribe recited from the Law: "You shall love the Lord your God with all your heart, and with all your soul, and with all your strength, and with all your mind; and your neighbor as yourself."

Jesus agreed. This was the most important part of the Law. It told how God wanted His people to live.

"You have answered correctly," Jesus told him. "Do this and you will please God."

But the scribe sought praise from Jesus and the others. He wanted to prove that he always kept this and the other laws of God.

He asked Jesus another question, "Who is my neighbor?"

The rabbis said that this Scripture meant your friends or all Israelites. They said it did not refer to people of other countries who did not worship as the Jews did.

Jesus did not agree with this interpretation. In order to help the scribe to better understand the Scripture he had quoted, Jesus told a story about a man who traveled from Jerusalem to Jericho.

The road from Jerusalem to Jericho was a dangerous one that wound around the hills. It was not well policed by soldiers, and many robbers made it their hideout. They would jump out on any passerby, especially one traveling alone. They would rob and often kill.

This man traveled alone, and as he rounded a bend, robbers jumped out on him. They robbed him of everything, even his clothes. They beat him and left him in the middle of the road. The poor man was in danger of dying there alone.

After a while a priest came down the road. He was busy thinking about his Temple service.

The poor man saw the priest. He was sure this religious leader of his own people would help him, but the priest did not seem to care. He saw the man, but he crossed over to the other side of the road and did not stop.

After a while a Levite came along. Once again the suffering man raised his head a little and feebly called for help.

But the Levite hurried on. He was afraid the robbers might be nearby and would jump out on him.

For many hours the man lay on the road. He had given up hope. Then he heard the sound of donkey's hoofs coming toward him.

It was a trader. The man rode one donkey and led another donkey which was burdened down with goods to sell. The wounded man expected no help, because this was a Samaritan. The Jews and the Samaritans were always quarreling over religion.

But the Samaritan did stop. He had pity on the poor, wounded man. He found healing oil and bandages in his provisions and used them to bathe and cover the wounds.

"Don't be afraid," he said. "The robbers have gone, and I will see that you get help. There is an inn further up the road."

The Samaritan put the man on his own donkey and led both donkeys along the road. When they came to the inn, the innkeeper helped the Samaritan put the wounded man to bed.

The Samaritan stayed at the inn that night, but early in the morning he had to start out on his journey again.

Before he left he gave the innkeeper money. "Take care of my friend," he said. "If you need to spend more money, I will repay you when I make my return journey."

After Jesus finished telling this story He had a question for the scribe. "Which of the three men was a neighbor to the man who was robbed?"

Jesus wanted the scribe to realize that a neighbor was anyone in need and that love was something you showed.

The scribe had to admit, "The one who showed mercy on him was his neighbor."

The scribe was puzzled. And yet this was the Samaritan. It was hard for him to believe that God wanted him to love foreigners.

"Go and act like this yourself," Jesus told the scribe. "Then you will be doing what the Law commands."

Luke 10:25-37

39. Jesus Gives a Prayer

The disciples often noticed Jesus at prayer. They knew He spent many nights in prayer. Often just before Jesus healed someone He spoke a word to His Father. They could see that Jesus was helped by prayer.

The disciples had also seen the religious rulers standing in the streets praying. These men didn't really seem to be talking to anyone but themselves. When anyone watched Jesus talk to God they knew that He was receiving help from God.

Often the disciples would say to one another, "Something really happens when Jesus prays. I wish I could pray like that."

One day after Jesus was finished praying in the presence of His disciples one asked Him, "Lord, teach us to pray. John the baptizer gave prayers to his disciples."

Jesus gave them a sample prayer to follow.

Father, hallowed be Your name.
May Your kingdom come.
May Your will be done on earth as it is
  done now in heaven.
Each day give us our food.
Forgive us our sins, for we forgive
  everyone who sins against us.
Lead us not into temptation.

Then Jesus taught His disciples many things about prayer. He said that prayer was very important to anyone who wanted to live in God's way, because all people needed God's help.

"You give to your friends, don't you?" Jesus asked them. "Supposing late one night you had unexpected company and nothing to give them to eat. Wouldn't you find a friend to ask help? You would go to your friend even if he were in bed and his house locked up for the night and ask to borrow some bread. God wants you to come to Him for help, because He wants to help you."

Jesus said that people should not hesitate to come to God in prayer. He said, "Ask, and it will be given to you. Seek, and you will find. Knock, and the door will be opened to you. Everyone who asks will receive. He who seeks will find. The door will be opened to him who knocks.

"You fathers give good things to your children when they ask. You are only men. How much more will God give help and guidance to those who believe in Him."

Jesus did not teach that God would give people anything they wanted but that He was always willing to listen and give what was best.

One day some men brought news to Jesus. "You must run away from here," they said. "We heard that Herod seeks to kill you." Perea was the territory of Herod Antipas.

But Jesus refused to run away from Herod. "I still have work to do here," He said. "And I know that I will be arrested and put to death in Jerusalem—not here."

There were many teachings Jesus wanted to give to His followers before His work on earth was over. He put some of these teachings in the form of stories such as these:

Once there was a rich man. He owned many fields. Each year the fields brought forth good crops. But this man never shared with anyone. He stored all that he could not use immediately. The time came when he had to build more and bigger storehouses to hold it all.

Finally the man said, "Now I have enough. I will stop work and enjoy my wealth."

That night God said to the man, "You have waited too long. Tonight your life will be over and who will have your wealth then?"

Jesus said, "This man was rich, but he was not rich toward God, because he did not share with others and help the needy. If he had made good use of his wealth, he would have had a good report to make to God."

In order to teach about God's forgiving love, Jesus told a story about a disobedient son:

Once there was a man who had two sons. The older son was very obedient. He always did as his father asked. He stayed at home and worked hard.

The younger son always seemed to be getting into trouble. "He has a mind of his own," people often said.

One day this younger son said to his father, "Father instead of waiting until after your death, I want all my inheritance now. I want to get away from here and go out on my own and make my fortune."

The father was sad. He knew the son was not ready for such a task. He knew the many temptations that would come to him, but he could see that his son had made up his mind. The father gave him the money.

The son was happy for a while. He went into another country where no one knew him or his family. He found it was easy to have friends, because he had money and would spend it on others. But when his money was gone his new friends left him.

Now that he had wasted his money the son had to go to work. He helped a farmer by feeding his pigs. A famine had come and wages were low. The son did not even have enough to keep himself well fed.

"How foolish I have been," he thought one day. "I wasted all my money on pleasure. I used it to do some things which were wrong. Now I have nothing."

He thought about his father's house. "Even the servants of my father have more than I have," he admitted.

Then he had an idea. He would go back to his father's house. "I am going to ask my father to hire me as a servant," he decided.

Even before the son got near the house his father saw that he was coming. He ran out to his son and welcomed him home. He refused to make him a servant, but he forgave him and made him a son once more.

"We will have a large feast," the father told his servants. "My lost son has come home."

The other brother was angry. "You are

g a large feast for this son who did wrong," he complained. "You have never given me a feast. Don't you appreciate me? I never went away."

"Of course I do," said the father. "I love you both. All that I have is yours, too. You could have had a feast any time. But your brother has learned a hard lesson. You should be as glad as I am that he has come back."

Jesus wanted His hearers to understand that God loves all, and will forgive those who repent. He wanted them to be as glad as God is when sinners turn from doing wrong.

Luke 11:1-13; 13:31-33; 12:16-21; 15:11-32; Matthew 6:9-15; 7:7-11

40. Who Can Come to Jesus

Jesus used all occasions to help people better understand God's way. He continued to tell stories that explained something about God's Kingdom.

One Sabbath a ruler who was a Pharisee invited Jesus to dinner.

Jesus told a story to the people who sat at dinner with Him. The story was about a very different kind of banquet. Most people, when they gave a good dinner, invited the most important people they could find; but Jesus wanted the people to know that God cares about all and all are wanted in His Kingdom.

In the story a man gave a great dinner. He invited many important people but they all found excuses not to come. They were not very good excuses. The man was angry that his invitations were refused. He told his servants, "Go out into the streets and invite anyone who will come—anyone at all."

The servants brought in all they could find. Many were poor people, some were the blind and lame beggars who often sat in the street.

They reported to their master. "We have brought in everyone we could find, but there are still empty places. We have more room."

"Then go out and find still other guests," said the man. "I want my house full. I want many to enjoy my banquet."

At another time Jesus told a story about two men who went to the Temple to pray. One was proud. He had joined the Pharisees and boasted of how well he kept all the difficult rituals and laws.

This Pharisee stood and prayed loudly, "God, I thank You that I am not one of those who are always breaking Your rules like this tax collector."

The Pharisee had noticed another man come up behind him. He knew that the other man collected taxes for Rome.

When the tax collector came towards the altar he did not go close up as the Pharisee had. He was bowed over and was truly sorry about some sin he had committed. He felt that he had done wrong and did not deserve to come to God and yet he wanted God's forgiveness.

And so the man prayed, "God, be merciful to me a sinner."

Jesus wanted His listeners to understand that those who come in humility and ask to be forgiven will find forgiveness from God. "The tax collector found forgiveness," Jesus told them. "God answered his prayer."

Jesus always spoke against pride. He believed that everyone was important—poor people as well as rich people, followers as well as leaders, women as well as men, children as well as grownups.

One day when Jesus was teaching a large crowd some mothers came with their children. The boys and girls walked a little ahead. The babies were carried in the arms of their mothers.

The disciples saw them coming and stood in the way. "Jesus is busy," they said. "He must teach men and women about God's Kingdom. He has no time for these small children and babies."

Jesus had seen the mothers coming. He heard what the disciples said and cried out, "You are wrong. I *do* have time. Let the children come to Me."

The boys and girls ran ahead to where Jesus was sitting. The mothers followed with quick step. The boys and girls crowded around Jesus, and He put His arms around them. He asked them their names and spoke to them about God and His love for them.

Each mother in turn held out her baby to Jesus. Jesus put His hand on the baby's head and asked God to bless the baby.

This took a long time, but Jesus did not mind. When he noticed the crowd stir impatiently, Jesus told them, "I want the children to come to Me. Do not try to keep them away.

"The Kingdom of God will belong to them. They find it easier to believe in Me. Those who are not willing to become like a child—one who is willing to trust and willing to learn—shall not enter God's Kingdom."

The people marveled. They had never realized how very important it was to help children know God while they were young.

From then on mothers did not hesitate to bring the children to talk to Jesus. Many of the children believed in Him.

Others who came to Jesus found it harder to become a follower. One person who found it too hard was a rich young ruler.

This handsome young man was interested when he heard Jesus preach. He came to Jesus and said, "Good master, what must I do to have this new life you talk about?"

"Live in ways that please God," said Jesus. "Keep the commandments."

Jesus reminded him of the commandments that told him how he should treat others. "Love your neighbor as yourself," said Jesus.

Jesus knew this young man was very rich, and he did not use his money to help others.

"I have always kept these commandments," said the man. Yet he felt he lacked something. "What is it I have not done?" he asked Jesus.

Jesus knew what the trouble was. This young man loved his riches too much. His love of possessions made him forget to care about others.

"You must give up your riches," said Jesus. "You care too much about your possessions. Your aim in life is to get more and more. Leave all of this. Give what you have to the poor, and join this band of disciples who go everywhere with Me."

It was a great invitation. Jesus knew this young man would make a good disciple. He could be a leader in God's Kingdom if he would forget his ambitions.

The young man thought about the money and possessions he had worked so hard to get. He thought about the fine house he wanted to buy and the many feasts and good times he expected to hold there.

He shook his head. No, he couldn't give up all this to follow Jesus and have a place in His Kingdom.

Jesus too was sad. "Many will fail to find God's Kingdom because they love possessions too much," He said.

Peter said, "We left our homes and our good business to follow you."

Jesus agreed. "Yes, I know, and you will be rewarded. You will find joy in being part of God's Kingdom. You will be repaid for your sacrifice. You will not be sorry you followed Me."

Jesus knew there were more important things than money and houses. There was a joy in serving God and doing His work that was greater than the joy of possessions.

Matthew 19:13-30; Mark 10:13-31; Luke 14:16-24; 18:9-30

41. A Brother Is Raised

Sad news came to Jesus around this time. Messengers from Mary and Martha told Him, "Lazarus is ill."

Jesus did not leave immediately, but two days later He told the disciples, "Let us go to Bethany. Lazarus needs My help."

The disciples were distressed. Bethany was only two miles from Jerusalem. "There is danger for you there, Master," they exclaimed. "The last time we were in Jerusalem, the leaders tried to stone you."

Then Jesus told them, "I have work to do. Lazarus has died. We must go to Bethany."

The disciples were unhappy and afraid. But Thomas told them, "Come, we can't desert Jesus now. Let us go and die with him."

The road from Jericho to Bethany wound up and around steep hills. When they approached the village, high in the hills, Martha came running to meet them. Someone had told her Jesus was coming.

Martha greeted Jesus. "Lord," she said, "if you had been here I know you could have healed by brother. He would not have died. Even now, I know that whatever you ask of God, God will do."

Martha had great faith in Jesus' power. Jesus assured her, "Your brother will rise again."

Martha was not sure she understood Jesus. She was not sure she dared to think Jesus meant Lazarus would rise now.

"I know that my brother will rise again on the day when all those who believe in God will rise to new life," she said.

"I am the resurrection and the life," Jesus told her. "Do you believe this?"

Martha said, "Yes, I believe that you are the Messiah God sent to us."

Then Martha hurried back to her house while Jesus and His disciples stayed outside the village. Martha told Mary, "Jesus is outside the village. He wants to talk to you."

For seven days after someone died, friends and relatives came to visit and express their sorrow. When all these people saw Mary and Martha hurrying out, many of them thought the sisters were going to visit the tomb of Lazarus, and went with them.

Mary ran to where Jesus stood with His disciples and knelt before Him. She was crying as she spoke to Him.

"Lord, if you had been here, my brother would not have died." Her friends and relatives began to cry also.

Jesus was troubled. How sad it was when loved ones went away. He asked, "Where did you put Lazarus?"

The friends said, "Come, see the fine tomb on the hillside."

They led the way to the hillside. A large rock was at the entrance of the cave-like tomb. Steps led down to the room where the tightly wrapped body lay.

When Jesus saw the place and heard the sobbing of the others, He too shed tears. Many in the crowd noticed this.

"How Jesus loved Lazarus," they said.

But others were critical. "Could not this man who opened the eyes of the blind man have kept Lazarus from dying?" they asked.

Now Jesus spoke in a clear, commanding voice. "Take away the rock."

Some of the men rolled away the rock. The people were wondering what would happen next. They knew that Lazarus had been dead four days. Even Martha was now thinking that nothing could be done.

Jesus looked to heaven and prayed aloud to God. "Thank You for hearing Me, Father," He prayed. "I know that You always hear Me when I pray, but I am praying aloud so that the people who stand here will be convinced that You have sent Me."

Then Jesus commanded loudly, "Lazarus, come out."

The people were frightened when they saw Lazarus stumble out of the tomb. The wrapped cloths made walking difficult. "Take away the cloths," said Jesus.

When they did this, they found Lazarus alive and well. Jesus had used His power from God to raise Lazarus from the dead.

The friends and relatives were all amazed. "Now we believe in Jesus," they cried. "He is truly the Messiah, the One sent from God."

Some of these people lived in Jerusalem. They told all their friends in the big city what had happened. When the Pharisees heard that Jesus had raised a man from the dead they were upset. The miracle did not make them believe in Jesus.

The Pharisees talked with the priests. "This man is showing so many signs and miracles that everyone will believe in him," they said.

The priests agreed. "This will cause a rebellion. The Romans will bring out soldiers against us and destroy our Temple. We must put Jesus to death before this happens."

Jesus knew of this plotting and so He and His disciples went away to a desert place for a little while.

In the meantime, other people in Jerusalem were talking about Jesus. Many asked, "Will Jesus keep the Passover this year? It is almost time for the Feast to begin."

In the Temple courts many were asking, "What do you think? Will Jesus come to the Feast?"

John 11

42. The Most Important Posts

One day Jesus told His twelve special disciples, "The time has come for us to go back to Judea. We will keep the Passover."

Jesus started down the road ahead of the disciples, walking swiftly and purposefully. The disciples were surprised and distressed. And when He slowed down for them to catch up with Him, and told them again what was going to happen, they were afraid.

"When we go to Jerusalem for the Feast of the Passover," He said, "I will be arrested and put to death. When this happens do not fear. I will rise again the third day."

The disciples refused to pay attention to this. They did not understand it at all.

On the road the old argument came up about places of honor in God's Kingdom. They still believed God's Kingdom would be like earthly empires with many princes and rulers over men.

That night when they made camp the mother of James and John came to visit. She talked with her sons, and they told her about this argument.

"You two should be the greatest in God's Kingdom," she said, "Come with me. I will ask Jesus about it myself."

So James and John followed their mother as she went and knelt before Jesus. "Rabbi, I have a request to make," she said.

"What is your request?" asked Jesus.

"When you sit on the throne in God's Kingdom, I want my sons to sit with you, one on your right hand and one on your left hand."

In an earthly kingdom these seats would show that the persons were next in authority to the king.

Jesus looked at James and John. They asked for the same thing.

Jesus said, "You don't understand God's Kingdom or the importance of what you ask. To be great in God's Kingdom means a willingness to suffer when one has to for God's truth, just as I am going to suffer. Are you able to do this?"

"Yes," they said eagerly. "We are able. We will do anything you ask."

Jesus sighed. The disciples would suffer persecution when they were left to carry on His work. Still Jesus said, "The honor you request is not for Me to give now. You must prove yourselves worthy."

The other disciples had gathered around. They were amazed when they heard what these disciples had asked. "What right do they have to ask for the best places?" they demanded.

Some became angry and talked among themselves about who was more worthy than James and John.

Jesus interrupted them. "You are still wrong in the way you think about God's Kingdom," He said.

He told them it would not be like the Roman Empire. Jesus said, "In our world the important men rule over others. They have authority over the lives of others. They are feared and obeyed. God's Kingdom is nothing like this."

The disciples listened carefully. Jesus was saying that their argument was not at all important. Would anyone be greater than another in God's Kingdom? Jesus went on to say that, yes, some would be greater than others. He told them who would be worthy.

"If you want to be great in God's Kingdom," Jesus said, "do the most service for others. Be like a slave in your willingness to work for and help others."

This was hard advice. The disciples did not know whether or not they wanted this kind of greatness.

Then Jesus reminded them how His own life had been filled with nothing but service for others. Often they had seen Jesus preach for hours when He was tired and hungry. Often they had seen Him go out of His way to heal one person. Whenever the crowds had come out to Him, He had helped them.

Jesus said, "Even I, the Son of Man, came to serve others, not to be served."

Now they were on their way to Jerusalem. Here Jesus would prove Himself to be the greatest servant. He would give His life for others.

Matthew 20:17-28;
Mark 10:32-45; Luke 18:31-34

43. A Rich Man Finds Salvation

About fifteen miles from Jerusalem, Jesus and His disciples made a stop at Jericho. This beautiful city was like an oasis in the desert. The climate was very warm, and many palm trees with their plump, brown dates lined the road. Mountains rose on one side and gardens and orchards on the other.

This was a busy road. Much trading took place in Jericho and merchandise was carried in and out of the city by caravans. Now many people were traveling through on their way to keep the Passover.

As they entered the city, crowds gathered around Jesus and walked with Him.

Blind people often sat on the busy street near the city gate and begged for money. A blind man sitting by the road heard many of the crowd talking about Jesus.

"Who has come?" he shouted to those passing him. "What is all the excitement about?"

People stopped and explained. "It is Jesus of Nazareth, the one who has healed so many."

Some said, "He is the Son of David, the Messiah."

The blind man called out for the help and healing he believed Jesus could give.

"Jesus, Son of David, have mercy on me!" he shouted.

Those who stood near rebuked him. "Don't disturb Jesus," they said. "Keep still."

But the man knew his one chance of healing was passing by. "Son of David, have mercy on me!" he shouted again and again.

"Be quiet," the people kept saying.

Jesus heard the man call, and stopped walking.

The people told Him, "It is a blind beggar calling."

"Bring him to Me," Jesus said.

Some of the men near the blind man took his arm. "It's all right. Come on, Jesus is calling for you," they told him.

When they brought the man Jesus asked him, "What is it you want Me to do for you?"

The man said, "Lord, I want my sight."

Jesus told him, "Receive your sight. Your faith has made you well."

Immediately the blind man looked around him and saw the crowd. He saw the face of Jesus who had healed him. He gave thanks to God.

The people around also gave thanks to God. Some had seen Jesus heal for the first time.

The man who had been blind followed close by Jesus and His disciples as they made their way into the city.

The people in Jericho heard that Jesus was coming. A large crowd gathered. Many were staying here on their way to Jerusalem. They lined the street to get a look at Jesus.

Zacchaeus, one of the chief tax collectors, had heard about Jesus but had never seen Him. Now he joined the crowd.

Jericho was on the main route from Perea to Judea and Egypt. Scented balm was made in the city and exported in large quantities to other countries. The men who collected the taxes on this trade would be rich indeed. The Roman government demanded so much money, and then the collectors could charge as much over this as they wished.

The crowd would not move aside and give Zacchaeus room to see, because they hated all those who collected the taxes. Zacchaeus was short, and he was about ready to give up and go home when he had an idea.

Zacchaeus noticed the low thick branch of a sycamore tree hanging over the road. Quickly he climbed up the tree and sat on the branch. Now he could see far down the road to where a group of people approached.

Zacchaeus was sure Jesus was the One so many tried to talk to at once. As Jesus came near, Zacchaeus looked closely at Him. He believed Jesus was a man who really knew God.

When He was below the tree Jesus stopped suddenly, looked up and saw Zacchaeus. He knew that Zacchaeus was a tax collector who probably cheated the people, but He believed in showing love to all. Jesus also knew that Zacchaeus needed help from God in order to change his ways.

Jesus called him by name. "Zacchaeus, hurry and come down. I would like to stay at your house while I'm here in Jericho."

Zacchaeus was overjoyed. Quickly he jumped down and led the way to the fine house in which he lived. As Jesus and His disciples followed, they heard the angry muttering of the crowd.

"Jesus chooses to stay with a tax collector. He honors a man who robs from the poor."

Jesus knew many of the people would feel this way, but He also knew that Zacchaeus needed His help and that he was ready for it. Some of the crowd had done as many wrong things as Zacchaeus, but they could not be helped, because they were not ready to change.

Jesus spent hours talking to Zacchaeus alone and with other members of his family. The next day Zacchaeus made an announcement before the crowd who came out to hear Jesus teach. His announcement showed that he had come to believe in Jesus, and this had changed his life.

"Lord," he said. "I am going to give half of all my wealth to the poor. I will examine my records, and if I have cheated anyone I will give him back four times as much as I took."

Jesus was happy to hear Zacchaeus' decision. He wanted all the people to realize that this was what being His disciple meant.

Jesus said, "Today salvation has come to Zacchaeus' house. The Son of Man has come to seek and to save those who have wandered from God's way and want to come back."

Luke 18:35-43; 19:1-9
Mark 10:46-52
Matthew 20:29-34

PART THREE
"HE GAVE HIMSELF"

The time had come for Jesus to give Himself for others. This was the part of God's plan which the people had not understood. The Messiah had not come to lead a conquering army but to give Himself for His people and so bring them back to God.

In the past some men had lived close to God and lived in many ways as God wanted; but now it would be possible to have an even closer relationship with God the Father. God was going to make it possible for men to work with Him in new and exciting ways.

Jesus had come to earth for this purpose. It was not only now that He was giving Himself for others. All through His life He had given Himself in love and service. Now it was time to go to Jerusalem.

For some time the religious leaders had been seeking to put Jesus to death, but Jesus had always escaped out of their hands. Jesus could have continued to escape, but He knew His time had come.

Outside of Judea and Galilee there were many places He could have taught in safety, but Jesus turned to go to Jerusalem because He knew it was God's will. He loved God His Father, and wanted to do His will. He loved men and wanted to be their Redeemer.

The religious rulers had united in opposing Jesus. Only a few of them wanted to protect Jesus or at least to give Him a fair trial without making up their minds ahead of time.

Many of the people believed in Jesus and were loyal to Him. Those who had been healed did not forget. But these were unimportant people. They had no power to make decisions.

Nevertheless the rulers were somewhat afraid of the great crowds who had followed Jesus. They said, "We must find a time when Jesus is alone with his disciples to arrest him. Otherwise there might be a revolt among the people. They might turn on us."

The rulers had another problem. They had the power to judge about religious matters and to punish offenders; but they did not have the power to pass a death sentence. Only the Roman ruler, Pontius Pilate could do that.

"We must convince Pilate that Jesus is against Rome and wants to start a rebellion," the rulers said.

So the plans were laid to arrest Jesus if He came to the Feast of the Passover. But it was really God's plan which was coming true. God had the future in mind. He knew that through His Son's death, men would find new life; they would find the power to overcome evil in their lives; and one day evil would be conquered and disappear from the good world God had made.

44. Jesus Comes to Jerusalem

After Lazarus was brought back to life he and his sisters were very grateful to Jesus and so were all their relatives. They decided to give a dinner in Jesus' honor. They held it in the large house of a relative called Simon. It was now six days before the Passover would begin.

Martha had made sure there were many good dishes of food for Jesus, His disciples, and the other guests. And she helped with the serving. She wanted to show her gratitude to Jesus by making this dinner a wonderful occasion.

Lazarus sat at the table and ate with Jesus. The twelve disciples were all there.

Mary found a special way to say "thank you" to Jesus. She had a pound of sweet-smelling oil with which people enjoyed soothing their tired feet. It cost a great deal of money, and Mary kept it in a beautiful alabaster jar.

In the middle of the dinner Mary came up to Jesus with the jar. She showed it to Jesus and asked to put some on His feet. As she opened the jar the sweet smell filled the room. She poured some out on Jesus' feet.

By then everyone had noticed. "How good it smells," they said. "It fills the air with its fragrance."

But one person was annoyed. Lately Judas Iscariot, one of the disciples, had been very discontented. He was not pleased with the kind of kingdom Jesus talked about. He had stopped trying to live in God's way.

It was Judas' job to keep all the money which belonged to them. This money had been given by followers who wanted to help. Lately Judas had been taking from this fund for his own desires.

Now as Judas saw the expensive oil being poured out he said, "This is a waste. Mary should have sold this ointment and then given us the money to give to the poor."

Mary was disappointed. She looked anxiously at Jesus. Had she done the wrong thing?

But Jesus said, "Do not rebuke Mary. She has done a good thing. There will be many chances in the future for you to help the poor; but I will not always be here."

During this week before the Passover, Jesus and His disciples planned to stay with Mary and Martha and go back and forth to Jerusalem. On the first day of this week Jesus and His disciples followed a footpath from Bethany that wound over the Mount of Olives to Jerusalem.

When they came near Bethphage Jesus had special instructions for two of His disciples.

"Go into Bethphage," He told them. "As you enter the village you will find a young donkey tied up outside that you may borrow."

"If anyone asks you why you are taking the donkey say, 'The Lord has need of it.' Then they will know you are from Me."

The disciples hurried away on their mission. They saw the house by the road and there out on the street a little donkey, a colt, was tied by the door.

The disciples went up and untied the animal. The people of the house who owned the donkey wanted to be sure the right people were taking it.

"Why are you untying our colt?" they asked the disciples.

"The Lord has need of it," they said just as Jesus had told them.

"It's all right," said the owners. "The Lord is welcome to our colt."

The disciples led the little animal back to where Jesus and the others were waiting. They took off their brightly colored cloaks and put them on the colt to make riding more comfortable for Jesus.

The colt had never had anyone ride him before this, but he took step after step and found that he could indeed carry Jesus.

Many of the people traveling to Jerusalem on the same road started to cheer. Jesus' disciples walked around Him as they continued towards the city.

Jesus had wanted to travel into Jerusalem in this way because an ancient prophecy about the Messiah was: "Your king will come to you in a humble way, mounted on a donkey."

The horse was an animal that made people think of war. Jesus chose the donkey because it was an animal that made people think of peace. Yet it would be a way of saying that He was the King the prophets had promised.

The crowds around Jesus became excited. Some put their cloaks on the mountain road for the donkey to walk over. Many broke off palm branches from nearby trees and spread them in the path or waved them in the air.

When they came to the descent of the Mount of Olives they could all look down on the city and Temple below. Then the people began to shout:

"Hosanna! Blessed is the King who comes in the name of the Lord!"

Jesus was glad for the words of praise, but He realized that the people did not understand His true purpose and what God's Kingdom would be like.

The crowd continued to shout and praise God for the wonderful works done by Jesus. In this way Jesus and the crowd came to the city.

Some of the excited palm wavers went ahead shouting and praising God. The crowds of people who stood about the city streets turned at the sound. They saw the crowd coming. They noticed Jesus on the donkey.

Some asked, "Who is this?"

But many knew Jesus. Some had been healed by Him. Some had been at the tomb when Lazarus was raised from the dead.

"This is Jesus of Nazareth, a mighty prophet," they said to all. "He even raised the dead to life."

At this many joined the praising crowd. They too reached up for palm branches. They waved them in the air or laid them in the street. They put their cloaks in the street. This was the way a king was greeted.

Many added their voices to the crowds who were singing out: "Glory and honor to the Son of David! Blessed is Jesus who comes in the name of the Lord. Blessed is the Kingdom of our Father David that is coming. Glory in the highest!"

It was a great entry into Jerusalem. It showed the rulers that many people did believe in Jesus; but it did not make them believe. They muttered their disapproval, but the crowds would not be silenced.

They continued to praise God and shout their welcome to Jesus: "Glory to God in the highest. Praise to the Son of David."

John 12:1-19
Matthew 26:6-13; 21:1-11
Mark 14:3-9; 11:1-11
Luke 19:28-39
Zechariah 9:9

45. Excitement at the Temple

The next day Jesus and His disciples went again to the city. Jesus went into the Temple courts and stopped by the booths of the money changers. He noticed the people coming to pay their Temple tax. He was sad that these men were still allowed inside the Temple courts.

The tax could only be paid with Jewish coins. Some people had foreign coins, because Jews came from many lands to keep the Feast. As these people had their money exchanged at the booths, they muttered that they were being cheated.

"The priests earn money in wrong ways," many of the people claimed.

Others were buying animals for the sacrifice. They exclaimed at how much the doves or lambs cost. "It is not right," many said.

Jesus too sighed at the injustices all around. It is always wrong to cheat people, but it was especially wrong to cheat them in the Temple and in connection with their worship of God.

Once again, as at the beginning of His work for God, Jesus spoke out against these men. He was angry that they were bringing disgrace to God's Name by their actions. He overthrew the tables of the money changers and chased out the men who sold the animals.

Jesus shouted at the men: "The Scriptures say, 'God's house shall be called a house of prayer,' but you have made it a den of robbers."

Then Jesus told the others how they should honor God's house. "It is a house of prayer for all people," He said.

As Jesus taught, some of the lame and blind beggars who sat at the gates to the Temple courts came up to Jesus for healing. Jesus spoke the words of healing to them. They went away walking and seeing.

Some boys and girls watched all of this. They had heard much about Jesus from their parents. Some had talked to Jesus. They believed He was the Messiah.

"Let's sing a song of praise to Jesus," several said. They gathered other friends together in a little group. Over and over they called out, "Glory and honor to the Son of David."

The children knew the Son of David meant the Messiah. The Pharisees who were there were angry at the song. They interrupted Jesus at His work.

"Do you hear what these children are singing?" they demanded.

"Yes, I hear," said Jesus. "I am glad for their song. The Scriptures say: 'Out of the mouths of children comes perfect praise to God.' "

Then Jesus warned the rulers that they were committing a great sin by rejecting Him as the Messiah. He did this by telling them stories and asking them questions.

Jesus said, "One man had two sons. One day he told the eldest, 'I want you to work in the vineyard today.' But the son said, 'I will not.'

"When the father had gone, the son thought about his refusal. 'I should not have refused my father,' he decided. 'I will go and work in the vineyard.'

"The father also talked to his younger son. 'I want you to work in the vineyard,' he told him. 'Yes Father. I will go right away,' said this son. But the son did not go. He found something else to do. Now which son did the will of his father?"

The religious rulers said, "The first son."

"You are right," said Jesus. "It matters what we actually do, not what we say we will do. Many of those you regard as sinners have come into God's Kingdom, but you have refused."

The next story was about a man who owned a large vineyard. He had to go into another country and so he rented the vineyard to tenants. They were supposed to care for the vines and gather the grapes when harvest came. Part of the harvest would go to the owner.

At the time of harvest the owner sent servants to get his share of grapes, but the tenants wanted to keep all the grapes for themselves. They killed the servants.

The owner sent other servants for the grapes. The same thing happened. Then the owner sent his son. "They will have respect for my son," he said.

But the servants said, "This is the heir. If we kill him we will have the vineyard for ourselves."

Then Jesus asked the rulers, "What do you think the owner should do to these tenants?"

The rulers said, "Such wicked men should be put to death, and the vineyard given to honest tenants."

Jesus rebuked them for rejecting His message. He reminded them of the prophets of God who had been put to death in the past.

"The Kingdom of God will belong only to those who believe God's message," He told them.

The rulers realized that Jesus had spoken against them because He knew they wanted to kill Him. They would have arrested Him there and then, but too many people were around who believed in Him.

Jesus then went on to criticize the rulers for their lack of love for others and their unwillingness to show mercy and give understanding. They were not good servants of God.

Jesus told a story about good and bad servants. Once a man who had three servants called them to him. He told them that he was going on a long journey and that they would need to care for all his business. He gave each servant a different sum of money. One received five talents, another two, and another one. A talent was about one thousand dollars. The servants understood that they were to invest this money so that their totals would increase.

Two of the servants got busy right away but one did no work. He hesitated to make trades because he was afraid he might lose the one talent he already had.

When the man returned to his servants he had praise for the two servants who had worked. They had doubled their money. But he was very angry with the servant who had not worked.

"You are no longer my servant," he told the man.

Matthew 21:12-16, 28-46; 25:14-30
Mark 11:15-18; 12:1-12
Luke 19:45-48; 20:9-19
Isaiah 56:7; Jeremiah 7:11; Psalm 8:2

46. Questions for Jesus

Each day in Jerusalem Jesus continued to teach by using stories. The crowds listened eagerly to what He had to say. Some were hearing Him for the first time.

Meanwhile the Pharisees had gathered together with other religious rulers. "We must find a good reason to arrest Jesus," they said. "We must get Jesus to say something which will get Him into trouble with the Roman authorities."

"We can ask Him some difficult questions," said one.

"I know," said another. "We can ask him about paying the Roman taxes. If he says we should not pay, the soldiers on the streets will report him. If he says we should pay them, the people will be angry."

"That's a wonderful plan," said the leaders, "but you must sound sincere when you ask, or he might not answer you."

Other men who were present were called Herodians. They were supporters of King Herod, and they would be quick to object if Jesus said a Jew did not need to pay taxes because God was his only king.

The group made their way to where Jesus was teaching. When he had an opportunity, one of them asked, "Teacher, we know that you always speak the truth and would not lie to protect yourself or others. We know that you are true in teaching the way of God.

"Now tell us, is it right to pay taxes to Caesar? Should we Jews pay taxes to this pagan government?"

The people around were frightened. They looked to see if any Roman soldiers were near.

But Jesus was not frightened. He realized that these men were trying to get Him into trouble with Rome.

"Bring Me a coin," said Jesus.

Several men got out money from the small pocket in the belts wound around their striped coats. One handed Jesus a coin. Jesus looked at the coin and held it up to the crowd. Then He asked them, "Whose picture is stamped on this coin?"

Some looked closer. "It is Caesar's picture," they said.

"Then it belongs to Caesar," said Jesus. "Give your ruler what belongs to him; but give God what belongs to Him."

Jesus used this question to teach an important lesson. Earthly rulers deserved obedience and respect, and everyone needed to contribute money to running a government. But God deserved love and loyal service. When it was impossible to do both, when a ruler wanted a person to disobey God, then God must come first.

The crowd was amazed at the wisdom of Jesus' reply. The Pharisees were angry and left. From that time on they were afraid to ask Jesus questions.

Then the Sadducees had a question for Jesus about the resurrection. They did not believe there was a life after death but the Pharisees did.

Jesus agreed that there was a resurrection for each person. "Do you remember the story of Moses and the burning bush?" He asked. "God said to Moses, 'I am the God of Abraham, Isaac and Jacob.' God is speaking of them as living people even though Moses lived after these great men."

Some of the scribes who believed in the resurrection had words of praise for Jesus. "Rabbi, you have spoken well," they said.

Then a scribe asked Jesus a question He had heard many times before. "Which is the greatest commandment?" the man asked.

Jesus answered as He had before, "There are two. The first is: 'You shall love the Lord your God with all your heart, and with all your soul, and with all your mind.'

"The second is, 'You shall love your neighbor as yourself.' These two commandments contain all that is most important."

The scribe said, "You are right, Rabbi. To obey these commandments means more to God than all the sacrifices and offerings we can bring."

Later that day, before they left the Temple courts, Jesus and His disciples sat down to rest. The chests which held the offerings of the worshipers were nearby.

Jesus watched as the people came and put in their money. Some men came dressed in expensive clothing. They made sure those who stood nearby noticed the many coins they put in the chest.

Jesus pointed them out to the disciples.

"How much they bring," one disciple said. "They are indeed helping to support our Temple."

Behind them came a woman who was dressed very poorly. She was known to be a widow. Jesus knew that she had very little money. Yet she had two coins for the chest.

Jesus smiled. "See that widow?" Jesus asked His disciples. "She really gave a larger gift than the rich men."

The disciples wondered, *How could that be?*

Jesus told them, "The rich men had plenty. They could have given even more money without going hungry or doing without things they needed. This widow has little money. In order to give to the Temple she had to sacrifice something she really needed. This made her gift great in the sight of God."

Mark 11:18; 12:13-44
Matthew 22:15-40
Luke 19:47; 20:40; 21:1-4

47. A Betrayer Appears

The Passover would begin with a special dinner on Friday evening after sunset. Then for a week the people would eat no bread with leaven or yeast in it.

Two days before the Passover began, the religious rulers had a meeting at the home of the high priest. They discussed ways of having Jesus arrested and put to death.

"We must do it before the Passover begins," they decided, "or there might be a riot among the people. By then many will be here for the Feast. Many of his friends from Galilee will have come."

"If only we could find and arrest Jesus some time when he is alone with his disciples," several priests said. Then the enemies of Jesus found unexpected help.

Judas Iscariot had been a dissatisfied disciple for some time. He had hoped that by joining with Jesus he would win a high post in His government when Jesus became ruler.

At last he was convinced that Jesus was not going to establish a kingdom of earthly power. He was very disappointed. The more he heard about a kingdom of love and peace the more he disliked it.

Judas also knew that the others suspected him of stealing. He decided he would get even with them all.

Judas went to the chief priests, "What will you give me if I deliver Jesus to you?" he asked.

The chief priests were surprised. They were glad, but they did not offer Judas much as a reward.

"Thirty pieces of silver," they said.

"I will do it," said Judas. "I will keep in touch with you and let you know a good time to arrest him."

"Find a time when not many friends are present," they told him.

Judas went back to the disciples and Jesus, whom he still professed to follow. He watched and listened closely for his chance to betray Jesus.

On Thursday many people started to prepare for the special dinner of unleavened bread, bitter herbs, wine, and lamb which was the Passover supper.

Two disciples asked Jesus, "Where do you want us to prepare for the Passover supper?"

Jesus told them. He had made arrangements with a loyal follower in Jerusalem to use the guest room on the roof of his house. The preparations were carried on secretly so that the enemies of Jesus would not know.

Jesus told these two disciples, "You must go to this person and tell him, 'The Teacher says, My time is at hand.' Then he will show you a large guest room furnished with a table and couches. Prepare the food for all of us."

Jesus knew that His enemies would soon arrest Him. He wanted to eat the Passover meal with His disciples. The two that He sent followed these instructions. They arranged the food and had everything ready when Jesus and the others arrived at the house Thursday evening.

When Jesus and the rest of the disciples came in they were hot and dusty. A basin of water and towels were nearby,

but no servants were there to wash the feet of the men. Open sandals and dusty roads always made the feet dirty.

None of the disciples wanted this job, and they pretended to forget about it. They found places on the couches, leaving the head place at the center of the table for Jesus.

The supper began. Jesus waited for one of the disciples to do this service. He had taught them so much about serving others; but they all continued to talk and eat.

Then Jesus got up and put off His cloak. He put the large towel about His waist. He filled the basin with water and knelt down. The disciples were too amazed to speak as Jesus took off each sandal and tenderly washed each foot and dried it with the ends of the towel.

When Jesus came to Peter this disciple cried out, "No, Lord. It isn't right for you to do this."

But Jesus insisted. When He had finished, Jesus spoke to them about what He had done.

"You call Me Teacher and Lord and you are right; and yet I have been willing to serve you by washing your feet, a task you all thought you were too good to do. I have given you an example. I was willing to serve you. You should be willing to serve one another, even in such a humble way as this."

The supper continued, and then Jesus gave a startling announcement. "One of you who is eating with Me is going to betray Me."

Jesus knew the way Judas felt. He knew that Judas had been to the chief priests, but even now He tried to help Judas change.

Everyone was shocked. To eat with someone was a sign of trust and friendship. It was awful to think that any of them would betray Jesus and yet continue to eat with Him.

But as the disciples gasped, they also wondered. Could it be themselves? In some future moment of weakness would they betray Jesus?

They began to ask Him, "Lord, is it I?"

Jesus would not tell them the name of the man. He repeated, "It is one at our table."

John was sitting next to Jesus. He leaned closer to ask, "Lord, who is it?"

Jesus still did not tell the name, but He whispered to John, "It is the one to whom I will give this choice portion of food."

Then Jesus handed a serving to Judas. He gave it as a way of showing favor to Judas, but Jesus could see that Judas no longer loved Him and that his mind was made up.

Jesus sighed as He looked at Judas. He saw a face which was filled with hate and desire for revenge.

"Do quickly what you are going to do," Jesus told him.

Judas could have returned and asked Jesus to forgive him, but he did not. He hurried away from the table. No one else knew that Judas was the betrayer. They thought Jesus had sent him on some errand.

Judas hurried down the steps and out into the dark street. It was night now, but Judas ran. He knew where he was going—straight to the chief priests.

Matthew 26:1-4, 14-25
Mark 14:1, 2, 10-21
Luke 22:1-13; John 13:2-30

48. A Last Talk With Friends

Before the dinner was over Jesus took a large piece of bread and broke it into smaller pieces for each disciple.

Jesus was about to give them a special way to remember Him that would have an important place in the church to come.

As He held the bread, Jesus prayed to God the Father. He thanked God for the bread and asked Him to bless it. He gave a piece to each disciple and said, "Take and eat this bread. It represents My body which is given for you."

The disciples ate the bread. Then Jesus took a cup of wine in both hands. As He held it up, He prayed. He thanked God for the wine and asked Him to bless it.

He said to the disciples, "Take this cup of wine and share it among yourselves. Drink it, for this represents My blood which will be shed at My death for the forgiveness of sins."

The disciples passed the cup around the table and each took a sip of the wine.

Jesus told them, "I shall not drink of the fruit of the vine again until I drink it with you in the Kingdom of God; but after My death keep this supper. Do it in memory of Me."

The disciples were very quiet. They knew that something very solemn and important had begun. They would always remember this moment and that Jesus had said, "My death is for you."

The dinner was over and the disciples got up. They quietly sang a psalm together. Without talking, they left the upper room and started out towards the Mount of Olives. Here they had planned to spend some quiet hours before returning to Bethany.

They walked down the narrow streets and out of the city gates into the open countryside. The moonlight shone among the gnarled hunched forms of the olive trees. In the quiet of the misty night they could hear their own footsteps.

Then Jesus had disturbing words. "Tonight you will all run away and desert Me; but when you do this, do not think everything is over. After I rise from the dead I will meet you in Galilee."

The disciples were shocked at these words. Only Peter spoke up. "Maybe the others will run away," he said, "but I will never desert you."

Peter was sure he had more love for Jesus than the others, but he was wrong. Jesus warned him, "Peter, before the day begins to dawn you will three times deny that you know Me."

Peter was still sure this would not happen. He was trusting in himself that he was strong enough to withstand temptation. He did not ask Jesus for help.

Jesus knew Peter's weakness and the weakness of the others, but this did not lessen His love for them. Now He said to Peter, "I have prayed for you, Peter. I have prayed that you will grow strong and be a help to others."

By this time they were well within the olive orchard. The disciples sat down and Jesus taught them for the last time before His death.

"Do not be troubled," He said. "Keep your faith in God and in Me. I have prayed to the Father for all of you. I am going away, but the Father will send you God's Spirit. He will help and guide you and give you the power you need to continue My work until I come back.

"Keep the teachings I have taught you and so show that you love Me. The teachings come from God. I have spoken as God told Me to speak. The person who loves Me will be loved by My Father.

"One day you will be with Me again. Remember, believing in Me is the way to God."

Then Jesus compared Himself and His disciples to a vine and its branches. "I am the vine, you are the branches," He told them. The branches of a vine receive food and strength from the vine. So the disciples would receive all their strength and help from Jesus. A good vine would bring forth good grapes. The disciples would show their faith by good deeds.

Jesus said, "God is glorified when you bear good fruit and so prove to be My disciples."

Jesus went on to tell the disciples as He had many times, "Love one another as I have loved you."

Jesus warned the disciples that it

would not be easy to carry on His work. The religious rulers who had been against Jesus would be against them. As the rulers had tried to stop Jesus, they would try to stop them.

Jesus assured them that He would always love them. "No man can have a greater love than one who is willing to die for his friend," He said, "and I will die for you."

Jesus called them His dear friends. Then He looked up to heaven and prayed aloud before the disciples.

"Father," He prayed, "the hour has come. Give glory to Your Son that Your Son may give glory to You."

Jesus knew that His death would bring men back to God. By dying for the sins of the world He was overcoming evil. It was not a moment of defeat, as the world thought, but a moment of great victory.

Jesus prayed for His disciples. "Keep these men who believe in Me from the evil of the world. Help them to be united in love."

Jesus thought about the many others who believed in Him and the many more who would come to believe because of their preaching.

He said, "I do not pray for these only, but also for those who will believe in Me through their word. I pray that they will all be united with us and with one another so that they will help others to believe in Me."

When Jesus finished praying He said, "Let us go a little farther." The disciples quietly followed as Jesus led the way.

Matthew 26:26-35
Mark 14:22-31
Luke 22:14-19, 31-39
John 13:37, 38; 14, 15, 16, 17
I Corinthians 11:23-26

49. Jesus Is Arrested

On the slope of the Mount of Olives was a garden called Gethsemane. Jesus had often met with His disciples here. It was along the road to Bethany.

"Sit here and rest," Jesus said as they entered the garden. Then He added to Peter, James, and John, "Come apart with Me and pray."

As they went farther on the path Jesus began to be very sorrowful. His spirit was heavy as He thought of the pain and shameful death ahead. It hurt Him to be rejected by His own people.

"Pray with Me," Jesus asked the three. They all lifted up their eyes to heaven. Jesus fell on the ground a little apart from the others.

Jesus needed strength from God to face what was ahead. The suffering and humiliation would be hard to endure, but this was not all that troubled Jesus. At His death Jesus knew He would represent all the sins of the world. Already this was a terrible burden within Him.

It was such a terrible prospect that Jesus prayed, "My Father, if You are willing, take this cup of suffering from Me; nevertheless not My will but Yours be done."

Jesus suffered in His body as well as in His spirit as He prayed, and God sent an angel to strengthen Him. Then Jesus went to talk to Peter, James, and John, but He found them exhausted from the excitement of the day. Instead of praying with Him, they had fallen asleep. It was close to midnight. Jesus could have easily escaped through the surrounding hills but He went back to praying.

Jesus talked to His Father about His coming death. He received the strength from God He needed. "Your will be done," Jesus told His Father.

Then Jesus got up. Through the trees he could see approaching lights. Judas had guessed that they would be here. Peter, James and John were still asleep.

"Get up now," Jesus told them. "The betrayer has come. Let us go to meet them."

The disciples were startled as they saw the large band of soldiers coming through the trees carrying torches and lanterns. Some were Jewish Temple guards sent by the Sanhedrin and some were Roman soldiers. They were armed with swords and clubs. Ahead of them walked Judas. He had told the soldiers, "I will give you a signal. The man I kiss will be Jesus."

Judas ran up to Jesus and kissed Him on the cheek. "Greetings, Rabbi," he said.

Jesus was gentle with Judas. "Friend, do you betray Me with a kiss?" He asked.

Then Jesus asked the soldiers, "Whom do you seek?"

The officers told Him, "Jesus of Nazareth."

"I am He," said Jesus. "Take Me, but let these disciples go."

Peter wanted to fight. He had a sword and used it now to strike at the first man he saw who happened to be the servant of the high priest. Peter cut off the man's ear.

Jesus rebuked Peter. "Put your sword up. I must drink this cup of suffering," He told him. Then He touched the man's ear and healed him.

Jesus spoke to the Temple guards. "Why have you come out for Me with swords and clubs as if I were a robber? For many days I sat and taught in the Temple, and you did not arrest Me."

The Temple guards could find nothing to say in answer. Then the Roman officers seized Jesus and bound Him.

When the disciples saw Jesus bound and being led away they ran as fast as they could so as not to be arrested. They were very frightened. Then Peter and John stopped. "We will follow at a safe distance," they decided.

They kept in the background as the band of soldiers led Jesus to the courtyard of the high priest. John's family was known to the high priest and his officers and he was allowed to come into the room where they had taken Jesus. Peter waited outside in the courtyard.

The soldiers first brought Jesus to the rooms of Annas who was father-in-law to the high priest. Annas had once been high priest himself, and he still had much influence and authority.

It was very early in the morning—not long after midnight—and still dark and cold in the courtyard. Peter's wool cloak did not keep him warm. He wandered over to where soldiers and servants were warming themselves by a brazier filled with hot coals which they had put on the tile floor.

They were talking about the Man who had been arrested and what the Sanhedrin was likely to do to Him. The fire felt good and Peter edged nearer. As the firelight flickered on his face one of the servant girls looked intently at him.

Then she cried out, "This man was with Jesus, the man they arrested tonight!"

Peter felt caught in a trap. He denied it. "I don't know him," he said.

Peter was ashamed, but he did not want to be arrested. He left the fire and walked closer to the gate. But the servant girl followed him.

She said to several men standing around, "This man is one of them."

Peter looked at the men in fear. "I don't understand what you mean," he insisted.

Then Peter had a worse fright. A man spoke up who was a relative of the man whose ear Peter had cut off. "Didn't I see you in the garden with Jesus tonight?" he asked.

"No, I don't know him," Peter shouted, and added a curse or two.

Then Peter noticed a faint streak of dawn appear in the sky. In the distance a cock crowed. Daylight had come. Then Peter remembered the warning of Jesus. As he realized the terrible thing he had done, he saw Jesus being led from one part of the building to another. Jesus turned and looked with sorrow and love at Peter. At this Peter broke down, and leaving the courtyard he wept bitterly.

Matthew 26:36-58, 69-75
Mark 14:32-54, 66-72
Luke 22:39-62
John 18:1-18, 25-27

50. Jesus Is Tried

Annas was an important man whom many feared to disobey. For some time he had been against Jesus and had urged the religious rulers to put Jesus to death. Now Annas wanted to talk to Jesus before He was brought before Caiaphas who was high priest at the time.

Jesus stood straight and tall before this man who hated Him. Annas questioned Jesus about His disciples and His teachings.

"You know what I have taught," Jesus told him. "I taught openly in the Temple courts and in the synagogues throughout the land. Many of these people heard Me teach. Ask them."

One of the officers of the high priest thought Jesus did not speak respectfully enough to such an important person. He struck Jesus. "That is no way to talk to Annas," he said.

"I have only said what is true," Jesus told them all.

Then Annas said, "I have had enough of this interview. This man must be brought before Caiaphas. Take him away."

Jesus was led into the room where the members of the Sanhedrin had gathered. They sat in a semicircle in front of Jesus. Caiaphas, the high priest, was in charge. They were waiting for Jesus.

Many of the chief priests were also there. They had brought men to speak against Jesus. These men accused Jesus of saying many things that were wrong, but one witness contradicted the other. This made their testimony worthless.

Then Caiaphas himself stood up. "Tell me," he said to Jesus. "Are you the Messiah, the Son of God?"

The high priest had heard that Jesus claimed to be the Son of God.

"I am," said Jesus. "In the future you will see Me sitting on the right hand of God and coming in the heavens in glory and power."

The high priest tore his clothes. Jews were supposed to do this when they heard blasphemy. Caiaphas cried out, "He has made himself equal with God. He has spoken blasphemy. We have no need for witnesses now. We have heard it for ourselves. How do you vote?"

The rulers cried out in anger. "He is worthy of death."

Two rulers who believed in Jesus, Joseph of Arimathea and Nicodemus did not vote against Jesus, but no one would listen to them.

Blasphemy was speaking against God or claiming to be God. According to the Law of Moses the punishment was stoning, but under Roman rule the Sanhedrin did not have the authority to put anyone to death. The Roman representative, Pontius Pilate, was the only one who could pass a death sentence.

For several hours Jesus was held prisoner until He could be brought before the Roman ruler, Pilate.

Pilate was the Roman procurator, a direct representative of Rome. He had been charged with keeping law and order in this part of the empire which was known to hate the Roman rulers. He was constantly on the alert to keep rebellion against the empire from starting.

Most of the time Pilate lived at Caesarea, but during the Passover he came to Jerusalem where so many Jews were gathered for the Feast. He brought extra Roman soldiers with him to help keep law and order, in this time when people's feelings ran extra high.

When Pilate was told that the Jewish rulers had a prisoner, he was concerned that this law and order would be disturbed. If the officials in Rome heard about any trouble in Jerusalem, they might take away his job or put him in prison.

The Jewish rulers knew that Pilate would not care about blasphemy or breaking the Sabbath. They needed to convince Pilate that Jesus was against the Roman empire and trying to overthrow it.

Roman soldiers brought Jesus into Pilate's house. The rulers waited outside. They would not go into Pilate's house themselves, because then they would not be able to eat the Passover that evening. Any Jew going into a Gentile home that day would be considered "unclean" and so be unable to keep the Feast.

Pilate came out to talk to the Jewish rulers.

"Who is this man you brought to me?" he asked them. "What has he done?"

The religious rulers had gathered together many people who hated Jesus. Now the rulers told Pilate, "This man is stirring up rebellion. He says we should not pay taxes to Caesar. He says that he is a king, the Messiah king."

Pilate had heard about the Jewish hope for a Messiah. As far as he was concerned it meant the Jewish hope to have an independent nation. He knew this could become a very serious matter, but he did not want to condemn Jesus without a hearing.

The Roman ruler went back to Jesus. Pilate wondered at the calmness and courage of Jesus as He stood there, His hands bound behind His back. "Are you the King of the Jews?" Pilate asked Jesus.

Jesus refused to argue in His own behalf. Pilate realized that the rulers had delivered Jesus out of envy and hatred. As he looked at Jesus, Pilate was not convinced that this Man was a danger to Roman rule.

"Don't you hear the many things your leaders say against you?" he asked Jesus. "Is it true? Are you a king?"

Jesus told him, "My kingdom is not an earthly one. If it were, I would have told My followers to fight for Me, to keep Me from being arrested. My kingdom is not of this world."

Pilate thought Jesus was a religious dreamer. "So you are a king then?" he asked, half smiling.

"I came into the world for this cause," Jesus spoke out.

Meanwhile Judas heard that Jesus had been brought before Pilate. Now he was sorry he had betrayed Jesus. He took the money back to the officials of the Temple.

"I have sinned and betrayed an innocent man," he told them.

The officials laughed at Judas. "Why should we care?"they asked.

Judas threw down the silver coins they had given him. He went out and killed himself.

Matthew 26:59-68; 27:1-14
Mark 14:55-64; 15:1-5
Luke 22:63-23:3
John 18:19-24, 28-37

51. Jesus or Barabbas

Pilate was convinced that Jesus did not mean to start a rebellion against Rome. Pilate believed Jesus to be a religious teacher who had disobeyed some Jewish law and made these religious rulers angry."

"I find no crime in this man," Pilate told the large crowd. The leaders were angry. "If he were not a criminal we would not have brought him to you," they shouted.

"Take him and judge him according to your own religious laws," Pilate told them impatiently.

"We can't," the rulers cried. "He is worthy of death, and it is against the Roman law for us to give a death sentence."

The crowd had become angry. Pilate wanted to help Jesus, but he did not want to get into trouble with the people of Jerusalem. He knew how important religion was to the Jews.

Now the religious rulers said, "Jesus has stirred up the people from Galilee to Judea."

When Pilate heard this, he thought he might get out of the responsibility of passing sentence on Jesus. "Is Jesus from Galilee?" he asked.

"Yes, he is from Nazareth," they told him.

"Then take him to Herod," Pilate told them. "Herod is the one who should be in charge of people from Galilee. That is Herod's territory."

Herod Antipas was in the city and staying close by. The Roman soldiers and the religious leaders took Jesus to this Roman ruler. For a long time Her-

od Antipas had wanted to see and hear Jesus. He was glad when the soldiers brought Jesus to him.

"Now I am going to see some miracle," Herod thought to himself. "It should be a good show."

But Jesus refused to perform any sign of power before Herod. He refused to argue and defend Himself.

Because he was disappointed, Herod began laughing at Jesus. The soldiers joined in.

"Take him back to Pilate," Herod ordered.

They returned to Pilate's house with Jesus. The crowd was still outside. Some of the priests had stayed with the people and urged them to keep on demanding the death of Jesus.

Again the religious rulers called for the Roman governor. Pilate again talked to Jesus. He was convinced that Jesus had done nothing worthy of death.

He told the people, "You brought me this man as one who is stirring the people to rebellion. After examining him, I do not find him guilty of your charge. Neither did Herod find him guilty for he sent Jesus back to us. Jesus has not done anything worthy of death. I will have him beaten and then release him."

The crowd shouted their disapproval. Then Pilate's wife sent a message to him. "Do not injure that righteous man. I have had a terrible dream which warns us of danger."

Pilate had heard that Jesus claimed to be from God. What if it were true? This frightened Pilate, but he was also afraid of the people. What if they sent a bad report about him to Rome?

Then Pilate had an idea. It was the custom at the Feast to release and pardon a convicted prisoner.

Pilate told the crowd, "There is a Jewish prisoner here accused of murder and of leading a rebellion against Rome. Do you want me to release this Barabbas to you as a favor at your feast time, or shall I release Jesus, who is called your Messiah?"

The religious rulers urged the people around them, "Ask for Barabbas."

These people were convinced that Jesus was a false teacher and deserved to die.

"Which of the two shall I release?" asked Pilate.

"Barabbas, Barabbas," the crowd shouted.

"What shall I do with Jesus who is called the Messiah?" he asked them.

"Let him be crucified," they shouted.

John 18:38-19:10
Matthew 27:15-22
Mark 15:4-13
Luke 23:4-19

52. Jesus Gives His Life

Pilate kept arguing with the crowd. "What evil has this man done?" he asked.

The crowd kept shouting, "Crucify him."

"It's no use," Pilate told his officials. "They demand the death of this man, and we will have trouble if we don't satisfy them."

He told the people, "Barabbas is released, and I have given orders that Jesus is to be beaten."

This was always done before a man was put to death by crucifixion.

Pilate wanted to show the crowd that he was not convinced of Jesus' guilt. He ordered a basin of water brought.

"I am innocent of this man's death," Pilate told them. He washed his hands.

"We will be responsible," the crowd shouted.

Inside Jesus was beaten. Soldiers laughed at Him and struck Him. They put a crown of thorns on His head and found a purple robe to put over His shoulders. Through it all Jesus did not strike back or even talk back.

Then Pilate called again for Jesus to come out before the crowd. He hoped that seeing Jesus with blood on Him from the beating would make them pity Him and ask for His release.

Pilate told them, "Here is the man."

The rulers shouted, "Crucify him, crucify him!"

"Take him yourself and do it," said Pilate.

"You know we're not allowed," the rulers replied. "Only you can have him put to death. We have our religious laws, and he has violated them. He has said that he is the Son of God."

Then one ruler cried out, "If you release this man you are not Caesar's friend. Anyone who claims to be a king has set himself against Caesar."

Pilate knew the rulers would report him to Caesar Tiberius, who was then emperor if he let Jesus go. Even though he believed Jesus innocent he said, "Very well. Jesus will be put to death."

Now the Roman soldiers were in charge. Two robbers were to be crucified that day as well as Jesus. The soldiers led them out to where the execution was to take place on a hill outside the city. Jesus carried His own cross on His back. On the way to the hill the soldiers stopped a man named Simon, from Cyrene, and made him carry Jesus' cross.

By now many friends and followers of Jesus had heard about the trial by night, but it was too late for them to protest. Besides, they had no power against the religious rulers and the Roman government.

The three crosses were put in the ground and the men hung on them. Jesus was in the center. It was a painful way to die, and it was a death reserved for only the worst criminals.

On top of Jesus' cross Pilate had commanded that a paper be attached that read: *Jesus of Nazareth, the King of the Jews.* The sign was written in three languages—Hebrew, Latin, and Greek.

Even in all this suffering Jesus did not turn against people. His heart was full of love and compassion to the end.

Soldiers of Rome surrounded the crosses and kept the crowd from getting close. The religious rulers were in the crowd and they taunted Jesus. Even the criminals on either side laughed.

"Jesus performed miracles before," they all laughed, "but he cannot save himself now."

The Roman soldiers joined in the mocking. Through it all Jesus had no words of hate or threat of revenge for any. Instead He prayed aloud: "Father, forgive them. They do not realize what a terrible sin they are committing."

The soldiers who guarded the crosses were given the clothing of the criminals. They noticed that Jesus had a fine cloak. "Let's roll dice for this," they said.

They cast the lots, and one man received the good cloak. They cared nothing for the suffering of the men.

One of the criminals spoke mockingly to Jesus, "If you are the Messiah, why don't you save yourself and us?"

The criminal on the other side had mocked Jesus earlier, but he had also watched how Jesus bravely suffered, without hate or anger. Now he said to the other criminal, "Aren't you afraid to talk that way seeing we are about to die and come before God? We deserve to die as criminals, but Jesus did nothing wrong."

Then the criminal turned to Jesus, "Lord," he said, "remember me when you come in your kingly power."

Jesus accepted the man as a believer. "Today you will be with Me in heaven," He said.

It grew very dark. The people were beginning to be afraid. Some women who had been followers of Jesus were in the front of the crowd. Mary, the mother of Jesus was there. The disciple John was close to her. She was sobbing.

Jesus wanted Mary to be well taken care of by one who believed in Him. He told John, "This is your mother." He told Mary, "This is your son." From that time on, John cared for Mary as though she were his mother.

The strange darkness lasted about three hours. After three in the afternoon, as the darkness was leaving, Jesus cried out loudly, "My God! Why have You forsaken Me?"

A little later, when it was light again, Jesus cried out again with a loud voice so all could hear: "Father, I give My spirit into Your hands." And He died.

One of the soldiers who was near Jesus was changed by Jesus' words. He no longer mocked. "Surely this man was innocent," he said.

When it was getting close to sunset, the religious rulers noticed that the Sabbath was just about to come. "We can't let these bodies stay here," they said. So they asked Pilate to hurry things up, and Pilate gave the order to the soldiers.

When they came to Jesus, they pierced His side with a sword.

Generally criminals were not given a good burial but Joseph of Arimathea, who had tried to defend Jesus in the Sanhedrin, went to Pilate and asked for permission to bury Jesus in a fine new tomb of his own.

Pilate gave the permission. Joseph had the body of Jesus taken from the cross. He wrapped it in fine linen. Nicodemus brought costly ointment to put on the body, and helped Joseph prepare Jesus for burial. It was the custom to put many spices and ointments on a body when it was buried.

Some of the women who had been followers of Jesus watched Joseph and Nicodemus, and they paid special attention to the tomb where Joseph put Jesus' body so they could find it again. Then they returned home to prepare additional spices.

The tomb was in a garden near the hill where Jesus had been crucified. They planned to return to the tomb with the spices very early on the first day of the week, after the Sabbath was over.

Matthew 27:23-61; Mark 15:14-47
Luke 23:22-26; John 19

53. An Empty Tomb

On the Sabbath (which is our Saturday) the disciples of Jesus met together in secret. They were filled with sorrow and their hopes for the future were gone. They were afraid of what the religious rulers might do to those who had believed in Jesus. They forgot what Jesus had said about rising from the dead.

But some of the religious rulers remembered that Jesus had said, "After three days I will rise again." They went to Pilate.

"We want you to put a guard at the tomb where Jesus was laid," they said. "We don't want his disciples to come and steal the body and then say he rose from the dead."

Pilate thought this was unnecessary but he gave in to them. He ordered soldiers to go with the rulers and take orders from them. The rulers told the soldiers to stay outside the tomb day and night until the three days would be up.

The first day of the week (Sunday) would be the third day. Very early, just as light was about to dawn on this day, the women who had prepared the spices came to anoint the body of Jesus.

They did not know that the soldiers were there and they asked each other, "How are we going to move the heavy rock at the door of the tomb. We really need a man to help us."

As they approached the hillside where the tomb was built into a cave, they noticed the Roman soldiers. Suddenly the ground shook beneath them.

They were very frightened and so were the soldiers. An angel from God appeared and rolled back the large flat rock at the entrance to the tomb. The women trembled and the soldiers fell down as though in a faint.

The angel said to the women, "Don't be afraid. I know that you seek Jesus, who was crucified. He is not here. He has risen from the dead as He said He would. Come, see the place where He lay."

The women followed the angel and looked inside the tomb. They went a few steps down into the tomb but it was empty.

They hurried out again. The angel told them, "Go quickly and tell Jesus' disciples that He has risen from the dead and that He will meet with them in Galilee."

It seemed too wonderful to be true. The women were not at all sure what to believe. One of them, Mary Magdalene, hurried away. She knew where Peter and John were staying, and she wanted them to come to the tomb.

At the same time the other women went on their way to tell other disciples what had happened. As they left the garden, Jesus met them.

"Greetings," He called.

Now the women believed because they could see Jesus for themselves. They fell at His feet and worshiped Him.

"Don't be afraid," said Jesus, "Go and tell My disciples to meet Me in Galilee."

The women hurried to some of the disciples who had gathered at the house of a friend. They told them about the empty tomb and how they had seen Jesus.

But the disciples thought the excited women had been frightened by some vision in the dark hours of early morning.

Meanwhile Mary Magdalene ran to Peter and John. She didn't believe the message of the angel. "They have taken the Lord out of the tomb, and we do not know where they have laid him," she cried out when she found them.

Peter and John immediately started out with Mary for the garden. Mary was weeping and the two disciples did not know what to think. In their anxiety, they both started to run. As they approached the tomb, they noticed the rolled-away rock.

John got there first. He was younger than Peter and could run faster. John stood at the top of the steps and looked down into the tomb where he could see the linen cloth was lying empty.

Peter came up, but he hurried down the steps. He saw the linen cloth and the napkin that had been around the head lying by itself and folded.

The two disciples looked at one another in amazement. The tomb was empty just as Mary had said.

They climbed the steps out of the tomb and into the bright sunshine. "We are going to the rest of the disciples," they told Mary; but she refused to move.

For a long while Mary stayed outside the tomb weeping. Then Jesus came and talked to Mary, but at first Mary didn't know that it was Jesus.

A voice said, "Woman, why are you weeping? Whom do you seek?"

Mary thought it was the caretaker of the garden. She said to him, "Sir, if you have carried him away, tell me where you have laid him."

Then Jesus called her by name, "Mary."

Mary recognized the voice of Jesus. "Rabbi!" she cried. She knelt and worshiped Jesus.

Then He was gone. Mary raced away. She found where all the disciples had gathered together. "I have seen the Lord!" she cried.

Matthew 27:62-28:10; Mark 16:1-11
Luke 23:56-24:11; John 20:1-18

54. On the Road to Emmaus

The Roman guards had to report to the religious rulers. They told them about the angel and the empty tomb.

The rulers were frightened. They assembled the Sanhedrin together to decide what to do. Then certain of the rulers gave the soldiers money.

"Take this, and tell no one what you have told us. If anyone questions you about this say, 'His disciples came and stole his body while we were asleep.' "

One of the soldiers said, "If Pilate hears this story, that we were sleeping on duty, we'll get into trouble."

"We will satisfy the governor," the rulers promised. "And we'll see that you don't get into trouble."

The soldiers took the money and spread the false story.

Meanwhile some of the special disciples and other followers of Jesus gathered together. Eagerly they talked about what had happened. They were still not sure that Jesus had risen from the dead. Peter and John had reported about the empty tomb, but so far none of the men had seen Jesus.

It was afternoon when Cleopas and another friend of Jesus said, "We are going to Emmaus." It was a village about seven miles from Jerusalem. The path wound over and around the hills.

As they walked, the two friends

talked about what had happened the past few days. They argued about the story the women had reported. They cried out their disappointment in how everything had ended when Jesus was crucified.

"We had so hoped that God's Kingdom would come through Jesus, and that we would be free from Roman rule," said Cleopas.

"Now what are we going to do?" asked the other.

Just then they heard steps behind them. A stranger came up beside them. They did not recognize Him, but it was Jesus.

"Greetings," said Jesus.

They invited the stranger to walk with them. As they walked they were silent.

"What was it you were talking about when I came along?" asked Jesus. "You seemed unhappy. Has a friend of yours died?"

The friends were amazed. "Don't you know about Jesus?" they asked. "Haven't you heard about what happened in Jerusalem just before the beginning of Passover?"

Jesus asked, "What happened?"

Cleopas said, "Jesus of Nazareth, a prophet mighty in deed and word, was put to death by our religious rulers. They crucified him. We were followers of his. We had hoped that he was the Messiah who would deliver Israel."

His friend said, "Then this morning some of the women in our group amazed us by telling us that the tomb where they laid Jesus was now empty. They said they had seen a vision of angels who said Jesus was alive."

"Two men of our group visited the tomb and found it empty, but they saw neither angels nor Jesus," Cleopas told Him.

Then Jesus reminded them of the words of the prophets that told how the Messiah would suffer and give Himself for others.

"It was necessary for the Messiah first to suffer and then enter into His glory," Jesus told them.

The friends were thoughtful. New thoughts about the Messiah were beginning to form in their minds. But still they didn't recognize Jesus.

By now they were in the village and had come to the house where they were going to stay. They stopped by the door and Jesus started to go on.

"Come in," Cleopas cried. "It is getting late."

"Yes, come in and have supper with us," said the other.

Jesus thanked them and came in.

When the food was ready they all sat down at the table. Jesus took up the bread and broke off a piece. He prayed the familiar prayer of blessing which He had used in the past. Then He gave a piece to Cleopas and the other.

On the hand that held out the bread they could see nailprints. Then they looked up at the Man they had not recognized before.

"Jesus," they cried. "Rabbi, it is you!"

Then Jesus vanished. They looked at one another in joy and wonder. There was no doubt in their minds now.

Matt. 28:11-15
Luke 24:13-31

55. The Risen Lord

"We must go back to Jerusalem and tell the others," Cleopas cried.

Quickly they ate the food and then started back over the dark rough road. "When Jesus talked to us from the Scriptures I felt that God was really speaking to my heart," said Cleopas.

"I did too," said his friend. "We should have realized that it was the Lord."

They walked quickly. When they came to the narrow street and the house where the disciples were hiding from the rulers they started to run. They dashed up the steps and found the disciples gathered together around the table in the upper room. Other followers of Jesus were with them.

Before they could tell them their good news some of the disciples spoke up. "The Lord has risen," they told the two. "He has appeared to Peter."

Peter said, "Yes, I have seen Him."

Then Cleopas and his friend told how Jesus had walked with them and how they had recognized Him when He broke the bread and asked God to bless it.

The door in the room was shut and locked because the disciples were still afraid of the religious rulers. Suddenly as they spoke, Jesus Himself, without warning, stood among them!

"Peace be with you," said Jesus.

The people in the room were frightened at the sudden appearance of Jesus. At first they thought they were seeing a ghost.

"Why are you troubled and frightened?" asked Jesus. "Why do you question? Look at Me. See the hands and feet that were hurt by the nails? You can touch Me. Make sure for yourselves that I am not just a vision."

Some did reach out and touch Jesus. They cried aloud with joy and wonder.

Jesus asked them, "Do you have something for Me to eat?" He wanted to prove to them that He was indeed alive.

One handed Jesus a piece of broiled fish from the table. Jesus ate it in front of them all.

They looked on in amazement. Then Jesus taught them some of the important truths He had given the two on the road to Emmaus.

"The prophets who told of the Messiah and His great glory and rule also spoke of His suffering, His death, and His resurrection. Now you are witnesses of what has happened. It is up to you to tell others."

Then Jesus vanished as He had before. The new body Jesus had did not have to depend on natural laws as earthly bodies do.

The friends of Jesus were happy. Now they had seen the Lord. But Thomas, one of the special disciples, was not there.

A little later in the evening Thomas came in. Eagerly the others told him what had happened. "We have seen the Lord," they insisted.

Thomas shook his head. How could he be sure all these friends had not seen some vision and not Jesus Himself?"

"Unless I see Jesus myself I won't believe," he said. "I am going to have to see the nailprints and touch Him for myself."

Thomas wanted to be sure about this. He realized that it was a very important thing and would make a great deal of difference in what must be done next. If Jesus truly were alive then His work that He had talked about was not over.

It was eight days later that Thomas was in the same room. The other disciples were there with him. They had made sure the doors were locked because they were still afraid the rulers might come looking for any who had believed in Jesus.

Suddenly Jesus again came. He stood before them and said, "Peace be with you."

The disciples greeted Him joyfully. Only Thomas was silent with wonder.

Jesus turned to Thomas and said, "Put your hand on My nailprints. Touch Me and make sure that it is I."

When Jesus spoke, Thomas did not need to do this in order to believe. He fell before Jesus and said, "My Lord and my God!"

Jesus accepted his worship. "You believed when you saw, Thomas," Jesus said to him, "but others in the future will believe in My resurrection even though they never see Me as you have."

During the forty days after the resurrection Jesus appeared to the special disciples and to other followers. Jesus appeared to His brother, James. From that time on James and the rest of Jesus' brothers and sisters believed in Him.

Jesus again spoke about a special meeting in Galilee. He mentioned a certain mountain with which they were familiar. They told all the followers they could about this meeting. They felt sure something special would happen then.

Luke 24:32-49; John 20:19-29
Acts 1:1-3; I Corinthians 15:3-7

56. "To All Nations"

The disciples from Galilee returned to their homes. They and many other followers of Jesus were waiting for the time to meet Jesus on the mountain.

One night Peter entertained James, John and other disciples.

Peter got up impatiently. "I am going to take out one of our boats," he said. "I'll see if I can catch some fish."

"We will go with you," said the others. A night out on the sea would feel good again.

Soon they were sailing over the dark waters. They stopped where they thought they would get a good catch and let down the net. Quietly they stayed there but nothing happened. They went on to another spot; but they did not catch any fish.

As the dawn was breaking a voice called to them. A Man stood on the shore whom they did not recognize, though it was Jesus. "Children," He cried, "have you caught any fish?"

"No, we have caught nothing," they called back.

Jesus called, "Cast your net on the other side of the boat and you will find some."

The disciples did this. Soon the net was filled with fish, so many that it was hard to bring it up.

John looked again at the shore. "It is the Lord," he said.

Peter was so eager to see Jesus he jumped into the water and swam to shore. John and the others brought the boat up on the beach. They dragged the heavy net with its burden over the sand.

When they came to where Peter talked with Jesus they found that Jesus had already built them a charcoal fire. Fish were cooking over the fire and bread was nearby.

"Bring some of the fish you have caught," Jesus said to them. "And come and have breakfast."

It looked good and soon the friends were having a happy meal together. Jesus passed out the bread and fish as He had done often before.

When breakfast was over Jesus had a question for Peter. Once Peter had boasted that he loved Jesus more than the others and would not deny Him; but Peter had denied Jesus three times.

Now Jesus asked, "Peter, do you love Me more than the others do?"

"I love you, Lord," said Peter. He did

not boast that his love was greater than the others.

Jesus asked Peter the same question two more times. Each time Peter confessed his love for Jesus.

Jesus said to him, "Feed My sheep, Peter." Jesus wanted Peter to be a teacher and a shepherd to other Christians. The other disciples were to do this work as well. They would be the leaders in the first churches.

Jesus left the disciples again, but the day came for the meeting on the mountain. The special disciples were there and many other followers of Jesus. About five hundred were gathered. Some of these followers of Jesus had not yet seen Jesus as the risen Lord.

As they waited there Jesus came to them. At first all could not see Him. Those who saw Him first fell on their knees in worship; but the others doubted. When Jesus came close to them, they too believed in His presence and acknowledged Him as their Lord.

After this Jesus spoke to His disciples about the work that was still to be done. He told them a new time had come. A new message was to be brought to the world. They were the ones who would spread it.

He told them: "All authority in heaven and on earth has been given to Me."

Jesus had been faithful in doing God's will. Now God had given Him glory and great power and authority in His plan to bring men back to Himself. It was Jesus, the Son, who was sending them out to do this work.

Jesus said, "Go and make disciples of all nations. Baptize them in the Name of the Father, the Son and the Holy Spirit. Teach others what I taught you. I want all My followers to obey these teachings."

This was a big job for the disciples, but Jesus assured them of His help.

"You will receive special power from God," He told them. "You will be My witnesses in Jerusalem, Judea, Samaria and to the end of the earth."

This was indeed a large task. They wondered; "Where should they start? What should they do next?"

"Wait for this special power from God," Jesus told them. "Stay in Jerusalem until God's Spirit comes to help you. You will not have long to wait."

After this Jesus left the ground and disappeared into the clouds. He returned to His place of honor and glory with God, the Father.

Those who watched Him go kept gazing into the sky. Then an angel appeared who said, "Jesus will come again. Do not stay here looking up into the sky. Do as Jesus told you."

The crowd started to move. They said to one another, "We must wait together in Jerusalem. From now on the only important thing for us is to be witnesses for Jesus."

John 21:1-17
Acts 1:6-12
Luke 24:50-52
Matthew 28:16-20
I Corinthians 15:6

PART FOUR

GOD'S PEOPLE, THE CHURCH

When Jesus was crucified, the rulers thought they had rid themselves of Him. They thought that they would hear no more about this Teacher and Miracle-worker of Nazareth. What they thought was the end was instead a great beginning—the beginning of the Church.

The disciples of Jesus became the leaders of a group of Jews who said that Jesus had risen from the dead and that this proved He was the Messiah. Many joined the group. The leaders of this movement worked wonders of healing in Jesus' Name. They spoke out boldly for their Lord.

For years these believers in Jesus continued to attend the synagogue and Temple services, but gradually they realized that the Church was something new. The Jews who did not believe in Jesus were against those who did.

As the word about Jesus spread, Gentiles received the good news and became part of the Church. There was a church in Rome, the capital of the Roman Empire. The missionaries who spread the good news used the well-paved Roman roads that linked all the important cities of the empire together.

The stories we read about in the Book of Acts took place during the first thirty or so years of the church's history. The Christians did not have an easy time. Those who opposed them were strong, and as the message spread, the opposition grew stronger.

Through all their troubles those who believed in Jesus had the strength to be faithful, but some had to give their lives rather than deny their belief in Jesus.

Jesus had said no evil power would be able to overcome His Church. It was true. In spite of everything the church grew. The believers had found the new life Jesus had talked about. They would not give it up when trouble came.

God had chosen the man, Abraham,

to start a new family, a family that would love and serve the One God. The family had grown into the nation of Israel and into this nation the Messiah had come.

Now those who believed in Jesus made up a new people of God, the Church. To make up this Church God would use not one nation, but people of all races and nations. All those who believed would be brothers and sisters to each other. They would have one Lord, Jesus, and God would be their Father and His Spirit would live in them.

57. The Church Is Born

Those who believed in Jesus returned to Jerusalem and waited for the help from God which Jesus had promised. The special disciples were there and many others, including Mary the mother of Jesus and Jesus' brothers.

For ten days they spent much time in prayer. John Mark's mother, Mary, opened her house to them. Then it was time for one of the important Jewish feasts, the Feast of Pentecost.

On this feast day the believers were gathered together in the room on the roof. They were praying. Suddenly they knew that God's promise had happened.

It was as though a mighty, rushing wind came into the room. Each felt power from God.

"God's Spirit has come," they all said. They praised God and were filled with a great happiness. They went out into the streets and began to talk to the people in other languages.

The crowds wondered. "What are these people so excited about?" they asked.

There were many people in the city for the Feast. Many Jews from other countries were there. Many from other countries who were Jewish converts had come. And they heard the disciples speaking their own languages, telling them about Jesus.

Then Peter stood up and began to talk to the crowds. They all gathered around to hear him.

"Today you see the promise of God come true," Peter told them. "God's Spirit has come to us and will come to others. This is the beginning of a new day, the day of the Lord that the prophets foretold."

Then Peter began to speak about Jesus. Many of the crowd had known and listened to Jesus. Some had been healed by Jesus or had seen Him heal others. Some had been in the crowd which had shouted, "Crucify him." Some of the religious rulers were there.

"Men of Israel, hear these words," said Peter. "You know the mighty works and signs which God did through Jesus of Nazareth. Yet you had Jesus put to death."

Many of the crowd recognized Peter as a disciple of Jesus. They wondered what he would have to say. Would he accuse the rulers of wrongdoing?

"God raised Jesus from the dead," Peter told them. "The prophets told about this long ago, and we are witnesses of this great event. We saw Jesus ascend into heaven, and He is there now at the right hand of God. It is Jesus who has sent God's Spirit to us. The promise of God's Spirit is for all who believe in Jesus."

Many of the crowd turned away. They did not want to hear any more about Jesus. But many stayed.

Some who had taken part in putting Jesus to death were ashamed. They were frightened when they heard about the resurrection. If Jesus truly were the Messiah, God would judge them for their great sin.

They asked Peter, "What should we do? Will God forgive us for crucifying the Messiah?"

Peter told them, "Repent and believe in Jesus. Be baptized in the Name of Jesus, the Messiah. Your sins will be forgiven, and you will receive God's Spirit."

Peter spoke on, giving out the good news. "The promise is for you and your children. It is for people everywhere who will believe in Jesus."

Many cried out, "We do believe in Jesus now. He is the Messiah. We want to be baptized."

The other disciples helped group these people together. That very day they were baptized in Jesus' Name. There were several thousand of these new believers.

It was the first church congregation. Many of these believers in Jesus lived in Jerusalem. They met together regularly. The disciples became known as apostles and were leaders in this new movement.

These believers were either Jews, or Gentiles who had followed the Jewish religion for some time. Now, as before, they faithfully attended the services at the Temple. They often went together.

Every day they found some time to meet in each others' houses. They listened as the apostles told them what Jesus had said and done. They prayed together.

They kept the meal of bread and wine to remember the death of Jesus. They did this at the close of a regular meal which was freely provided by those who had more money than the others.

Some of those who believed in the apostles' teaching were wealthy and some were very poor. Those who had money cared about the poor ones. They even sold some of their own possessions in order to give to them.

The believers in Jesus felt that they belonged to each other in a special way, and they were glad to share all that they had. They enjoyed meeting together and worshiping God together.

Others noticed how they loved each other. They had words of praise for this small but growing group of people who confessed Jesus as the risen Messiah.

Acts 1:12-14; 2

58. A Lame Man Walks

It was the time of the evening sacrifice and many went to the Temple to pray. Peter and John joined the crowd of worshipers who were heading for the Gate Beautiful. The gate was called this because its plates of silver and gold were thicker and more costly than the other gates to the Temple courts.

Ahead of them a lame man was being carried by relatives who set him down outside the gate on the mat they had brought. All day he would hold out a small bowl for coins. He hoped to receive gifts from those who entered the Temple courts.

Peter and John were at the gate now and the man held out his bowl. "Please, some coins," he said. "Please help."

Peter and John stopped. They looked closely at the man. "Look at us," they told him.

The man looked up into these kind, strong faces. He thought they would give him a good gift. Peter's words surprised him.

"I have no silver or gold, but I give you what I can. In the Name of Jesus, the Messiah, get up, walk!"

Peter took the man by his right hand and raised him up. The man felt strength in his legs. He tried and found he could stand. He walked and jumped as he followed Peter and John into the Temple courts.

People were surprised to see the lame beggar who had been sitting every day at the Temple gate, now walking and shouting. The man praised God for his healing. He kept close by Peter and John as they made their way forward.

The people called to each other. "Come on, let's find out what happened." They crowded around Peter and John. When they were in Solomon's portico the apostles could walk no farther because of the crowd. People were staring at Peter and John as though they were men of divine power.

Then Peter spoke. "Don't look at us in this way," he said. "It was not our power that made the lame man walk."

Peter used this time to talk about Jesus. "God sent Jesus, the One whom all the prophets told about; but you and the rulers delivered Him to Pilate and had Him put to death.

"God raised Jesus from the dead. We know this, because we saw Him. It is the power of Jesus which made the man walk. We called on Jesus' Name, and He heard us and made the man walk. You have seen this yourself."

Peter spoke out boldly. "You and the rulers had Jesus put to death out of ignorance, because you did not realize He was the Messiah. Now repent and accept Jesus as your Messiah, so that your sins may be forgiven. He was sent to you and to all people."

Some of the rulers were in the crowd. They were annoyed. They had thought they had heard the last about Jesus.

The Sadducees were especially angry. They did not believe in resurrection for anyone, and now Jesus' disciples were saying that Jesus had actually come alive from the dead. They would convince the people that there was a resurrection and that Jesus was the Messiah. They must be stopped.

The Sadducees went to find the Temple guards. "Arrest these men who are speaking in the Name of Jesus," they ordered.

The guards took Peter and John and the healed man and led them to a place where prisoners were kept. It had grown late. "Tomorrow you will come before the Sanhedrin," the guards told them.

Meanwhile many of the crowd left the Temple courts talking excitedly. "These men are right. Jesus is the Messiah. The fact that they saw Jesus risen from the dead and the miracle of the lame man proves it."

A great many people became believers in Jesus as a result of Peter and John's witness that day.

Early the next day the Sanhedrin gathered. All the chief priests were there, including Annas who had questioned Jesus. The man who had been healed was brought before them. The prisoners Peter and John were brought into the room.

"By what power or by what name did you heal the lame man?" the rulers asked the two.

Peter gave a speech in answer. God's Spirit gave him the courage to be bold. "Rulers of the people, by the Name of Jesus of Nazareth, the Messiah, whom you crucified and whom God raised from the dead, in His Name this man was healed.

"You rejected and condemned Jesus, but God has given Him great glory and power. Through Jesus alone salvation will come to all those who believe."

The rulers were surprised that Peter spoke with such boldness. He had never been to their school for rabbis, and yet he spoke with authority from the Scriptures.

The prisoners were told, "Go outside the room, and we will talk together and decide what must be done to you."

When Peter and John and the healed man had gone out, the rulers talked together. "We can't deny this miracle," they said. "All the people saw what happened."

One said, "But it must not go farther. We do not want people believing in Jesus. Let us warn them against ever speaking in Jesus' Name again."

They called to the guards, "Bring back the prisoners."

When the men were brought in again, the rulers said, "You must never speak or teach in the Name of Jesus again. Now you may go."

But the apostles would not be silenced. They said, "You will have to decide whether it is right to listen to you rather than to God. As for us, we cannot be quiet about the things we have seen and heard."

Acts 3; 4:1-22

59. The Church Grows

While the two apostles were before the Sanhedrin, the believers in Jerusalem prayed for them. They were still gathered together in one of their homes when Peter and John came in.

"The authorities could not keep us," Peter told them, "but they were very angry. They threatened us and told us never to speak in Jesus' Name again.

"We must pray that God will give us all strength and courage to continue our work as witnesses for Jesus."

The believers prayed: "Lord, You know what the rulers threatened. Help us to speak out with boldness. Continue to heal and to work wonders in the Name of Jesus so that more will believe."

As they prayed each one felt strength from God and His Spirit filled them. After the meeting they went out and talked to many about Jesus. They continued to meet together and take the special supper. They taught the new converts all the teachings of Jesus.

The church grew in size and in strength. Its members felt that they were all of one family because of their belief in Jesus. They shared generously with one another so that not one of the believers suffered from a need for food or clothing.

In order to do this some of the wealthy men sold some of their property and gave it to the apostles to give to those in need.

One of the believers who had become a teacher of others was Barnabas. He was a Jew who had been born on the island of Cyprus. He was also a Levite, a man who helped in the Temple.

Barnabas sold a field which belonged to him. Many had brought part of such sales to the apostles, but Barnabas brought the whole amount.

"Distribute this among our brothers who are in need," he told the disciples. In this way Barnabas and the other believers obeyed Jesus' teaching to show love for each other.

Then a man called Ananias and his wife Sapphira thought of a way they could seem to be very generous, and yet have some money for themselves. They decided that they too would sell some of their land and give the money to the church. They received a very good price.

"We don't need to give all this to the church," said the husband. "We'll tell Peter we sold the land for a smaller amount and that we are giving all the money to help those in need but we will keep some of this money for ourselves."

Sapphira agreed. But Peter was not deceived when Ananias brought the gift to the church and said it was the full amount.

"Why are you lying, Ananias?" he asked. "I know that you sold the land for more money than this. You did not have to give *any* of this money to the church, or you could have given only part of the money. It was up to you. But it was very wrong of you to lie. God is not pleased with you. You lied not really to men but to God."

Ananias was frightened as he listened to these words. Suddenly he collapsed. When they got to him he was dead.

Later that day Peter talked to Sapphira. He asked her, "Did you sell the land for so much?"

"Yes," lied Sapphira.

"God's judgment will come on you for your lie," Peter told her. "Why did you and your husband agree to try and deceive God?"

When she heard these words, Sapphira collapsed. She too, was dead.

The people of the church were frightened. They realized that God wanted members of the church to live righteous lives.

All this time the apostles continued to preach and teach about Jesus. They went regularly to the Temple worship and often spoke to the crowds gathered in Solomon's portico. Believers got into the habit of gathering there. As the worshipers at the Temple listened to Peter and the other believers, many became convinced of the truth about Jesus and His death and resurrection.

Sick people were often brought to these meetings, and Peter and the other apostles healed them in Jesus' Name. Soon people from outside the city heard about the healings and came to hear these new teachings. Often they brought sick people too.

The Sadducees had hoped the people would grow tired of the apostles' teachings and ignore them; but they saw that the opposite was the case. They watched the crowds gather in Solomon's portico.

"These men must be stopped," they said.

One day when the apostles were teaching, Temple guards came and arrested them and put them in prison. The next day the rulers planned to bring them before the Sanhedrin.

During the night though, the apostles escaped. An angel of the Lord opened the prison doors. "Go back and preach in the Temple," the angel said.

The next morning the apostles were again in the Temple courtyard speaking to the people who had come for the morning sacrifice.

Meanwhile the Sanhedrin had gathered. The high priest was there and many important Sadducees. An important rabbi called Gamaliel was also there who was known throughout all the country as a wise man.

When they were all seated the rulers told the officers, "Bring in the prisoners."

The officers went to the prison. The guards let them in, but to their amazement no one was inside.

"The prisoners have escaped," they cried.

The officers had to bring back this word to the rulers. "We don't know how it happened," they said.

The rulers were embarrassed and angry. "Now what will happen if word of this gets around?" they muttered to each other.

Then other officers came in with a report. "The men whom you put in prison are back teaching the people," they said.

"Bring them here at once," ordered the rulers.

The officers soon came back with the apostles. "We told you emphatically not to teach in this Name," the high priest said, "but you have filled all Jerusalem with your teaching. You want to incite the people against us, because we had Jesus put to death."

Peter and the other apostles had only one answer. "We must obey God. It is more important to obey God than men. God raised Jesus whom you put to death, and through Him wants to give repentance and forgiveness of sins to all. We are witnesses of these things.

The Sadducees were enraged when they heard this. Several shouted out that the apostles should be put to death.

Then Gamaliel spoke up. He asked that the prisoners be put out of the room so that he could speak to the rulers.

"Take care, rulers of Israel," Gamaliel told them. "Other men have claimed to be the Messiah or some special leader of the people, but in time the people grew tired of them or they were slain by the Romans.

"Leave this group alone. If this movement is of men it will die; but if it is of God nothing will stop it. We would not want to be found fighting against God."

The rulers had respect for this famous rabbi and agreed to take his advice. They called back the apostles.

"We do not want you to speak any more in Jesus' Name," they told them. "As punishment for disobeying you will be beaten."

The apostles suffered their punishment. They were not angry or bitter as they returned to the believers. They remembered that Jesus had suffered. They remembered how Jesus had said His followers would sometimes have to suffer for His sake, and they were thankful to be considered His faithful followers.

Instead of being unhappy they rejoiced and told the others, "We will continue to speak of Jesus."

The apostles and the other believers in Jesus continued to win others to their way. They met in each others' houses to encourage each other and to learn more of what Jesus taught.

Acts 4:23-32; 5

60. Stephen: Faithful to Death

As the church grew in numbers, a problem arose. Most of its members had been born in Judea and spoke Aramaic, but some had been born outside Judea and spoke Greek. These were called Hellenists or Greek Jews. The Greek Jews brought a complaint to the apostles.

"Our people are not given their share of the money for the needy," they said.

The apostles knew how important it was for the believers to live in harmony. They called for a general meeting.

The apostles told the people, "Distributing the money to the needy is taking too much of our time. We want to spend all our time praying for God's power and blessing, preaching to those who do not know Jesus and teaching when believers gather together."

They suggested a plan. "Elect seven men from among all of you to do this work of giving to the needy. Make sure they are men who are wise and who are faithful in their witness for Jesus."

The believers thought this was a good idea. In this way the Greek Jews would be represented. Among the seven who were chosen was a Greek Jew called Stephen.

The seven men came before the apostles in the presence of all the believers. The apostles laid their hands on them and prayed. They asked God to help these men to be faithful servants in this special office in the church.

From then on the apostles spent all their time spreading the good news about Jesus. Many believers were added to the church every day. Many of the priests in Jerusalem became believers.

All the believers told others, but some became well known as preachers. Stephen often spoke to other Greek Jews. He told them that Jesus was the Messiah and that they must believe in Jesus and His teachings.

Some of these Greek Jews became very angry at this new teaching. They spoke against Stephen to the other people and to the rulers. "This man speaks against the Law of Moses," they declared.

One day when Stephen was preaching, some of his enemies came up to him, seized him roughly and dragged him away to the rulers. Stephen stood trial before the Sanhedrin.

Witnesses came to speak against Stephen. "He is against the Law of Moses," they said. "He does not have respect for the Temple. He wants to change our religion."

The rulers looked at Stephen. His face was full of the holiness that comes from living close to God.

The high priest asked Stephen, "Is this so?"

In answer Stephen preached a sermon. He reminded the Jews that their history had started with Abraham. God had worked with His people before the Law was given through Moses. And even then God's people had not always obeyed Moses.

Stephen quoted Moses as saying that a greater prophet than himself would come and that they must listen to this prophet. He recalled how God's people had not at first worshiped in a temple but in a tent. He told the rulers that

where they worshiped was not as important as obedience to God.

"In the past our people rejected the many prophets God sent to them," said Stephen. "These prophets spoke of the coming Messiah, but many of them were killed. Jesus the Messiah came and you rejected and killed Him.

"You rulers speak of the Law as so important, and yet you do wrong and fail to keep the Law."

This made the rulers very angry. Instead of defending himself, Stephen had accused them. As they looked with hatred at this tall figure standing before them, Stephen's face glowed.

He gazed up to heaven where he saw a vision of Jesus. Stephen cried out, "I see the heavens opened and the Son of Man standing at the right hand of God."

At this all the rulers and other people present covered their ears. With a cry they rushed at Stephen. There was no sentence passed or rules of order observed. They dragged Stephen out of the room and onto the street.

"He has spoken blasphemy," they cried as they headed for the gates of the city. Outside they bound Stephen and prepared to stone him.

The first to cast the stones were the witnesses who spoke against him. These men laid their cloaks at the feet of a young Pharisee called Saul. Then they threw the first large stones. After this any in the mob might throw stones.

Stephen faced death bravely. He prayed aloud, "Lord Jesus, receive my spirit." Before he was knocked unconscious by the flying stones he again prayed, "Lord, do not count this sin against them."

Acts 6, 7

61. Philip Spreads the Good News

After the death of Stephen the Jews who did not accept the apostles' message banded together in an effort to stop the new teaching. One of the leaders of the opposition was Saul the young Pharisee who had watched Stephen die.

This young man had a great desire to keep the Law of Moses perfectly, and he thought these followers of Jesus would destroy this Law. Saul often informed the rulers as to where believers gathered. He himself led the soldiers who arrested the people worshiping in the Name of Jesus.

Saul had been born far to the north of Jerusalem in Tarsus, but he had studied under Rabbi Gamaliel in his famous school at Jerusalem. Saul knew much about the Scriptures. The other Pharisees spoke highly of him.

Because of the arrests, many believers left Jerusalem, but the apostles stayed there and continued to teach. The church in Jerusalem met regularly. They kept in touch with the believers in other places.

Most of those who left Jerusalem were Greek Jews or converts, people of other nationalities who had become Jews in religion. These believers left the place of danger, but they did not stop talking about Jesus. They told everyone about the new life that was possible because Jesus had died for them.

Philip had been a teacher among the followers at Jerusalem and had been one of the seven men chosen to distribute money to the needy. Now he went to the city of Samaria and preached about Jesus. The Jews had always despised the Samaritans, but Philip realized that this was all in the past. The good news was also for these ancient relatives of the Jews.

In Samaria Philip preached to great crowds. Everyone came out to hear this new message and to see the miracles. Like the other leaders in the church, Philip had the power to heal in Jesus' Name. Great joy came to the people because of Philip's work. Many believed, were baptized, and formed a church.

The apostles in Jerusalem heard about this new church. The report said that many Samaritans were eager to hear the good news about Jesus and God's Kingdom.

The believers in Jerusalem were surprised that Samaritans would be able to believe in Jesus and be a part of the church. "We ought to go to where Philip is preaching and see this for ourselves," said some of the apostles. Peter and John agreed to visit the church in Samaria.

When Peter and John talked to the believers gathered in Samaria they were convinced that these people did believe in Jesus. This made the two apostles very happy. They prayed for the people and asked God to bless this new work. God sent His Spirit on the Samaritan believers, just as He had at Pentecost. Peter and John welcomed the Samaritans into the church.

One of the Samaritans who believed in Jesus was a magician, Simon. He was impressed by the miracles of Philip and by the power of God's Spirit that he saw as a result of Peter's praying.

"How much money will you take," Simon asked Peter, "to give me the pow-

er of God's Spirit so that I can use it?"

"Simon," Peter said sternly, "you are absolutely wrong. You cannot buy God or His power. Nor can you have any of it. Repent, be sorry for your wrong attitude, and ask God to forgive you and change you. Or you will be trapped in your wrong thinking."

John and Peter spent some time teaching these new believers before they returned to Jerusalem. On the way back they preached to many Samaritans themselves.

Soon after this Philip had a great adventure. An angel from God told him to leave Samaria and travel down the road that went from Jerusalem to Gaza. The midday sun was hot and the road was dusty. It was a deserted area, and Philip was surprised when a chariot approached.

The chariot was coming from Jerusalem. Philip could see a dark-skinned man seated in the chariot. He was reading aloud from the version of the Jewish Scriptures which was in the Greek language.

Philip was interested. He ran up to the chariot. He could tell by the rich chariot and the clothes of the driver that the man within was an important person.

"Do you understand what you are reading?" Philip asked him.

"No, I don't. I need a teacher," said the man. "Come up into the chariot."

Sitting beside the man on the chariot, Philip found out that he was a native of Ethiopia, an important official to the queen of one of the Ethiopian kingdoms. The Ethiopian had long been interested in the Jewish religion. He had just been to Jerusalem to see the worship in the Temple for himself.

The man showed Philip where he was reading. It was the scroll of Isaiah where the prophet told how the Messiah would suffer and die for sin.

"Does the prophet speak of himself or another man?" asked the Ethiopian.

"He is speaking of Jesus, the Messiah," said Philip. Then Philip told the official all about Jesus, His death and resurrection. He told him how believers in Jesus had gathered together to form the church. He told him how Jesus had said to preach about Him everywhere to all people and to baptize those who believed.

The man listened intently. This was the truth he had been waiting so long to hear. "Is this good news for me also?" he asked Philip.

"Yes," Philip told him, "if you believe in Jesus."

"I do," the Ethiopian assured Philip. "I believe Jesus is God's Son." Just then he noticed that they were passing a river. He called for his driver to halt.

"Look," he said to Philip, "here is water. Could I be baptized now?"

Philip was happy. "Yes," he said. "Let's get out of the chariot."

The official from Ethiopia was baptized and became a believer. He went back to his kingdom in Africa a happier man. Philip went on to other towns up along the coast, preaching about Jesus and winning many people.

Years later Philip went to live in Caesarea. He worked in the church in this city and in the surrounding areas. Always Philip loved to be the first to tell someone about Jesus.

Acts 8; 22:3, 4; 26:9-11
Galatians 1:13, 14

62. A Foe Becomes a Friend

Many groups of believers in Jesus had been formed outside the city of Jerusalem. There was a group as far north as Damascus.

Saul, the Pharisee, was a leader in arresting believers. He told the religious rulers, "Give me written permission to have the believers in the synagogue at Damascus arrested. We will bring them here to Jerusalem to be tried before the Sanhedrin."

The rulers were pleased with this young man. "We will give you letters to those in authority at Damascus," they promised.

As he traveled the road to Damascus, Saul thought about how these believers in Jesus were trying to change his Jewish faith. He was angry.

Saul believed he was doing what God wanted, but lately, in the very bottom of his heart, a doubt had started to grow. When they came near Damascus the men with Saul were surprised and startled by a blinding light from heaven. Saul fell to the ground and he heard a voice say, "Saul, Saul, Why do you persecute Me?"

"Who are you?" asked Saul, not daring to look up.

"I am Jesus whom you are persecuting," said the voice.

Then Saul looked up. There in the surrounding light was the risen Lord. Now Saul knew. What the apostles had preached was true. Jesus *had* risen from the dead. He was the Messiah.

Jesus spoke to Saul. "Get up and enter the city. There someone will help you and show you what you are to do. Saul, I have chosen you to be a great worker for Me instead of a worker against Me."

When Saul started to rise the men helped him. Saul groped with his hands. "I can't see," he cried.

The men were amazed and distressed. Their young leader was blind. They helped him into the city.

Saul told the men he wanted to be alone. They found him a room. Saul stayed in the room for three days without eating. All this time he prayed.

Now Saul knew that the only thing for him to do was to become a follower himself. It was important for all the Jewish leaders and people to realize that Jesus was the Messiah.

The rulers in the synagogue in Damascus had heard that Saul was coming to arrest those who believed in Jesus. The believers had heard about it too.

About three days later the leader of the group of believers, Ananias, was wondering what they ought to do. The Lord brought a strange message to Ananias in a vision.

"Ananias, I have a task for you," He said.

"I am ready, Lord," said Ananias.

Then the Lord said, "Go to Straight Street and to the house of a man called Judas. There you will find a man named Saul praying. Go in and lay your hands on him, and he will receive back his sight."

"But Lord," said Ananias, "Saul is our enemy. This is the man who has come from the chief priests in Jerusalem. He is going to arrest all those who believe in You."

The Lord said, "Go. I appeared to Saul on the road. Now he believes. This man is going to be a great worker of Mine. He will preach about Me to many—Jews and Gentiles."

Ananias was fearful and yet he obeyed. He found the house and was brought to the man he feared. His enemy was blind and praying for help.

Ananias went over to Saul. He put his hands on Saul's head. "Brother Saul," he said, "the Lord Jesus who appeared to you on the road sent me to you. Receive your sight."

Saul looked up. He could see again. Ananias talked to Saul about Jesus. Saul assured him that he now believed in Jesus as Lord and wanted to join the group of believers.

"You must be baptized," Ananias told him. "Come, we will go to the other believers."

Saul met some of those who believed in Jesus and was baptized. He had dinner with them. They were surprised but overjoyed at this change. It proved to them that God had great power and was working with them.

"I must talk to the people of the synagogue," Saul said.

On the Sabbath Saul got up to speak. The members were amazed. The man they thought had come to arrest the believers now told them that he was a believer in Jesus. "Jesus is the Son of God," Saul said.

Then Saul wanted time to be alone with God. He went away into a nearby deserted place. Here he spent much time in prayer. He thought about how he could best tell the story of Jesus to others.

When Saul returned to Damascus he became a part of the church there. He preached in the synagogue. Saul reminded the Jews of many of the prophets' words and convinced many that Jesus was the Messiah.

After about three years, the rulers of the synagogue in Damascus gathered together. "We must kill this traitor," they decided.

But word got to the believers. The leaders of the church talked to Saul. "Your life is in danger. You have much work for God in the future. You must save yourself."

"I will leave," Saul promised.

"But," one said, "the leaders of the synagogue have persuaded the governor to have soldiers guarding the city gates day and night. They are instructed to arrest you."

Another said, "My house is built on the city wall. We can let Saul out of the window on the other side of the wall."

The believers agreed. Saul came with them to the house on the wall. They tied ropes to a large basket and Saul got inside. Then they lowered the basket out of the open window.

Soon Saul was safely on the ground outside the city. Quietly he waved good-by to his friends and returned alone to Jerusalem.

Saul knew there was trouble ahead. Those who had been his friends would hate him. He no longer had a chance to become a leader of the Pharisees and a famous, respected rabbi.

But Saul was still happy. There was joy in his heart. Now all the doubt and guilt was gone. He had found Jesus to be his Lord. From now on it only mattered for him to serve Jesus, the Messiah.

Acts 9:1-26; 22, 26
Galatians 1:15-24
II Corinthians 11:32, 33

63. Peter Visits the Churches

As soon as Saul returned to Jerusalem he visited the church there; but he was not welcomed. The believers were afraid it was a trick. They thought Saul was only pretending to believe in Jesus. It was discouraging for Saul. Now he had no friends.

The teacher Barnabas knew about what had happened in Damascus. "Come," he told Saul, "we will go to the apostles."

Barnabas told the apostles about Saul's vision on the road to Damascus. "Then Saul preached in the synagogue and many came to believe in Jesus," Barnabas told the leaders of the church. "Saul was so successful that the religious rulers got the governor of the city to post guards at the gate in order to arrest him."

The apostles believed the word of Barnabas and Saul. They rejoiced that God had brought salvation to one who had been their enemy.

Saul stayed in Jerusalem for fifteen days. During this time he preached to the Greek-speaking Jews. Since he came from Tarsus, Saul knew Greek even though he was a Jew. Tarsus was known for its goatshair cloth which was used to make tents, and as a boy Saul had learned the trade of weaving this cloth.

During his brief stay in Jerusalem, Saul talked to Peter, and to James the brother of Jesus, about the work of the church and all that was yet to be done.

But it was too dangerous for him to stay. Those who hated Saul the most were in Jerusalem.

"I will go back to my home in Tarsus," Saul told the apostles. "I can preach about Jesus there."

Some of the believers in Jerusalem went with Saul as far north as Caesarea. From there the new apostle continued on alone back to Tarsus, taking the good news about Jesus with him.

For a while there were no more arrests of believers in Jesus. More were added to their groups in Judea, Samaria, and Galilee. Peter found time to visit some of these churches along the coast of the Mediterranean Sea.

At Lydda there was a man who had been paralyzed and could not walk. He had kept to his bed for eight years. Peter visited the sick man. "Aeneas," he said, "Jesus, the Messiah, heals you. Get up now."

The man tried to get up out of bed, and found he could. He stood up and walked again and went out into the town. Many of the people in Lydda believed in Jesus because of this miracle.

While he was at Lydda, Peter received urgent word from some of the believers in Joppa, an important seaport town.

"Please come to us without delay," they said. "One of our members has just died. She was a good woman who always showed love to others. She spent all her time helping people. Now she has left us, and everyone is weeping."

Peter listened to the message and went back with the men. It was a trip that took about three hours. When they arrived at the house, they climbed the stone steps and went into the room on the roof where Dorcas was lying on the bed. Around her were many widows from the church at Joppa.

"Look," they said to Peter, "these are some of the good clothes Dorcas made for us. She was a woman who really lived in the way Jesus taught."

The cloaks and jackets Dorcas had made showed skill and care.

Peter told them all to leave. Then he knelt and prayed. In Jesus' Name he asked God to give him the power to bring life back to Dorcas. Then he looked over to where Dorcas lay. "Dorcas, get up," he said.

The woman opened her eyes. She sat up in bed. She looked over at Peter, and the apostle helped her to stand.

Peter called to the others, "You can come in now."

The men and the widows came back. There was Dorcas standing by Peter. The believers of Joppa were very happy. They praised God for the power of Jesus that was at work among the leaders of His church. They told everyone they knew about it.

The people of the town wondered as they saw Dorcas alive and well. She again began to sew clothes for the needy. Many Jews of the city believed in Jesus as the Messiah and joined the church there.

Galatians 1:18-24
Acts 9:26-43

64. Good News for a Roman Officer

In Joppa Peter stayed at the house of a man called Simon. Simon was a tanner and his house was by the sea. Often Peter went up on the roof, away from people, so he could pray and think about God's work and all that Jesus had said and done.

One day Peter was on the rooftop. He had prayed for a long while. Suddenly he realized that he was very hungry. He went down the steps and asked Simon's wife if she could get him something to eat.

"Of course. I'll bring it up to you on the rooftop," she told Peter.

When Peter returned to the rooftop he looked out toward the sea and the sky. Then a vision came to him. A large sheet was let down before him. On the sheet were many animals which Gentile people sometimes used for food but which the Law of Moses said the Jews could not eat. This food was called "unclean."

Peter heard a voice, "Here is food to eat."

Peter shook his head and turned away. "No, Lord," he said, "I have never eaten unclean food."

Then the voice said, "You must not call unclean something which God has made clean."

This same vision appeared three times. Peter was puzzled. He knew God was giving him a message in this vision, but he was not sure of its meaning.

"Could it be that we no longer need to keep these laws about food?" he wondered.

Then Peter looked down. At the gate to the courtyard three men waited. Peter heard them ask, "Can you tell us if a man called Peter is staying here?"

God's Spirit spoke to Peter, "Go with these men. I have sent them."

Peter hurried down the stairs. He opened the gate and let the men inside the courtyard. "I am Peter," he said. "Why are you looking for me?"

One man was a Roman soldier, the other two were servants. They had a long story to tell Peter.

"We come from Cornelius, a centurion in the army of Rome, who is stationed in Caesarea. Cornelius and his family believe in the God of the Jews and observe their hours of prayer. He gives alms to the needy and is well spoken of by the Jews of the city. Yesterday an angel from God came to Cornelius and told him to send for you, because you had a message for him."

Peter knew that most Jews would think it wrong to entertain these men or go with them to a Gentile house, but he invited the men in.

"Stay overnight with us," he told them, "and tomorrow I shall go back to Caesarea with you."

The men talked with Simon and his wife and met other believers. Peter asked several members of the church at Joppa to come with him on this trip.

The next day they started north towards Caesarea, a journey of more than forty miles. The following day they arrived in this important city where most of the people were Gentiles.

When they came to Cornelius' house they found that they were expected. Cornelius had gathered his family, servants, and other relatives together. They all welcomed Peter into the house and asked him to speak to them.

"You know that strict Jews refuse to come into Gentile homes," Peter told them, "but God sent me a vision that told me all homes and people are clean in His sight. When these men asked me to come, I was glad to come to you. Now, what is it you want me to do for you?"

Then Cornelius told Peter about the angel who talked to him. "Four days ago I was praying in my house," he said. "A man in bright clothing came to me saying, 'Cornelius, God has seen all the good you do for others and your prayer has been heard. God knows you want to know more about Him. Send to Joppa for a man called Peter who is staying with Simon, the tanner.'

"Immediately I sent these men to ask you to come to us. Now we are gathered together. What does God want you to tell us?"

Peter realized how very important this occasion was. The good news about Jesus was for Gentiles as well as Jews.

Peter began to preach. "I realize now that God has no favorites. In any nation those who acknowledge God and do what is right are acceptable to Him.

"We are believers in Jesus. We were with Him and saw His deeds. God anointed Jesus of Nazareth with the Holy Spirit and gave Him great power. He went about doing good and healing all who were oppressed, for God was with Him."

Peter told the company of Gentiles how Jesus had met death but that God had raised Him from the dead.

"We saw Jesus after He rose from the dead," Peter said. "Jesus told us to preach about Him to all people. Through Jesus you can receive forgiveness of sins."

Acts 10:1-43

65. The Gospel Goes to Gentiles

Cornelius, his family, and the others who listened believed Peter. They praised God and assured Peter and his friends that their faith was real. Then God's Spirit came to them, just as He did to all the disciples in Jerusalem on the Day of Pentecost.

The believers from Joppa were amazed. "These men have received God's Spirit," they said.

Peter agreed. "They are one of us," he said. "What should keep them from being baptized?"

"They should be baptized as Jesus commanded," said the others.

The baptism was held that day. Peter stayed several days in Caesarea. He taught these new believers many things about Jesus and how they were expected to live now.

This group of believers made up the first Gentile church. Before this only Jews and Gentiles who had been converts to the Jewish religion had made up the church.

In Jerusalem the believers heard that Peter had gone to visit and had eaten with Gentiles. They heard that these Gentiles had become believers in Jesus.

Some of the members did not like it. They did not mind admitting Gentiles into the church when the Gentiles were Jewish in religion; but they did not want to admit any who were outside the Jewish faith.

When Peter came back to Jerusalem they criticized him. "The Law says not to eat with Gentiles," they reminded him.

Peter told the members of the church the whole story about his vision and his visit to Cornelius. "These Gentiles received the Spirit of God when they believed in Jesus, just as we Jews did," he said.

Peter had brought some of the believers from Joppa. They told the same story.

Those who criticized were silenced. The church at Jerusalem rejoiced. "Then the message is to the Gentiles too," they decided.

Not long after this, word came to the believers in Jerusalem that more Gentiles were coming into the church. Greek Jews at Antioch in Syria had preached to Gentiles and many had believed in Jesus.

The leaders in Jerusalem said, "We want to be sure these Gentiles who come into the church from idol-worship really understand the Christian message."

The church at Jerusalem decided to send Barnabas to Antioch. They asked him to send back a report on the church there and to stay and teach the new believers.

Antioch was a large, beautiful city and the third in importance in all the Roman Empire. Most of the people were Gentiles, but there were also many Jews and many Gentiles who belonged to the synagogues.

Barnabas was pleased when he came to the church at Antioch. The believers were living in harmony with one another and were faithful in telling others about Jesus. Under his preaching a great many more Gentiles came to believe in Jesus. But all these new Christians did need teaching. Those who had not been raised in the Jewish faith did not know the Old Testament Scriptures.

Barnabas decided he needed help for this work. He heard that Saul was still faithfully preaching about Jesus around his home in Tarsus, less than one hundred and fifty miles away. He remembered that Saul was well educated in the Scriptures.

Barnabas went to this city in the hills to visit Saul and he asked for his help. "Come to Antioch and help me teach these Christians," he said. "There is so much they need to know about the One God and the prophets He sent. They need to know all that the apostles have taught about Jesus and what He means to us."

Saul agreed to leave Tarsus and go back with Barnabas. For a year they taught at the church in Antioch. Both Saul and Barnabas understood Greek customs and could speak the Greek language. Under their leadership the church in Antioch grew even more.

So many people believed in Jesus as the Messiah or Christ that they began to be called Christ-ians—Christ's followers—by those who didn't believe.

Although Antioch was a long way from Jerusalem, the Christians thought of themselves as brothers who belonged to one church because they all believed in Jesus.

One day the Christians at Antioch heard sad news from Jerusalem. A famine had come to Judea and many of the Christians were in need.

The believers at Antioch said, "We must help our brothers in Jerusalem. Let's take a collection and send a gift of food to them."

Everyone thought this was a good idea. They gave generously. With the money they bought the necessary food. Saul and Barnabas were chosen to take the gift to Jerusalem. It had been about fourteen years since Saul had been in the big city. Arrangements were made for the journey.

Acts 10:44-11:30
Galatians 2:1

66. Peter Is Put in Prison

The believers in Jerusalem were in trouble. Herod Antipas was banished to Gaul and his rule over Galilee was given to his nephew Agrippa. Herod Agrippa was the grandson of the first Herod. Besides Galilee he was given rule over Judea and Samaria.

Agrippa had been educated in Rome, but he was a Jew. He wanted to prove to the religious rulers that he believed in the strict keeping of their religion. Herod knew that the religious rulers were against those who accepted Jesus. He decided to win their approval by arresting some of Jesus' followers.

First he arrested James, the brother of John, and some others. These he had put to death. Then he arrested Peter and put him in prison.

It was close to Passover time and Agrippa planned to bring Peter to judgment immediately after the Feast. Meanwhile he made the guard on Peter extra sure.

Four men would take turns each watch of the night. Inside the cell, Peter was chained to two of these soldiers; the other two watched outside the door.

It looked as though Peter would have to give his life as James and Stephen and other believers had done.

Every day the church at Jerusalem gathered together and prayed for Peter. They met at the home of Mary, the mother of John Mark.

This was a wealthy family and they owned a fine large home. Jesus and His disciples had often met there, and it was one of the first places in Jerusalem where believers gathered regularly.

They prayed that Peter would have the strength and courage he needed. They prayed that Peter would be released if it were God's will, but that in any case the church would grow.

On the night before his trial Peter was asleep in his prison cell. The soldiers to whom he was chained lay beside him. Suddenly a bright light flooded the dark cell and an angel from God appeared before him. He made the chains fall off Peter's hands.

"Get up quickly," the angel said. "Put on your clothes and sandals. Don't forget your cloak. Follow me."

Peter hurried and made himself ready to walk out, but it all seemed like a dream. The soldiers on guard paid no attention as the angel led Peter past them. When they came to the iron gate that led to the street, the gate opened. The angel led the way through the gate, and Peter followed him down the street. Then the angel vanished as quickly as he had come.

Peter looked around. There were no guards. He felt the cool night breeze. The ground was firm beneath his feet. It was not a dream. He was really free. The trial would not be held tomorrow because Peter would not be there.

"The Lord sent His angel to rescue me," Peter said to himself. "Now I must find the believers and let them know that I am safe."

Peter headed for John Mark's house as a likely place. The gateway to the courtyard was locked. Peter knocked loudly.

Rhoda, a servant girl who had been stationed nearby, came to the gate to find out who was there. When Peter spoke to her, she was so excited and overjoyed at hearing Peter's voice that she forgot to unlock the gate. Instead she ran to the house and up to the room where the Christians were gathered. They were praying.

Rhoda interrupted them. "Peter is at the gate," she cried.

"You're crazy," some said. Others thought she had seen some kind of vision.

Then they listened. They could hear a loud knocking on the gate. It wasn't safe for Peter outside.

Several of the believers followed Rhoda back to the gate. "It is Peter," they cried. They opened the gate for the apostle.

Peter went up to the room and told the believers how he had been rescued by the angel.

"The Lord delivered me," Peter told them. "Now I must leave this city. Tell this story to James and to the rest of the church who are not here."

James, the brother of Jesus, was the head of the church at Jerusalem. The believers were happy to see that the apostle was safe. They assured him that they would continue to remember him in their prayers.

Peter sadly said good-by to them. "I will see you again," he promised, "but for the time it is best for me to leave Jerusalem. I will go and visit other churches."

Not long after these events Herod Agrippa met sudden death. Instead of his young son, Agrippa, being given his rule over the Jews, another procurator was sent from Rome.

The Jews did not like this, and from that time on restlessness and rebellion against Roman rule grew in Jerusalem.

Acts 12:1-24

67. Sent Out to Tell Others

When Saul and Barnabas returned to Antioch from Jerusalem they brought a young man with them—John Mark, a cousin of Barnabas. John Mark had been faithful in serving God in the church at Jerusalem which often met at his house. Now he wanted to do more work for God.

There were several very good teachers in the Antioch church. The members wanted to share what they had with others.

"There are many who have heard nothing of Jesus," they said. "Teachers are spreading the story in many places. We should send some out from our church."

The Christians at Antioch were especially concerned about the people of Asia. Most of these people still worshiped the Greek and Roman idols. Magnificent temples had been built in honor of these gods. People would journey many miles to worship at these famous shrines. But in spite of all their worship and sacrifice they did not know the peace and joy that came from being right with God. This could only come from having faith in Jesus, the Messiah.

The Christians prayed for God's guidance and God made it known that Saul and Barnabas were the ones to go out and tell others in these pagan cities. The leaders of the Antioch church laid their hands on the missionaries and prayed that God would help them and keep them safe.

Saul and Barnabas spoke to the people in Greek. They told them that Jesus was the Christ, the Greek word for Messiah. Saul became known by his Roman name, Paul. He soon proved to be a truly great preacher.

John Mark went with Paul and Barnabas and helped in the work. First the missionaries sailed for the mountainous island of Cyprus, some sixty miles south west of Antioch. This was the old home of Barnabas. Most of the people worshiped the Greek goddess Venus, but there were Jews on the island who had several synagogues.

The missionaries went and spoke to the Jews in the synagogue at Salamis. They visited other towns and villages. Then they came to Paphos which was the seat of government and the center for the pagan religion. In this city the Roman governor of the island became a Christian along with many others.

The missionaries then took a ship northwest to Perga on the coast of Asia Minor, a voyage of about one hundred and seventy-five miles. At this time John Mark left them and went back to Jerusalem.

Paul was disappointed to lose a helper, but they continued with the trip. They went north over the mountains to another city called Antioch of Pisidia. This was the chief city of the Roman province of Galatia. Throughout their journey the missionaries used the fine Roman roads.

On the first Sabbath in Pisidian Antioch the missionaries went to the synagogue and joined the other Jews in their worship of God. After the Scriptures had been read, the rulers of the synagogue asked if one of the visitors would like to give the sermon.

Paul got up and preached to the assembly. He reminded them how God had cared for His people in their past history. "God sent us prophets and kings," said Paul, "and now He has sent us a Saviour, Jesus, the Messiah He promised.

"The rulers in Jerusalem did not recognize Jesus as the Messiah. They had Him put to death, but God raised Him from the dead. He appeared to the disciples who had been with Him in Judea and Galilee.

"Now we bring you good news. Through Jesus you can find forgiveness of sins." Paul closed with a warning. "Do not close your ears to my message as many did to the prophets of old."

As the people left the synagogue, they spoke about what Paul had said. Many told the missionaries and the rulers of the synagogue, "We want to hear more about this next Sabbath."

Some of the Jews believed the message and wanted to hear more from the missionaries right then. The missionaries talked about Jesus and answered many questions.

The next Sabbath the synagogue was full and overflowing. All wanted to hear Paul, but the synagogue rulers were jealous. They spoke to the people and contradicted what Paul had told them.

Paul spoke up. "We wanted the people of the synagogue to hear the message first," he said, "but this good news is also for Gentiles. Now we are going to preach to them."

Paul went into the marketplace and wherever he could gather a crowd. He told anyone who would listen about Jesus. Many of these Gentiles left their idol worship and turned to Jesus. They joined the Jewish believers and made a church.

Paul and Barnabas preached in the city and in surrounding areas. More believers joined the group.

But the rulers of the synagogue wanted the missionaries to leave. Some important women of the city were members of the synagogue. The rulers urged these women to complain about Paul and Barnabas to the city officials.

"These men are disturbing the peace of our city and preaching strange religious teachings," the women told the officials.

The officials wanted peace in the city. They gave in to these citizens and told the missionaries to leave. Paul and Barnabas said good-by to the new Christians.

"Remain true to the Lord Jesus," Paul told them. "We will come and visit you again, and we will expect the church to have grown."

Acts 12:25; 13:1-48

68. Mistaken for Gods

Paul and Barnabas left Antioch Pisidia and went east to the city of Iconium. They attended the synagogue service and spoke to the members about Jesus. Many of the Jews and the Greek converts believed the message. The missionaries stayed in the city and continued to teach, and more and more joined the church.

The rulers of the synagogue and the other Jews who did not believe were angry, because so many of their members had joined this group. They spoke against the missionaries to the Gentile people of the city.

Some of the people of the city took up for Paul and Barnabas and those who followed them, and some agreed with the Jews who did not believe. In time there were enough against Paul and Barnabas that they planned to form a mob and stone them. The missionaries heard of the plan and made ready to leave the city.

They encouraged the Christians to continue to meet, to keep the Lord's Supper, and to pray together. They told them, "We are going to preach the good news of Jesus to other people."

Paul and Barnabas headed south towards Lycaonia and the cities of Lystra and Derbe. There was no synagogue and only a few Jews at Lystra. Most of the people knew nothing about the One God who made heaven and earth and the Law He had given through Moses.

Paul and Barnabas preached faithfully and some believed their message. A Jewish widow called Eunice, who had been married to a Greek, joined the church. She lived with her mother, Lois, and her son, Timothy. These women had faithfully raised the boy in Jewish beliefs.

Timothy knew the Scriptures well. Paul and Barnabas became good friends with this family.

The missionaries preached in the marketplace where people often gathered to talk and to hear men give speeches on many different subjects. One day Paul noticed a crippled man sitting in a safe place by a stall.

Paul had noticed that this man always listened intently. He could tell that the man was beginning to believe the message. Paul spoke to him, "Stand up on your feet."

Suddenly the man knew that he could. He got up. The crowds gathered around. They had never before seen such a miracle.

The people understood the Greek language, but they usually talked in a language of their own. Now they shouted out in their language, which neither Paul nor Barnabas could understand.

"The gods have come down in human form," they cried. "These men are gods, or they could not have made this crippled man stand and walk."

The crowds continued to exclaim among themselves. Because Barnabas was older they thought he was Zeus the greatest of the Greek gods. Because Paul spoke so well they decided that he must be Hermes or Mercury, the messenger of Zeus.

"We must make a sacrifice to them," some began to say. "Let's get the priests."

The priests who led the people in worshiping the idols believed their story. They made animals ready for sacrifice by putting garlands of flowers around their necks. They brought them to the missionaries. The people began bowing before Paul and Barnabas.

Finally the missionaries realized the awful mistake. "Stop," shouted Paul. They both tore their clothes as a sign of distress. "Why are you doing this? You must not worship us. We are men like yourselves."

Finally they quieted the crowd. Paul told them, "Our message to you is that you should turn from these idols. Worship the living God who made heaven and earth. It is God who has given you rain and sun and food to eat. Your worship and gratitude should be to Him."

The missionaries continued their work in Lystra and a church was formed. Then trouble came. Some of the Jews who had opposed the missionaries in Antioch and Iconium banded together and traveled to Lystra.

These men turned some of the people in Lystra against the missionaries. They led a mob which threw stones at the men. Barnabas escaped, but Paul was hit by many of the stones.

When Paul fell down, the crowd cried, "We have killed him." They dragged Paul down the street and out of the city gate. There they left him.

But Paul was not dead. When some of the Christians of the city went out to take care of his body, they discovered that he was still alive. Full of joy they helped him back into the city where Barnabas was waiting in one of the Christian's homes.

The family took care of Paul's wounds. That night both missionaries rested, but early the next day they continued on their journey and came to the city of Derbe.

Acts 13:51-14:20; 16:1, 2
II Timothy 1:5

69. A Church Meeting at Jerusalem

In Derbe many believed the message and a church was started. Here Paul and Barnabas found no opposition and were allowed to teach in peace.

After some time Paul said, "Let's go back to the churches we started. We must be sure they are still meeting. No doubt those who opposed us have been unkind to them."

"It is dangerous," said Barnabas, "but we should go. We must be sure God's work is done well."

So the missionaries retraced their steps. They visited the churches at Lystra, Iconium, and Pisidian Antioch. In all these places they found believers still meeting.

The missionaries encouraged them saying, "God is with you in spite of the troubles others bring because you believe in Jesus."

In each church the missionaries appointed leaders who would watch over the affairs of the church and lead in the work of telling others. They prayed with each group of believers, asking that God would give them strength to be true to Jesus.

The disciples returned to Perga and then went to Attalia on the coast. Here they boarded a ship which took them back to Antioch without stopping at the island of Cyprus.

The news soon spread among the Christians at Antioch that Paul and Barnabas were back. The missionaries had been gone about a year and a half. The church gathered together to hear the report.

They all wondered, *Had many converts been made? Had the Gentiles accepted the good news about Jesus and turned from their idols?*

The missionaries told the Christians what happened in each city. "Many have come to know Jesus," Paul told them. "The Gentiles are eager to hear about the One God and Jesus Christ whom He sent. Now they know freedom from the fears their pagan religion gave them."

Paul and Barnabas stayed at Antioch for some time. One day some Christian teachers came to Antioch from Jerusalem and other places in Judea.

They told the Gentile Christians, "You should have gone through the ritual of becoming a Jew before you were baptized. You should keep all the Law God gave through Moses."

Paul and Barnabas disagreed with them. "It is not necessary," they said. "These rituals and ceremonies cannot make us right with God."

There was a sharp disagreement, and many of the members of the church were confused. "We must get together with the apostles and discuss this," they said.

Paul, Barnabas and other leaders of the church at Antioch decided to return with these teachers to Jerusalem.

On the way Paul and Barnabas stopped at churches in Phoenicia and Samaria and told them that many Gentiles had been converted in Asia Minor. In all these places the Christians rejoiced at this news.

In Jerusalem they were welcomed by the church leaders. Paul and Barnabas lost no time in telling them what had happened in Asia Minor.

There was a group of Christians in the church who insisted, "But first they should have become Jews and told to keep the rituals of our faith."

Paul disagreed. He believed that the church was a new movement and that the old rituals were no longer necessary. Faith in Jesus as the Christ was now most important.

Finally a meeting was held in Jerusalem at which all the apostles along with many believers were present. (This was somewhere around the year 49.) There was a lot of discussion. They had all heard about the missionary journeys to the Gentiles.

Then Peter got up. He agreed with Paul. He told those who had assembled, "You remember when I first preached to the Gentile, Cornelius. He and his family became Christians. The Lord Jesus has brought salvation to all, not just to Jews."

Then Paul and Barnabas had a chance to tell all the details about their trip. Paul told them that many Gentiles had believed and had shown by their changed way of living that they had received God's Spirit.

James the head of the church in Jerusalem had spoken out for keeping all the Jewish Law. Now he said, "The prophets of the past declared that through the Messiah the Gentiles would one day come to know the true God. Now we must not trouble these Gentile Christians by making them go through the ritual of becoming a Jew. But let us ask them to observe a few of our customs."

James then mentioned a few Jewish customs he thought very important but which would not be hard to keep.

Paul and Barnabas agreed to this compromise. All the leaders at the council agreed. They were sure God's Spirit had led them to make the right decision. They were glad that this quarrel had been resolved.

Some said, "Let us send some of our best teachers back with Paul and Barnabas to report to the Christians there."

Judas and Silas were chosen. The leaders of the Jerusalem church wrote a letter to the Christians of Antioch, especially to those who had been converted from idol-worship.

It said:

> Dear brothers who are Gentiles,
>
> Some teachers came to you from Jerusalem and confused you. We did not send these teachers. We have had a meeting, and we have decided that you do not have to keep all the rituals of the Jewish faith.
>
> We are sending teachers along with our beloved brothers, Paul and Barnabas, who risked their lives to preach about Jesus, so that you can talk to them yourselves. We do ask that you keep a few Jewish customs and that you live good lives.

When the letter was heard by the Christians at Antioch they accepted the message. They rejoiced at the outcome of the meeting. They listened to the teachers, Judas and Silas, preach from the Scriptures.

In a little while Judas and Silas returned home to Jerusalem. Paul and Barnabas continued as teachers in Antioch. *Acts 14:20-15:35*

70. The Gospel Goes to Europe

One day Paul said to Barnabas, "I wonder how the churches in Cyprus and Asia are doing. Let us take another journey and visit each one."

Barnabas agreed. As they discussed their plans Barnabas said, "My cousin John Mark wishes to come along."

Paul disagreed. "I don't want John as a helper. He left us soon after we started the journey. We need helpers who will stay with the work."

When Barnabas insisted that John come, the two missionaries quarreled. "We had better divide the work," said Barnabas. "I'll take John Mark to Cyprus and visit the churches there."

Paul decided to ask Silas, the teacher from Jerusalem, to come with him. Silas agreed, and they made their plans to visit the churches in Asia Minor. The leaders of the church at Antioch agreed with these plans. They prayed with all four missionaries and asked God to help them in their work.

Barnabas and John Mark sailed for Cyprus. Paul and Silas headed for Asia

Minor by land. They passed through Syria and Cilicia and visited churches on the way. The Christians in these churches were helped by their preaching from the Scriptures.

The first stop was Derbe and then Lystra. At Lystra Paul found that the young Timothy had become a faithful worker in the church. All the Christians at Lystra and Iconium knew him and spoke well of him.

"Do you want to help us in this missionary work?" Paul asked the young man.

Timothy told him, "I want to use all my talents to serve the Lord Jesus. I want to tell people who have never heard about Him."

Paul and Silas were glad to have this young Christian. He went with them as they visited the churches in that area. As they talked to each congregation, they told them about the church meeting at Jerusalem. They read the letter the Jerusalem church had sent to the Gentiles.

Paul was glad to see that these Gentile Christians had remained true to the Lord and had not returned to idol worship.

Now it was time to go to new territory. The missionaries prayed that God would lead them in the right direction. They traveled down to the port of Troas, a fine Roman city. Here Luke, a doctor who was also a Christian teacher, joined them. Later Luke wrote down the adventures of the missionaries in what we know as the Book of Acts.

At the seaport of Troas Paul received the guidance he needed. He had a dream in which a man said to him, "Come over to Macedonia and help us."

The next day Paul told the others about it. "God's Spirit is leading us into the lands across the sea," he said. "We must go to Macedonia."

This was an important decision, because it brought the good news about Jesus to Europe. The missionaries took a ship that sailed across the Aegean Sea to Macedonia. They journeyed inland ten miles to Philippi, one of its most important cities.

There were very few Jews in Philippi. The missionaries discovered that there was no synagogue.

On the Sabbath Paul said, "Let us look to see if there is a congregation worshiping by the river. When there is no synagogue, our people often worship in such a place."

Outside the city gate by the banks of the river the missionaries found a group of women praying. They were Jews. Paul and Silas preached to them that Jesus was the Christ.

One of those who believed the message was Lydia, a Jewish convert. She was a wealthy woman who had much influence in the city. She and her family were among those who were baptized that day.

The missionaries said good-by to the group and promised to visit and preach to them again the next Sabbath.

Lydia asked them, "Where do you stay? I have a large house. Please come and stay with me."

Paul, Silas, Timothy and Luke accepted her invitation. They went to stay with Lydia. Her home was open not only to the missionaries but to any who wanted to hear the Christian message. More people came to believe in Jesus, and a church was formed.

Acts 15:36-16:15

71. In Jail for Jesus

One Sabbath the missionaries walked to the place of prayer by the river. A girl and two men approached.

There was something strange about the girl. She was a slave, and these men were her owners. They made much money from this girl, because people believed she could see into the future. She was sick in her mind.

The girl had heard something about the missionaries and their work. "These men are servants of God," she called out. She repeated this many times. From then on every time she saw the missionaries she called after them.

Paul knew the girl was very unhappy and needed to be healed. Finally one day he spoke to her and healed her in the Name of Jesus. From then on the girl acted normally. No one would pay to have her tell their future.

The men who had used the girl to make money were very angry at the missionaries. They seized Paul and Silas and dragged them into the marketplace. They told everyone what Paul had done.

"These Jews are teaching a strange religion," they cried. "We don't want them in our city."

Many of the crowd agreed with the men. They started to hit Paul and Silas as they marched them before the rulers of the city. "These Jews are disturbing our city," they told the magistrates. "They preach a new religion and talk against our gods."

Even in front of the rulers, the crowd kept on attacking Paul and Silas. The judges did not give the missionaries a chance to defend themselves or explain their teaching. "Beat them and put them in prison," the judges declared.

Soldiers took Paul and Silas away. They were severely beaten with rods and then pushed into a dark prison, sore and bleeding.

"Keep these men who started this riot safely," the official told the jailer who guarded the prison.

The jailer put them in the dark inner prison and fastened their feet in the stocks so that they couldn't move.

In spite of their pain, Paul and Silas did not feel that God had deserted them. They remembered that Jesus had suffered, and they knew that the leaders of the church must be willing to suffer if the message was to be spread abroad. They encouraged themselves by singing some of the hymns the Christians sang when they gathered together.

They also prayed, and in their prayers they thanked God for the message of forgiveness through Jesus which they could preach. It was so interesting to the others that everyone was awake listening to them, even though it was midnight.

Suddenly there was an earthquake and the foundations of the prison were shaken. The floor beneath them trembled, the doors were jarred open, and the chains fell off all the prisoners. The stocks on the missionaries' feet opened up. But everyone was so startled that no one moved.

The earthquake woke the jailer up. When he saw that the prison doors were open, he took out his sword and was

about to kill himself. He knew the officials would put him to death for letting the prisoners escape.

But Paul called out, "Do not harm yourself. We are all here."

The jailer called for someone to bring torches, and they rushed into the inner prison. It was true. All the prisoners were in their cells. The jailer recalled the message the missionaries had been preaching about Jesus. He wanted the same faith as these men.

"What must I do to be saved?" he asked.

"Believe in the Lord Jesus," Paul told him.

The jailer was grateful to Paul for not escaping and for stopping him from killing himself. He brought Paul and Silas into his own house. The women there washed the wounds of the missionaries and gave them food.

"Now tell us more about Jesus," said the jailer.

Paul preached to the entire family, including the servants. They received his message and wanted to be baptized. That night the missionaries baptized them all.

When it was light, soldiers came from the judges. "Our officials have decided to let these men go," they said. "They are to leave our city."

But Paul objected to the way they had been treated. "We received no trial, and now you want us to leave secretly as though we had done wrong. We are Roman citizens, and it was against the law to have us beaten."

Everyone in the Roman Empire was not a Roman citizen. Besides those born in Rome and certain other cities, citizenship was granted only to certain worthy people. Some people paid a lot of money to become Roman citizens. Citizenship gave the person certain privileges. Paul's father had been a Roman citizen, and so Paul had inherited this right.

The judges were frightened when they heard that these Jews were Roman citizens. They had broken the Roman law by beating them.

The judges went to Paul and Silas. "We are sorry," they said. "We will go with you to the gates of the city to protect you. The people are stirred up against you. It would be dangerous for you to stay."

Paul and Silas agreed to leave under their protection but first they visited Lydia. Many of the believers had gathered in her house.

Paul encouraged the Christians to continue to meet. He assured them he would come back some day and see how they were growing as a church. He promised to write to them. Luke stayed behind as a teacher for these Christians.

Then Paul, Silas and Timothy left Philippi, the first European city they had visited.

One of the letters Paul later wrote to these Christians said: "I thank God every time I remember you. From the first day you heard the good news about Jesus you have been faithful to Christ. You are partners with me in telling the story of Jesus to others."

Acts 16:16-40 (20:6)
Philippians 1:3-5

72. From City to City

Next Paul and his helpers went to Thessalonica, about one hundred miles southwest. It was an important, busy city. Here there was a synagogue, and they went there on the Sabbath to preach.

The congregation listened as they talked about Jesus and quoted what the prophets had said about the Messiah. "Jesus did all this," Paul argued.

Many of the Jews and the Gentile converts believed the message, but not all. Those who did not believe became jealous of the way the missionaries had become leaders.

About three weeks after the missionaries first came these people banded together. "We must get rid of these men," they said. "We don't want them in our city. If we chase them out, things will be as they were before. We will be the leaders again."

First they told the missionaries they could no longer preach in the synagogue. So the Christians found a house they could use for worship. Jason, one of the converts, opened his house for meetings. He also invited the missionaries to live with him while they were in Thessalonica.

The Jews who did not believe talked to many Gentiles in the marketplace. "See those men?" they asked, pointing to Paul and Silas. "They are speaking against Caesar. They say that a Man called Jesus is King."

These enemies stirred up people to join together and go after the missionaries. It was an excited mob that came up to Jason's home. The missionaries were not there, so they took Jason and dragged him and some of the other Christians who were with him to the court.

The rulers of the city heard their case. "Men have come here with a strange message," the accusers said. "They are visiting many cities and turning everything upside down. They cause trouble wherever they go. Jason has received these men into his house."

"Tell us more about the message these men bring," said the rulers.

"They go against the laws of the emperor. They say that there is another king, Jesus."

This disturbed the rulers. They did not want Roman soldiers to have to come and put down an uprising.

They told Jason, "You must promise that you will have these men go at once."

Jason agreed. He knew that the Christians would continue to meet together after the missionaries had gone.

That night Jason told the missionaries, "You must leave here tonight. These enemies will stop at nothing. They are lawless men."

Paul and Silas agreed. They continued on to Berea, about fifty miles away. The first thing they did was to preach in the synagogue. Here they found the members eager to hear their message. Their minds and hearts were open. When Paul and Silas preached to them about Jesus and quoted from the prophets, the members, both Jews and Greeks, looked up the words of the prophets in the copies of the Scriptures they had.

They talked about these things among themselves. They were not afraid of new ideas and only wanted to know the truth. Many of them became Christians, including many of the important women of the city.

Back in Thessalonica, the enemies of Paul heard that a church had been formed in Berea. They were angry at Paul's success. These men journeyed to Berea and talked to the people of the city. They planned to form another mob and attack the missionaries, but the Christians heard about it.

Since rabble rousers spoke mainly against Paul, Silas told Paul, "You had better leave. We will stay for a while and watch over the work here."

Paul agreed. "I will go on," he said. "I will send word to you later."

Some of the Christians went with Paul as far as a port on the coast. Paul had decided where he would go. "I will take a boat now and go to Athens," he told the Christians. "Tell Silas and Timothy to come and join me as soon as they can."

Paul journeyed to Athens by sea and then by land. He was eager to see this city which even then had a great history. It was still considered an important place and a center for pagan religion. Great artists and teachers lived here. From all over the Roman Empire students came to study at the university.

The Greeks and Romans worshiped many gods, all of whom had a temple or an altar at Athens. People from all over the empire came here to worship before the idols.

The statues of the gods were very beautiful, but Paul could only think of what they represented and the fact that these people worshiped images which they themselves had made.

Pagan religion held much fear for its people. It taught that gods and spirits were everywhere. If these gods were not given proper honor they would harm the people. The worshipers often wondered if they had left out some of the gods who ought to be honored. At one place Paul found an altar which said, "To An Unknown God."

These people needed to know about the one true God and Jesus Christ whom He had sent. Paul planned to tell them.

Acts 17:1-16, 23
I Thessalonians 1, 2

73. In the Midst of Idols

On the Sabbath Paul preached in the Jewish synagogue at Athens. During the week he spent time in the marketplace speaking to different people.

The marketplace at Athens was a busy and beautiful place. There were many decorated porticos, each with its statues and altars. From the crowded streets of the market place one could look up to the famous temple, the Acropolis, which stood on top of the hill.

People came here, not only to shop, but to discuss topics of the day. Teachers used the marketplace to gather an audience.

Paul argued with the people about their worship of idols. He tried to make them see that God was spirit and could not be worshiped in this way. After some days had passed, more and more people gathered around to hear Paul.

Some of the well-known teachers came to hear what Paul had to say, but they were not impressed.

"He is speaking nonsense," they said.

Others said, "This man speaks about a strange new religion. We ought to hear more of what he has to say." They liked to hear new and strange ideas.

They asked Paul, "Come, tell us all about this new teaching."

Paul gladly agreed and they led him to a courtroom where the leaders of the city sometimes met to judge cases. This was an outside place called the Areopagus, and teachers sometimes used it as a classroom.

Here teachers, students and men and women gathered to listen to Paul. These people did not know the Scriptures, so Paul began by talking about their own religious beliefs.

"Men of Athens," said Paul, "I have noticed many idols and altars in your city. I know you think religion is very important. I found one altar which said: 'To An Unknown God.' I want to tell you about the God you do not know."

Paul went on to tell them about the One God. He said, "God made the world and everything in it, including ourselves. God does not need anything from us in the way of temples and altars. He is the Lord of heaven and earth.

"It is God who has given us the gift of life, and so we should not think that we can make idols that represent God. God is too great to be represented in this way. What God does want is for us to be thankful to Him and to receive Jesus whom He sent. If you seek the true God, you will come to know Him."

Paul went on to tell them about Jesus' death and resurrection. The teachers laughed at the idea that a man could rise from the dead. Only a few wanted to hear more on another day.

Paul was discouraged, but as he was leaving the court a few people gathered around him. "We believe what you say," they told him. "We want to turn from the worship of idols."

Paul was happy that at least some people had accepted the message.

Not long after this Paul journeyed on to Corinth. Since Silas and Timothy hadn't come yet, he sent word for them to join him in this city.

Many people lived in Corinth. It was

a few miles inland from the sea, but because it had two neighboring towns for seaports, it became a wealthy trading center. The people worshiped the goddess Venus and were known for their immoral ways.

Soon after Paul's arrival he made friends with two Jewish Christians, Aquila and his wife Priscilla. They were newcomers in Corinth.

These two Jewish Christians had left Rome when the Roman Emperor Claudius had ordered all Jews to leave. A church had already been founded in the capital, and Aquila and Priscilla had learned about Jesus Christ through it.

Paul had been taught the trade of making cloth for tents. Aquila and Priscilla also worked at this trade. Paul stayed with them and earned money to continue his missionary work by helping them weave the goatshair cloth.

Every Sabbath the three of them attended the synagogue service. Paul preached at every opportunity he could. He told the members of the synagogue that Jesus was the Christ.

Silas and Timothy joined Paul at Corinth. They brought good news from Philippi and Thessalonica. The Christians there were meeting faithfully every Lord's Day, the first day of the week. More believers had been added to their groups.

Paul was so glad for this news that he wrote the Christians a letter, telling them how much he loved them, how glad he was they were still believing in Jesus in spite of persecution. He encouraged them to be faithful and to live the way God wanted.

"Do good to everyone," he told them.

"Always rejoice. Pray constantly.

"Thank God for whatever happens to you.

"And the God of peace will keep you safe till Jesus comes again."

Paul had good news to tell Silas and Timothy also. "Many here in Corinth believe," he said. "Crispus, the ruler of the synagogue, and all his family believe, and have been baptized."

Soon the Jews who did not believe began to make trouble. They were angry that their ruler had joined the Christians.

Paul told them, "We won't preach in the synagogue again. You have rejected the message."

One of the Christians, Titius Justus, whose house was next to the synagogue said, "Come and meet in my house."

From then on the Christians met there. The members of the synagogue found a new ruler, a man called Sosthenes. But eventually Sosthenes too believed in Jesus as the Messiah.

The church continued to grow. The Lord encouraged Paul and Silas to continue to work hard in this city. For a year and a half they worked among these people. During this time Paul wrote another letter to the church at Thessalonica.

Then a new proconsul, the Roman ruler, came to Corinth. The Jews who were against Paul thought this was a good time to make trouble for the missionaries.

They seized Paul and brought him before the ruler, Gallio. "This man is persuading other Jews to worship God in ways that are contrary to our religious laws," they said.

Paul was about to speak in his defense, but the Roman proconsul interrupted. "You should only bring those here who have been guilty of some crime," he said. "You must settle your own religious quarrels among yourselves." Gallio ordered them to leave the court.

Paul and Silas continued their work at Corinth, but the time came when they had to move on. Priscilla and Aquila had helped Paul in many ways. They were Christians who were able to teach others. Now these teachers asked Paul if they could continue as missionary helpers. Paul and Silas were glad to have their help.

The missionaries went back across the Aegean Sea and stopped at Ephesus in Asia Minor. Paul talked to the Jews in the synagogue at Ephesus. Some were interested. "Will you stay a little longer and teach us more?" they asked.

"I will leave these good teachers, Aquila and Priscilla, with you," Paul said, "but I must go and greet the church in Jerusalem. Then I will report to my friends in the church at Antioch; but if God wills I will return."

Acts 17:17-18:21
I Thessalonians
II Thessalonians
I Corinthians 1:1, 14-16

74. Riot in Ephesus

Paul did not forget his promise to the Ephesians. He visited Jerusalem and then spent some time at home in Antioch. Then he started out on another missionary journey.

First he visited some of the churches in Galatia and Phrygia. He encouraged them to continue to live in the Christian way. After listening to Paul preach, the Christians felt stronger. They were more determined to try to win people to Jesus.

Then Paul went back to Ephesus. Aquila and Priscilla welcomed him back and told him about a preacher called Apollos who had come to Ephesus.

"We were able to help him to better understand the Christian way. He did not know about baptizing in Jesus' Name," they said. "Now he has gone to Corinth. The Christians there have been greatly helped by him."

Paul preached in the synagogue at Ephesus. When many believed, those who did not accept the teaching started quarrels.

Paul had found that when this happened it was best for the Christians to meet in a separate place. In Ephesus the Christians found a school they could use. It was operated by a man called Tyrannus. For two years the Christians met here daily to worship God and to hear Paul preach about Jesus.

The Christians in Ephesus told others of Jesus and brought them to hear Paul. People came from all the surrounding area. As a result churches were formed in other cities in Asia Minor, including one in Colossae.

By God's power Paul was able to heal the sick in Jesus' Name. This made many believe the truth of the Christian message.

The church in Ephesus became strong. Many joined, but there were also many enemies of the work. Sometimes the leaders were in danger.

Ephesus was an important center for pagan religion. It was the most important seaport of Asia Minor. Many came by boat to see its famous temple to the goddess Diana. There was also a fine theater, a stadium, and a public library in the city.

Most of the people of the city believed in magic spells to protect themselves from evil spirits. The Christians came to realize that this was wrong. Many who had books which told how to perform these magic rites came together and burned them.

Those who were still idol-worshipers watched the huge bonfire. They wondered that the Christians were no longer afraid of evil spirits. Some of them were influenced to become Christians themselves.

A silversmith called Demetrius was alarmed at how many people had turned from idols to the Christian way. When visitors from afar came to the temple of Diana they liked to take home small copies of the temple or a small statue of the goddess.

Demetrius gathered all the silversmiths together. "How can we make a living if all the people of Ephesus become Christians?" he asked them. "No one will want our statues. Besides, what right have these foreigners to come here and change our ways?"

The other men agreed. Demetrius told them, "It is not only in Ephesus. This message is being brought to all Asia. Paul has persuaded many in all these countries to give up their worship of idols. The time might come when this wonderful temple of ours will be empty. No one will believe in Diana."

Some of the men who really believed in the pagan religion became very upset at this. They cried out, "Great is Diana of the Ephesians!"

"Let's get these Christians who want to destroy our goddess," some shouted.

"We will kill Paul," others cried out.

They all rushed out into the street shouting out to those around them how the missionaries were trying to destroy their temple, and their religion.

More people joined them crying out, "Great is Diana of the Ephesians," until they became an angry mob. Then the crowd spotted two of Paul's missionary helpers, Gaius and Aristarchus who came from Macedonia. They dragged these men into a large theater.

Here thousands of people gathered to see plays performed. Now many came to see what the riot was about. The excited mob made so much noise it was hard for anyone to figure out exactly what was happening. All they knew was that some people were trying to injure their temple, their goddess and therefore their city.

Word about the riot spread to some of the Christians. They went and told Paul. "I will go right away and talk to the people," Paul said.

The Christians said, "No, it would only make matters worse, and they might kill you. They are all so angry that they would not listen."

Paul still wanted to go, but the Christians begged him not to leave his house. Meanwhile some of the rulers of the city came into the theater. They asked the leaders of the mob, "What is all this about? What do you have against these men?"

One shouted one thing; another shouted something else. Then the people began to argue among themselves. Many did not even know what the riot

was about or why they had gathered in this theater.

Some of the Jews were afraid there would be an attack on all who did not believe in idols. They urged one of their number, Alexander, to speak to the crowd in their defense.

Alexander got up before the people and tried to speak, but the crowd recognized him as a Jew. They knew that the Jews had always been against idol worship.

Someone began to chant, "Great is Diana of the Ephesians." The crowd took up the chant. For nearly two hours nothing else was heard in the theater.

Finally the people grew tired of chanting. The rulers of the city got them to be quiet. At last their spokesman could be heard.

"Men of Ephesus," he said, "we all know that ours is the greatest temple to Diana in the world. We do not need to worry that we will lack worshipers. We do not need to fear these men who preach new things. They have not said anything against our goddess that we rulers have heard.

"If Demetrius has a case against these men we have our courts of law. If we hear anything more of this it must be on the days when the courts are open and done in an orderly, lawful way."

The crowd had quieted now and many started to leave. The silversmiths were angry, but they knew that nothing else could be done at the time. Gaius and Aristarchus joined the other Christians. They told Paul all that had happened.

Paul encouraged the Christians to be faithful to Christ no matter what the danger might be. "We are fighting against strong enemies," he said, "but God is with us."

Acts 18:18-19:41
Colossians 1:1-9
II Corinthians 1
Ephesians 6

75. Paul Starts for Jerusalem

For a long while Paul had been planning further missionary work. He wanted to visit the churches in Macedonia and Greece and then go down to Jerusalem. From there he wanted to make the long voyage to Rome. Some day he hoped to journey westward to Spain and preach about Jesus there.

While Paul was in Ephesus he sent two helpers, Timothy and Erastus, to visit the churches in Greece and Macedonia. They were to receive a collection for the poor people in the church at Jerusalem.

Around this time Paul wrote a letter to the church at Corinth. He asked them to receive Timothy warmly and he told them about the collection.

He wrote: "I am suggesting to all the churches that on the first day of every week you put some money aside. Then when it is time to take the money to Jerusalem the gift will be ready."

He also promised these Christians that he would come and see them himself. He said that he would spend some time with them and not just pass through.

Some people in this church were quarreling. Some were angry at Paul and said he was not a good teacher. Paul urged them to act like Christians and love each other.

He said: "Be watchful, stand firm in your faith, be courageous, be strong. Let all that you do be done in love."

Paul had been at Ephesus for about three years. Soon after the riot he made ready to leave. He would keep his promise to visit the church at Corinth and the other churches of Greece and Macedonia.

Timothy and Erastus had returned from their travels, and now they joined Paul on this trip. For several months they traveled many miles by sea and land through Greece. They stopped at different places to encourage the Christians.

The trouble at the church in Corinth had not been settled. Paul had sent a helper, Titus, to talk to them. Now Titus joined them. He told Paul and the others that there was peace at Corinth.

During his travels Paul found time to write to different churches. He would answer their questions about the faith and help solve differences that arose. He wrote again to the Corinthians telling them he was glad their quarrels were over and that he would see them soon.

Paul spent the three winter months in Corinth. He helped these people who had turned from idol worship and immoral living to better understand the Christian way and to live in love and peace with each other. While he was here Paul wrote to the Christians in Rome, telling them of his plans to come to them.

Paul still had enemies. He planned to take a special ship which took Jewish pilgrims to Jerusalem, but he heard that some men on the ship were seeking to kill him. Paul and his friends decided to go to Jerusalem another way and they returned through Macedonia.

Certain Christians from the churches which were sending the gift of money to Jerusalem went with the missionaries. At Philippi they found Luke faithfully taking charge of the church there.

Paul remained in Philippi with Luke to celebrate the Feast of the Passover with the other Jewish Christians, but the rest of the party went across the sea to Troas. After the Passover Luke joined Paul on the trip to Jerusalem. The others were waiting for them at Troas.

On the first day of the week Paul met with the Christians of Troas and took the Lord's Supper with them. It had become the custom now for Christians to meet on this day as a way of remembering that it was on this day that Jesus rose from the dead.

In all the churches they were willing to listen for hours as Paul explained the Scriptures. Here at Troas the night before Paul intended to travel on, they stayed past midnight as Paul continued to preach.

The next day Paul told the party. "I want to be in Jerusalem for the Feast of Pentecost." It meant that they could not waste time.

"We will take a ship that does not stop at Ephesus," some suggested, "or else the Christians there will want us to stay with them for at least a few days."

"I'll send word to the leaders of the church at Ephesus," said Paul. "They could come and meet us at Miletus when the ship stops there."

The ship sailed down the coast passing many small islands. When they stopped at the seaport of Miletus the leaders from the church at Ephesus met with Paul and his party. The Christians loved Paul and were glad to at least receive a message from him if he could not come to their city.

Paul spoke to the Ephesian leaders. He reminded them of the years he spent with them as their teacher. He reminded them that he had worked at his trade of tentmaking in order to earn money for himself and his helpers. He told them that they too should work hard so as to earn enough money to help those in need. He reminded them of a saying of Jesus which had been handed down from the apostles: "It is more blessed to give than to receive."

Paul told them, "Now I am going to Jerusalem. I know there is danger, but I believe God wants me to go back there. That is all that is important to me. I only want to go and preach about Jesus wherever He sends me.

"You are leaders in the church of the Lord. Teach and help those under your care. Love them as a good shepherd loves his sheep. I know God will be with you."

Then they all knelt down on their knees and prayed together. They prayed for Paul and the others who were going to Jerusalem. They prayed for the church at Ephesus and the other churches.

When they said good-by the leaders could not help crying. They were sad that this great man whom they loved so much would be facing the hatred of his worst enemies.

Acts 19:21, 22; 20:1-38
I Corinthians 1-4, 6, 13, 16:1-13
II Corinthians 1, 2, 7, 12, 13
Romans 1:13, 15:22-29

76. Back in Jerusalem

Paul and the other Christians continued on their way to Jerusalem. At Patara they changed ships. They sailed past the island of Cyprus and went on to the ancient port of Tyre where cargo was unloaded. It was necessary to wait a week here and they stayed with Christians.

The church at Tyre was glad to see them and to hear about churches in other places. They had heard much about Paul. They were surprised that he was going back to Jerusalem. "It is too dangerous," they said. They tried to get the missionary to change his mind, but Paul would not. He felt sure it was God's will for him to continue.

Paul wanted to see the apostles in Jerusalem and give them the gift from the different churches. He wanted to celebrate the Feast of Pentecost in the city that was sacred to him.

On the day when they had to return to the ship, many of the Christian families went with them to the dock. They knelt together on the beach and prayed for each other. They prayed that the work of the church would continue to grow.

From here the ship sailed to Ptolemais, which was its last port. Now the rest of the journey to Jerusalem would be made by land. In Ptolemais there were Christians to visit. They put the travelers up for one night.

The next day they went on to Caesarea where Philip had worked for years as a preacher. They stayed at his house.

While they were at Caesarea one of the Christians who was known as a prophet came from Judea. He told Paul, "The religious rulers will put you in prison if you go to Jerusalem."

They all begged Paul not to continue. "Those who hate you the most are there," they said.

Paul said, "Please don't try to persuade me not to go. I am willing to go to prison if I have to. I am willing to die for Jesus if it is necessary."

Those who were traveling with Paul said, "The will of the Lord be done."

Some of the Christians at Caesarea joined their party. Two days later they all arrived in Jerusalem.

The leaders of the church in Jerusalem were glad to see Paul and the other Christians. They were thankful for the gift that was brought.

"We want to hear all about the churches in Macedonia, Greece and Asia," they said. "We will have a meeting tomorrow. Will you come? All the Christian leaders of Jerusalem will be here."

They promised. The next day Paul and the others reported their success in preaching to the Gentiles. Paul did most of the speaking.

The leaders were overjoyed to hear how many Gentiles had become Christians and that the number was still growing. They were glad to hear that these people who had turned from idol worship now lived good lives.

Then James and some other leaders talked to Paul about a problem. "There are thousands of Jews in our church. We love God's Law and the Temple, and we know that you do too. But many of our people think that you no longer love God's Law and that you speak against it. Some say you influence Jewish Christians to ignore all Jewish customs."

These Jewish Christians understood that the converts from idol-worship did not need to become Jews and keep Jewish customs. But they believed Paul was now trying to persuade Jewish Christians to leave these customs too.

Paul still loved the Temple and the worship there. It was one of the reasons he had wanted to be in Jerusalem for the Feast of Pentecost.

He told the leaders this. Then James had a suggestion. "We have four members who have made a vow to the Lord, but they do not have the money to pay for the special sacrifices. It would prove that you still love Jewish worship if you paid their expenses and made a vow yourself."

Paul was glad to do this. For seven days Paul and these four Christians went to the Temple every day. They offered the sacrifices and prayed. No one questioned Paul or the men with him. Because they were all Jews, they went into the inner court, the Court of Israel.

The Jewish Christians were glad to see that Paul still loved the Temple worship. But when the seven days were almost complete, trouble came.

Some Jews from Ephesus had come to keep the Feast. One day they recognized

Paul on the street. They noticed that Paul was walking with a Gentile Christian, one who had never been a Jew.

The next day these men saw Paul in the Temple. They did not wait to find out for sure. They thought Paul had brought this Gentile Christian into the inner court of the Temple which was against the Law. It was a serious offense which was punished by stoning.

As soon as they saw Paul, these men rushed up and grabbed him. "Men of Israel," they cried out in order to get the attention of the crowds of worshipers. "This is the man who teaches against our Law and our Temple throughout Asia. He has now defiled our Temple by bringing Greeks here within the sacred place."

The outer court was the Court of the Gentiles. A high wall with doors separated the two. Signs on the wall read: "No one who is not a Jew may enter. The punishment for disobeying this law is death."

The other Jews believed these men and dragged Paul out of the Court of Israel. Some picked up stones to hurl at him.

Roman soldiers were stationed in a nearby tower. They noticed the riot and reported it to their commander. The soldiers thought it was a revolt against Roman authority. The commander himself led the soldiers into the Temple courts. The men stopped beating Paul when they saw the soldiers, but they did not let him go.

The commander arrested Paul and ordered the soldiers to bind him with chains. "What did this man do?" he asked the crowd.

Many of the crowd did not know. Some shouted one thing and others something else.

"I can't understand what they are shouting," the commander complained. "Let's take this man to the barracks."

The crowd was still angry and the soldiers had to carry Paul out of the Temple courts to keep him from being killed. As they climbed the stairs to the tower Paul asked permission to speak.

The commander was surprised that Paul spoke to him in Greek. "I am a Jew born in Tarsus," Paul told him. "Let me speak to the people. I must explain to them why I am here."

The commander gave permission and Paul turned on the stairway and spoke to the crowd below. He told them that he was a Jew who had studied under the famous Gamaliel. He told them about his vision on the road to Damascus.

The people listened with good attention. But then Paul said, "The Lord who appeared to me told me to preach the story of Jesus, the Messiah, to the Gentiles. It is God's will that they too have a chance to believe."

At this the crowd grew angry again. "Away with him," they shouted. "He isn't fit to live."

Acts 21:1-22:52

77. A Plot Against Paul

The commander, Lysias, had Paul brought into the barracks. He was going to have Paul beaten, but then he heard that Paul was a Roman citizen. He told the other soldiers to go out so that he could talk to Paul alone.

"Tomorrow we will call the Jewish leaders together and bring you before them," he said. "Then we will find out exactly what charge they bring against you."

Paul was kept in the barracks. On the next day he was led out by Roman soldiers to where the Sanhedrin met. They had gathered as ordered.

Ananias, who was now high priest, had charge of the meeting. Paul looked intently at these religious rulers. He proclaimed himself innocent of doing or saying anything against the Law or the Temple.

"Brothers," he said, "all my life I have lived in good conscience before God."

It was confusing to the Roman officers. They could not understand why the rulers were angry at Paul. The more Paul proclaimed himself innocent, the more angry the rulers became.

Paul knew that most of the Sanhedrin were Sadducees but many were Pharisees. He hoped to get the Pharisees on his side.

"I was raised and educated as a Pharisee," he told the assembly. "I am on trial now because I believe in the resurrection of the dead."

Paul was referring to the resurrection of Jesus, but the Sadducees did not believe in any resurrection. They started to talk against the belief in a resurrection. This angered the Pharisees on the council.

Now they were quarreling with each other instead of considering Paul's case. Many of the Pharisees made speeches about why they believed in a resurrection.

The Roman commander could not understand the case. He commanded the officers, "Take Paul back to the tower."

The officers had to force some of the council members away from Paul in order to take Paul safely out of the court.

Paul was taken back to his cell in the barracks. That night the Lord spoke to him. "Take courage. You have witnessed about me here in Jerusalem. You must also tell your story at Rome."

When daylight came Paul felt better. He was sure now that he would get to Rome and be able to preach about Jesus there.

As daylight was breaking over the city, a band of some forty Jews met together. They were members of a group who worked against Rome.

"We must see that Paul is put to death," they said.

One suggested, "Let us make a vow that we will neither eat nor drink until we have killed Paul."

The others agreed. The first step in their plot was to go to the chief priests and other religious rulers. They told them, "We have bound ourselves by a vow that we will taste no food till we have killed Paul. We need your help.

"Send to the Roman commander. Tell him you want to see Paul in order to ask him questions about the charge made against him. We will be waiting along the way to kill him. He will never reach this place."

The rulers agreed to this wicked plot, but word of what they were planning leaked out. Paul had a sister and a young nephew who lived in Jerusalem. This young man heard about the plot.

"I must save my uncle," he decided.

The nephew hurried to the tower where Paul was imprisoned. He asked the soldiers, "May I see the prisoner, Paul? He is my uncle."

The soldiers allowed the boy to come in and talk to Paul. "Uncle," cried the boy when they were alone, "the rulers are plotting with men to kill you. They are going to ask for you to be brought to them and then these men will jump out at you on the way."

Paul praised his nephew. "You have been loyal and brave," he said. "Now I want you to tell the commander exactly what you told me."

Paul called out for the soldiers who were on guard. A captain came to the cell. "Take this young man to the commander," said Paul. "He has something important to tell him."

The captain took Paul's nephew to the commander, Lysias. "Sir," he said, "the prisoner, Paul, asked me to bring this young man to you. He has something to tell you."

The commander took the young man by the hand and brought him to where they could talk privately. "What is it that you have to tell me?" he asked.

The young man told his story. "My uncle is in great danger," he said.

The commander was surprised. Paul was an important prisoner to the Jews. Paul was also a Roman citizen with certain special rights. Lysias would have to be very careful. He did not want to get into trouble with his superiors.

"You may go now," the commander told Paul's nephew. "I will see that your uncle is protected, but you must tell no one of this visit."

The young man promised. Lysias had decided what to do. He would send Paul to the procurator of Judea who was now Antonius Felix.

The procurator lived in Caesarea and here Paul would be safely away from those who sought his life. The religious rulers would have to go to Caesarea to accuse Paul at a trial.

Lysias sent for two captains, "Get a guard ready," he told them. "Tonight you will take the prisoner Paul to Felix."

Acts 22:23-23:24

78. Paul Before Felix

A bodyguard of four hundred foot soldiers and seventy soldiers on horses took Paul to Antipatris, about half the way. The horsemen rode with Paul the remaining distance to Caesarea.

When they came to the procurator's palace they brought Paul before this Roman governor. One of the captains handed Felix a letter written by the commander, Lysias.

The commander wrote Felix:

> This man was seized by the Jews. He was about to be killed by them when I and my soldiers came upon them and rescued him. He is a Roman citizen.
>
> I brought him before the Jewish council and discovered that their charge against him concerns their religious laws. I could not see that he deserved death or imprisonment.
>
> When I discovered that there was a plot against this man's life I sent him to you. I am going to order his accusers to come before you and say what they have against him.

The governor read the letter. He told Paul, "I will hear your case when your accusers arrive from Jerusalem."

Then Paul was led away and put into a guarded room in the fortress which was part of the palace.

Five days later the high priest, Ananias, and some selected members of the Sanhedrin came to Caesarea. They brought along a professional speaker called Tertullus to make their speech against Paul. The governor, Felix, greeted these important men of Judea. When he was ready to try Paul before them, he called for soldiers to bring in Paul.

When Paul was in the room Tertullus got up to make his speech. He began with words of flattery for the Roman ruler. Then he spoke against Paul. "This man is an agitator," he said, "a troublemaker among all the Jews throughout the world. He is a ringleader of the sect of the Nazarenes. When he disobeyed the laws of our Temple we seized him. Ask him yourself if this is not true."

The Jews who had brought Tertullus spoke out in agreement.

The governor told Paul that he could now speak in his defense.

Paul told him, "I am glad to make my defense against these charges to the Roman ruler. I went to worship in the Temple at Jerusalem. These men did not find me arguing or stirring up a crowd in the Temple, in their synagogue, or in the city. I was worshiping and performing my vow in the Temple according to the Law.

"I do worship God according to the way they call a sect, but we of this way believe all that is written in the Law and the prophets. I came to Jerusalem with gifts of money for those other Jews who belong to this way.

"Some Jews from Ephesus said I had brought Gentiles into the Temple, but this was not true. Now these men from Ephesus are not even here to make their charge. Let these rulers from Jerusalem say what wrong I have done, and let them prove their charge."

Felix knew something about the Christian way. He suspected that Paul had been unjustly charged, but he did not want to make the religious rulers angry by declaring his decision immediately.

"I will make a decision about this when Lysias, the commander, comes here and I can talk with him," he told them all.

The religious rulers had to be content with this and returned to Jerusalem.

Paul had to remain at the fortress. "Any of your friends may come and visit you," he was told. "They can bring anything you might need."

Felix had married a Jew, and he talked to his wife, Drusilla, about Paul. Drusilla was the daughter of Herod Agrippa I. "I am curious about this Christian way," Felix told her. "Let's have Paul explain it to us."

Paul was glad to preach to Felix and Drusilla, but he did not try to flatter them with his message. He knew that Felix often took bribes and in other ways governed unjustly. He knew that Felix had married Drusilla before her first husband had died.

Paul told them the Christian way was one of right living and self-control and that in the future God would judge those who did wrong.

Felix was alarmed. He wondered, "Was there really a God who knew about his wrongdoings?" If this were true, terrible judgment might come to him. He knew he was guilty of many sins.

Paul told him how to find forgiveness, but Felix did not want to change. "I have heard enough for now," he said. "I will listen to you again some other time."

The days went slowly by. Visitors came to Paul and Felix noticed this. "If I keep Paul here, they will surely offer me money for a decision in his favor," Felix thought. This is what so many people had done in the past.

Paul and his friends realized that the governor expected this, but they would not do it, because it was wrong.

Often Felix sent for Paul saying that he wished to talk to him. He really hoped that Paul would bring him money.

For two years Paul stayed in Caesarea and Felix gave no decision about him. Then a change was made. Another man was appointed procurator. Before Felix left he decided that he would do nothing to help Paul.

Acts 23:23-24:27

79. Paul Appeals to Caesar

Soon after Porcius Festus took over his new office he visited Jerusalem and talked with the religious rulers. To rule in peace the new procurator wanted the cooperation of these leaders.

The chief priests and other important men told Festus about Paul. "This man disobeyed our religious laws," they said, "but Felix would not listen to us. The man is still in prison in Caesarea.

"As a favor to us, send him here to Jerusalem so that he might be tried for this offense before our court." The men planned to have Paul killed while he was making the trip.

The new governor hesitated. He did not want to anger the men, but he suspected that they plotted against Paul. He wanted to know about this case before he gave permission.

"I know that Paul is a prisoner at Caesarea," Festus told them, "but I know little of the case. I am going back to Caesarea shortly. Let men of authority come with me, and they can accuse Paul in the court there."

The religious rulers agreed and appointed certain men. Several days later they journeyed back with Festus to the governor's palace and the fortress where Paul was kept a prisoner.

The next day Festus sat on his seat of judgment. He ordered Paul to come to the court for another trial. When Paul was brought in he noticed the Jews from Jerusalem who had come to accuse him.

Now these men were permitted to speak. They told the governor, "This man speaks against our Law. He stirs up the people against us and other religious rulers. He disobeyed the laws of our Temple."

But the men had no proof.

Paul defended himself. "I have done nothing against the Law or the Temple. Nor have I spoken against Caesar."

Festus realized that there was no proof against Paul. *He ought to be allowed to go free,* Festus thought. But the governor did not want to make enemies of these Jewish leaders.

The governor told Paul, "The Jewish leaders want you to come to Jerusalem to be tried before the Sanhedrin, which takes care of religious matters. Do you wish to do this? I will come along and be at the trial to make sure all is done properly."

Paul knew that he could never get a fair trial before the Sanhedrin. He said, "I am standing in this Roman court where I ought to stand trial. I have done no wrong. As a Roman citizen I have the right to appeal to Caesar and be tried in Rome. I appeal to Caesar."

Festus was surprised at Paul's boldness. He went aside and talked to some of his advisors. When he sat down again he said, "You have your request. You will go to Caesar."

In order to send a prisoner to the emperor in Rome the governor needed to write a letter and say why this was a serious case. Festus could not understand exactly what it was the religious rulers insisted Paul had done.

Around this time Herod Agrippa II came to visit. He was the son of the Herod Agrippa who had put Peter in prison. His sister, Bernice, was with

him. They came to welcome Festus to his new post.

The emperor, Nero, had given Agrippa II rule over much Roman territory. Agrippa professed to be a Jew in belief, but he had many Roman ways and much praise for the Roman emperor.

Festus told them about Paul. "You know a great deal about Jewish matters," he said. "I need help in explaining to the emperor just what Paul is supposed to have done.

"We had a trial here, but the charges were nothing like I had supposed. It had to do with their religion and concerned one called Jesus. The leaders said Jesus was dead but Paul said He was alive."

"I would like to hear Paul's defense," said Agrippa.

"You shall hear him tomorrow," Festus promised.

The next day Paul was brought before these important visitors. It was a formal occasion and many important men of the city were there.

Paul was glad when he looked around. Here was a good chance to tell many about Jesus.

Festus addressed Agrippa and the rest of the assembly. "This is the man against whom the Jewish leaders brought charges. He asked to be sent to Caesar and that is what I am going to do. I have brought him here before you, and especially before our worthy Agrippa, so that we might all better understand this matter."

Agrippa was a more important Roman ruler than Festus, so now Agrippa said to Paul, "You have permission to speak for yourself."

"I am glad to speak before you, Agrippa," said Paul, "because I know you are familiar with the customs and beliefs of the Jews."

Once again Paul told his story. He told them all how he had once persecuted the Christians. Then the risen Lord had appeared to him and he had become a Christian himself.

Paul told them, "Jesus spoke to me and told me that I was to tell of this vision to others, to Gentiles as well as Jews. I was not disobedient to the heavenly vision. I preached about Jesus throughout Asia and many Gentiles came to believe in Him. It is for this reason that the Jewish leaders want to kill me."

Paul went on talking about Jesus.

At last Festus interrupted him. "Paul, you are raving!" he cried. "We did not ask you to preach to us."

"I speak the truth," said Paul. "Agrippa has heard about these things. The message of Jesus has been preached openly throughout this part of the world."

Then Paul asked Agrippa, "Do you believe the prophets? I am sure you do."

Agrippa was surprised at the direct question. "Are you trying to make me a Christian?" he asked.

Paul said, "I wish you and everyone here were a Christian."

After this Agrippa got up as a signal that the meeting was over. Festus and Bernice left with him.

Together they talked about Paul. "This man has not done anything worthy of death or imprisonment," they agreed.

"You could have set him free," said Agrippa, "but now that he has appealed to Caesar he will have to go to Rome."

Acts 25, 26

80. A Storm at Sea

Plans were made to send Paul and other prisoners to Rome to be tried before the emperor's court. Roman soldiers under the command of an officer called Julius were in charge of the prisoners. It was probably in the fall of the year A.D. 60.

It would be a long sea voyage and there was no ship sailing directly to Rome. They took a ship which was planning to sail along the coast of Asia Minor. Luke and Aristarchus from Thessalonica went with Paul. The first stop was Sidon.

Here Julius treated Paul and his friends kindly by allowing them to visit Christian friends in the city.

From Sidon the ship sailed east of the island of Cyprus because the winds were rough. At the port of Myra in Lycia the company had to change ships.

Julius found a ship which was bound for Italy and ordered the soldiers to bring the prisoners aboard. This ship came from Alexandria in Egypt. It carried passengers and a cargo of grain.

Sailing was always difficult. Ships of this time depended on the winds to drive them to their destinations. When the winds blew against the ship, it had to change its course. After difficulty, they reached a harbor called Fair Havens. They stayed here, hoping that the weather would get better, but instead it grew worse.

October came, and soon the autumn would make the seas even more dangerous. Sailors reckoned the sea dangerous from the middle of September to the middle of November. From November to the middle of March no ships sailed at all.

Paul had gone on many voyages and he knew this. He spoke to Julius about it. He was with the captain and the owner of the ship at the time.

"Sirs," Paul said, "we should stay here for the winter or we will lose our cargo and perhaps the ship and our lives."

The captain and the owner wanted to continue. "We still have time to make a safe trip as far as Phoenix," they said. "There is a better harbor there." The Roman officer listened to them.

"We will head for Phoenix in Crete and spend the winter there," they decided. The ship sailed off. The trip was supposed to take about twelve hours.

At first it seemed as though the winds were in their favor. The south wind blew gently. They sailed along the coast of the island of Crete. Then suddenly a wind, a northeaster, came from the land and caught up the ship so that it was driven entirely off course. The waves tossed the ship about so that even the experienced sailors were helpless in its grasp.

The storm raged throughout the night. The next day they made the ship lighter by throwing some of the cargo overboard. The storm still raged. All those on board helped to throw the furniture and utensils overboard and to take down all the sails.

For thirteen days the sun did not come out by day nor the stars by night. They were lost without these aids to navigation. The sailors were afraid they would be driven upon fearful sandbars

along the north African coast. All gave up hope of their lives—all except Paul.

The people were so frightened that they hardly took any food. Finally, after two weeks Paul came forward and said, "Men, take heart. The God I worship sent an angel to tell me that no lives would be lost on this voyage. I have faith in God. We will all be saved. We must try to land on some island."

The next night a few of the sailors said they thought the ship was nearing land. They measured the depth of the water and found it to be twenty fathoms. In a little while they measured again and found it to be fifteen fathoms. They were fast approaching the land.

"We will be cast upon rocks," the sailors cried in alarm. "Let down the anchors. We will stay at this spot until daylight comes."

The sailors had decided secretly among themselves to try to escape the ship in a small boat. While the others thought they were casting out the anchors, they lowered the small lifeboat into the water. But Paul and many others were awake, and Paul discovered them.

Paul hurried to Julius and his soldiers. "We will be lost if the sailors leave the ship," he told them.

Quickly the soldiers jumped to action. They cut the ropes by which the small boat was being lowered. The lifeboat quickly drifted away. The sailors were forced to stay and attend to their duties.

Finally daylight dawned. Paul urged the others to eat. "You will need strength to get the ship to shore. Do not fear. God has promised to spare us."

Paul began to break pieces of bread off a large loaf. He prayed to God and thanked Him for the food.

The others followed Paul's example and took bread and other food. Altogether there were two hundred and seventy-six persons on board.

When the meal was finished they threw what remained of the ship's cargo out into the sea. A light boat would be easier to row to shore.

Ahead of them was a small bay and a strip of beach. "We can bring the ship ashore there," the sailors said.

They cut away the anchors and hoisted the sails. The men began to row carefully to shore, but they were not able to bring the ship safely to the beach. The prow of the ship struck a sandbar and remained immovable while the stern of the ship was broken to pieces by the dashing waves. Now each one must make for shore the best he could.

The soldiers cried out, "We must kill the prisoners or some of them might swim away and escape."

"No," shouted Julius. He liked Paul and wanted to be sure he was saved.

Julius ordered, "Those who can swim throw yourselves overboard and head for shore. Those who cannot, find some planks from the ship to help you get to the beach."

The orders were obeyed. Swimming or floating they got to the land. On shore a roll call was made of the prisoners. They were all there. The sailors and the passengers were all safe on the beach. The ship was destroyed, but their lives had been saved.

Acts 27

81. Arrival in Rome

It began to rain in this strange lonely place. "How cold it is," many said. "We must try to build a fire."

Then someone shouted, "Look, people are coming!"

People who lived on the island came to greet them. They listened with amazement to their story of escape.

"You are on the island of Malta," they told them. "Come, we will get you dry wood for a fire."

Paul set to work with the others in looking for dry sticks. As he brought a bundle over to the fire, a viper crawled out of the bundle and bit Paul's hand. Paul shook the snake into the fire.

Some of the people of the island saw and whispered to one another. "This man must be a murderer. Even though he escaped drowning, he will now die because of his misdeeds."

They waited for Paul to show signs of being poisoned by the snake; but nothing happened. Then they changed their minds about Paul completely. "He must be a god," they said.

Publius, the Roman ruler of the island, and the people of Malta were friendly to the shipwrecked travelers who had been forced to stay with them. Publius invited Paul and his friends to visit him for three days.

Some time after this Publius' father became very ill with a high fever. Paul went to visit him. He prayed, putting his hands on him, and asked God to heal him in Jesus' Name. The man's fever left him.

All the people of Malta became excited over this. Many brought their sick to Paul. He healed them in the Name of Jesus. Paul used this opportunity to tell them about Jesus.

In three months it was safe to take another ship on to Rome. This ship had been on the island all winter, waiting for the good sailing weather to return.

Those whom Paul had helped brought him farewell gifts which Paul and his friends took on board. They would have to supply all their own needs while Paul waited for his trial.

The seas were calm as they sailed north to Italy. They made several stops along the way. Puteoli in Italy was the last port for the ship. The cargo of grain was unloaded at this important market. The rest of the way to Rome would be by land along the famous highway, the Appian Way. They would walk one hundred and thirty miles.

The Christians in Rome had heard that Paul was coming. They had never seen Paul, but he had sent them a letter several years before which had contained a wonderful sermon on the Christian faith.

They were eager to see this man who had brought the Christian message to so many. Some of these Christians traveled about forty miles out of the city along the Appian Way to meet Paul. Another group met them thirty miles from the city.

This welcome and the Christian love it showed made Paul very happy. He felt greatly encouraged. Even though he was a prisoner, he was going to see Rome and have a chance to tell his story there. He thanked God for keeping His promise to bring him here.

When the company arrived in Rome, Julius spoke well of Paul to the authorities. The letter Festus had sent also spoke well of him. Paul was allowed to rent a house of his own, but a Roman soldier would always be chained to him. Paul was told that friends could come and stay with him at any time.

One of the first things Paul did at Rome was to send word to the leaders of the Jewish synagogue. He asked them to come and visit him. Ten years before the Emperor Claudius had ordered all the Jews to leave Rome. Later that order was cancelled and many Jews returned. Now there was a synagogue and a church at Rome.

Three days later the Jewish leaders came to visit Paul. Paul told them, "Brothers, I had done nothing to harm our people, but the leaders in Jerusalem delivered me to the Roman authorities.

"I do not want you to think I have anything against my own people. I would like to tell you more about my belief in Jesus, the Messiah."

The leaders told him, "The rulers at Jerusalem have not sent us any letters about you. Nor have any who come from Jerusalem said anything to us about you. We have heard many things against those who believe in Jesus, but we are willing to listen to your explanation."

The Jewish leaders made arrangements to come back another day and bring other Jews with them. When the day arrived the largest room in Paul's house was filled with the Jews of Rome.

Paul spent all the day talking to them. He quoted from the Law and the prophets and tried to convince them that Jesus was the Messiah.

Some were convinced by Paul's sermon but others were not. They began to argue among themselves. As they departed Paul said to those who had not believed, "You have closed your ears to the message of God just as your ancestors refused to listen to the prophets.

"The good news about Jesus will go to the Gentiles. They will believe and become a part of the Kingdom of God."

Acts 28:1-28

82. Paul, the Prisoner

For more than two years Paul was kept under guard in Rome. Day and night he was chained to a soldier. He was not allowed to leave the house; but anyone could come and see him.

Paul welcomed all visitors Jews or Gentiles, Christians or unbelievers. He encouraged and instructed the Christians and preached about Christ to the others. Paul talked about Jesus to the different soldiers who were sent to guard him. Many people of Rome believed in Jesus because of Paul's work.

Paul also wrote to many of the churches he had founded on the missionary journeys. Sometimes he wrote on parchment, sometimes on papyrus paper. In these he answered questions, gave words of encouragement, and told the Christians not to worry about him.

To the church at Philippi Paul wrote;

> I want you to know, brothers, that what has happened to me has really advanced the work of Christ. The message has become known to many of the soldiers. The Christians here at Rome are encouraged when they see that I am ready to suffer for Jesus. It made them brave, and they speak to many about Jesus.

At the close of this letter Paul sent greetings from all the Christians in Rome, including those who lived or worked in the palace of the emperor.

Luke, Timothy, John Mark and others who had worked with him spent some time with Paul in Rome. At times Paul opened the house for preaching and everyone was invited to come.

One day a young man named Onesimus was present. He knew Paul, but he hoped that Paul would not recognize him. He was a runaway slave.

Onesimus listened to Paul. He had heard about Jesus from his master who was a Christian and a leader in the church at Colossae. This church had been started by Christians converted at Ephesus while Paul was preaching there. His master, Philemon, had preached about Jesus to all his relatives and slaves and many had become Christians.

Onesimus had refused to become one of the church. He was bitter and unhappy about being a slave, even though he had a kind master. One day he found a chance to run away and he took it. He stole money from his master and made off.

In Rome Onesimus had hoped to lose himself in the big city. He knew the Roman laws said he could be put to death for escaping and that anyone who sheltered him would be punished. Freedom did not prove to be as wonderful as the slave had thought, because he was always afraid of being arrested.

Onesimus knew that Paul preached about God's love. As he listened Onesimus wondered if Paul could in some way help him, but he was afraid to ask. What if Paul sent him back to his master?"

Paul and his helpers did recognize Onesimus, and Paul spoke kindly to him. Onesimus told him the whole story.

"Stay with me for a while," Paul told him. "Later we shall decide what we should do."

The slave stayed with Paul and served him faithfully. Paul taught him about the Christian way. One day Onesimus told him, "I want to become a Christian."

This made Paul very happy. "You have been a great help to me," he told Onesimus. "I wish I could keep you here, but it would not be right."

"I know," said Onesimus. "I broke the law, and I should go back to Philemon, my master."

Paul comforted the young man. "Do not fear," he said, "Philemon is a good Christian. He will forgive you I am sure. One of my helpers is going to Asia and you can travel with him. I will send along a letter to Philemon."

Paul wrote to Philemon:

> I thank God when I remember you as I pray. I hear such good reports of you and the other Christians who meet in your home. Now I have a favor to ask of you. I ask you to forgive and take back, Onesimus.
>
> Onesimus is now a fellow Christian. Even though he wronged you, forgive him and treat him as a brother. This is the Christian thing to do.
>
> Onesimus was a poor servant when he was at your house, but he has been a good servant to me. I would like to keep him here with me, but I would not do that without your consent.
>
> Receive him as you would receive me if I came to your house. If he has taken any money from you, I will repay you. When I am released from prison I will come and visit you.

In this difficult period of waiting, not knowing what would happen to him, Paul never remained discouraged for long. He hoped to be released, but he was ready to die if need be.

At one time Paul felt sure that death was near. He wrote to Timothy:

> I am ready to die; the time has come. I have fought the good fight. I have finished the race. I have kept the faith. The Lord will reward me as He will reward all those who faithfully serve Him.

Acts 28:30, 31
Philippians 1:12-18; 4:21-23
Philemon
II Timothy 4:6-8

83. Letters to Churches

At first the message of Jesus' life, death and resurrection was only spoken by the apostles. Those who heard and believed their message told others. For a time nothing was written down.

As years passed the Christians realized that they needed a written record of what Jesus had said and done. Different ones wrote down some of the events of the life of Jesus. We have four of these accounts of Jesus' life, called Gospels, in our Bibles.

Another kind of Christian writings were the many letters Paul and other Christian leaders sent to the churches. Most of the time these letters were written to one person or to one church. Sometimes they were written to all the churches in one area.

In any case the letters were copied by hand and sent around from church to church. When Christians gathered to take the Lord's Supper and to worship together, their leaders read from these letters because they contained valuable Christian teaching.

Many of these letters were lost as years went by but some were handed down. Some of these letters were later accepted as part of our New Testament. These particular letters had been such an inspiration to the Church that it was decided that they deserved a place in the Holy Scriptures.

These writings helped to explain the Christian faith to those who had recently become Christians. They gave instructions to the churches on how they should choose leaders and what the leaders should do.

The writers spoke of Jesus in words of praise and worship. They said that Jesus, the Christ, was head of the Church. They were servants under Christ, but sent by Him to tell others. They were like shepherds and their flocks were made up of other Christians.

The letters urged the Christians to live in the way that Jesus had taught. There were words of encouragement for times of persecution. There were instructions for living in the way God wanted every day.

Here are a few quotations from some of these letters.

From Paul's letter to the Romans:

> Let love be genuine. Hate what is evil. Hold fast to what is good. Love one another with brotherly affection.

From Paul's letter to the Ephesians:

> Let all bitterness, anger, lying, and hatred be stopped. Be kind to one another. Forgive one another as God forgave you.

From Paul's letter to the Colossians:

> Whatever your task, do it with enthusiasm, as a service to the Lord. Remember you are serving the Lord Christ.

From Paul's first letter to the Thessalonians:

> Respect those who are your Christian teachers and leaders in the work

of God. Esteem them very highly and love them. Be at peace with each other.

From the letter to the Hebrew or Jewish Christians:

Show hospitality to strangers. Remember those who are in prison and those who are ill-treated and help them. Do not think having money is the most important thing. Be content with the good things you have.

From the letter of James the brother of Jesus:

Be doers of the word and not just one who listens. Help orphans and widows. Show no partiality. Welcome the poor as well as the rich.

From the first letter of Peter:

Always be prepared to make a defense to anyone who calls you to account for your faith in Christ. But do it with gentleness and respect. Do what is right. Then when you are falsely accused, your life as a Christian will make them feel ashamed of their lie. It is better, if necessary, to suffer for doing right than for doing wrong.

From the first letter of John:

Let us not love in word or speech but in deed and in truth. This is God's commandment, that we should believe in the Name of His Son Jesus Christ and love one another, just as Jesus has commanded us.

God loved us and sent His Son to die for our sins. If God so loved us, we also ought to love one another.

Romans 12:9, 10
Ephesians 4:31, 32
Colossians 3:23
I Thessalonians 5:12-13
Hebrews 13:2, 3, 5
James 1:22, 26; 2:1
I Peter 3:15-17
I John 3:18, 23; 4:9, 11

84. The Church Is Promised Victory

In the year A.D. 62 James, the head of the church in Jerusalem, was put to death by orders of the high priest, Ananus. It was just after the death of the procurator, Festus, and there was much confusion in the city. There was a strong feeling of rebellion against Roman-appointed officers.

Paul was put to death in Rome, perhaps around A.D. 64. At this time the Emperor Nero started a drive to get rid of all Christians in Rome. The Apostle Peter was put to death around the same time.

The church had won many members. Nero and other Roman officials thought it was a threat to their power over men.

In Jerusalem, feelings against Rome grew stronger as the years went by. When open rebellion broke out Roman soldiers fought the rebels. In A.D. 70 the emperor Vespasian had the city of Jerusalem and the beautiful temple completely destroyed. Jews were no longer allowed to live there.

The Christians escaped from Jerusalem before this happened. They went

to other places and became a part of other towns and villages and churches. From the time of the fall of Jerusalem, the church and the synagogue were always separate. Christians realized that theirs was a new faith, no longer part of the Jewish religion.

The Christians did not have the favor of the Roman government. Times of persecution against them grew stronger as the years passed.

The Roman rulers used pagan religion to further the power of the government. Temples had been built in many places dedicated to Rome and the emperor. Now the Roman rulers grew proud and demanded that people worship at these shrines. It was no longer a matter of choice.

Around A.D. 93 the emperor Domitian demanded that he be called "Lord and God." Many Christians refused to do this and chose rather to die. The government called the Christians traitors because they refused. It became a crime to be a Christian.

The leaders of the church encouraged its members to be true to the Christ. They said, "Jesus was willing to suffer and die for us. Stephen, James, Paul, Peter and other Christian leaders have been willing to give their lives rather than deny that they believed in Jesus."

The Christians found hope in their belief that Jesus would come again as He had promised. They believed this would happen very soon, and that then God's Kingdom would fully come to earth. This gave them courage to continue to meet in Jesus' Name.

The church leaders assured the persecuted Christians that they would find strength and courage from Christ Himself. "He is always with His church," they said.

In many different messages they proclaimed that God would deliver them. They said the church would be victorious over all the evil opposition which now surrounded them.

One message of encouragement to persecuted Christians was sent by John to seven churches in Asia Minor. John was a prisoner on the Island of Patmos because of his Christian faith. He and many other Christian prisoners were made to work in the quarries there.

John had suffered much rather than deny his loyalty to Christ. In spite of present persecutions, he still believed that the church would have the victory.

The Christians had come to call the first day of the week on which they met together the Lord's Day, because it was the day on which Jesus Christ the Lord, was raised from the dead.

One Lord's Day John was praying and thinking about Christ and the Church, when he had a vision. In this vision Christ appeared to John, shining in all His heavenly glory. He gave John a message for each of these seven churches.

Each letter encouraged the Christians to remain true. A few included words of warning against living in unchristian ways. But all were assured of Christ's love for them and His willingness to forgive those who repented.

Then John had a vision of heaven. He heard a song of praise to God:

"Holy, holy, holy, is the Lord God almighty."

In this vision John saw a great multitude of people from all tribes and nations standing before God's throne.

They worshiped and called out:

"Victory belongs to our God who sits upon the throne and to Jesus."

All the angels joined in the worship chanting:

"Blessing, and glory, and wisdom, and thanksgiving, and honor, and power, and might, be to our God for ever and ever. Amen."

Then John was told that these were Christians who had been persecuted for their faith. Now they were in God's presence and would serve God and know only happiness.

When John wrote to the churches he warned them that troubles for the Christians would not soon be over. In fact, he said, events would grow worse for the Church. But John insisted that the Kingdom of God was still going to come on earth.

John told them of voices from heaven chanting:

"The kingdoms of the world have become the kingdoms of our God and His Christ. He shall reign forever and ever."

Christians were persecuted by Rome during the reigns of several emperors, although some were not as zealous in doing away with them as others. In Rome the Christians met secretly in burial caves called catacombs. In spite of all this opposition, the church grew in numbers and influence.

The emperor who most hated the Christian faith and tried to destroy it entirely was Diocletian. This was A.D. 303. But then, in A.D. 312, the emperor Constantine said Christianity was a legal religion and that its believers should not in any way be harmed. Before he died, Constantine became a Christian.

From then on the Church grew in influence. About a hundred years later, the Roman Empire crumbled, as other empires had in the past; but the church of Christ lived on.

The good news about Jesus spread throughout Europe. Wherever Christian teachers went they helped the poor and tried to help the sick. They remembered how Jesus had healed the sick.

As centuries passed the Christian influence made people more concerned for others. Many beautiful churches, hospitals and schools were built.

When the new world was discovered, the Christian message was brought to it. Today about one third of all the people in the world profess the Christian faith.

But there is still work to do. There are still people who do not know about Jesus Christ. Christians are needed to tell them—they are needed wherever people need to know more about God and His love as shown in Jesus Christ. They are needed wherever people are cold and hungry and ill. Christians remember that Jesus cared about these people when He was here on earth, and they care and do what they can to help.

Christians still believe Jesus taught about the Kingdom of God, and that He will come come to set up the Kingdom on earth. All around the world they still pray to God the prayer Jesus taught:

"Thy kingdom come:
Thy will be done on earth as it is in heaven."

Revelation 1-3; 4:8; 7:9-17; 11:15

QUESTIONS FOR DISCUSSION

The following are questions which can be used in any small informal group. Some families using the book for family devotions could use them to talk together about the things of God. These are not questions on factual information nor are they meant to be "yes" or "no" questions. Sometimes there is no correct or incorrect answer. The questions are meant to start children and adults thinking about the meaning of each story for themselves. Hopefully, they will stimulate other questions for thought and discussion.

Occasionally instead of a question a suggestion is given for a project or report to be done by the family or the group together. You will probably find these projects of most help with older children.

Story 1

1. Bring together some books written for children on science. Leaf through them and each try to find five things which make you wonder at the power God showed in creation. Give yourself five minutes.
2. Does God still feel the world He made is good?
3. What do you think is good? What is not good?
4. How did God plan for life to go on?

Story 2

1. What brought sorrow into the world?
2. What brings trouble to individuals today? Are we ourselves always responsible?
3. How should we feel toward the world of plant and animal life around us?
4. What kind of responsibility do we have toward animals?

Story 3

1. Why did God accept Abel's offering and reject Cain's offering?
2. When does God reject an offering of mine?
3. What did Jesus teach about our brothers and our offerings?
4. How do we know that there was civilization in this time of man's history?

Story 4

1. In the history of other ancient peoples there are stories of a great flood. See if you can find out about some of these stories.
2. Why did God have to judge those who did wrong?
3. Are people ever judged for doing wrong today?
4. Are nations ever judged today?

Story 5

1. How do you think it came about that men started to worship idols?
2. Languages change and grow. Think of some English words which have come from another language.
3. Why does the Bible have to be translated?

Story 6

1. Why do you think Abram was discontented with his religion?
2. Why do you think God wanted him out of Ur of the Chaldeans?
3. Why did this step require a lot of courage from Abram?
4. What do you think the servants had to say about the trip and its purpose?

Story 7

1. What does this story tell us about Lot as a person?
2. What remarks might the herdsmen of each group have made about Abram after the parting?
3. What made Abram sure God's promise would come true?
4. Could Abram have quit at any time and gone back to Ur? What kept him going?

Story 8
1. Did Sarai act wisely? In what way was her attitude right or wrong?
2. To what extent was Hagar wrong?
3. Where did Abram make his mistake?
4. How did God make things right?

Story 9
1. What does this story tell me about what kind of friends to have?
2. What could have kept Sodom from being destroyed?
3. Why do you think Lot found it easier than the others to believe?

Story 10
1. See the questions under story 8 and apply them to this story also.
2. Do we sometimes get into trouble because we think we know more than God? Name some such times.
3. Why is jealousy in the family not pleasing to God? Can a jealous person be happy?

Story 11
1. Why was it important that Isaac not marry a woman of the Canaanites?
2. Why do you think Rebekah would make a good wife and mother?
3. Can we pray about anything?

Story 12
1. Describe Jacob as though you knew him and were telling a friend about him.
2. Do the same for Esau.
3. What was important about the birthright?

Story 13
1. Do mothers ever do wrong? Did Rebekah do wrong?
2. Did Esau have a right to be angry?
3. What does this story tell me about how I should treat others?
4. Are we always "paid back" for the wrong we do?

Story 14
1. Do we ever think that we have "left God behind"? Is there any place we can go where God isn't there?
2. How did Jacob know that God had forgiven him?
3. Should we make promises to God as Jacob did or should we tell God we love Him without making any kind of "bargain"?
4. Why should we give anything to God when He has everything?

Story 15
1. Has it ever happened to you that someone did to you what you did to them or to someone else? What can we learn from this experience?
2. What do you like or dislike about Rachel? How do you feel about Leah?

Story 16
1. Does it always pay to work hard?
2. How did God help Jacob?
3. Did Jacob have a right to complain?

Story 17
1. In what ways are the brothers different in this story from the last time they saw each other?
2. How can we make good use of difficult times which come to us?
3. Do you think that God sends difficult times to us so that we can learn, or do they come by accident?
4. Why was God pleased with Jacob?

Story 18
1. What was wrong in this family? How was each one to blame?
2. Why did Joseph's dream make the brothers angry?
3. What was important about the coat?
4. Why might Joseph be afraid of life in Egypt?

Story 19
1. Did Joseph have reason to doubt that God was with him?
2. Have you ever been accused of something you didn't do? What is the best way to act at such times?
3. Do you think Joseph is growing in God's way even in this pagan land? If so, why?

Story 20
1. What enabled Joseph to become such a success?
2. Do you think success will go to his head and make him conceited or cruel?
3. Does God want us to be a success?

Story 21
1. Why didn't Jacob want Benjamin to go? What does this tell us about Jacob and Joseph?
2. How do we know that the brothers did not forget but often thought about what they did to Joseph?
3. Do you think Joseph's test was a good one? Why?

Story 22
1. How do we know the brothers have learned from their past experiences?
2. Why did Joseph find forgiveness possible?
3. Do you think Joseph wise or foolish to be so loving and forgiving?

Story 23
1. Do you think the Hebrews were as faithful to God while in Egypt as they could have been?
2. In what ways does it help us to be around people who love and worship God?
3. How do we know all the Egyptians were not as cruel as the Pharaoh?

Story 24
1. Was Moses right in feeling sympathy for his enslaved people? Then why was what he did wrong?
2. You are a Hebrew trying to convince the others that God still cares about you. What would you say?
3. Why didn't fame in Egypt appeal to Moses?

Story 25
1. Why was Moses surprised to be called by God?
2. What made him feel inadequate?
3. What helped to convince the people? Later stories will show whether or not it was a deep conviction.

Story 26
1. What made Pharaoh so hard to convince?
2. Why do such things as earthquakes and floods cause people to think about God?
3. If you were an Egyptian do you think you might become a believer in the Hebrew God? Why?

Story 27
1. Why did the Passover become an important holy day?
2. What stories do you remember from the New Testament about the Passover?
3. What is the special supper Christians keep? What does it mean?

Story 28
1. What did the fiery cloud mean to the people?
2. In what way did God give them special help? Does God do things like this today?
3. Do you think these people will never doubt God's power again?

Story 29
1. Does this experience of having faith, then not having it and then getting it and then losing it again still happen to people today? Can you think of times?
2. Why were the people foolish in thinking God wanted them to die? Do people today ever think as foolishly as this?
3. How does God provide food for us?
4. How about the other things we need for life?
5. What is our part in getting the things we need?

Story 30
1. Why was Jethro's advice good?
2. If you were one of the leaders around Moses what would you say should be the qualifications for a judge?
3. Where can we go for advice when we have a problem? Are there poor as well as good places to go? Name some.

Story 31
1. What makes a mountain, or a building or anything else "holy"?
2. How do we know that, at the beginning of the story, when the elders made their promise they were not sincere?
3. What circumstances helped to make the people fashion and use an idol?
4. What were some of the things Moses found out about God through this experience?

Story 32
1. Why is it good to have a "place" of worship when God is everywhere?
2. Do you think the people were now sincere in their desire to worship God? Do presents prove sincerity?
3. What was necessary to build the place of worship besides gifts that could be handled?

Story 33
1. Why should the good news that the land was valuable and therefore worth defending bring dismay to the people?
2. Would God have given them the land if they had believed?
3. What do you think of the idea of a new captain and a return to Egypt?
4. Do people today ever prefer comfort to freedom?

Story 34
1. Moses is known today as one of the greatest leaders the world has ever known. What do you think made him great?
2. What do you think it means that Joshua had God's Spirit within him?
3. What was Moses' special warning? Keep this in mind in the light of future stories.

Story 35
1. Contrast the attitude of the people in this story with that in story 33.
2. Why did Joshua want them to be sure to tell their children about crossing the river as well as other events that would one day be history?
3. Does God help nations today?

Story 36
1. Why do selfish interests hinder people from doing God's work in the best way?
2. What in this story tells us that each individual is important?
3. Did you ever know of someone who spoiled the work a group was doing? How can we keep ourselves from being like this?

Story 37
1. Does God always help those with the best equipment? Does He always help those with the poor equipment?
2. Why did God bring judgment to the people of Canaan?
3. Did God promise never to bring judgment to the people of Israel?

Story 38
1. Why did the people grow careless in their worship?
2. How did their neighbors make it difficult for them?
3. Why is it important for us to have friends who live in Christian ways?

Story 39
1. Which is better, a few people who believe in what they are doing or a large number who are willing to give some time and thought to the work but have many divided interests?
2. What is the meaning of Gideon's test for the soldiers? Why was it a good one?
3. Was Gideon's answer to the messenger's greeting justified?

Story 40
1. In what way was Samson weak? How was he strong?
2. If Samson had acted in stronger ways how would this story be different?
3. Make up a different story, making Samson act in ways which were more what God wanted.

Story 41
1. What made Naomi lose her faith in God's care?
2. What contributed to Ruth's success?
3. Do I have to do anything if God answers my prayers for help?

Story 42
1. How did both Ruth and Naomi work to solve their problem?
2. Does God expect us to work as well as pray?
3. Name some people from other lands who have played an important part in our history.

Story 43
1. What good part can children play in a home? How can they make their parents happy?
2. How can young boys and girls serve in the church today?
3. What kind of things is it right to ask God to give us?

Story 44
1. How do we know Eli was a poor father?
2. What might he have done wrong?
3. How do we know he is doing a good job training Samuel?

Story 45
1. Were the Philistines right or wrong about the ark?
2. In what way were the Israelites wrong about the meaning of the ark?
3. Is God present only at church or at religious services? How do we know?

Story 46
1. Why did the people want a king?
2. What were the reasons against the idea?
3. Keep this story in mind and decide in the light of future stories whether having a king was good for the people.

Story 47
1. What was there about Saul which made him appear to be a good king?
2. What country uses the phrase "Long live the king" in their patriotic ceremonies today?
3. Does God choose kings or political leaders today?

Story 48
1. Why was Saul in the wrong?
2. Make up a good prayer for political leaders.
3. If leaders are so important, how important are followers?

Story 49
1. Had Saul learned a lesson from his previous mistake? How do we know?
2. Do people ever make the same mistake today?
3. What might have happened if Samuel had given up trying to lead the people?
4. What happened instead?

Story 50
1. If you had met David as a young boy what might have helped you think he would be a good leader?
2. What had David learned as a shepherd which would help him later on? Keep this in mind as you hear future stories.
3. What does it mean that God looks on the heart?

Story 51
1. What do you think helped to make Saul sick?
2. Does anger and jealously ever make you sick?
3. Why was this an important step in David's future?

Story 52
1. Was it faith that made David reject the armor, or was he trying to "show off"?
2. Was David entirely untrained?
3. Do we ever need courage like David?
4. How can we find help?

Story 53
1. Pretend two of you are David and Jonathan and talk about the court and other things the friends might have talked about.
2. What made Saul's love turn to hate?
3. What causes broken friendships?
4. How can this be avoided?

Story 54
1. If God had important plans for David, why is he in such danger?
2. Does David show signs of beginning to doubt God's love?
3. Has God ever promised that those who love Him will be spared all trouble?

Story 55
1. In what different ways and at what times did Jonathan show his love for David?
2. Tell about some friends who have helped you a lot?
3. How can you be a good friend?

Story 56
1. Why did David spare Saul?
2. Did David want to be king?
3. Should David have stayed and fought Saul?

Story 57
1. Why did David have a right to expect help?
2. What kind of person was Nabal? Do you know any people like him?
3. What did Jesus teach about giving to others?

Story 58
1. What was David trying to teach Saul.
2. Why was it so hard for Saul to believe?
3. Who had the best soldiers David or Saul? Why?

Story 59
1. How was David's problem of loyalties solved?
2. Are there times when we can do nothing but wait? Name some.
3. How did David prove a just leader in this story?

Story 60
1. Did David become king right away?
2. Is it also true today that God's will sometimes takes time?
3. Someone tell in their own words how David became king.

Story 61
1. How do we know that David cared about the religious faith of his people?
2. Why was the ark important?
3. Why did David want a Temple?
4. Why did Nathan think it wasn't important?

Story 62
1. In what different ways was David different from other kings of his time?
2. What thoughts, do you suppose, crossed Mephibosheth's mind as he was being brought to David?
3. Did David do more than was expected of him? What was his reward?
4. What is the best reward that comes from being extra kind?

Story 63
1. What was wrong about David's attitude?
2. How did one wrong thought lead to others and to wrong deeds?
3. Are our thoughts important?

Story 64
1. How did Nathan show himself a good prophet?
2. How did his story refer to David?
3. What did David do that was right?
4. What should we do when we realize that we have done wrong?

Story 65
1. How did David's sin affect his family and bring trouble to him?
2. What kind of person was Absalom?
3. Why would Absalom have made a poor king for God's people?

Story 66
1. How did Absalom return his father's kindness?
2. How did David show himself to be a good father?
3. Was David a coward in this story?
4. How do we know David still trusts God?

Story 67
1. What was wrong about Adonijah's ambition?
2. Is how we get something as important as getting it?
3. Is it wrong to want success?

Story 68
1. What makes it seem as though Solomon will be a good king?
2. What do you think about David's advice to Solomon?
3. Do you know what you want to be a success at? Have you ever asked yourself why you want to do it?

Story 69
1. Have someone pretend he is a tour guide and lead the rest through the Temple describing and explaining about it.
2. Why was it good for the people to have a Temple?
3. Might it be possible for the Temple to come to mean too much to them? Keep your answers in mind for future stories.
4. How important is the church building?

Story 70
1. How many promises did Solomon break and to whom?
2. Why was Ahijah's message which he brought from God good?
3. Does God care who our rulers are? Will He take the ruling power away from some men in our time as He did in Bible times?

Story 71
1. Write a letter giving Rehoboam advice on how to handle the crisis.
2. What does it mean to be a leader? Can a leader have anything he wants or do anything he wants?
3. Name some modern-day leaders you think are leading in ways God would approve.

Story 72
1. What did Jeroboam lack as a leader for God's people?
2. Is it ever good to be influenced by others?
3. When is it not good?
4. What was wrong with the pagan worship?

Story 73
1. How did Asa please God? Name all the ways.
2. Why was Syria a poor friend to trust?

3. Why did Asa get angry at the prophet Hanani?
4. Syria's "friendship" with Israel and then with Judah should help us learn about being friends today. Can you "buy" a friend? If someone is false to or lies about another friend, can I be sure he is a true friend to me?

Story 74
1. What was Omri's big mistake?
2. Why do you think this will cause trouble later on?
3. Why was Jehoshaphat wise?
4. How important is teaching in the church?

Story 75
1. Pretend you lived in Elijah's time. Describe him to a friend.
2. Does God ever reward us greatly when we have done just a small kindness?
3. Where did Elijah get his power? Name some others who have had like power.

Story 76
1. Obadiah proved his love for God in how many ways?
2. Write up the contest as it would appear in the daily newspaper.
3. After the miracle some people still worshiped Baal. What excuse do you think they probably gave?

Story 77
1. Who was right—Ahab or Naboth? Why?
2. How would you describe Jezebel?
3. In what different ways did God try to bring Ahab back to doing right?

Story 78
1. How did the wrong kind of friendship get Jehoshaphat into trouble?
2. Do you know any modern true stories about young people getting into trouble because of friends?
3. What good were prophets who said only what the king wanted to hear?

Story 79
1. Why do you think Elisha will make a good prophet?
2. Why did the prophets accept Elisha as their leader? What did the signs represent?
3. Name some signs we can see in Christian leaders today which help us believe they have God's Spirit?

Story 80
1. If you lived in these days would you have preferred to live in Judah or Israel? Why?
2. Why did Jehoshaphat give so much attention to laws and courts when the kings of those days had such power?
3. How important is law and order today?
4. Why is it so important to have honest judges?
5. When should we praise and thank God?

Story 81
1. Was it a "big" thing the woman and her husband did? Why do you think Elisha was so pleased?
2. What kind of thoughtfulness do we like others to show us?
3. Think of three things you can do to show thoughtfulness to someone today.
4. Does it "pay" to be kind to others?

Story 82
1. Why was Naaman's first reaction foolish?
2. Why was Elisha's servant wrong?
3. Should we never take payment for something we do for others?
4. Why is it sometimes nice to do something and receive only thanks?

Story 83
1. What went wrong with Jehoshaphat's good plan? How do you think he could have prevented this?
2. Is it good to be influenced by relatives?
3. When should we make up our own minds and when should we be influenced by what others say?

Story 84
1. Why were many dissatisfied with Ahab?
2. Why do we know that Athaliah's religion was not a good one?
3. Is murder ever right?

Story 85
1. How had God used a man to keep Athaliah's wickedness from achieving its purpose?
2. If God was with Jehoiada why did he need the help and protection of the army?
3. Will God help our national leaders?

Story 86
1. Why was it important to keep the Temple in repair?
2. How could Joash have avoided being influenced by those who wanted pagan worship?
3. Can we ever depend on godly friends too much?
4. How can we be a strong Christian who is able to stand alone and not have to depend on others when temptation comes?

Story 87
1. Why did the prophets think the times bad and the court officials think they were good?
2. Do leaders today sometimes make this same mistake?
3. What did Hosea learn from his own experience?

Story 88
1. Why did Amos hesitate to go North?
2. How would you put Amos' message in your own words?
3. What do you think Amos would say to us if he visited our country?

Story 89
1. Why didn't Jonah want to leave home?
2. Are there people today who think only their own country is worth saving or worthy of God's love?
3. Does God love everybody?
4. Why wasn't Jonah pleased at his success?

Story 90
1. Pretend you are a reporter for a newspaper and report what Isaiah said happened to him in the Temple.
2. Did God still love the people? How do you know?
3. Did Isaiah just talk about religion or about politics as well?
4. Why should Christians be concerned about what political leaders do?

Story 91
1. Why were the small nations afraid of Assyria?
2. How do we know God cared about these people in trouble?
3. Do there always have to be big nations who want to harm smaller nations?

Story 92
1. Why was worrying about protection a poor thing for Ahaz to be doing?
2. What do you remember about the Samaritans from New Testament stories?
3. Why did God allow Israel to be destroyed seeing the people were the people of God?

Story 93
1. What made Hezekiah a good king?
2. Why was it so important how the people worshiped?
3. What important events are to be remembered as part of the Christian faith?
4. Why is it important to worship together with others?

Story 94
1. What did Micah find wrong with his country?
2. What did he have to say about the future?
3. Do you believe that this will happen?
4. Who works for peace in the world today?

Story 95
1. Why wasn't it good to trust Babylon?
2. What did Hezekiah learn from this national crisis?
3. What lessons have you learned through particular times of trouble?

Story 96
1. What did Manasseh do wrong?
2. What made him change for the better?
3. Why didn't Manasseh's change make more of an impression on the practices of the people?
4. Can we always undo harm we have done?

Story 97
1. Why do you like Josiah?
2. Why is it important to learn about God as a child?
3. What was Jeremiah's message?
4. Was there any hope for the people?

Story 98
1. Was the message from God a happy or an unhappy one?
2. Why had the scroll been lost? Whose fault was it?
3. Could the Bible become lost if no one read it anymore or considered it important?

Story 99
1. Why did Jeremiah's relatives find fault with him? Why did they like the "high places"?
2. Why was it hard to be a small nation in these days?
3. How had Josiah helped his people?
4. From the stories of kings you have heard so far what do you think makes a good ruler?

Story 100
1. Why was Jeremiah always getting into trouble?
2. Do we have leaders today who think it more important to obey God than powerful rulers?
3. Why did the priests think God would never destroy the Temple?
4. Why were they wrong?

Story 101
1. What disturbed Habakkuk?
2. How would you answer someone who said, "If God loved us He would not allow anyone to suffer"?
3. Did being a prophet mean that the message was true?
4. Did Habakkuk ever come to understand everything God did? Does anyone understand this today?

Story 102
1. Did it pay the king to burn the book?
2. Was Jeremiah discouraged in his work for God?
3. Why was judgment coming to the people?

Story 103
1. Was Jeremiah patriotic to write such a letter?
2. Should we be loyal to anything our country does which is not what we think God wants?
3. Why is it more important to have God's laws within us than on paper?

Story 104
1. Why was Jeremiah put in prison?
2. Why did the king keep asking his advice?
3. Make up a good prayer for us to pray about our own country.

Story 105
1. What advice would you have given Zedekiah?
2. What made Jeremiah still have hope?
3. Should Christians have hope for the future of our world?

Story 106
1. What was good and what was bad about Babylon?
2. How did God still show His concern for His people?
3. Why did the people blame their ancestors? Were they right?
4. Does one generation sometimes make it hard for another generation?

Story 107
1. Pretend you are a Jewish boy in the court. What would you say to Daniel about his stand?
2. Why did Daniel think he should keep the laws about eating?
3. What contributed to the success of Daniel and his friends?
4. Does it always pay to stand up for our beliefs?

Story 108
1. Why was the dream important?
2. What kind of ruler was Nebuchadnezzar?
3. Do you think God's judgment is going to come to him?
4. Are evil men always punished right away?

Story 109
1. Why wouldn't Daniel's friends bow before the image?
2. Why did their faith impress the king?
3. How can we make our faith attractive to others?

Story 110
1. Why did God's judgment come to Babylon?
2. Does God still judge nations?
3. Do you think God is pleased with everything our nation has done in the past?

Story 111
1. Why did Daniel have enemies?
2. What was Darius' mistake?
3. Why does pride still get people into trouble?
4. Could Daniel have prayed anywhere?

Story 112
1. You ask a wealthy Jewish merchant why he doesn't want to return—what does he say?
2. Did those who stayed behind still believe in God?
3. Do you think the people learned any good lessons from being taken away from their homeland?

Story 113
1. Why was the unfinished Temple a bad sign?
2. What were some of the discouragements the people faced?
3. Are there sometimes dangers and delays when we try to do God's work?
4. Does this mean that God is not with us?

Story 114
1. Why do you think the king liked Esther?
2. How do we know Mordecai is a loyal subject?
3. Name some people you have read about who became a great success after coming from humble beginnings.
4. How can such people be used by God?

Story 115
1. Was Haman right in his charge against the Jews?
2. If you were Esther what would you say to the king?
3. How do we know God is helping His people?

Story 116
1. Tell the story so far from Haman's viewpoint? Is he a proud or a humble person?
2. If any Jewish people live near you find out how they keep the Feast of Purim.
3. Can you think of anyone in history who was used to save the lives of many others?

Story 117

1. What did Malachi find to complain about? Was he too harsh with the people?
2. Why do we need teachers like Ezra?
3. Why was it important that everyone believed the same things about God and worshiped in one way?
4. Are we never to be friends with people who are not Christians?

Story 118

1. Why was Nehemiah needed?
2. What is the best thing to do about jealousy from others?
3. To get this accomplished, what is needed beside influential leaders?

Story 119

1. What helped the people to have courage?
2. Do good people also have to be wise?
3. What did Jesus say about having goodness and wisdom?

Story 120

1. Why was the Law more important than ever before?
2. What did God want the people to do rather than cry?
3. How can we prove to God that we are really sorry when we have done wrong?

Story 121

1. Why were the synagogues important?
2. Who do you know that went to a synagogue as a child and then later taught in one?
3. Who was the Messiah? What does the word mean?

Story 122

1. In what way is our worship the same and in what way is it different from worship in the Temple?
2. The psalms still give inspiration to hymn writers. Get a hymn book and see if you can find a hymn based on a psalm.
3. Make up a psalm together praising God for His love and care.

Story 123

1. Make up another psalm thanking God for all the things you most enjoy in His world.
2. Why is it a good idea to learn psalms and some other passages from the Bible?
3. See how many of the passages quoted in this story you can memorize. Perhaps you can set them to music.

Story 124

1. What did you learn last Sunday in Sunday school?
2. Is it possible to go each Sunday and still not learn truths from the Bible?
3. Print or have someone type the passage from the Song of Solomon on a large sheet of paper. Draw or paste pictures to illustrate it and so make a hanging for your room.

Story 125

1. What important lessons did Job learn?
2. How can troubles make us stronger?
3. Does everyone have trouble or only those who try to live in God's way?
4. If we believe in God what advantage do we have?

NEW TESTAMENT

Story 1

1. In what ways were people ready for the Messiah?
2. In what ways were they not ready?
3. What makes parents happy about their children?

Story 2

1. Why do you think God chose Mary to be Jesus' mother?
2. Why was Jesus' birth special?
3. Which prophets had foretold that the Messiah would be born?

Story 3
1. How did the people feel about Zechariah's vision and the new baby?
2. What work did God have for John to do? Remember this as you read the later stories.
3. Is the message about the Messiah—Jesus—still good news?
4. Who brings this message to others today?

Story 4
1. What do you like best about the Christmas story?
2. You have heard this story so often, can you tell it in your own words?
3. Why was the birth of Jesus good news?

Story 5
1. Others were in the Temple. Why didn't they recognize the Messiah as a baby?
2. Why wasn't everyone glad about the birth of Jesus?
3. Why doesn't the message of Jesus make everyone glad today?
4. In what way is Jesus a king?

Story 6
1. What important part does Joseph play in the story of Jesus' birth?
2. Why was it important that everyone not know that Jesus was the promised Messiah of the Jews?
3. How was God making His promises come true?
4. How was He showing love for His world?

Story 7
1. In what ways was Jesus' childhood like your own?
2. Why would you have liked Jesus for a playmate?
3. In what ways was the home of Mary and Joseph a good home to grow up in?
4. Besides the school, where did Jesus learn?

Story 8
1. What was special about a trip to the Temple?
2. Why were the rabbis impressed with Jesus?
3. Do you remember your first visit to church? Tell about it or about some religious service that made you feel especially close to God.

Story 9
1. Describe the preacher John to a friend. Pretend you lived in these days and you want your friend to come hear John.
2. How did John say God wants people to live?
3. What did John say about the Messiah?
4. Why was Jesus greater than John?

Story 10
1. Why did Jesus want to be baptized?
2. Why do you think everyone who heard John did not immediately believe in Jesus as the Messiah?
3. Why doesn't everyone believe in Jesus today?

Story 11
1. Why was it important that Jesus win this victory?
2. Why was it important **how** Jesus did God's work?
3. Can we do what we think is God's work and do it in the wrong way so that we do wrong when we mean to do right?
4. How can we prevent this?

Story 12
1. What was the special meaning of this miracle Jesus performed?
2. Why did Jesus perform miracles?
3. Does God work through people today? How do we know?

Story 13
1. What do you think might have impressed Nicodemus enough that he came to see Jesus?
2. What was wrong in the Temple?
3. Was Nicodemus brave or a coward?

Story 14
1. Did it pay John to do God's work? Do you think he was sorry?
2. Why didn't Jesus mind going through Samaria?
3. Are there places you wouldn't go because you don't like the people or don't think they are good enough?

Story 15
1. What was the "water" Jesus spoke of?
2. What made Jesus forget about food?
3. Can we help others to come to know Jesus?

Story 16
1. Jesus had the power from God, what did those who asked for help need?
2. Do we need faith before God can help us?
3. Why were just miracles not enough?
4. What good did the miracles do?

Story 17
1. Pretend you are a native of Nazareth who has always known Jesus. What would you say to help convince the important people of the synagogue that Jesus was the Messiah?
2. How do we know that the people of the synagogue did not love other groups of people and did not realize God's love was for all?
3. Why couldn't Jesus do much in this town?
4. Do you think Jesus stopped loving His old friends of Nazareth?

Story 18
1. Why did Jesus need helpers seeing He was God's Son?
2. What do you think helped the fishermen to decide?
3. What did Zebedee have to give to the work? What did he sacrifice?

Story 19
1. How did Peter's family help in God's work?
2. Why were so many in need of healing?
3. Does God heal people today?

Story 20
1. Why was Jesus able to forgive sins?
2. Pretend that you live in Jesus' day. Write a letter to a friend telling how you went to see and hear Jesus.
3. If you become ill does it help to pray or is going to a doctor enough?

Story 21
1. How should you choose your friends?
2. Why did Jesus care about Matthew?
3. How did Matthew prove worthy?
4. Should we look only for friends who can help us or also find friends we can help?

Story 22
1. Why were the rulers angry? What did they consider most important?
2. From this story what did Jesus think was most important?
3. How should Sunday be spent?

Story 23
1. Why did the rulers consider Jesus dangerous?
2. Does this prove that Jesus was popular and successful with the people?
3. What was wrong about the way the rulers thought about the Sabbath?
4. Do people today ever think of rules and regulations as more important than people?

Story 24
1. Who did Jesus say would be happy?
2. Do we need to work if God will provide for our needs?
3. What would the people in God's Kingdom be like?

Story 25
1. Why did John find it hard to believe?
2. Did John fail in his work for God?
3. Did anyone else in the Bible have power from God to heal the sick?
4. Why should this power help people to believe in Jesus?

Story 26
1. Why do you think it was hard for Jesus' family to believe?
2. Why was God's Kingdom like something small?
3. Why was God's Kingdom like a pearl?
4. In what prayer do we mention God's Kingdom?

Story 27
1. What power did Jesus demonstrate in this story?
2. Why did some find it too difficult to follow Jesus?
3. Do some people find it too difficult to serve God today? Why?

Story 28
1. Why is it important to have faith?
2. Did miracles convince everyone?
3. What helps people believe in Jesus today?
4. Can we do anything to help others believe?

Story 29
1. Think about the missionaries you have heard speak or have heard about. What are they like? What kind of people are they?
2. What do missionaries today do to help others come to know Jesus?
3. Why are these ordinary men able to do what Jesus had done in healing the sick?
4. Were these men glad they were in Jesus' work?

Story 30
1. How does this story show us that Jesus cares about people's physical needs?
2. Does Christian work today sometimes include feeding the hungry?
3. Could the boy have refused to share his lunch? What would have happened then?
4. Why did Jesus refuse to have the men make Him king?

Story 31
1. How does this story show that Jesus cared for all people?
2. Are all people of equal worth to God?
3. What does this say about how we treat people of other races or nationalities?

Story 32
1. Why was Peter's confession important?
2. Why is it important for us too to believe what Peter said about Jesus?
3. Why did Jesus warn the disciples of His coming death?
4. Why were some people losing faith in Jesus?

Story 33
1. How did this experience increase faith in the disciples?
2. What does this experience tell us about Jesus?
3. If you could have talked to the disciples that lacked faith, what advice would you have given them?

Story 34
1. What was wrong with the questionings of the disciples?
2. Do Christians today ever quarrel about the same thing? How can we prevent this?
3. What did the story of the sheep and the shepherd tell us about God and ourselves?
4. What lesson did the story of the king and his servants tell?

Story 35

1. When did the lepers find that they were healed? How had they demonstrated their faith?
2. Why does God want us to express our thanks when He can read our hearts?
3. Make a list of things you have seen or experienced today for which you thank God.
4. Why did His enemies have trouble doing away with Jesus?

Story 36

1. Why did the blind man get into trouble?
2. Can we get into trouble when we do what is right?
3. What makes the story have a happy ending?

Story 37

1. What lesson can we learn from these two sisters?
2. Does God still want missionaries to go out preaching and healing?
3. How can we help this kind of work?
4. Are there still less workers than are needed to do God's work around the world?

Story 38

1. Who is your neighbor?
2. Is there anyone God says you may be excused from loving?
3. Do you think the scribe lived differently after this talk with Jesus?
4. Do we sometimes hear and understand the truth and still not live by it?

Story 39

1. What was different about Jesus' use of prayer?
2. Why is prayer important to us?
3. What does the story about the son who left home tell us about ourselves and God?
4. Why was the other brother wrong to be angry?

Story 40

1. In Jesus' story, why was one prayer better than the other?
2. What does the story of the dinner tell us about God's Kingdom?
3. What kind of trouble can love of possessions bring to a person?
4. Does this mean that we shouldn't pray about things we need or ask God to help us succeed in school or in our work?

Story 41

1. How do we know the two sisters did not lose their faith in God or in Jesus?
2. Why were Jesus' enemies especially angry about this miracle?
3. How do we know Jesus cares when someone we love dies?

Story 42

1. How is God's Kingdom different from the Roman Empire or even from our United States?
2. What was wrong with the mother's request?
3. What does God do when we ask for wrong things?
4. Do we always know what is best for us and therefore what to ask for?

Story 43

1. Why did Jesus care about Zacchaeus?
2. Were the people right in disliking all tax collectors?
3. How did Zacchaeus show his change of heart?
4. How can we prove that we really believe in Jesus and what He taught?

Story 44

1. How might it be argued that Mary's gift was good or not good? What do you think of her gift?
2. What important part did the man who owned the colt play in the story of Jesus' life?
3. Was the praise of the people sincere?
4. How did Jesus show Himself a King not only in this story but in all His life?

Story 45
1. What was wrong at the Temple?
2. What do you think King David who had first thought of the Temple would have said about the Temple of Jesus' day?
3. Why did Jesus' stories make the rulers angry?
4. Could the rulers even then have repented and believed in Jesus?

Story 46
1. Why was the question about the tax a dangerous one?
2. What do we owe our country and what do we owe God?
3. What is the greatest commandment?
4. How can we put this command into our lives everyday?

Story 47
1. How can Jesus be betrayed today?
2. Why was Peter shocked at what Jesus did?
3. Do you think this story means we should wash each other's feet? If not what does it mean we should do for each other?

Story 48
1. What is the meaning of this special supper Jesus had with His friends?
2. Why do we observe the Lord's Supper today?
3. Why was Peter wrong?

Story 49
1. Why did Jesus need to pray at this time?
2. How could Jesus' friends have been more helpful?
3. How did Jesus show love for others even in this time of crisis?
4. What made Peter fail?
5. What is the difference between the failure of Peter and that of Judas?

Story 50
1. What was the main fault of the rulers in how they treated Jesus?
2. What kind of man was Pilate?
3. Could Judas have repented and come back to Jesus?

Story 51
1. Why didn't Jesus show Herod some sign?
2. What was the purpose for the signs and miracles Jesus had performed throughout His life?
3. Do mobs do wrong today? Why is it easy for mobs to act suddenly and unjustly?
4. Are people ever wrongly condemned by a crowd today? Are some even killed?

Story 52
1. Did Pilate clear himself of blame?
2. Are rulers responsible for what people under them do today?
3. How do we know that Jesus continued to have love for people?
4. Do you think that Joseph of Arimathea and Nicodemus, as important men, did all they could have done for Jesus?
5. Do we always do all we can do?

Story 53
1. What is the glad message of Easter?
2. What does it say about life and death for us?
3. When had Jesus told His disciples all this would happen?

Story 54
1. Why did the rulers think a guard necessary? Did they have more faith in Jesus' promise of resurrection than the disciples?
2. Why didn't Cleopas and his friend recognize Jesus right away?
3. Do you think you would have found it easier to believe if you had lived in these times?

Story 55
1. Tell what you think the disciples said to Thomas about their experience?
2. What was good and what was bad about Thomas' attitude?
3. How do we know that this appearance of Jesus was not just the appearance of a ghost?

Story 56
1. What did Peter find out at the breakfast?
2. What does this tell us about Jesus and ourselves?
3. What happened on the mountain?
4. Why was this so important for the centuries that have come since?

Story 57
1. What was different about the church?
2. When did Jesus say He would start the church, that it would be His?
3. What is the evidence that the church was not just an idea good religious people had to stay together in an organization?
4. What helped so many to believe on this feast day?

Story 58
1. What was different about the way Peter and John healed the lame man from the way Jesus healed?
2. Why were the rulers angry about such a good deed?
3. What was in Peter's message which was good news?
4. What did he say that was a warning?
5. Who did Peter say was responsible for Jesus' death?

Story 59
1. Pretend you live at this time. Tell a friend about this new group of people who believe in Jesus.
2. If the church was of God why were the members having trouble?
3. What made the disciples show more courage than they did before the death of Jesus?

Story 60
1. What was Stephen's sermon about?
2. Why did it make the rulers so angry?
3. In what way was Stephen's death like the death of Jesus?
4. Why would Stephen be counted a good Christian, a good follower of Jesus?

Story 61
1. Why was it good that many followers of Jesus left Jerusalem?
2. Why were some believers surprised that some Samaritans received God's Spirit?
3. Who said the Gospel was to go to Samaria?
4. What people should hear the Gospel today?

Story 62
1. Why did Ananias need a lot of faith and courage?
2. Is it possible today to believe that we are doing what God wants and be wrong?
3. What do you think Saul told his former friends who were still against the followers of Jesus?

Story 63
1. Why were some believers disturbed by the conversion of Saul?
2. How did Peter get such power from God?
3. What were some of the things which were making the church grow?

Story 64
1. What did Peter's vision mean?
2. How did Cornelius get his prayers answered?
3. Think of some time when God used someone to answer a prayer of yours.

Story 65
1. Why did some believers wonder that Cornelius and his family received God's Spirit?
2. What were some of the things Barnabas would teach in Antioch?
3. Why did one group of believers think it was their business if famine affected another group?
4. How do different churches help one another today?

Story 66
1. Did God always deliver the Christians put in prison as He did Peter?
2. Why did Peter leave the city? Was he cowardly in doing this?
3. Does God always answer our prayers for the safety of godly men and His work prosper?

Story 67
1. What was different about the trip taken by Saul and Barnabas and the past trips taken by Saul or by other apostles?
2. Why did the missionaries go first to the Jews?
3. How could the church grow without Paul and Barnabas there to oversee everything?

Story 68
1. Does this story tell us that good Christian families can sometimes be found in pagan places?
2. Why were Paul and Barnabas so upset about the mistake of the people?
3. What made Paul's work dangerous?
4. Is it sometimes dangerous today to have ideas different from the majority?

Story 69
1. Why did the missionaries feel they should revisit instead of going to new places?
2. What important question was settled at this big church meeting in Jerusalem?
3. What made Peter agree with Paul?
4. Why was this meeting especially important for Christians today?

Story 70
1. What new area was reached in the spread of the church?
2. Why is this important to us?
3. What made Timothy a good helper?
4. How did Lydia help? Was this important?

Story 71
1. What angered the people against the Christians?
2. When do people sometimes get angry at what the Gospel teaches today?
3. What impressed the jailer so that he wanted to become a Christian?
4. Are people ever put in jail for good causes today?

Story 72
1. How did jealousy cause trouble for the Christians?
2. Does jealousy ever cause trouble in your class or in your home?
3. Why did Paul feel the people of Athens needed to know about Jesus?

Story 73
1. Why did the people in Athens find it hard to believe Paul?
2. What help did Paul find in Corinth which he did not have in Athens?
3. How can we all help Christian leaders, teachers and preachers?

Story 74
1. Do riots ever make sense?
2. How did the Christians show courage?
3. Why were the silversmiths upset?
4. When does the desire to keep making money sometimes lead people to do wrong today?

Story 75
1. Why is it bad when quarrels come into a church?
2. Why was there danger for Paul in Jerusalem?
3. Why did the Christians worship on Sunday?

Story 76
1. What good news did Paul bring to the church in Jerusalem?
2. Why did Paul go to the Temple and worship there?
3. Was Paul guilty of what the crowd said he had done?

Story 77
1. How did a young man help to fulfill God's plan for the growth of the church?
2. Can you think of any other true story or something from your own experience when a seemingly little thing resulted in a lot of good?
3. What gave Paul courage?

Story 78
1. Why did Felix keep Paul in prison?
2. Would it have been all right for Paul's friends to have bribed the Roman for such a "good cause"?
3. How did it help Paul to be a Roman citizen?

Story 79
1. If you were defending Paul and telling his story to a Roman ruler what would you say?
2. Do you think Agrippa at least partly believed in Jesus?
3. Did arresting Paul keep him from preaching and the Gospel from spreading?

Story 80
1. How did God show that He was with Paul?
2. Why was travel by water more dangerous in those days?
3. How do Christian teachers travel today? What other modern inventions do they use to spread the Gospel?

Story 81
1. How do we know that Paul was not discouraged in his work for Jesus?
2. Why was Paul glad to be in Rome?
3. What were some of the things you think Paul said to the Jewish leaders in Rome?

Story 82
1. What good did Paul do in prison?
2. What kept him from giving up?
3. What do you think happened to Onesimus? Write down an ending to this story.

Story 83
1. How can letters written so long ago help Christians today?
2. Pick out the quotation in this story you think most helpful and make a wall motto of it.
3. Do people still write books to help us understand the teachings of Jesus better? Name some of them.
4. Why are we glad these first Christians decided to write?

Story 84
1. Why do you think the church grew so rapidly?
2. Why did it successfully endure persecution?
3. What is God's promise for the future of our world?
4. What is the meaning of John's vision of people before the throne?